The Origin of Capitalism in England
1400–1600

Historical Materialism Book Series

The Historical Materialism Book Series is a major publishing initiative of the radical left. The capitalist crisis of the twenty-first century has been met by a resurgence of interest in critical Marxist theory. At the same time, the publishing institutions committed to Marxism have contracted markedly since the high point of the 1970s. The Historical Materialism Book Series is dedicated to addressing this situation by making available important works of Marxist theory. The aim of the series is to publish important theoretical contributions as the basis for vigorous intellectual debate and exchange on the left.

The peer-reviewed series publishes original monographs, translated texts, and reprints of classics across the bounds of academic disciplinary agendas and across the divisions of the left. The series is particularly concerned to encourage the internationalization of Marxist debate and aims to translate significant studies from beyond the English-speaking world.

For a full list of titles in the Historical Materialism Book Series
available in paperback from Haymarket Books, visit:
www.haymarketbooks.org/category/hm-series

The Origin of Capitalism in England

1400–1600

By
Spencer Dimmock

Haymarket Books
Chicago, IL

First published in 2014 by Brill Academic Publishers, The Netherlands
© 2014 Koninklijke Brill NV, Leiden, The Netherlands

Published in paperback in 2015 by
Haymarket Books
P.O. Box 180165
Chicago, IL 60618
773-583-7884
www.haymarketbooks.org

ISBN: 978-1-60846-485-2

Trade distribution:
In the US, Consortium Book Sales, www.cbsd.com
In Canada, Publishers Group Canada, www.pgcbooks.ca
In the UK, Turnaround Publisher Services, www.turnaround-uk.com
In all other countries, Publishers Group Worldwide, www.pgw.com

Cover design by Ragina Johnson.

This book was published with the generous support of
Lannan Foundation and the Wallace Global Fund.

10 9 8 7 6 5 4 3 2 1

Library of Congress Cataloging-in-Publication data is available.

Contents

Introduction

If capitalism is defined as an economic system in which businesses produce to sell on the market either domestically or overseas, then capitalism has always existed if in less efficient forms. If this definition is accepted, both the pre-history and the history of capitalism would amount to the history of commerce and commercialisation – that is, the recounting of increasing efficiencies in production and exchange through technological innovation, related changes in the organisation of production and distribution, and the geographical expansion or globalisation of trade. The question therefore of capitalist *origins*, the subject of this book, would be beside the point.[1]

This book begins with the premise that rather than simply an economic system, capitalism is a specific historical form of social system or *society* with its own specific economic logic, *fundamentally* distinct from earlier historical forms of society – and indeed from non-capitalist societies in different parts of the world today. This is because, like all other historical forms of society, capitalism has a unique structure of class relations, and it is this structure which determines its specific economic system and therefore specific patterns of economic development. In other words, it is the struggle to make a living by opposed interests within the established structure of class relations that determines the nature of economic development (or non-development). Capitalism and other historical forms of society are therefore necessarily defined in *political* terms. For example, capitalism is the only form of society in history in which the majority of people and their families are entirely dependent on others for waged employment in order to survive. It is in that dependency, and the consequent imbalances in power in the work-place, that there lurks the political relationship. This contrasts with other *non*-capitalist forms of society, such as feudalism and absolutism in medieval and early modern Europe and Asia, in which the majority of people and families held land, were largely self-subsistent in food that they produced themselves, and had therefore to be coerced by more directly political means by lords, monarchs and emperors into paying various forms of rent and taxation. And it contrasts with slavery in ancient and early medieval Europe, and New World societies such as North America between the seventeenth and nineteenth centuries, in which large sections of the population were neither wholly self-subsistent nor free to seek waged employment, but coerced by political means into forming part of the constant capital of their masters' production process and bought and sold

---

1 For example, a recent self-styled 'definitive' history of capitalism traces the 'rise of capitalism' from ancient Babylon and the first known traders: Neal and Williamson, 2014.

like other investments.[2] It follows therefore that any historical account of economic growth, development and transformation will have to firmly integrate these fundamental political relationships at the centre of the analysis.

This book is about how the capitalist form developed out of the feudal form in England. It is about how the majority of people in England came to no longer work the land for a living, having done so for thousands of years, and were forced instead to seek employment either from farmers or in industry and service; in other words, how the lives of the majority of people changed from subsistence farming in which they had a permanent means of supplying at least their basic needs, to one in which they were dependent on others for employment in order to supply those needs. A fundamentally similar process is going on today elsewhere in the world, the most obvious example of which is China. Millions of people are being rapidly uprooted from their subsistence plots and communities in the countryside, and are migrating to the vast new cities that are being built in preparation for them. The Chinese Communist Party that is directing these changes had a blueprint of already existing capitalism which it has applied, but there was of course no such blueprint for the English; these fundamental changes in England were the unintentional result of pragmatic adaptations implemented blindly.

This book is comprised of both an intervention in a long-standing debate and the presentation of original research on the origin of capitalism in England. England is particularly significant in this debate because while forms of capitalist production developed in the medieval urban centres of Italy and Flanders, and it is arguable that capitalist social-property relations developed in the northern Netherlands from the fifteenth century, England was the first country in which a transition from feudalism to capitalism was sustained from the fifteenth century through to modern industrialisation in the eighteenth and nineteenth centuries. As such England's capitalist origins have often been treated as a model with which to compare and understand origins and transitions to capitalism in other countries, past and present. In fact, England's transition to capitalism appears in stark contrast to the rest of Europe in the medieval and early modern periods, including those countries such as Italy, Germany, France and parts of the Low Countries which were more advanced in terms of trade and urbanisation in the medieval period and beyond. These countries only underwent a transition to capitalism after fully-fledged agrarian capitalism had already developed in England and it was developing its Industrial

---

2   See Post 2011 for a brilliant recent discussion on the fundamental characteristics of slavery
    and the obstacle it posed to capitalist expansion in North America in the mid-nineteenth
    century.

Revolution. Because of the central place England often has within the debate, it is very important to be clear about the nature of the transition in that country. Yet recent contributions to the long-standing debate by historians have served to confuse rather than to illuminate.[3] One of the aims of this book is to subject these recent contributions to a detailed critique and to promote a consensus on the nature of the origin of capitalism in England, not only among professional historians and social scientists, but for the benefit of anyone wanting to know more about the fundamental aspects of the society in which they live and desiring to put themselves in a better position to reflect upon its past and future.

The phrases 'the origin of capitalism' and 'the transition to capitalism' are often used interchangeably. The focus of this book is on the 'origin' because it wishes to place emphasis on a period of historic rupture, the key stage marking the beginning of the transition from a non-capitalist to a capitalist society without necessarily referring to a completed transition. If it is recognised that capitalism had a beginning, and that it is not simply a term that describes a higher form of 'commercial society' that has existed since ancient times, it should be concluded that capitalism is another specific form of society with a beginning and an end like all other previous specific forms.[4] If this conclusion is drawn, discussions about the future of capitalism can be informed by knowledge of how such permanent historic ruptures occur, right down to the names and motivations of individuals and classes who created or attempted to resist them.

The discussions in the following chapters cover a historical trajectory from the Viking invasions of the late Anglo-Saxon period to the parliamentary enclosures of the eighteenth and early nineteenth centuries. The argument of this book however is that capitalism in England both originated and became prominent in the two centuries between 1400 and 1600; in other words, its origins were largely late medieval. The decades around 1400 witnessed the widespread transference across the whole of England of the feudal lords' home farms or 'demesnes' to the wealthier peasantry. This was an unprecedented development. Following the 'English Rising', or 'Peasants' Revolt', of 1381, the decline of serfdom and therefore the decline of a major source of their livelihoods and of important controls over the peasantry, lords sought new ways to maintain the level of income to which they were accustomed and which enabled them to reproduce themselves as lords. These farms represented

---

3   Rigby 1995, Whittle 2000, Hatcher and Bailey 2001, French and Hoyle 2007.
4   See the discussion in Wood 2002, pp. 1–8, and more recently and succinctly in her 'Foreword' in Post 2011.

approximately twenty to thirty percent of the best land in the country. They were leased and the new leaseholders were compelled to produce competitively for the market upon taking up the leases; previously their production strategies had been fundamentally geared to subsistence. Linked to this earlier development, the progressive uprooting of the English peasantry from the middle third of the fifteenth century was driven fundamentally by the mutual interests of lords and their farmers, and in many places a social transformation had taken place by the 1530s. As a result, England's economic and demographic patterns were by this time diverging from those on the continent. In the decades around 1600 the generation of large capitalised farms out of fragmented peasant-organised, subsistence-based production had proceeded to such an extent, albeit unevenly across the country, that they were by then the typical feature of English agrarian society. The political and economic interests of large farmers who were powerful locally, a commercial aristocracy and a centralised state government had by 1600 become firmly committed to the future of the new system.

The book is divided into two parts. Part I is comprised of a series of discussions that amount to a defence of the work of Robert Brenner. It is my contention that Robert Brenner has produced the most convincing thesis yet on the fundamental characteristics of feudal and capitalist societies, and on how capitalism developed from feudalism. In the earlier 'Brenner Debate' on the transition from feudalism to capitalism, Guy Bois described Brenner's approach as 'political Marxism' because in his explanation of historical development Brenner prioritises specific class structures rather than specific economic systems.[5] The label has stuck ever since and, although inadequate, it does usefully distinguish his approach from other forms of Marxism. Brenner defines specific societies such as feudalism and capitalism by their structure of class relations and the specific way in which the surplus product or surplus labour is extracted from the producer by the non-producer – that is, from peasants by feudal lords in feudalism, and from wage workers by capitalist entrepreneurs in capitalism. In sharp contrast to orthodox Marxist approaches, Brenner does not confine his application of class, or what he terms 'social-property relations', to the vertical class relationship or surplus-extraction relationship between lords and peasants or between wage workers and capitalists. For Brenner the rivalry and competition amongst lords and between states in feudalism, and

---

5   Bois 1985, pp. 115–16. Bois's criticisms were in fact far harsher than this summary suggests. He accused Brenner of abstracting class struggle from the feudal economic system in an ideological and voluntarist fashion. Brenner's orthodox Marxist and non-Marxist critics have deployed this criticism ever since and I address it in Chapter Two below.

amongst capitalist entrepreneurs and between states in capitalism, is at least as important a factor in determining historical change. Brenner's approach provides for an immensely rich understanding of these societies, their peculiar patterns of development and their susceptibility to crises. Routinely hived-off disciplines such as social, economic and political history, are necessarily and genuinely integrated. For example, with regard to feudalism, the development of political and judicial institutions, the fragmentation or consolidation of sovereign authority, warfare and the accumulation of territory on a national or international basis, all had an impact on relationships between lords and peasants and on the nature of production at the level of the manor, and the latter had a simultaneous impact on the former. A broad core of human life is apparent here as the analysis takes account of the choices that people have to make in order to reproduce themselves within their own families, communities and social classes, with all of the economic and political decision-making this entails within particular historical contexts. The misreading of Brenner's thesis by historians and social scientists of all political colours – his application of class as social-property relations in particular – has meant the potential of his approach for a richer and more integrated view of medieval and early modern society has been foreclosed, and this has led to decades of wasted time in the understanding of transitions to capitalism.

Hence Part I of this book is a detailed engagement with Brenner's work on the transition in England, in which I respond to his critics. It begins with an outline and statement of what Brenner's thesis actually is. In my experience of working in academies, English historians and students find the debate on the transition and Brenner's style rather daunting. Because of the complexity of the task that Brenner set himself, namely the comparative economic trajectories of countries in Europe in the medieval and early modern periods, he writes in a deliberately systematic way in order to be as theoretically rigorous as possible and to avoid contradiction and misinterpretation. This strategy has not always been fruitful, so in Chapter One I spell out aspects of the thesis that have caused problems for historians in the past.

My defence of Brenner in subsequent chapters is both theoretical and historical in nature, and incorporates the findings of recent empirical studies. Chapter Two discusses critiques of Brenner's use of class or social-property relations as a prime mover or first cause of economic and social change. While the commercialisation thesis in its various forms, or the 'rise-of-the market' approach adopted from Adam Smith, generally holds sway among economic historians, there has been a distinct turn among English non-Marxist economic and social historians to pluralist approaches which do not privilege any factor (class, population or commercialisation). Others have their own unique

theories, as we shall see. In Chapter Three I examine the fundamental differences between feudal and capitalist societies. I address doubts about whether
these societies are as fundamentally distinct from each other as Brenner insists.
Brenner defines feudalism by the *political* or extra-economic extraction of the
surpluses produced by landholding peasants, and he defines capitalism by the
economic extraction of the surpluses produced by wage workers. In capitalism
direct political controls through imposed forms of serfdom (unpaid services
and numerous other fines, monopolies and restrictions) are not necessary to
secure the means to exploit workers because workers are forced to sell their
labour power on the market as a means to secure employment. Historians
point out however that, given that half of the English peasantry by the end of
the thirteenth century were freeholders and not serfs, Brenner's thesis of political or extra-economic extraction in feudalism would appear, on the face of
it, to be inadequate. Nevertheless I aim to demonstrate that as long as the
peasantry – free and unfree – remained subjected to the manorial regime there
was always the potential for lords to impose new demands on peasants that
were characteristic of serfdom. Free and unfree peasants were also neighbours
and interrelated by marriage, and so disabilities for the latter substantially
affected the former. In Chapter Four I discuss endogenous and exogenous
causes of 'the crisis of feudalism' in Europe between the late thirteenth century and the middle of the fourteenth century, and the role of this crisis in
subsequent developments, whether these developments turned out to be in
a capitalist direction or otherwise. Chapter Five examines the nature of the
security of property in England during the transition. We are often informed by
economists and economic historians that capitalism requires a stable, secure
environment to encourage entrepreneurs to take risks and invest in long-term
projects. So was the origin of capitalism facilitated and characterised by a new
era of secure property in the fifteenth century? Or did it feed on new tenurial insecurities following the decline of serfdom? Chapter Six aims to identify
which social agents were responsible for generating capitalism's origins. Was
capitalism generated from below by the initiatives and rebellions of peasants?
Or, alternatively, was it a top-down imposition by lords or seigneurial authority? Were peasant struggles against their lords therefore motivated by a desire
for capitalism, or were peasant communities generally anti-capitalist in outlook and behaviour? Chapter Seven is a detailed periodisation of the transition
in medieval and early modern England, with a particular focus on the chronology of the expropriation of the English peasantry from the land. Identification
of the key period of expropriation can help us explain the causes of the historic
rupture in feudalism and the *qualitative* transformation from feudalism to capitalism. I aim to demonstrate that it is the 'long fifteenth century' – a period

of relative commercial and demographic downturn – which is the most significant for these epochal changes. Finally, in Chapter Eight, I address recent orthodox Marxist critiques of Brenner in order to illuminate major differences in Marxist approaches to the origin of capitalism. This is particularly important, and I have given it extensive treatment, because Brenner's distinctive 'political Marxist' approach is usually misinterpreted by non-Marxist historians because they read it through the prism of orthodox Marxism. These recent orthodox Marxist critiques are particularly prone to severe misreadings of Brenner's thesis. Their foundation is a political project geared towards a socialist revolutionary 'event', and this colours their approach to history and theory. As a result they repeat the tendency to teleology, technological determinism and a simplified approach to class that hampered the earlier twentieth-century tradition. It is my hope that once these two very distinctive approaches are more readily recognised, historians and social scientists both within and outside of the Marxist tradition will read Brenner on his own terms.

Part Two is a detailed case study based upon original research on the origin of capitalism in a region of Kent in south-east England c. 1400–1600.[6] The survival of evidence for this rural, small-town society and its region between the fourteenth and the sixteenth centuries is remarkable. Indeed, evidence of this quality survives for much of medieval Kent, and yet this county has been largely ignored by medieval economic historians, and has found little place among the empirical findings usually marshalled in contributions to the debate on the transition in England. When Kent is mentioned in the context of the debate, such as in a discussion on the chronology of enclosure of peasant land into large farms, it is usually assumed that no transition was really necessary there: the land was already enclosed during the medieval period, albeit into small peasant subsistence holdings, and it had strong commercial links with London and the continent. One need only introduce the Black Death and a free land market and capitalism was sure to follow. It will hopefully become clear from this study that this assumption has been entirely misplaced.

The chapters in Part II are mostly assembled in chronological order. The evidence is interrogated largely in the light of questions thrown up in Part I. I aim to demonstrate in Chapter Nine that Lydd, a parish containing a small market town and several manors, was densely populated, and it was a community (or set of interlinked communities) with long-established political institutions in the first half of the fifteenth century. There was no indication of the enforced

---

6 This section began as my doctoral thesis on the origin of capitalism: Dimmock 1998. Some of its findings have already been aired briefly in short essays and reviews: Dimmock 2001; Dimmock 2007a; Dimmock 2007b.

engrossment and progressive uprooting of the peasants, artisans, fishermen and petty traders from their holdings that was to come in the second half of the century. Chapter Ten examines the motives and methods of those responsible for engrossment and enclosure in the fifteenth and early sixteenth century. Chapter Eleven reconstructs the form of society that had emerged by c. 1530 as the direct result of these momentous developments, and it assesses the extent to which agrarian capitalism had already emerged by then. Chapter Twelve traces the continuity of the expropriation of peasant land and commons in the second half of the sixteenth century. It addresses the thesis that there was a hiatus in the enclosure movement between 1530 and 1580, and assesses the extent to which state protection of peasant property was successful in this period. Chapter Thirteen looks at attempts to legitimise the authority that emerged from the social transformation in Lydd by 1530. I argue that an economic crisis in the 1520s and increasing threats posed to coastal communities in Kent by Henry VIII's wars led to attempts by the new capitalist farming interests, in conjunction with the centralising Tudor state, to seek to close the widening cracks in social relations with appeals to national unity and common purpose in the form of an unprecedented four-day festival and drama of St. George held at Lydd in 1533. All quotations from original sources have been translated from the medieval Latin and from fifteenth and sixteenth-century English into modern English.

This book is dedicated to Robert Brenner and to Christopher Dyer. Their perspectives on the transition to capitalism in England are not always in agreement, but while studying this topic I have found that a dialogue between the rigorous theoretical analysis of the former and the detailed problem-orientated empirical studies of the latter has been a fruitful approach. I wish to acknowledge and thank Ralph Griffiths and Louise Miskell of the College of Arts and Humanities at Swansea University for allowing me to use the University's research facilities as an honorary research fellow. I also wish to thank Marie Bevan for helping me with library materials, Charles Post for his useful comments on an earlier draft of this book, and David Broder, Danny Hayward and Rosanna Woensdregt for their friendly help in seeing the final draft through to production.

PART ONE

A Defence of Robert Brenner

∴

CHAPTER 1

Robert Brenner's Thesis on the Transition from Feudalism to Capitalism

The purpose of Robert Brenner's work on the transition from feudalism to capitalism has been to answer two important questions posed by earlier seminal theories on demographic cycles and on economic development in medieval and early modern Europe. They are, first: given the impressive growth of towns and trade between roughly 1050 and 1750, why was most of the European economy characterised not by capitalist development but by demographically-driven cycles that were marked by falling labour productivity in agriculture? Second: why was it that in the late medieval and early modern period a few countries and regions, namely England and the northern Netherlands, achieved a breakthrough to self-sustaining growth in the face of these same demographic patterns and the same economic (and cultural) context? In other words, why during this period did economic development in these rather small polities take the form of a transition from feudalism to capitalism while in the rest of Europe it did not? Why, indeed, was the transition to capitalism the *exception*? The brief answer for Brenner lies in the different structures of novel feudal class (or social-property) relationships that were established in different regions of medieval Europe, particularly in the tenth and eleventh centuries, and the consequent changing balances of class forces – of class power – in the following centuries. A longer answer will be given shortly, but first it is necessary to outline those theories to which Brenner objects in order to illuminate the distinctiveness of his own thesis.

i   Ahistorical Perspectives

Brenner's critics have charged him with displaying either a wilful ignorance of demographic causation, or with being dismissive of the role of population in determining historical change. Yet it will become clear that Brenner recognises the importance of the demographic model derived from Malthus and Ricardo and applied in more recent times to medieval and early modern Europe by historians such as Michael Postan and Emmanuel Le Roy Ladurie. These historians identified a relationship between demographic cycles – that is, long-term patterns of rising and falling population, with key periods of growth and decline in economic development, and with changing patterns of income distribution across Europe between 1100 and 1750. Rising population between 1100 and 1300 led to rising rents, falling wages, the severe fragmentation of peasant holdings and declining labour productivity due to overpopulation on a finite resource: the land. The Malthusian 'check' to this crisis in the fourteenth century, which took the form of famine and plague, caused a massive decline in population and set in train the reverse experience of declining rents, increased wages and increases in the size of land holdings. Then from the mid-to-late fifteenth century to the early seventeenth century, rising population led to the same trend experienced between 1100 and 1300 and with similar consequences.

This Malthusian theory, as applied to medieval and early modern Europe, identifies important materialist foundations to economic and social change, and key historical trends, which Brenner incorporates into his thesis and analysis. But for him it is ultimately ahistorical because it seeks to apply a transhistorical model of demographic fluctuation to the *whole* of Europe between 1000 and 1750. Certain societies, for reasons relating to their changing social-property structures, were generating their own divergent demographic patterns from the fifteenth century and these patterns are not accounted for by the Malthusian model. Different economic outcomes were experienced in different regions while subject to the same demographic trends. Brenner pointed out that the model cannot therefore in itself *explain* the historical trends it has identified, and this is most clearly demonstrated by the fact that it cannot account for why these trends held for most of Europe but not for England and the northern Netherlands. Additionally the Malthusian 'check', according to the theory, should have brought the population back into a more favourable relationship with the available resources following the famine and plagues of the early and middle decades of the fourteenth century, and should have immediately led to a new 'up-phase' of demographic and related economic expansion. But this new 'up-phase' had to wait a century until about 1450 in continental Europe – much longer in England. Brenner argues that the reason for this was 'because the operation of the feudal economy encompassed a balancing not merely of peasants' requirements for subsistence with the potential output of medieval agriculture, but of lords' requirements for "political accumulation" with peasants' potential surplus'. So the drastic decline in the numbers of peasants meant a *potentially* similar decline in income for the lords from rents and dues. However, the *actual* extent of the decline in lordly incomes was dependent upon whether lords had the capacity to extract more from the surviving peasants or the power to take property from other lords in order to compensate. Both scenarios were likely to lead to the disruption of production and further demographic decline rather than a return to a population and resources equilibrium.[1] In other words, the outcome of the 'Malthusian crisis' in the four-teenth century was determined by the established structure of class relations rather than a homeostatic mechanism balancing populations with resources. Moreover, the population ceiling itself in medieval Europe, rather than simply being established by the available resources and technology, was determined by the surplus extraction relationship between peasants and lords. The greater the capacity lords had to own property and to extract the peasants' surplus product, the more peasants' consumption and ability to develop the produc-tive forces was reduced. Hence the appearance of overpopulation occurred at different densities in different regions because the number of peasants able to survive on a particular allocation of resources varied with income and the related ability to develop or apply existing technology.[2]

Since the 1970s, the demographic model has fallen out of favour among historians, and the most prominent current theories of economic develop-ment are derived largely from particular interpretations of the work of the eighteenth-century economist Adam Smith. Put crudely, they view economic development, where it was not held back by political barriers, as largely *driven* by the rise of the market and trade. Commercialisation leads to the division of labour and more efficient methods of production and productive organisation. The key to this broader development is the assumed natural propensity of peo-ple in all historical societies to seek to maximise the gains from trade: they do so by specialising their production in response to changing commodity prices, and in competition with others they accumulate surpluses and systematically invest in innovations in order to increase productivity. For Brenner this theory accounts for modern capitalist economic growth given certain prior condi-tions, but it cannot account for economic growth either before or during the feudal period in medieval Western Europe. Most importantly for our purposes it cannot account for the origin of the transition from feudalism to capital-ism or for the origin of the transition to the conditions in which the causes of modern growth are seen to occur. So for Brenner the Smithian model is also transhistorical, and therefore ahistorical because it assumes the presence of specific economic laws and capitalist mentalities operating in a generalised way in all periods of history. Brenner is also critical of the more recent mani-festations of this theory, the authors of which neglect the important findings of the demographic model. Indeed the demographic model grew out of a cri-tique of the original unilineal 'rise of the market' model which assumed that commercial development automatically led to the decline of serfdom through

---

1   Brenner 1985b, pp. 223–4; Brenner 2001, p. 288.
2   Brenner 1985b, p. 223.

the change from labour rents to money rents, and a concurrent breakthrough to modern growth through the progressive commercialisation of agriculture. And yet Michael Postan had long demonstrated that commercialisation in late medieval and early modern Europe often led to *tighter* feudal controls on peasants and the *strengthening* of feudalism, rather than modern economic growth. Clearly the processes of commercialisation and urbanisation could lead to an intensification of serfdom rather than its decline as lords sought to control labour in market areas in order to ensure the supply of food to feed cities (such as Paris) or where increasingly commercialised large-scale production of grain was developed for export in response to demand from the growing world market (such as in eastern Europe).[3]

Brenner has been equally critical of the orthodox Marxist theory of economic and social change which he argues is derived from Marx's work of the pre-*Grundrisse* period. Brenner argues that Marx in this period was strongly influenced by Adam Smith, and that his famous statements in the *Communist Manifesto*, *The German Ideology* and *The Poverty of Philosophy* provide ample licence for an all-encompassing transhistorical, ahistorical theory of economic change.[4] Applications of this theory claim to account for the transition from feudalism to capitalism as well as for a potential transition from capitalism to socialism. The key assumption is that that there is a tendency in *all* historical societies for the productive forces (that is, techniques of production, trade and markets and the organisation of the labour process) to improve the productivity of labour and therefore generate economic growth. As a result of the development of the productive forces, class structures are formed and are eventually transformed from below so that a new revolutionary class with a greater capacity to benefit from these changes appears, and a new society or mode of production based upon a new class structure emerges out of the conflict against the remnants of the old. Again as with the above critique of recent non-Marxist applications of Adam Smith, Brenner argues that the inherent tendency for the productive forces to develop holds well for economic development within capitalism – and no doubt he would agree that it provides a framework for understanding the potential for a transition out of capitalism. This is because it is *only* in capitalist societies with capitalist social-property

---

3 Brenner 1985a, p. 25.
4 As we shall see in Chapter Eight, Marx maintained his transhistorical theory into his mature work, and this led to contradictions with his developing theory on the specificity of class relations in particular societies and the specific laws of motion determined by them.

relations that there is an inherent drive to improve the productivity of labour by developing the productive forces:

> only under such a structure of social-property relations, are the economic actors not only left free to act as they deem best, but also – and most fundamental – rendered dependent upon the market for their inputs, thus subject to competition in production to survive, and therefore compelled on pain of extinction to seek systematically to maximise exchange value through specialisation, accumulation, and innovation, and moving from line to line to meet changing demand, meanwhile subordinating all other goals to exchange value maximisation.[5]

As Brenner has aimed to demonstrate, this subjection to competition in production in order to survive as a result of market dependency does not exist in feudal and in non-capitalist societies generally past and present. In feudal Europe the development of the productive forces was fundamentally based upon peasant possession of land and only partial market dependence due to necessarily limited market integration. In feudalism, both peasants and lords are shielded from the implications of full market dependency and are therefore also shielded from the need to systematically improve labour productivity in order to cut costs. Having said this, a constant increase in technology beyond the level available in feudal societies, even before 1300, was not necessary for the transition to capitalism. For Brenner the fundamental origin of the transition in England took root in the demographic and economic 'down-phase' of the fifteenth century, a time when for the most part the productive forces were relatively stagnant. Social and economic remodelling conducive to capitalist development took place in *this* context, not in one of technological advance.[6] Factors other than new technology in the development of the productive forces were behind the transition to capitalism in its early stages. What historians of agrarian revolution sometimes regard as new agricultural techniques introduced in the early modern period had in fact long been available in the medieval period. However, Brenner argues that for reasons specific to feudal social-property relations they were neither widely nor systematically applied to the key purpose of improving labour productivity.[7]

---

5 Brenner 2001, p. 278.
6 Brenner 1986, pp. 46–7, n. 45.
7 Brenner 1985a, pp. 32–3; Brenner 1985b, p. 233.

ii   Historical Materialism and Social-Property Relations

Brenner's account is influenced by Marx's mature works, *Grundrisse* and *Capital.* Brenner argues that in these works Marx rethought his earlier Smithian assumption of the primacy of the productive forces in economic development. Marx now placed much greater emphasis on the specificity of social relations and economic patterns in particular societies, namely feudalism and capital-ism, and on what he called their internal logic and 'solidity'. Marx now argued that in pre-capitalist societies like feudalism the immediate goal of peasants and artisans was subsistence rather than to increase wealth, and to reproduce themselves in their communities. For peasants, this was made especially dif-ficult because lords aimed to reproduce themselves, and their own communi-ties, largely at the peasants' expense. Attempts to specialise on a permanent basis in order to profit from market opportunities would lead to market depen-dence, and peasants viewed this strategy as too risky. Marx also now rejected the Smithian idea of primitive accumulation which assumed that the invest-ment of accumulated wealth from trade was the fundamental precondition for generating capitalist economic development and the transition from feu-dalism to capitalism. Rather than accumulated wealth from trade dissolving feudal relations, for Marx this 'so-called primitive accumulation' could only be the process by which the peasantry were divorced from the land.[8]

For Brenner it is the acknowledgement of the specificity of these patterns in different societies that is at the heart of historical materialism, and one can-not over-stress this point in a defence of his work. In a recent paper Brenner argued that historical materialist theory and history offer a means to resolve and transcend problems in the ahistorical materialist perspectives, whether Marxist or non-Marxist. There is no such thing as a transhistorical economic rationality. Every historically evolved mode of production and society, whether feudal or capitalist, has its own micro-economics. In Brenner's words, 'the specific form of socio-economic behaviour that individuals and families will find to make sense and will choose will depend on the society-wide network of social relationships – society-wide constraints and opportunities – in which they find themselves'.[9] Crucially for Brenner, what determines these individual and family choices and behaviour is what Marx called a society's relations of production, and what Brenner calls social-property relations or a society's macro-structure. It is central to the aim of this chapter to under-stand what Brenner means by social-property relations, and what he has also

---

8   Brenner 1989, pp. 285–8.
9   Brenner 2007, pp. 57–8.

termed relations of *re*production, and its distinction from the term 'relations of production'. This is particularly important, because the core of the criticism of Brenner stems from an unfortunate and frustrating misunderstanding of its usage.

When Brenner speaks of class structure in medieval Europe he is referring to a structure of class relationships which taken together constitute feudal social-property relations. Specific feudal social-property relations were established during the tenth and eleventh centuries and developed as the outcome of earlier inter-aristocratic conflict and warfare, as well as the class struggle between lords and peasants during the break up of the Carolingian Empire on the continent and the break up of the Anglo-Saxon 'great estates' in England. Social-property relations, which vary fundamentally in their nature in different societies or modes of production, are constituted by both the 'vertical' surplus-extraction relationship between appropriators and direct producers (such as lords and peasants, or capitalist entrepreneurs and landless workers), and by the 'horizontal' relationships among the appropriators themselves (aristocratic feudal lords or capitalist entrepreneurs) and among the direct producers themselves (peasants or landless wage workers). In his most recent paper Brenner asserted that 'if anything' the horizontal relations were more critical.[10]

Brenner prefers 'social-property relations' to 'social relations of production', the traditional term used by Marx and Marxists for class structure because, first: 'relations of production' generally refers to the vertical exploitative or surplus-extraction relationship only; and second, '[it] is sometimes taken to convey the idea that the social structural framework in which production takes place is somehow determined by production itself, that is, the form of cooperation or organisation of the labour process'.[11] What Brenner sees as the 'disastrous' implications of the formulation 'relations of production' has been that the significance of the property relationship between appropriators and direct producers, that is, the unequal allocation of land in feudalism, has not been fully appreciated, and the wider political organisation and power of the non-producers (monarchy and aristocracy) over the producers (peasants) has been mistakenly separated conceptually from class relations to another sphere, namely the political superstructure.

Brenner argues that the assumption therefore, widespread among Marxists, is that a mere technical change in the immediate process of production will lead to, if not select by itself in some way, a new appropriate division of labour to

---

10   Brenner 2007, p. 58. See also Comninel 1987, pp. 166–8.
11   Brenner 2007, p. 58.

apply it and therefore create new relations of production. In other words, in this formulation, new class structures are the *product* of technical changes in some kind of automatic response by socio-technical managerial relations in the *immediate* process of production to commercial and demographic forces – that is, to price fluctuations and changing patterns of supply and demand. In this way the transition from feudalism to capitalism can be seen simply in terms of the introduction of free labour by lords as a technological response to improve productive efficiency.[12] In his critique of Sweezy and Wallerstein, Marxists who were both strongly influenced by the work of Adam Smith, Brenner analysed the logic of their position in which the productive forces are seen as the primary determinant of historical process. He argued that as a result of the latter position,

> their accounts of the transition from feudalism to capitalism end up by assuming away the fundamental problem of the transformation of class relations – the class struggles this entailed – so that the rise of distinctively capitalist class relations of production are no longer seen as the basis for capitalist development, but as its result . . . the transition to capitalism is seen to occur as a smooth lineal process – which is essentially no transition at all. Given the rise of exchange and the techno-economic imperatives of the development of the productive forces under commercial pressures, the rise of capitalist social relations is reduced to a formality.[13]

Brenner argued that for these Marxist historians whose analyses vary little from Adam Smith, 'the historical problem of the origins of capitalism becomes that of the origins of trade-based division of labour', along the lines that Marx laid out in *The German Ideology*. Like Smith, their accounts of the transition from feudalism to capitalism are rooted in the initial establishment of trade routes. Following Henri Pirenne, 'for Sweezy . . . it is the re-establishment of Mediterranean commerce after the Mohammedan invasions; for Wallerstein (who follows Frank), it is the great voyages of discovery and conquests which paved the way for the rise of the world market'.[14] For Brenner there cannot be a straightforward determination of economic and demographic forces by technical changes or improvements in production because the application of techniques is dependent upon not only the desirability and opportunity but

---

12   Brenner 1977.
13   Brenner 1977, pp. 38–9. See also the critique of Cohen in Brenner 1986.
14   Brenner 1977, p. 40.

crucially the *ability* of lords or peasants to make the changes, and not only as individuals and families but as lordly political communities in fundamental conflict with peasant political communities. As he says, 'Economic needs or desires cannot explain their own satisfaction, nor can opportunities account for the capacity to take advantage of them'.[15]

It is important to be clear at the outset that Brenner's approach to the structure of class relations was very substantially developed after his first paper in 1976 when he made his first challenge to the transhistorical approach of the demographic interpreters. It is his follow-up paper in 1982 in which he responded to critics, and his critique of Adam Smith in his paper 'Neo-Smithian Marxism' in 1977, which formed the basis of his work subsequently.[16] This is rarely recognised and has led to continuing confusion among critics. In the first paper readers could certainly be forgiven for interpreting Brenner's approach to class as concerned only with the vertical relationship by which is meant 'the property relationship' or 'surplus-extraction relationship' between lords and peasants. While he was explicit about the significance of the horizontal relationship among the peasantry, he was not explicit about that same relationship among the lords and monarchy.[17] Nevertheless, clearly in this first paper the relationship between monarchy and aristocracy was fundamentally linked to the nature of the surplus-extraction relationship between peasants and lords. In this first paper the theoretical and historical framework and analysis was broadly concerned with two main issues: first, the relationship between agrarian class structure and 'long-term economic development in late medieval and early modern Europe'; and second, the breakthrough from 'traditional' economies to self-sustaining growth or 'more generally "the transition from feudalism to capitalism"'.[18] As an important development, however, and almost certainly influenced by contributions in the original 'Brenner Debate' by Rodney Hilton and Guy Bois, the second paper in 1982 specifically targeted the complexities of the feudal social-property system, feudal evolution, feudal crisis, and more specifically the transition from feudalism to capitalism.[19] In the second paper,

---

15   Brenner 1985b, p. 282.

16   The papers of 1976 and 1982 were published together in Aston and Philpin 1985. They are therefore referenced here as 1985a and 1985b respectively.

17   Brenner 1985a, p. 11.

18   Brenner 1985a, p. 30. In this first paper the earlier debate among Marxists on the transition from feudalism to capitalism was virtually unmentioned. Brenner was more concerned with a critique of the demographic interpreters and to specify the relationship between class structure and economic development. For the earlier debate see Hilton (ed.) 1976.

19   With regard to Brenner's first paper, Bois concluded that 'the idea of feudalism is totally absent from [Brenner's] article': Bois 1985, p. 116.

the relationships among feudal lords and between feudal lords and feudal monarchies, their social cohesion and processes of political centralisation and state formation, now joined centre stage in the historical process with struggles between political communities of feudal lords and political communities of peasants. The driving force of history was now explicitly not simply the vertical class-struggle dialectic between producers and appropriators, peasants and lords – which has often been the fundamental charge of critics against Brenner – but the closely interconnected horizontal relations within the main classes. The development of capitalist social-property relations was no longer simply a question of the 'breakthrough' to self-sustaining growth, but rather the problem of a 'transition' from one specific set of social-property relations to another. Overall, the second paper was 'a more fully developed interpretation of the problems of European feudal evolution and of the transition to capitalism'.[20] As we will see in the following chapter most critics did not, it seems, wish to follow Brenner beyond the first short paper.[21]

As outlined in his 1982 paper, Brenner's historical materialist approach, in contrast with the ahistorical materialist approaches outlined above, takes seriously Marx's emphasis in his later critique of classical political economy on the specificity of modes of production. Brenner asserts that specific structures of social-property relations, feudal or capitalist for example, will give rise to specific strategies for the *reproduction* of these relations. In feudal society, in common with most pre-capitalist societies, and in fundamental contrast with capitalist society – a system which appears as the antithesis or negation of feudalism – the vast amount of production was agrarian or land-based, and the vast amount of land was held or possessed (though rarely owned outright) by peasants or relatively small-scale cultivators. First and foremost, peasants produced for family subsistence and marketed only surpluses beyond their needs for reproduction and their financial obligations to lords.[22] For feudal lords to derive a steady income, they were therefore forced to coerce the peasantry to give up the surplus from the produce of the peasants' holdings. Additionally, in order to limit the market in free labour, lords forced peasants to work on the lords' own land, the home farm or demesne. The relationship determining the

---

20   Brenner 1985b, p. 216.

21   See especially my critique of John Hatcher in Chapter Two.

22   Marx saw this as a key feature of pre-capitalist society. He noted that peasants produced
      independently of the lord who had no entrepreneurial input and so in this respect they
      had more leeway in their productive activities as skilled agriculturalists – even those who
      were servile – than the wage-dependent working class which he saw around him: Marx
      1991, pp. 791–2.

economic *re*production and survival of these main classes was therefore of a political or extra-economic nature. This relationship was in fundamental contrast to that in capitalism where the economic reproduction of the main classes is fundamentally, although by no means entirely, of an economic nature due to its mediation by the market. In other words, in capitalism, workers' labour power is bought and sold in the market place, and is not *directly* coerced by political communities, which is typically the case in feudalism.[23] This political or extra-economic relationship was at the core of reproduction strategies of lords and peasants in most parts of medieval Europe.

Peasants desired to maintain the possession of their lands and in the best conditions possible. Brenner argues that the desirable conditions for peasants were full property rights on the land and payment of a small fixed, non-economic rent. However, as they demonstrated in clear examples of class conflict in the fourteenth century, peasants had visions and practical demands for the entire removal of lords and the manor.[24] This was by no means a desire for capitalism. Peasants aimed to achieve this goal towards better conditions vis-à-vis their lords by strengthening their local communal organisations or institutions of self-government, and by defending the force of custom in their lord's manorial and borough courts; not by specialising and competing against each other on the market. One cannot examine peasants' strategies for reproduction in a political vacuum: the pressure from lordship had a crucial determinant effect on peasants' lives and their approach to production and community.

The lords' goal was to maintain or improve their controls over the peasants' surplus, and also over peasants' bodies, in order to restrict a market in peasant labour power, thus avoiding competition between lords and thereby improved conditions for peasants. Lords did so by strengthening serfdom, and by generating income channels through their broader manorial jurisdictional capacity – founding market centres and small towns or boroughs, for example. The ability for lords to strengthen serfdom (squeeze and control the peasantry) could only be achieved by an increase in their military and legal powers. Their means for achieving this was what Brenner describes as 'political accumulation'. It was the accumulation of territory, government offices, and political alliances that determined the level of power feudal lords and monarchs wielded not only

---

23   For Marx wage labour in capitalism is still coerced, even though the surplus is not extracted extra-economically. As he said: 'in essence it always remains forced labour – no matter how much it may seem to result from free contractual agreement'. Marx 1991, pp. 818–19.

24   For example, Hilton 1973.

over each other but over peasants. Political accumulation and state building increased social cohesion amongst lords but it was difficult because of the decentralised, fragmented nature of power in feudal societies which forced lords to compete with each other for power, resources and peasants.[25]

For Brenner, feudal social-property relations gave rise to other strategies for reproduction. Peasants' most pressing concerns were the survival of their families and the continuity of the family line in the property they possessed, and they had to do this in very challenging conditions. This point cannot be emphasised too strongly. As Brenner says, 'the price of business failure was intolerable', and if peasants got this wrong they faced debilitating poverty and potential starvation. So peasants tended to have large families to ensure security in old age; and where the size of holdings allowed, peasants tended to subdivide holdings in order to provide the means for young heirs to get married early and set up for themselves. This strategy served both to enable the continuance of the family line and to ensure young heirs were not a burden for too long on their parents. This occurred even where the custom was primogeniture. Rather than specialise, peasants typically diversified their production of necessities to meet as many of their subsistence needs as possible and to avoid market dependence and the insecurity it brought in the face of potential bad harvests. They marketed only surpluses, if there were any.

For lords, in addition to political accumulation through warfare, state building, and hegemonic display[26] which enabled them to maintain their status and

---

25   Benno Teschke has taken further Brenner's emphasis on the importance of horizontal relations within the feudal social-property system through an examination of the correspondence between these relations and the broader international geopolitical order. Because of the essential competitive nature of feudal lords and monarchies and the requirement to redistribute peasant surpluses among themselves, 'the geopolitical system was characterised by constant military rivalry over territory and labour between lords, and within and between their "states". The geopolitical dynamic of medieval Europe followed the zero-sum logic of territorial conquest. The form and dynamic of the "international" system arose directly from the structure of social-property relations': Teschke 2003, pp. 46–7.

26   For a useful recent synthesis on the ostentation and extravagance of the political and domestic culture of the English nobility and the crown see Harris 2005, pp. 107–19, 433. Aside from the lavish 'trophy' castles built by the newcomers to the English nobility in the first half of the fifteenth century to celebrate the wealth and status that they attained through office or war, a period when noble incomes had received a shock from the decline of serfdom, Harris describes the households of the nobility in general as 'first and foremost a statement of lordship, of the virtues of magnificence and largesse, and the vices of pride, extravagance and oppression ... As a proportion of disposable income the household rarely cost less than fifty per cent and could rise towards seventy five per cent'.

political power both in relation to other lords and to the free and unfree peasants on their estates, their main strategy for reproduction was 'extensive' economic growth. Because peasants possessed the vast majority of the land, and because of the political nature of the relationship between lords and peasants, lords were denied any opportunities to invest productively on land outside of their demesnes in order to increase the labour productivity of the peasantry. They were therefore *compelled* to extend their lands by taking them from other lords (and monarchs) or by new colonisation in which peasants were encouraged to break new ground either by being offered favourable tenurial terms or by the use of force. As a result of these reproduction strategies,

> feudal economic development manifested a two-sided conflictive interaction: between a developing system of production for subsistence through which the class of peasant possessors aimed to reproduce themselves and provide for the continuity of their families, and a developing system of surplus extraction by extra-economic compulsion for nonproductive consumption, by which the class of feudal lords aimed to reproduce themselves as individuals and as a ruling class.[27]

These reproduction strategies were determined by feudal social-property relations and, specific to these relations, these in turn determined overall demographic and economic development patterns peculiar to feudalism from the establishment of these relations in the tenth and eleventh centuries to around 1300. These patterns were rapid population growth,[28] the extension of production and colonisation of new lands, urbanisation and the increasing sophistication of international trade due to lordship demands for military equipment and other luxuries, and increasing political centralisation and state formation. In turn however these specific feudal development patterns led to specific feudal forms of crisis. Feudal crises were characterised by the following:

---

27   Brenner 1985b, p. 232.
28   Demographic expansion in the period following the establishment of feudalism (that is, between 1100 and 1300) can be contrasted with a decline in population between the sixth and eighth centuries in the post-Roman early medieval period. Demographic decline appears to have corresponded with weakening aristocratic power over peasant populations. Indeed, in the three centuries before the 'caging' of peasant villages into manorial cells, peasants typically had a good deal of autonomy from their aristocratic neighbours. Wickham argues that 'in the last two millennia the period 500–800 was probably when aristocratic power in the west was least totalising, and local [peasant] autonomies were greatest – taking into account regional differences ... this is one of the main markers of the specificity of the earliest Middle Ages': Wickham 2009, pp. 215–17.

overpopulation and severe underemployment on materially finite and jurisdictionally defined resources; declining *labour productivity* in the face of limited application of available techniques despite the increased *land productivity*
from the increase in worker inputs in the thirteenth century (a period which
saw population expansion, partial commercialisation and dependency);
reduced demand for manufactured goods, and a consequent decline in urban
production and trade; a declining rate of increase in the feudal levy on peasants over time; and an increase in warfare as lords sought to compensate for
the reduced income derived from an increasingly debilitated peasantry. These
elements of feudal crisis led to a downward economic spiral through the
increased fiscal and jurisdictional pressure on peasant production which had
already been pushed beyond the capacity that resources allowed. This crisis
was compounded by terrible weather between 1315 and 1318 which caused a
series of bad harvests, animal disease, and famine which killed 10 percent of
the population. Then a series of devastating plagues in 1348–9 and again in the
1360s killed half of the population of Europe.

There is an increasing tendency among historians to view the full impact of
this weather and plague as a 'shock', or 'shocks', which were wholly exogenous
or independent of the feudal crisis. One historian has in fact argued that these
shocks were the only crisis that occurred.[29] Brenner agrees that there was a
strong exogenous impact on the feudal crisis, but he argues that it was the
crisis of overpopulation, malnutrition, and the increased impositions on peasant production and warfare which were determined by feudal social-property
relations that left peasants inordinately exposed to famine and infection in
this period. This explains why the impact of plague and weather on European
societies was so extensive and so deep. There is also a tendency to see warfare as an exogenous shock in this period, and yet those historians who follow this line can do so only by avoiding Brenner's thesis that conflict between
and among ruling classes is dialectically integrated within the broader social-
property relations.

The feudal crisis appeared at different times in different places and the
outcome of the crisis in different regions was also divergent. The outcome
in England was the origin of the transformation of feudal to capitalist social-
property relations and to consequent patterns of Smithian economic growth.
By contrast the rule elsewhere was continued feudal or absolutist social-
property relations which determined feudal and non-capitalist forms of development, and led again to feudal forms of crisis in the seventeenth century.
A crucial point for Brenner is that the development of capitalist social-property

---

29   See my critique of S.R. Epstein in Chapter Two.

relations in England was the *unintended consequence* of lords and peasants acting in class conflict with each other with the purpose of reproducing each other *as they were*. Capitalism in its formative stages in the fifteenth century was not something that was desired by a revolutionary class from below.

These divergent evolutions in different countries, and their divergent outcomes from the feudal crisis in the face of precisely the same demographic and economic developments, were the result of differences in feudal social-property relations as they became established in the tenth and eleventh centuries out of the fragmentation of the Carolingian empire. Key for Brenner was that from their establishment the *overall* character of these feudal social-property relations remained resilient and was not altered or shaped by these demographic or economic fluctuations, even if the balance of class power did of course change sharply in changing demographic contexts. Key factors within feudal social-property relations in medieval Europe which led to divergent economic outcomes in different countries and regions were as follows: the unequal allocation of property between peasants and lords when these relations were first established; the ability of lords to maintain this unequal allocation of property; and the lords' level of political cohesion and organisation. These factors determined the lords' capacity to coerce versus the peasants' own level of self-organisation and power of resistance over time. With momentous implications, they therefore conditioned the ability for either class to benefit at different times from demographic patterns or economic stimuli.

iii   Medieval and Early Modern Europe in Comparative Perspective

To demonstrate his thesis that the establishment of varying forms of feudal social-property relations across Europe from c. 1000–1100 conditioned subsequent demographic, economic and political evolution, Brenner employs a rigorous and systematic comparative method. In his earlier papers he examined the differences between the evolution of England and France and more widely between the evolution of western and eastern Europe. More recently he compared the evolution between different regions within the Low Countries, and between the Low Countries and elsewhere.

Brenner argues that the precocious centralisation and cohesion of lords and monarchy in England in the Anglo-Saxon period, an outcome of the organisation of resistance to the Scandinavian invasions, and most especially Norman developments in state construction following the conquest of the whole of England in the late eleventh century, placed Anglo-Norman and subsequently English lords in a comparatively better position vis-à-vis the peasantry than lords in polities such as France and western Germany. Good indications of the relatively favourable position of English lords are the comparatively large demesnes that they maintained throughout the medieval period, and their retention of powers to maintain or increase arbitrary rents and fines (characteristic of serfdom) over much of the peasantry before the mid-fourteenth century, and for a few decades after the Black Death. The English demesnes amounted to some twenty to thirty percent of the best land in the country. These factors enabled English lords to keep their incomes in line with inflation for much of the period of demographic and economic growth at the expense of the peasantry between 1100 and 1300. However, this sustained increase in the level of surplus extraction reduced peasants' ability to invest and maintain sufficient land and animals, and this was an important factor in the decline of labour productivity by the early fourteenth century. Indeed, early fourteenth century England is characterised by declining peasant labour productivity, reduced peasant demand for manufactured goods, the levelling-off of lordship income after extensive production had reached its limits, and the onset of feudal crisis. By contrast, in much of France, for example, lords' political communities were less cohesive due to the excessive decentralisation and fragmentation of political power. As a result lords in France had relatively small demesnes which only amounted to between eight and twelve percent of the land, and they could not maintain the capacity to enserf the peasantry through the thirteenth century. This was in fact a period of peasant gains in France with regard to the achievement of communal self-government in the villages, and the achievement of fixed rents and dues and full proprietorship of the land. So in France, in contrast to developments in England, lords could not keep abreast of inflation and at various points in the thirteenth century population and lords' incomes stagnated, well before the period of exogenous shocks.

The outcome of the feudal crisis and exogenous shocks in England left lords weakened in the century after the Black Death due to the scarcity of labour and heightened peasant resistance. This weakening led to the decline of serfdom in the decades around 1400. The English lords still suffered from decentralised power even though they were comparatively more cohesive and linked more closely as a class to the interests of the monarchy than they were in France. However for Brenner the 'trump card' for the English lords was their retention of large demesnes and their feudal powers over customary property, and this was achieved in no small part by support from the monarchy and state. Unlike French and German lords who faced greater restrictions from their respective monarchies that increasingly wielded greater autonomous (absolutist) power, English lords could legally attach vacant customary land in order to consolidate and increase the size of their demesnes further, and thereby increase the area of land under leasehold tenure and thus subject to commercial rents. Equally important was their ability to control the remainder of the customary or copyhold tenure and turn it into the equivalent of leasehold or commercial rents. They did so by imposing arbitrary fines on inheriting peasants or when tenancies were changed or renewed. Again this outcome was in contrast to that in France – and especially Germany – where peasants had gained full proprietorial rights on the land and the hereditary rights of peasants were given legal sanction by royal justices: for the French and German monarchies it was necessary to protect peasant customary holdings in order to tax them. Hence the customary holdings were not subjected to limited terms and arbitrary entry fines.

In a context of heightened class struggle from the late fourteenth century, and in the face of a greatly reduced peasantry that was prospering due to low food prices and low rents, English lords were compelled to lease out their demesnes in order to maintain themselves as lords in the late fourteenth and early fifteenth century, as well as their incomes. This entailed the transference (within the four decades between 1380 and 1420) of between one-fifth and one-third of all cultivable land in England to peasants, merchants and lesser gentry, although the vast majority of it went to wealthy peasants. The result was the beginning of the transformation of feudal social-property relations into what would turn out to be capitalist social-property relations. The new demesne lessees were compelled to specialise and produce efficiently for the market in competition with one another in order to gain a big enough return to pay for the lease and gain profits. They did so in mutual relationship with lords who found it in their interests to help their tenants become successful. Labour productivity gains in agriculture were already evident in the early fifteenth century with the reversion to pastoralism, but in the second half of the fifteenth century sheep farming expanded in symbiosis with the rural cloth industry in England in response to increasing domestic and foreign demand. This was facilitated by an enclosure movement that sought to accumulate the remaining small peasant copyhold tenures. The insecurity of the latter enabled farmers and lords to make inroads into them on a significant scale already before 1520. As a consequence, there was a parting of the ways, from late fifteenth century onwards, between English and western European economic and demographic patterns. Mass anti-enclosure rebellion by English peasants and artisans in the sixteenth and early seventeenth centuries had the potential to 'clip the wings of agrarian capitalism' but this ultimately failed. So capitalism originated in the English countryside and capitalist social-property relations continued to develop in the shell of landlordism. The replacement of subsistent agricultural production and village manufacture with competitive leasehold led to ongoing increases in labour productivity and an agricultural revolution which was able to support increasing numbers outside of agriculture. The rate of urbanisation in England (and the Netherlands) between 1500 and 1800 was not matched elsewhere in Europe, and 'the separation of manufacturing from the peasantry was the indispensable foundation for dynamic industrial development, and ultimately the industrial revolution'.[30]

There was no growth of a bourgeois class in direct opposition to old feudal lordship driven by commercial expansion and growth of the productive forces which then defeated the latter in the 'bourgeois revolution' of the mid- and late seventeenth century, as has often been contended. Instead feudal lordship became 'bourgeois' itself. These commercial landlords, who now leased land on market-sensitive leases, and defeated militarily attempts by peasants to halt the enclosure movement, were a fundamental part of the newly emerging capitalist system in its triad form which – unintentionally – they helped to create. This period also saw an increase in the power of lords over capitalist farmers, their tenants. The latter had had the better of the new developments before the early sixteenth century, but that was about to change as demand for land increased and competition for leases dramatically improved landlords' rental income. In the mid and later seventeenth century English lords were as responsible for breaking the remaining extra-economic prerogatives of monarchy and its allies as the 'bourgeoisie' that grew up in the shell of their estate system.[31]

As stated above in the discussion on developments in England, political sovereignty was excessively decentralised and fragmented in France and western Germany compared to England, and the resulting competition and rivalry between territorial lords and state-building princes and monarchs enabled peasants to develop strong political communities and hereditary property. After the feudal crisis in France and western Germany, faced with an entrenched peasantry on the land which was able to resist new impositions characteristic of serfdom thanks to protections issued by the state, alternative 'absolutist' centralised state systems were developed in which the extra-economic extraction of the peasant surplus remained fundamental. In the face of a highly organised free peasantry, many lords saw their best option for reproducing themselves by office holding in an increasingly centralised monarchical system. Instead of extracting a surplus through rents and dues at the manorial level they could now benefit from more efficient taxing of the peasantry at the state level. This inevitably led to the return of a downward spiral of declining peasant productivity and warfare as this new form of surplus extraction

---

30   Brenner 1985a, pp. 46–54; Brenner 1985b, pp. 246–64, 270–2, 291–319; Brenner 1996; Brenner 2007, pp. 8–9, 104–11.

31   Brenner 1989; Brenner 1993, 'Postscript'.

prevented peasant investment in improvements, particularly when the population rose rapidly again from the middle of the fifteenth century, and plots
became fragmented once more. The majority of hereditary peasant property
in France and western Germany was undermined in the long run, although
in a different way and with consequences different to those in England.
Increasingly fragmented plots due to rising population, overtaxation, and peri-
odically devastating warfare and famine (which hit France much harder than
England), forced peasants into debt, and in the north and west the majority
were forced to sell their hereditary holdings. Due to massive hikes in taxation to pay for its geopolitical interests, the state, which had earlier protected
peasant property from legal eviction, paradoxically served to undermine it.
By the seventeenth century, large holdings were accumulated as in England,
with commercial farmers employing wage labour, particularly in the Paris
basin. Outwardly it would appear that these developments were the same as
in England, but these wealthy farmers were also heavily taxed by the state and
church as the vast weight of taxation fell on the peasantry rather than on the
nobility and bourgeois. Seigneurial rents were also very high. Moreover, these
large farms were situated in a sea of fragmented smallholdings, and lords and
farmers found it was in their best interests to draw high rents from fragmented
plots and engage in labour-intensive farming given the abundant availability
of underemployed labour, rather than invest capital in labour-saving technology in order to increase labour productivity. Even at the time of the French
Revolution, the situation was fundamentally the same. The vast majority of the
French population remained on the land, the majority paying short-term rents,
supported by rural industry and other work.[32]

The persistence of so-called 'backwardness' in eastern Europe into modern times was the result of the re-enserfment of the peasantry by the lords in
response to the demographic downturn of the fourteenth century. By striking
contrast this downturn aided the *decline* of serfdom in the west, as we have
seen. Feudal settlement in east-Elbian Germany and Poland occurred later
than in the west during the demographic 'up-phase' of the twelfth and thirteenth centuries as German lords sought to extend their lands by conquest
and colonisation in the east in time-honoured feudal fashion. To achieve this
settlement lords were forced to offer peasants favourable tenurial terms in
order to induce them to emigrate eastwards, and at this stage German peasants fared better in terms of their legal status than their western counterparts.
However, as a consequence, the nature of peasant settlement was far more

---

32   Brenner 1985a, pp. 54–63; Brenner 1985b, pp. 69–72, 242–64, 284–91, 299–319; Brenner
       1996; Brenner 2007, pp. 91–3, 101–3.

individualistic than that in the west, and communal peasant productive organisation and peasant structures of self-government and political and military
organisation were weaker. This made it difficult for peasants to resist new
feudal extra-economic demands made on them by their lords in the fifteenth
century, even though in theory demographic conditions should have provided
them with more leverage.[33] This achievement by the German lords was facilitated by their own unprecedented high level of self-organisation which was
specifically designed to prevent inter-lordship rivalry: 'As in much of western
Europe, lords thus revived the system by which they coercively took a surplus
from the peasantry by profoundly expanding the scope and cohesiveness of
their political communities, extending the long-term feudal evolutionary process by which there emerged over time in every region of Europe ever larger
and more powerful feudal states'.[34]

Regions and polities within the Low Countries witnessed strikingly divergent paths during the late medieval and early modern periods. As a major hub
in medieval European trade, the inland southern Low Countries contained the
largest urban populations in Europe during the medieval period. These placed
unrivalled demand on agriculture, and yet this region followed a similar trajectory as France and Germany. Competition between the 'state' (the count of
Flanders) and the towns who were allied on the one hand, and the Flemish
nobility on the other, resulted in a weakened aristocracy. Following rebellions
in the 1320s against the seigneurial reaction to the crisis in lordship revenues,
a free peasantry emerged alongside the increasing development of a tax-office
state. The presence of massive urban demand for food and raw materials for
industry enabled the fragmentation of holdings to create the densest population in Europe as high levels of technology were applied to holdings. As in
France and Germany, especially after 1600, due to indebtedness and the inability of their fragmented holdings to support them, peasants were forced to sell
up and take up leases. But there was no tendency to build up large holdings.
Small peasants could compete with larger ones by reducing consumption and
living standards and adding proto-industrial sidelines. So the proportion of
smallholdings increased even with leasing. Greater surpluses were thus created by lowering living standards and intensifying labour rather than investing
capital in innovation, hence long-term increases in land productivity at the
expense of labour productivity, and no possible transition to capitalism.[35]

---

33   Brenner 1985b, pp. 272–84; Brenner 1996; Brenner 2007, pp. 93–5, 103.
34   Brenner, 2007, p. 95.
35   Brenner 2001, pp. 304–8.

In the maritime area of the northern Netherlands and parts of maritime Flanders Brenner argues that two distinct forms of capitalist social-property relations emerged, although with contrasting evolutions. The first, which is less well known and less researched, was on the clay soils of maritime Flanders, and on the Frisian coast in the Zeeland archipelago in the northern Netherlands. The capitalist social-property relations that developed there seemed to take the form of landowners leasing to large tenant farmers on the English model. The origin of this form, in maritime Flanders at least, was the reclamation of the coastal areas by the count of Flanders and his aristocratic followers. Given the presence of the great urban markets of Flanders and Brabant, these lands appear to have been farmed commercially from the outset, either directly by the lords themselves or leased to large market-dependent tenants with the capacity to invest. During the late medieval period the maritime Flanders region appears to have been devoted to large-scale cattle breeding, holdings increased in size averaging over 20 hectares (approximately 50 acres), and they grew larger in the sixteenth and seventeenth centuries. On the clay soils of the Frisian coast in the northern Netherlands, high-value bread grains were produced on similar capitalist tenant farms.[36]

The second form of capitalist social-property relations that Brenner argues developed in the Low Countries was in the adjacent maritime northern Netherlands, although they were the result of a very different evolution to their establishment in other parts of the region and in England. Settlement by peasants following the remarkable reclamation of land from the sea occurred with minimal involvement of lordship. As elsewhere, the goal of Dutch peasant reproductive strategy was to achieve full free peasant property producing for subsistence, and to diversify produce. In this case they were helped by powerful village organisations that developed with the requirement to regulate the complex drainage systems. But the drainage of the land had ecological affects on the exposed peat, and as early as the thirteenth century there began an extended process of ecological degradation. Along with a rise in sea levels after 1350 the land became too wet to grow bread grains, and after 1400 there was an agricultural crisis. As a result, '[t]hrough ecological processes strikingly analogous in their effect to "the so-called primitive accumulation" that deprived agricultural producers of their land in England, Dutch peasants were thus separated from direct access to their means of subsistence'.[37] However although they could not use the land for subsistence they mostly continued to own the land. But having become market-dependent for their inputs these small owner

---

36   Brenner 2001, pp. 311 n. 18, 320–2.
37   Brenner 2001, p. 310.

occupiers with 16–18 hectares were subjected to competitive production and forced to specialise and invest in increased labour productivity. Thus the unintended consequence of the reclamation of the peat lands by peasants engaging in feudal rules of reproduction was for these peasants to transform themselves into capitalist farmers, and for the surplus population to become wage-earning proletarians. At the same time, from the second half of the fourteenth century, large towns developed in this region for the first time:

> Unlike anywhere else in Europe, the subjection of the agricultural producers to dependence on the market and the rise of a large market dependent population involved in trade and industry in towns occurred to a very large extent as part of a single process of agrarian transformation. The emergence on the one hand, of Dutch clothmaking, brewing, shipping, shipbuilding and peat digging – much of which was orientated to export – and, on the other, of Dutch dairy and cattle raising were thus two sides of the same extraordinary process of ecologically-driven separation of the direct producers from their means of subsistence leading to the transition to capitalism, and they must be understood together.[38]

By 1350, 23 percent of Holland's population was located in the towns – but by 1500, as a result of this transformation, it had reached 50 percent. During the early modern period holdings were not subdivided and they grew, although they were still not very large in comparison with those in England. The surplus, proletarianised population left the land for the expanding towns and industry.[39] From the outset of this transformation, the presence of huge markets for dairy produce in the inland southern Low Countries was certainly fortunate, as was the rapid rise at the same time of commercialised grain production in eastern Europe, which enabled farmers and the increasing non-agricultural population to buy food relatively cheaply, increase their discretionary expenditure and thereby increase demand for the agrarian and non-agrarian produce of the region.[40] In the long run Brenner argues that capitalist development became 'stymied' in comparison with England because of the Netherland's heavy dependence on food imports and – because of its trading dominance – its greater commercial integration into the feudal economies of Europe and their cycles of declining productivity. The Dutch economy had grown much faster than the English on the basis of this trading dominance, but the English

---

38   Brenner 2001, p. 309.
39   Brenner 2001, p. 313.
40   Brenner 2001, p. 312.

economy (which by contrast was geared fundamentally to its domestic market for industrial goods) was self-sustaining, 'leading to ever-increasing industrialisation marked by the movement of an ever-increasing proportion of the labour force out of agriculture', and as such had the capacity to overtake the Dutch.[41] Nevertheless Brenner argues that throughout the early modern period, both countries saw continuing increases in labour productivity which allowed a progressive increase in the proportion of non-agricultural population; a continuing rise in the population without hitting a Malthusian ceiling; and a separation of industry from agricultural household production into specialised industrial districts which became large industrial towns.[42]

Criticism of Brenner's thesis and analysis as presented in outline in the foregoing has been extensive and often heated. I respond to these critics in the chapters that follow, and while doing so I examine the application of Brenner's thesis in more detail.

---

41   Brenner 2001, pp. 332–4.

42   Brenner 2007, pp. 108–9. For a more detailed study on the remarkable regional diversity of early medieval settlement, and the consequent economic and social developments in the Low Countries as a whole, see Van Bavel 2010. This important new work firmly supports Brenner's perspective on the centrality of social-property relations in economic and social change.

The Prime Mover of Economic and
Social Development

The focus of criticism against Brenner from a number of leading historians of English medieval society has been on his assertion that class (social-property relations) is the prime mover or fundamental determinant of economic and social development. Indeed many now regard the concept of a prime mover in historical analysis, whether class, population or the rise of the market (commercialisation), as illegitimate. In his early paper in 1976 Brenner had criticised demographic historians by arguing that their theory of historical causation simply replaced the Smithian 'key variable' of the rise of the market with their own population-resource driven demographic cycles. While doing so they either rejected class as a concept, or treated it as a dependent variable. Critics, including those same historians who used to privilege demographic fluctuations in historical causation, accuse Brenner of doing the same with what they regard as his own 'key variable' of class and class struggle. Many lines have been written recently on the virtue of a pluralist approach whereby all economic and social factors have equal validity in determining a historical outcome and should be taken together without privileging any particular element of causation. What is interesting is that while these historians criticise the concept of a prime mover, Brenner's use of class in particular, they do so in different ways and this illuminates fundamental flaws in their critiques. Misreadings of Brenner abound, and this is further illustrated by the work of one influential historian whose critique as we shall see below cannot actually identify a prime mover in Brenner's work. Others, while wishing to join in with the pluralist turn, still privilege the market, and cannot see beyond it.

i   J. Hatcher and M. Bailey: The Case for Pluralism I

While certainly no Marxists, John Hatcher and Mark Bailey have been cited as representing a move towards acknowledging the contributions of Marxist historians because in a recent work they presented *class* as a historical determinant of equal importance to population and commerce.[1] In their own words

---

1   Wickham 2007, pp. 34–5, referring to Hatcher and Bailey 2001. This is more surprising than it sounds. For example, in 1999 Andy Wood could state that 'H.N. Brailsford's comment of

Hatcher and Bailey have described the Marxist, historical materialist, approach as 'commendably ambitious' as 'it opens up the possibilities of constructing a comprehensive overview which maps and measures the multiplicity of inter-connections between political, social, economic, legal, cultural and religious institutions, ideologies and practices and of providing explanations of eco-nomic and social change which take them fully into account'. For them the Marxist contribution has also been 'in seeking answers to some of the biggest questions which confront medieval historians, and in searching for the roots of capitalism and the origins of industrialisation in the fundamental changes in agrarian structure, conditions of tenure, and relations between landlords and tenants, which took place within the Middle Ages'.[2]

However for Hatcher and Bailey the ambition of historical materialism is not matched by what they see as a focus by Marxists on class as the prime mover which determines and drives the 'multiplicity of interconnections'. According to them, Marxists have resorted to 'ingenious gyrations' in order to avoid what they view as the obvious flaws in trying to demonstrate the cen-trality of class.[3] For Hatcher and Bailey, Brenner's application of historical materialism is one of the least convincing. They argue that he belongs to an older Marxist tradition constituted by Maurice Dobb and Evgeny Kosminsky which mistakenly equates feudalism with serfdom, and locates the instability and collapse of feudalism 'almost exclusively' in the struggle for rent and the destructive exploitation of the unfree peasantry. They assert that the strength of the argument of this old defunct Marxism derives directly from its simplicity which is achieved by denying the significance of economic and demographic forces, and by focusing selectively on particular components of the feudal sys-tem. This old tradition is set against a more reputable set of 'Neo-Marxist vari-ants' which is, according to them, represented in the work of Perry Anderson and of medieval historians Guy Bois and Rodney Hilton. Anderson is praised for his eclecticism while Hilton and Bois are applauded as 'Marxists who place considerable weight on changes in the whole mode of production, and thus propose broader and subtler interpretations of the forces at work in medieval

---

almost forty years ago that "historians are as shy in confronting the fact of class as were nov-elists of the last century in facing the fact of sex" still holds true': Wood 1999, p. 16. When I defended my Ph. D. thesis in the same year, the external examiner's first question was to ask why I had chosen to use such an old-fashioned concept as class – although admittedly his tongue was firmly pressed in his cheek. Still now, a recent collection of studies by English medieval economic historians is notable for its virtual absence of the word class: Dodds and Britnell (eds.) 2008.

2   Hatcher and Bailey 2001, p. 95.
3   Hatcher and Bailey 2001, p. 120.

society. By doing so they are able to create explanations which are more sensitive to the surviving evidence of the period and which allow more emphasis to be given to the influence of economic, demographic and commercial forces'. However even these explanations are insufficient, because 'as they draw closer to the complexities of real historical experience these more flexible and inclusive models lose much of their brute intellectual strength which cruder models derive from their simplicity'.[4]

The problem for Hatcher and Bailey's critique is that their basis for the dismissal of Brenner, and the so-called 'old Marxist' tradition, as distinct from a so-called more reputable although still flawed new Marxist tradition, derives from their interpretation of his application of class as an exclusive, autonomous driver of change without reference to economic and demographic forces. Brenner's theory and analysis has been elaborated and strengthened since his first paper in 1976, yet Hatcher and Bailey's critique of him rarely strays beyond this first polemic which was written specifically to challenge the dominant Malthusian consensus. Moreover, their fire is specifically targeted at the paper's introduction where Brenner lays out his use of class as prime mover and the utility of demographic explanations of change. Hatcher and Bailey argue that this introduction points to class not only as prime mover, but as an autonomous force driving history along without any significance given to the rises and falls in population and markets. The offending section of Brenner's introduction is worth quoting in full:

> It would be my argument then that different class structures, specifically property relations or surplus extraction relations, once established, tend to impose rather strict limits and possibilities, indeed rather specific long-term patterns, on a society's economic development. I would contend that class structures tend to be highly resilient in relation to the impact of economic forces; as a rule they are not shaped by, or alterable in terms of, changes in demographic or commercial trends. It follows therefore that long-term economic changes, and most crucially economic growth, cannot be analysed adequately in terms of the emergence of any particular constellation of relatively scarce factors unless the class relationships have first been specified; indeed the opposite outcomes may accompany the impact of apparently similar economic conditions. In sum, fully to comprehend long-term economic developments, growth and/or retrogression in the late medieval and early modern period, it is critical to analyse the relatively autonomous processes by which

---

4   Hatcher and Bailey 2001, pp. 76–91.

particular class structures, especially property or surplus-extraction relations, are established, and in particular the class conflicts to which they
do (or do not) give rise. For it is the outcome of such class conflicts – the
reaffirmation of the old property relations or their destruction and the
consequent establishment of a new structure – that is to be found perhaps the key to the problem of long-term economic development in late
medieval and early modern Europe, and more generally of the transition
from feudalism to capitalism.[5]

Later Brenner concludes more forcefully that the model of demographically
driven economic forces 'simply breaks down in face of comparative analysis.
Different social and economic outcomes proceeded from similar demographic
trends at different times and in different areas of Europe. Thus we may ask
if demographic change can be legitimately treated as a cause, let alone the
key variable'.[6]

In the first quote Brenner is not minimising the significance of demographic
and economic patterns. He is simply saying that they do not by themselves
alter or modify class structures, as viewed in accordance with his application of
social-property relations that I have discussed at length in the previous chapter. Because once these relations are established, as feudal structures were in
the tenth and eleventh centuries as the result of previous class struggle and
warfare, they produce a resilient though not unchanging framework of relationships which condition subsequent demographic and economic evolution.
For Brenner, the demographic and economic forces influence *the balance* of
class forces, but the key point here is that the nature of this influence on class
forces, and the outcome of the struggles that resulted, were conditioned by
the established though not unchanging social-property relations; specifically
by the prior distribution of property between the classes of lords and peasants, and the capacity of the monarchy and lords to coerce in the face of peasant organisation and resistance: 'It is this prior distribution and capacity to
coerce that structured the significance of demographically determined market forces'. Brenner argues that it is enough to show that, in different countries, this prior distribution of property and capacity to coerce determined
entirely different historical outcomes in response to similar demographic and
economic contexts.

Brenner asserted that class was a 'relatively autonomous' factor in historical causation, but he does not mean 'autonomous' in the sense that class has

5   Brenner 1976, pp. 11–12.
6   Brenner 1976, p. 21.

no connection to demographic and economic forces, a perspective which of course would be absurd. Indeed, in the introduction to his second essay, where he sought to take account of criticisms of the earlier paper as well as elaborating his thesis, he states that demographic and commercial trends 'acquired their economic significance for the distribution of income and the development of the productive forces only in connection with specific, historically developed systems of social-property relations and given balances of class forces'. He also put it another way to ensure that class was to be given primacy: 'changes in relative factor scarcities consequent upon demographic changes exerted an effect on the distribution of income in medieval Europe only as they were, so to speak, refracted through the prism of changing social-property relations and fluctuating balances of class forces'.[7] Although Brenner clarified his position in this way, Hatcher and Bailey, in their recent critique, have ignored the explanations that Brenner made twenty years earlier, and have ploughed on regardless, accusing Brenner of deflecting rather than answering criticisms. They prefer to relegate Brenner's explanations to a footnote in which readers are referred to the work of Steve Rigby.[8] It was in fact Rigby who tutored these two historians in historical materialism as they acknowledge in their preface. I attend to Rigby's critique of Brenner below.

Hatcher and Bailey's key criticism of Brenner concerns the constrasting level of power English lordship enjoyed before and after the Black Death. Brenner had argued that during the inflationary period of the thirteenth century and early fourteenth century English lords, with their relatively large allocation of property and relatively greater capacity to coerce the peasantry, had been able to maintain their incomes at the expense of the peasantry. In this period, the heavily-weighted land to labour ratio due to overpopulation greatly favoured the lords as labour was increasingly plentiful and cheap, and peasants had less bargaining power with which to maintain themselves. Also, in the face of increasingly open peasant resistance in the late thirteenth and early fourteenth centuries, this was a period of victories for English lords in open legal battles. As a rule the English peasants were unable to get their dues fixed and effectively gain full proprietorship of their holdings at the expense of the incomes of the lords. By contrast in France, although subject to the *same* demographic pressure as English peasants, French peasants gained the upper hand at various points in the thirteenth century and managed to get their dues fixed from quite early on in the century, and they possessed a far greater proportion of the land. The lords' incomes therefore fell away as the fixed rents became

---

7   Brenner 1985b, pp. 213, 218.
8   Hatcher and Bailey 2001, pp. 74 n. 12, 108 n. 83.

increasingly low in the face of inflation during the economic and demographic up-phase of the thirteenth century. In England, after the severe reduction in population caused by the Black Death, the land to labour ratio strongly tilted towards the peasantry. During the seigneurial reaction to this increased level of peasant bargaining power, English lords were able to hold their own between the late 1340s and the 1370s with support from the crown, but the repetition of demographic shocks in the 1360s and 1370s served to heighten competition between lords for peasant tenants, and led to intensified peasant resistance which culminated in the rebellion of 1381. The result was the decline of serfdom in England and its virtual disappearance by 1440. In France, the Black Death could, theoretically, only improve the position of the peasants vis-à-vis the lords, but the reduction in aristocratic income and the resulting economic 'downward spiral' due to warfare on French soil led to the widespread devastation of villages.[9]

Now Hatcher and Bailey ask the following simple question, and they argue that Brenner's thesis stands or falls on the answer: why were lords so strong in England before the Black Death and not afterwards? If such a striking change in fortunes had nothing to do with the Black Death and the demographic downturn then '[in] order for Brenner's model to establish its validity, these sharply contrasting situations would have to be solely due to changes which occurred independently in the structure and power of the two conflicting classes'.[10] But as I have explained in the foregoing, Brenner does not see class and class struggle as an autonomous force driving history without regard to, or independent of, demographic and economic forces, a position that Hatcher and Bailey strangely persist in attributing to him. For Brenner the balance of class forces between lords and peasants in England was altered in favour of the peasants

---

9   Conflict in France between peasants and lords in the decades after the Black Death took a different form to that in England. It did not arise from a seigneurial reaction aiming to maintain serfdom because that had already been severely attenuated in most places in France. What amounted to class genocide on both sides in the Jacquerie of 1358 was the outcome of either the inability or wilful lack of desire on the part of French lords to defend French peasant lands against the English. French peasants often had to fight the armies of English (and Welsh) knights themselves and, it must be added, with notable victories: Cohn 2006, pp. 34–8. It is also notable that class conflict also took different forms in the two countries in the sixteenth century: in England peasants fought to resist enclosure and extortionate inheritance fines that were undermining their property, while the French peasants fought against increasing taxation by the absolutist state, the latter having supported peasant property against the lords in order to maintain its main tax base: Brenner 1976, p. 57.

10   Hatcher and Bailey 2001, p. 109.

in the context of the demographic downturn; it *was* influenced by changes in population. Although the English ruling class was relatively cohesive compared to its counterparts on the continent, power or sovereighty in England was still decentralised into lordship jurisdictions, a characteristic of feudal Europe as a whole. As such, English lords had to compete with each other for peasants, and the latter vacated lands previously held by harsh tenures because of the abundance of vacant freehold land elsewhere. But Brenner's point is that the overall framework of English class relations (social-property relations) established three centuries earlier, and still resilient in terms of property allocation and the capacity to coerce and resist, remained directly determinate in the outcome of the conflicts arising from the demographic crisis.

To be perfectly clear on this, we perhaps need to place greater stress on the analytical distinction in Brenner's explanation between the overall framework of established social-property relations (the macro structure of society), and the balance of class forces in changing economic and demographic contexts to which the allocation of property, jurisdiction and power gave rise. The balance of class forces was of course sensitive to changing economic and demographic contexts; but social-property relations, although not unchanging over time, were resilient. If social-property relations are *fundamentally* changed, then so is the whole society, along with the demographic and economic patterns specific to it.

Aside from this, and to return to Hatcher and Bailey's question, Brenner does not seek simply to answer the question of 'why were English lords strong vis-à-vis the peasantry before but not after the Black Death' because, as we have seen, such a question is misleading. The significance of demographic patterns in historical causation in a particular country can only be adequately demonstrated in comparative terms. Hence Brenner is more interested in why English lords remained *relatively* strong in comparison to lords in France vis-à-vis the respective peasantries and, more importantly, why England developed capitalism while France and virtually all of the rest of Europe did not. This is the key point which Hatcher and Bailey are not willing to address, even though such questions formed part of the commendable historical materialist repertoire that they had earlier praised. Brenner's answer is as follows: although their position vis-à-vis the peasants in the late fourteenth century and throughout the fifteenth century had weakened, English lords maintained their large allocation of property and relative cohesion in connection with the monarchy, in spite of the decline of serfdom. They still directly controlled at least twenty to thirty percent of the best land in lowland England through their demesnes. They had the jurisdictional capacity to draw in vacant land to enlarge their demesnes still further due to the demographic downturn and the movement of peasants away from harsh tenures. And, they were able to prevent the customary peasantry from gaining almost full freehold rights over their holdings which amounted to another third of the land. Although the private jurisdiction of lords in England was weakened with the decline of serfdom and mobility of the peasant population, it was nevertheless maintained, if nonetheless in an attenuated form. However this weakening was compensated by the development of the legal structure of the Justices of the Peace from the fourteenth century which gave lords powers as royal justices, posts which they and their retainers could use to enhance their power locally.

In the face of the decline of serfdom and fixed customary dues English lords were able to maintain and subsequently enhance their incomes by leasing their large demesnes to the wealthier peasantry. While this option was taken under duress and it weakened their *direct* controls over their demesnes, it maintained English lords as a class and marked the beginning of the transition from feudal to capitalist social-property relations. In mutual relationship with a section of the peasantry who were now developing capitalist farmers, lords increased their rental income while the successful of these farmers who were now subject to competition and so compelled to improve productivity increased their profits. As a result, demographic and economic patterns displayed a divergence from the continent as early as the end of the fifteenth century.

Hatcher and Bailey's construction of a distinction between a newer more reputable and an older much less reputable Marxist tradition and their association of Brenner with the latter is a false one.[11] For the benefit of students to whom their book is targeted Hatcher and Bailey might provide a second edition after the critique of Brenner has been thought through again, and after other errors such as their attribution to Marx of Proudhon's curious philosophical conclusion that 'property is theft' have been removed from the text.[12]

---

11   This is not the place to discuss the work of Dobb and Kosminsky, both of whom remain of great importance. It is worth pointing out here, however, that Hatcher's serious misinterpretation of Brenner and Marxists generally leads him to misinterpret Hilton's point in his contribution to the 'Brenner Debate' that it 'would take an utterly blind historian who would ignore the demographic factor in the shaping of the economic and social developments of the period': Hilton 1985, p. 131. Hatcher views this statement as forming part of Hilton's credentials as a Neo-Marxist variant and as a criticism of Brenner's thesis: Hatcher and Bailey 2001, p. 120. On the contrary this was an indirect criticism by Hilton of Hatcher's absurd assumption. In the same paper Hilton professed a broad agreement with 'Brenner's emphasis on the overall determining role of social relationships': Hilton 1985, p. 119 n. 4.

12   Hatcher and Bailey 2001, p. 104. The point these authors are trying to convey here with this incorrect attribution is that Marx's approach to property and rents was moralistic and

If Hatcher and Bailey are genuinely serious about applying historical materialism, then they are obliged to give Brenner and Marx a much fairer hearing. They might also be advised not to begin their presentation of historical materialism with quotes from Stalin.[13]

ii   S.R. Rigby: The Case for Pluralism II

While sympathetic to aspects of Brenner's thesis, in particular the recognition of class structure and class conflict as an important aspect of feudal society which he has done much to emphasise in the mainstream historiography of Britain in the last two decades, Steve Rigby is also an advocate of a pluralist approach towards historical causation, specifically on the lines of Max Weber and J.S. Mill. As such he rejects Brenner's claim that class has primacy in historical causation. Unlike Hatcher and Bailey however, Rigby recognises and defends Brenner's incorporation of demographic change in his account of late medieval social change. In his work, Rigby agrees with Brenner's thesis that demographic and commercial trends 'acquired their economic significance for the distribution of income and the development of the productive forces only in connection with specific, historically developed systems of social-property relations and given balances of class forces'. However, as Rigby says, this quote is compatible with a pluralist approach to historical causation. On the face of it class is not given primacy, but is seen simply *in connection with* demographic and economic determinants. But Rigby does not regard this as a rare inconsistency in Brenner's presentation of his thesis nor, to be fairer to Brenner, as part of the beginning of a more detailed clarification of his thesis in the same paper which does categorically give class or social-property relations primacy. As I mentioned above, Brenner was at pains at the beginning of his 1982 essay to stress the importance of the demographic factor in his thesis in response to criticism of his earlier paper. This is something that Postan and Hatcher and now Hatcher and Bailey ignore. Rigby in fact regards it as a softening or qualifying of Brenner's earlier position, and he views it as 'another' example of a

---

    not therefore objective and economic. On the contrary, Marx was severely critical of such
    idealist approaches: this was exemplified in his critique of Proudon's idealist philosophy
    in his *The Poverty of Philosophy*. Hatcher and Bailey clearly remain confident of their
    analysis and representation of Marxism and Marxist historians in 2001, because Bailey
    recently advertised it in support of his latest paper on the relative insignificance of
    serfdom in England: Bailey 2009, p. 430.

13 Hatcher and Bailey 2001, p. 68.

Marxist professing the primacy of class in theory, while the analysis involves a form of explanatory pluralism.[14]

The problems with Rigby's critique of Brenner begin with his misunderstanding of Brenner's use and meaning of class structure as social-property relations. He has Brenner saying that the outcomes of struggles between peasants and lords, rather than rises and falls of population, constitute 'the key variable' in explaining social change.[15] This is a mistake, and it severely hampers his whole critique. To begin with, social-property relations – the macro-structure of a society – cannot be described in terms of objective key variables as can indices of population and commercialisation, and this point will be developed later. Second, social-property relations are not simply constituted by the vertical class relationship between lords and peasants. In common with all of Brenner's (less sympathetic) critics is the absence in Rigby's critique of any recognition of Brenner's incorporation of horizontal relations within social-property relations – that is, of the relationships *within* the main classes.

This absence is most clearly demonstrated in Rigby's critique of Brenner's account of the relative ability for peasants to resist lords in different periods. Hatcher and Bailey ask the question, why were English lords strong before the Black Death and weak afterwards? Rigby, as part of an attempted critique of the 'internal logic' of Brenner's thesis, asks the question that Croot and Parker asked in the earlier 'Brenner Debate': why, *unlike the French peasantry*, were village communities in England not strong enough to resist their expropriation by lords in the sixteenth century, and yet were able to resist the seigneurial reaction in the post-Black Death period?[16] As Rigby says, Brenner's answer is that by the early sixteenth century the French monarchical state guaranteed peasant freehold property rights in the land, a guarantee it achieved while in competition with French lords for the peasants' surplus. Brenner also of course pointed to the relative weakness of the French lords vis-à-vis the peasantry from the establishment of feudal social-property relations in France in the tenth century. Excessively decentralised jurisdictions were consistent with lords' relatively small demesnes and a relatively limited capacity to coerce the peasantry. The strategy of the French state served to protect its own taxation base (the mass of peasantry) from excessive dues imposed by the lords' private jurisdiction. This was a process which had begun during the feudal crisis in the thirteenth century in France, and the outcome was absolutist state

---

14   Rigby 1995, pp. 127–44; Rigby 1999, p. 155; Rigby 2006, pp. 1–30.
15   Rigby 1995, pp. 127, 138.
16   Rigby 1995, p. 140.

centralisation that developed as a more effective form of extra-economic surplus extraction in which lords came to play a key role. Because he sees only the
vertical class relationship between lords and peasants as constituting Brenner's
social-property relations, Rigby argues that, in Brenner's analysis, the French
state is relatively autonomous and is attributed an *independent* role in social
change *outside* of the class-productive relations of lord and peasant. In Rigby's
words, this role of the French state therefore represents for Brenner 'a deus ex
machina', a god conveniently, but illegitimately, introduced from outside the
model in order to make the model work.[17]

The crux of the problem for Rigby in this critique is that in his account of
medieval society 'class relations are defined in terms of the Marxist typology
developed by G.A. Cohen'.[18] It appears therefore that Rigby is viewing Brenner's
thesis through the prism of G.A. Cohen's orthodox, techno-functionalist
Marxism, a Marxist perspective that Rigby is critical of, for good reason. In stark
contrast to Brenner, Cohen advocates the primacy of the productive forces in
social change, specifically developments in technology, and like all orthodox
Marxists his work displays a conceptual separation between a society's economic base and superstructure, in this case between peasant property and
relations of production (economic base) and state politics (superstructure).[19]
So when Brenner says, 'In France strong peasant property and the absolutist
state developed in mutual dependence', Rigby, by taking Cohen as his Marxist
model and mistakenly associating this with Brenner, can only conclude that
there arises an explanatory pluralism from this because, in Cohen's terms, the
peasantry and the state cannot be mutually dependent because they belong
to two separate spheres, base and superstructure. But with Brenner's political
Marxist model there is no explanatory pluralism, because this mutual relationship between the French state and the peasantry was a specific attribute of
developing French feudal and absolutist social-property relations as they had
come to be by the early sixteenth century. These sixteenth-century social-property relations can be traced back to their establishment in decentralised feudal
form in the tenth century and to their increasingly centralised absolutist form
as the outcome of crisis from the thirteenth.

Another example shows how Rigby's questioning of the internal logic of
Brenner's thesis leads him to difficulties. Unlike Hatcher and Bailey, Rigby
takes on board Brenner's comparative approach but still finds his thesis wanting. Brenner pointed to the relative strength of peasant communities in west-

17   Rigby 1995, p. 140.
18   Rigby 1999, p. 155, referring to his analysis in Rigby 1995.
19   See Cohen 1986, pp. 11–22, and Brenner's response in the same volume, pp. 23–53.

ern Europe (England, France and western Germany) in contrast with those in eastern Europe (east Elbian Germany and Poland). This formed part of the explanation as to why those in the west were able to resist lordship during and after the feudal crisis and destroy serfdom in the fifteenth century in England (and earlier in France) while at the same time in the east a previously free peasantry were enserfed even given the same demographic context as the west. Brenner pointed to the communal peasant productive organisation that was required to regulate open field agriculture in the west, an organisation that was associated with long-settled strong peasant (political) communities and common fields. This contrasted with the east which developed later as part of a colonial extensive development and where peasant productive organisation was far more individualist, without common fields, and where communities were as a consequence less politically cohesive. Another factor contributing to the relative strength of communities in east and west is that in the west lords' manorial organisation was more fragmented with more than one lord having jurisdiction over a single village. This situation potentially gave peasants a political advantage because they could exploit inter-lordship competition. In the east villages usually came under the jurisdiction of a single lord, thus potentially enabling the latter to achieve greater controls.

Rigby counters by arguing that these open field villages in England were also areas of strong manorialised lordship, meaning lords had greater controls through serfdom, and he rejects on empirical grounds the comparison of fragmented jurisdiction in the west compared to the 'one village one lord' model in the east. Thus for Rigby it follows that manorialisation (strong lordship) and strong peasant communities would appear to be complementary rather than in opposition. Moreover, for Rigby it follows that if common field agriculture cannot *per se* be taken as independent evidence of a peasant community strong enough to resist landlords, then we run the risk of lapsing into a circular argument: 'the western European peasantry won its freedom because it was stronger than the peasant community in the east. How do we know that it was stronger? It must have been because it managed to win its freedom'.[20]

The first point to make in defence of Brenner is that Rigby cannot reject on empirical grounds that villages in the west tended to have more than one lords' jurisdiction cutting across them. This was not always the case, but it was the most common experience. In England, for example, early feudal settlement from the tenth and eleventh centuries onwards led to a tendency over time towards fragmented lordship. Subinfeudations over the centuries – through royal wardship rights, politico-military favours and aristocratic and royal

---

20   Rigby 1995, pp. 138–9.

grants to the church and elsewhere – meant that lands and jurisdictions often switched hands and became subdivided. As Bruce Campbell has pointed out recently, 'only a minority of manors were so neat and tidy'.[21] Second, because strong lordship and manorialisation, on the one hand, and strong peasant communities on the other tended to coexist in the west, it simply does not follow that the two were complementary rather than in opposition. Rigby's point here causes unnecessary confusion. Brenner is not concluding that peasant communities must have been stronger in the west simply because they won their freedom. The relative strength of these peasant communities would be seen in England when the land-labour balance tilted towards them after the Black Death. In the post-crisis, post-Black Death demographic context the western lords' capacity to subject the peasantry to low wages and robust impositions characteristic of serfdom had been weakened significantly. In this context these peasant communities in the west that were of long standing with long traditions of self-organisation and self-government, much of which was related to communal open field farming, struggled successfully to destroy serfdom.[22] In the same demographic context in the east the lords' capacity to enserf a more recently settled, less politically organised (and yet previously free) peasantry was clearly far greater. This is not a circular argument; it fundamentally demonstrates Brenner's position on the primacy of social-property relations in historical causation in this period.

Moreover, Rigby's argument fails to take into account the broader implications of social-property relations as both vertical and horizontal. Open-field, politically cohesive communities, were *only one factor* in determining the strength of peasants vis-à-vis their lords. Equally important was the political organisation and cohesion of lords and state which determined individual lords' jurisdictional strength and the practical power to coerce the peasantry. What is at stake here is not simply the immediate production relationship between lords and peasants but the evolution of the state and its relationship with the broader ruling class. We therefore can disallow Rigby's simple isolation of elements such as 'open-field agriculture' in the west in comparison with

---

21   Campbell 2006, p. 191.

22   This is not to say that strong peasant organisation was dependent upon open-field agriculture. In England the so-called individualist farming in the south-east based on divided severalty should not be compared to the type of single farm single plot type in eastern Europe, and this I hope to demonstrate in my study of Kent in Part II. While open fields and crop rotation were not typical, each tenant contained a number of these plots that were scattered over the manor to ensure diverse land use – pasture and arable for example. This militated against farm isolation and provided for a good deal of cohesion, if not perhaps the level of cohesion achieved in the open fields.

more individualist agriculture in the east as a means to undermine the logic of Brenner's thesis. Nevertheless, Brenner's example of long-standing open-field organisation as *one aspect* of why evolution was different between east and west is a useful and valid one.

Rigby falls back on the philosophy of Mill and Weber as the basis for his case for pluralist causation. He follows Mill's dictum that all causes–class organisation, population changes, commercial developments–have equal weight and that historical outcomes are the sum resultant of all of them. Citing Weber's point that it is impossible to quantify the relative importance of the causes, he argues that it is therefore futile to try to isolate one of them because that is inevitably the result of our subjective perceptions.[23] Rigby can only fall back on this line of thinking in his critique of Brenner if he has Brenner saying vertical class struggle is the key variable in historical causation, rather than, say, the rise of markets or demographic fluctuations, which of course Brenner does not. Brenner does not try to *quantify* the relative importance of the causes; that would be impossible as Weber says. In advocating the primacy of social-property relations Brenner advocates the social basis of change, and he rejects the dubious historical method of abstracting objectively measured indices such as population or market influence from social relationships and giving them a direct or equal causal influence. As I began to argue in relation to Hatcher and Bailey's critique above, social relations are not objective variables, and cannot be measured or tested in this way. They are of a different order. People, active in their social relations, vertical and horizontal, as individuals, in families and in politically organised communities, *experience* changes in population levels, urbanisation, and in the proliferation of markets, technical developments in production and exchange. To paraphrase E.P. Thompson, people experience these determinations and then act in conscious ways, limited or guided by their relationships.[24] The focus must always be on human agency, history conceived as human beings in their social and productive activities, the relations among themselves, and between themselves and their material environment.

---

23   Rigby 1995, pp. 141, 144.

24   Thompson 1978, p. 106. Christopher Dyer has put the distinction in another way. His conclusions on the processes of transition from feudalism to capitalism point to 'the social basis of change, against a background of fluctuations in population, prices, wages and rents': Dyer 2007, pp. 1–2. Elsewhere he argues that 'the emphasis is placed on decision-making in all sections of society' rather than on the rises and declines of population: Dyer 2002, p. 12. One could substitute Dyer's 'decision-making' within social relations for Brenner's 'rules for reproduction', both of which amount to the same thing. This approach is less theoretically rigorous but it may present a more accessible starting point for some.

Rigby argues that the futility of advocating a primary cause in social change is somehow 'demonstrated' by the 'Brenner Debate', 'whose participants often seemed to be talking past each other'. But as has hopefully been shown in the foregoing, the reason earlier and more recent critics such as Rigby, Hatcher, Bailey – and others we will come to mention – are talking past Brenner is because they misinterpret his thesis in demonstrably stark ways. Hatcher, who was a participant in the earlier debate, persists in doing so even after Brenner's explanations in his second paper, and even after Rigby showed support for Brenner's position on the role of demography in his thesis, against Hatcher. Rigby is talking past Brenner, not because Brenner advocates a prime mover, but because he misinterprets both Brenner's use of class as social-property relations and Brenner's Marxism more generally.

Rigby concludes with:

> [I]t is impossible to isolate one presiding element in what was actually a complex interaction and mutual feedback between many interrelated factors. Nor was class struggle necessarily leading history to some particular direction or to some particular goal, such as capitalism. There is no overarching sociological theory which allows us to predict the outcome of such class struggles in advance; all we can do is to make such outcomes intelligible with historical hindsight.[25]

Rigby's critique of orthodox Marxism is well put here, and he elaborates on it elsewhere.[26] I defend Brenner against recent challenges to his thesis by 'productive forces' or orthodox Marxists in Chapter Eight. Brenner's work is particularly damning of this kind of teleology, and yet Brenner is, inadvertently I think, being tarred with the same brush. For Brenner, capitalism came about as the result of class struggle, the processes of the destruction of serfdom and the expropriation of the peasantry; not as 'some particular goal' on the part of either lords or peasants, but, to labour the point, as an unintended consequence of struggles between lords and peasants to maintain themselves *as they were*, in order to reproduce their way of life.

iii   S.R. Epstein: State Formation and Market Integration

Unlike the foregoing critics of Brenner, S.R. Epstein argues that Brenner does not in fact incorporate a prime mover into his thesis. According to Epstein,

---

25   Rigby 1995, p. 144.
26   Rigby 1998.

Brenner's whole thesis is based around access to property, and that for Brenner capitalism came about simply through lords evicting the peasantry from their property. He states that Brenner's interpretation suffers from,

> the combination of a narrow form of 'property rights romanticism' whereby property rights to land determine the existence of markets and the path of technological change, and of 'typological essentialism', which defines the feudal economy in terms of only one characteristic (property rights to land) deemed to represent its essential qualities ... Brenner's problems stem from his excessively narrow definition of feudal property rights – that is, of enforced rights to income streams – in terms of property [rights] to land, which excludes all the 'extra-economic' rights of lords to extract rents from transactions (production and trade), and which therefore deprives his model of an endogenous source of change and short circuits the question of how markets in feudalism actually arose. Significantly, Brenner never discusses the emergence of markets in either feudalism or capitalism, appearing simply to assume that capitalist markets followed the emergence of new property rights to land with the expulsion of the peasantry.[27]

So, for Epstein, Brenner's thesis has no endogenous source of change, no built-in prime mover. First, given Brenner's detailed construction and application of social-property relations as prime mover, this charge is baffling. Second, far from excluding all extra-economic rights of lords to extract rents, for Brenner these rights are at the core of understanding the relations between a peasantry which possessed the vast amount of the available material resources (land), and feudal lords who had no entrepreneurial input in peasant production. Lords could survive only by extracting peasants' surplus by extra-economic means; their ability to do so was generated by their own political organisation. In fact Brenner's emphasis on extra-economic surplus extraction relations as key to feudalism is something he comes under fire for, and this point will be addressed in the next chapter. The final charge from Epstein that Brenner never discusses the emergence of markets in either feudalism or capitalism is simply another black and white misrepresentation. After all, one of the main questions that Brenner's thesis seeks to address is why there was no transition to capitalism on the continent before 1750 despite centuries of huge market demand? Brenner also explained in detail the essential symbiotic relationship between major urban centres and the luxury or military trade for the non-productive consumption of feudal lords. The luxury trade was integral for lords

---

27   Epstein 2000, p. 5.

as a class in providing military equipment and luxury produce geared to household display and consumption which was an essential part of feudal patronage in order to gain and maintain followers. In other words, they needed it to
fight. The origin of capitalism for Brenner owed a good deal to the stimulation
provided by the Antwerp entrepot from the middle of the fifteenth century
for English woollens, as well as to the equally if not more important domestic
demand in England.

Epstein's thesis can be firmly located within a Smithian commercialisation perspective. His thesis on the causes of economic growth and the transition to capitalism is based around the idea that political constraints inherent
in feudalism, namely fragmented institutions or jurisdictions, stifled the
potential for Smithian-type growth in the feudal economy. The transition to
capitalism therefore entailed the lifting of these barriers to enable modern
economic growth to take its natural course. The factors and processes determining the lifting of these barriers were those conducive to institutional
political centralisation. For Epstein, institutional political centralisation
led to, or equated to, market integration, and market integration promoted
cheaper trade and reduced transaction costs and the marketing burdens on
peasants. Reduced transaction costs for peasants provided incentives for
them to specialise, compete, improve productivity and generate modern
growth. England did not become the first capitalist country because the
state backed the lords to evict the peasantry from their property from the fifteenth century, but rather because constitutional changes from the late seventeenth century unified institutions and secured absolute property; the rest
of Europe followed suit from the late eighteenth century. More will be said
of Epstein's thesis below because it is a radical challenge to Brenner. While
containing elements of the old 'rise of the market' theory, which sees capitalist attitudes towards production immanent in all periods, an argument
which Brenner has extensively criticised, it explains the unlocking of these
attitudes and strategies in novel ways. For now it is sufficient to recognise
that Epstein's attack on Brenner is essentially targeted at Brenner's apparent
lack of understanding of markets and their promotion of economic change
and growth.

Epstein's critique that Brenner never discusses the emergence of markets
in either feudalism or capitalism relies on Brenner saying that peasants were
averse to markets. According to Epstein, Brenner thinks that peasants only
went to market because they were forced by lords to exchange their produce
for cash in order to pay their money rents and dues. They did not need the market because they held – Epstein incorrectly says they 'owned' – their property,

and their strategy was to use it for subsistence.[28] Although Epstein is wrong to say that Brenner viewed peasants as market-averse, the close connection between peasant possession and peasants' prioritisation of subsistence-based farming, rather than specialisation and market dependence, is of course part of Brenner's historical materialist argument that particular societies have their own micro-economics. This contrasts with Epstein's ahistorical materialist argument that assumes specifically capitalist micro-economics in all societies. As a corollary to Epstein's rejection of Brenner's focus on peasant subsistence holdings as central to feudal social-property relations, he also rejects Brenner's statement that the typical peasant holding was a virgate (25–30 acres typically) or half a virgate (12–15 acres typically), the size required for subsistence. Epstein counters on empirical grounds Brenner's core argument that peasants' produced for subsistence by showing evidence of large sections of the peasantry with very small holdings and large numbers of landless peasants in the thirteenth century.[29] For Epstein it follows that peasants were typically market dependent rather than subsistence-orientated, and he points to the innovative nature of the peasantry in developing different types of produce, including rural-based industrial produce for the market. For Epstein these developments are indicative of the potential for Smithian growth in the feudal economy.

Against Epstein, any rural historian of medieval England, including Hatcher, Bailey and Rigby, would point to the importance of the subsistence-based virgate holding as the backbone of peasant holdings, particularly outside of counties in the south-east.[30] The problem facing Brenner and others was that

---

28   Epstein 2000, p. 4.

29   Epstein 2000, pp. 4, 47.

30   See Dyer 2007, pp. 25–6, 65, 129. Even in late thirteenth-century England when population peaked and as a result holdings became fragmented there were 4000 households holding a yardland or half a yardland living within the trading hinterland of the small towns of Evesham and Pershore in the west Midlands. In places like Kent holdings were more fragmented but still primarily subsistence-based. Dyer says that the yardlanders and half-yardlanders were the most substantial peasants but there were too many of them to be called an elite: these were the backbone of the village, paying the most tax, producing most of the food, serving on juries and filling manorial offices. They framed the bylaws in their interests. They were very much the dominant culture of the village and so of peasant society. Accumulation and polarisation in the different situation of the fifteenth century led to radical changes to this picture by 1500. By that date in much of the midlands, south and north-east of England, 'those with 15 acres formed a relatively poor minority, whereas in the late thirteenth century they lay near the centre of the social spectrum'. See also Bailey 2009, p. 435: he argues that in the thirteenth century, 'Villein holdings throughout

because of increasing overpopulation during the thirteenth century, subsistence holdings became increasingly divided, and the resulting underemployment, the lack of applied technology, and lordship burdens imposed on the peasantry, led to a crisis of subsistence in which peasants were increasingly forced into petty commercial agriculture and proto-industry. But for Brenner this does not contradict the essentially subsistent nature of peasant strategies towards production. As he recently said of the late thirteenth century:

> A greater proportion of the peasantry than ever before was rendered at least partially dependent upon the market. Nevertheless, (usually partial) market dependence for these peasants led not to any breakthrough toward modern economic growth, but an intensification of long term trends toward stagnation and decline...The peasants' turn to commercial agriculture and proto-industrialisation should therefore not be understood, in Smithian fashion, as a voluntary attempt to secure the gains from trade in response to growing market opportunities, but rather as a second choice, made under duress, as the only way to survive in the face of insufficient land to cultivate food grains.[31]

In his critique of what he considers to be Brenner's thesis, Epstein makes one erroneous charge after another, and includes Brenner in his general critique of the apparent agreement among historians that the Black Death – an 'exogenous shock' – marked a watershed in the transition to capitalism. After the Black Death, which Epstein equates with 'the feudal crisis' because he rejects the idea of a subsistence-based crisis in the late thirteenth century, he has Brenner saying that in England only 'the development of agrarian capitalism required the expulsion of the self-sufficient and market-averse peasantry from the land'.[32] For Epstein then it follows that,

---

England tended to be held in standard size units (often 15 or 30 acres) to facilitate the administration of the complex package of rents and services attached to them'. Campbell quotes figures taken from the Hundred Rolls of 1279. He finds that 60 percent of tenanted land was made up of holdings of at least 30 acres. These formed the top 20 percent of holdings. A further 20 percent of holdings accounted for 30 percent of tenanted land and contained between 15 acres and 30 acres. Thus towards the period of population peak in the late thirteenth century, as much as 90 percent of the entire tenanted land area of midland England was at or around subsistence level: Campbell 2005, p. 48.

31   Brenner 2007, pp. 78–9.
32   Epstein 2000, p. 54.

the transition to capitalism was set in motion by factors external to feudalism itself, as indeed follows logically from the assumption that feudalism possessed no internal dynamic for growth. Brenner sees the deus ex
machina as the balance of class power determined by historically contingent national characteristics ('the peculiarity of the English').[33]

Now flourishes like this might look good, but they only serve to misrepresent
and confuse. Brenner does not see the transition to capitalism as set in motion
by the Black Death and therefore by a factor external to feudalism. To begin
with, Brenner does not equate the feudal crisis with the Black Death; the feudal crisis was – to repeat – a subsistence crisis, and crisis of feudal incomes
from the late thirteenth century. The outcomes of the feudal crisis, which this
exogenous shock served to confirm and seriously exacerbate, were worked out
in a unique way in England because of its unique social-property relations,
especially the lords' retention of large demesnes, the power to draw in vacant
peasant land, and powers to maintain controls over customary land in order
to ensure peasants did not gain full property rights. On this point alone we
can reject Epstein's premise that in terms of the logic of Brenner's thesis the
transition had to be set in motion by factors external to feudalism. And we
can reject it on the grounds that for Brenner feudalism did of course possess
an internal dynamic for growth. His point is that given feudal social-property
relations, and feudal strategies for reproduction, peasants who held the vast
majority of the land produced for subsistence as a safety-first strategy, and
lords, unable or unwilling to invest in production, saw their best or most logical means of gaining income through squeezing the peasantry and by extensive growth through conquest and developing new lands through colonisation.
This internal dynamic for growth, given feudal social-property relations and
feudal strategies for reproduction, led to feudal forms of crisis: overpopulation,
limited application of available technology and declining labour productivity,
intensified warfare and so on.

With regard to the actual transition to capitalism, because Epstein does not
address Brenner's thesis that economic and social change in medieval society
was determined by feudal social-property relations, particularly by the struggle
between lords and peasants' opposed rules for reproduction, he is unable to
appreciate Brenner's conclusion that the development of agrarian capitalism
was the result of the unintended consequence of this struggle. Relegating his
criticism of this key point to a footnote Epstein states the following:

---

33   Epstein 2000, p. 54.

In Brenner's formulation, England escaped feudalism because, unlike elsewhere, the strongly centralised state sided with the feudal lords in evicting the peasantry after the Black Death. However he does not explain the 300 year hiatus between the feudal crisis after 1350 and the full transition to agrarian capitalism in the seventeenth century. Brenner implies that capitalism arose in England through historical chance, a curious position for an avowed Marxist, since Marxism's main distinguishing feature compared with rival social science accounts is its brand of technological determinism.[34]

Here again Epstein views the Black Death as a key driver, and he seems to have Brenner saying that lords and monarchy got together and evicted the peasantry in 1350, thereby leaving unexplained the 300 year wait for the full transition to agrarian capitalism in the seventeenth century. The state certainly backed the lords in the immediate aftermath of the Black Death in order to place controls on wages and shore up lords' local powers as royal justices. But, as Brenner says, there was no real movement to undermine peasant property until the second half of the fifteenth century. Indeed, the peasantry as a whole had enjoyed a 'Golden Age' of prosperity for much of the fifteenth century, something that Epstein recognises elsewhere but seems to see it in contrast to Brenner's thesis.[35] Also, Brenner had never argued that the state backed the lords in evicting the peasantry. He was concerned to show that the state was unable to provide security for peasant copyhold property until at least the late sixteenth century; this is an entirely different thing. Lack of security on peasant holdings following the decline of serfdom allowed lords to charge flexible entry fines on copyholds in line with commercial rents or leaseholds, and enable the consolidation of plots by the wealthier peasants who usually also held the large demesnes by lease.[36] This process began in the fifteenth century but it was uneven across the country; there was no hiatus. Not surprisingly these very striking errors on Epstein's part leave him in no position to appreciate Brenner's meaning of the emergence of capitalism as an unintended consequence of struggle. Brenner does not 'imply' this, it is key to his thesis of the transition and to his perspective of historical materialism as has been argued in detail above. There was no capitalist class within feudalism breaking through the fetters of the old relations towards an intended outcome of capitalism; there could not be given feudal social-property relations and the

---

34   Epstein 2000, p. 5 n. 14.
35   Epstein 2000, p. 56.
36   The security of peasant tenure is the subject of Chapter Five.

micro-economics these generated. All that is left for Epstein to do is to question, like Rigby, Brenner's credentials as a Marxist through the technological determinism of Cohen that we came across earlier. But this will not do as a serious critique. The fact that Epstein never quotes Brenner is a problem too; the target of his critique often appears to be a paper tiger with which to contrast his own superior work.

Now because Epstein's critique of Brenner falls flat on many counts, it does not necessarily follow that his own account of the transition to capitalism is flawed. He may simply have a better explanation. To that we can turn now and give a fair hearing.

For Epstein 'pre-modern growth was to a large extent "Smithian", instigated by growth in demand which reduced transaction costs (because of economies of scale in commercial services) and increased potential gains from innovation'.[37] Feudalism placed constraints on this growth, a direct result of the decentralised, fragmented jurisdictions of feudal lords. These constraints took the form of significant burdens on peasants in the form of serfdom, but they also created monopolies, drains on markets, and 'coordination failures' (different laws, weights and measures etc.) which were a feature of 'non-integrated markets'. For Epstein, these constraints on Smithian growth were one side of the internal logic of feudalism. The other side of this logic was warfare which Epstein says 'was just as much part of the internal logic of feudalism as jurisdiction exploitation'.[38] Warfare was the product of jurisdictionally fragmented lordships and decentralised states, the driver of territorial expansion, political centralisation and state formation, and, as a consequence, of institutional unification and market integration. Market integration reduced transaction costs, made buying and selling cheaper, and thereby stimulated specialisation and improved production for the market. In Epstein's words:

> Although the main goal of feudal territorial expansion through warfare was to broaden the lord's political and economic resource base, it also benefited the wider economy by increasing jurisdiction integration and reducing transaction costs within the new territory ... it also reduced the costs of modifying existing property rights and introducing new institutions: it lowered seigniorial dues, abolished or seriously weakened rival feudal and urban monopolies ... systematised and territorialised fragmented legal codes and legislation, weights and measures (coordination failures), limited opportunities for pillage and warfare and reduced

---

37 Epstein 2000, p. 7.
38 Epstein 2000, pp. 50–1.

rulers' opportunities to act as autocratic 'stationary bandits' against their subjects. State formation was thus a major cause – possibly the major driving force – of market integration and Smithian growth before the nineteenth century.[39]

So for Epstein, feudalism contained within itself not only the problem of constraining Smithian growth, namely jurisdictional fragmentation, but its own solution, namely state formation through warfare which acted as an inbuilt driver towards market integration and the dissolution of these constraints. Fragmenting jurisdictions on the one hand, and state formation through warfare on the other, were 'two countervailing forces' in which the latter 'won out'.[40] Epstein distinguishes his theory from other recent (Anglo-American) Smithian or 'commercialisation' theories, by asserting that they see Smithian growth in abstraction to institutional contexts; they describe Smithian growth, they do not explain it. They see the unilineal rise of the market as a contradiction to feudalism which therefore breaks through feudal fetters. He sees market integration and the rise of market influence as an endogenous process working within feudalism – that is, within feudal institutional contexts.[41]

Before we move on to look at how Epstein applies this thesis, a few points need to be highlighted. To begin with, readers may feel some familiarity with it after the previous discussion on Brenner's own thesis of social-property relations as prime mover. With Epstein, we have vertical relations between lords and peasants in the form of significant burdens placed on the latter by the former; and we have horizontal relations among lords and between lords and states which represents the real driver, lifting the constraints imposed by the vertical relations. So while subjecting Brenner's own thesis to a curt caricature as solely focussed on access to property and without a prime mover, or without an endogenous source of change, Epstein has borrowed most of Brenner's framework of social-property relations and made it work for himself in a novel way. To make it work on his terms Epstein declines to acknowledge any class struggle dynamic in the relationship between lords and peasants, even given his recognition of the significance of the extra-economic burdens placed on peasants. In fact he displays no understanding of how these burdens came to be there in the first place. Not surprisingly therefore he also fails to see how political centralisation and state formation through warfare has any bearing on, or any determinate relationship with, this class struggle. Instead

---

39   Epstein 2000, pp. 51–2.

40   Epstein 2000, p. 52.

41   Epstein 2000, p. 49 n. 29.

jurisdictional fragmentation and lordship constraints on peasants are taken as a given; they are *just there* with the unintended consequence of increasing transaction costs; and warfare occurs simply because of jurisdictional fragmentation, an unintended consequence of which is market integration and reduced transaction costs.

For Epstein there was no subsistence crisis or feudal crisis at the end of the thirteenth century. He does recognise that there was a downturn in the economies across medieval Europe at the end of the thirteenth century and early fourteenth century before the equally widespread exogenous shocks of bad harvests and famine between 1315 and 1322 and 1348–9. However, he states that there was no link between increasing population densities and poverty; on the contrary increased population led to higher land productivity and increased use of technology, even 'probably' higher *labour* productivity. For Epstein as we have seen, the problem was lack of market integration. Lack of market integration prevented peasant innovation and specialisation for the market because of high transaction costs. High transaction costs made it costly to trade and acted a disincentive to innovate or specialise. So for Epstein the so-called feudal crisis was instead made up of the exogenous shocks just mentioned but these had a different effect on the economy than that which Brenner argued.[42]

The processes of political centralisation and market integration had indeed made some progress since the eleventh century. These processes came to a head in the late thirteenth century. It is Epstein's view that warfare intensified in this period for *this* reason, not because of the levelling-off of lordship income due to feudal crisis as Brenner argued. For Epstein, warfare had positive as well as destructive effects. Where historians including Brenner, Campbell and others view warfare as destructive of human power, property and peasant incomes through increased taxation to pay for the wars, Epstein sees it as a stimulus to state formation, the development of new institutions (centralised tax administrations), and therefore the driver of market integration. Indeed, if it was not for those exogenous shocks, Epstein suggests there would have been a continuity of the slow evolutionary path between the eleventh and fourteenth centuries lifting constraints, unifying institutions, and promoting 'a higher growth path', presumably towards capitalism. Instead, the exogenous shocks set in train a far more rapid period of change, of 'creative destruction', which was driven by heightened political and economic struggle. Epstein avoids the implications of the class war across Europe in the second half of the fourteenth century for his thesis, preferring to relegate to a footnote his point that 'the eruption concerned longstanding issues over limits, prerogatives

---

42   Epstein 2000, pp. 38–49.

and duties of the state'.[43] Instead he concludes that the demographic collapse and process of creative destruction 'raised the western European economies to higher growth paths'. For him this is demonstrated by higher population growth rates across Europe after 1450 compared to before 1300, and he suggests that the creation of a new dynamic equilibrium in the period of state formation and market integration after the Black Death 'may have marked the most decisive step in the continent's long trajectory towards capitalism and world hegemony'. Hence the post-Black Death period was one of greater consumption, monetary improvements, language unification, reduction in costs of capital, and increasing innovation and specialisation.[44] Urbanisation increased generally and marketing and distribution systems improved. However while these improvements occurred in more backward economies, 'including possibly England', there was a decline in more developed economies like Italy and Flanders. Epstein has no explanation for this diversion in fortunes except – perhaps – that this diversion indicated 'that these regions were facing structural barriers to further growth'.[45] What these barriers were we are not told.

Now it is true to say that there has been a good deal of recent research which has generated a more positive view of the feudal economy before the early fourteenth century, particularly with regard to the improved use of technology by peasants under pressure from holding division, and the relationship between high population and high land productivity and output. There is now a consensus that peasants were more sensitive to the market and to price signals than is generally allowed under the so-called 'pessimistic' view.[46] This research and its implications for the integrity of Brenner's thesis will be discussed with other empirical challenges in the chapters that follow. For now it is sufficient to point out that improved *land* productivity is not the same as improved *labour* productivity; and that the former was only won through greater numbers of labourers which ultimately led to declining labour productivity. Brenner, who has always stressed this point, is strongly supported in this view by Campbell who draws on recent work suggesting that due to underemployment there was a 60 percent drop in male labour productivity in England between 1209 and 1309, and that 'it was lower between 1270 and 1329 than at any other time between 1209 and 1869'.[47] Could a situation that militated against Smithian economic growth be presented more starkly?

43   Epstein 2000, pp. 54–5, 55 n. 48.
44   Epstein 2000, pp. 57–62.
45   Epstein 2000, pp. 62–3.
46   For a useful discussion see Dyer 2005, pp. 7–45.
47   Campbell 2005, pp. 64–5.

Let us look at some of the main points that Epstein regards as the product of this new post-Black Death 'dynamic equilibrium', particularly as it relates to England, the country in which agrarian capitalism first emerged. First, it is true that consumption increased per head but not overall, and there were productivity gains in sheep farming as lords leased out their demesnes to wealthy peasants; this was indeed the context of emerging capitalism in England as Brenner had argued. But historians specialising in medieval England would not recognise this acceleration of population after 1450. In England population growth was stagnant up to 1520 with no significant growth before 1540, and in this way it showed a clear divergence from the continent. They would also not recognise an increase in urbanisation in England before the second half of the sixteenth century, although there was a qualitative restructuring between provincial centres, small towns, rural industry and London. Manufacturing deserted the larger towns in the fifteenth century where it was traditionally based in the medieval period, and it developed in rural industrial areas. The larger towns and London developed as distribution centres for rural manufactures. Historians would also be hard pushed to acknowledge any decisive increase in market integration and state formation in England between the Black Death and the late fifteenth century. England had already been precociously centralised in the eleventh century and had developed a highly unified parliamentary, legal and royal state apparatus by the late thirteenth century as we have seen earlier. It is true that there were developments in political integration in the century after the Black Death: the increasing definition of parliament as an institution and the establishment of its functions; the laicisation of the civil service; the extension of local magistracy through the legal system of the Justices of the Peace to middling landowners – that is, to the gentry below the higher nobility or peerage – and to major medieval merchants; and the extension of the franchise to yeomen or 'forty shilling freeholders'.[48] There was also a change in outlook by the English monarchy in 1415 from the traditional feudal ideal of the 'brotherhood of Christian chivalry' among the nobility of the whole of western Europe, to the idea of the English 'nation' as God's chosen people in a holy war against France. It is at this point that the red

---

48   Before the Tudor period, commissions were run on an ad hoc basis and were still headed by the leading nobility or their retainers. And the apparent extension of the franchise to forty-shilling freeholders in 1429 was in fact designed not to extend the franchise but to exclude non-propertied elements. This was apparently a response to the disruption of recent contested elections by the latter, as well as probably a reflection of the increased wealth and status of the peasant elite by this time: Harriss 2005, pp. 45–52, 66–74, 167–71.

cross of the crusading banner of the feudal nobility of Europe was adopted for
St. George of England.[49]

However, the first half of fifteenth-century England is also characterised by
the golden age of the peasantry and disunity among the increasingly small and
exclusive group of leading nobility. This disunity was exacerbated by decisive
defeats in the wars with France, particularly in 1453 which marked the end of the
'Hundred Years' War' and the beginning of the English civil 'Wars of the Roses'.
And while more of the 'nation' may have been drawn into the public sphere,
the ability of the English state to draw revenues from taxation – a key indicator
of centralised polity – declined markedly as the level of finance derived from
customs fell in tandem with the huge drop in exports of English wool. This
traditional export, prized on the continent, was replaced with that of woollen
cloth from the late fourteenth century, but the crown balked at raising the tax
on cloth as this would have been self-defeating because of the serious affect
on the ability of English cloth producers to compete with the Low Countries.
Direct taxation continued as it had done from the early fourteenth century;
experiments in poll taxes between 1377 and 1381 were abandoned after they
triggered the national rebellion of 1381.[50] On the continent processes of state
unification towards absolutism (the tax/office state) occurred rapidly from the
early fourteenth century, and while the up-phase of the economy in the late
fifteenth and sixteenth centuries led to increased commercialisation, the continent did not display a high growth path towards capitalism. On the contrary,
as Brenner argued, what was displayed was the reinforcement of peasant property which, under pressure from increased state taxation, led to another cycle
of overpopulation, declining productivity and a downward destructive spiral
of warfare leading to the 'general crisis of the seventeenth century'.

The problems with Epstein's thesis on the process of progressive state
centralisation and market integration through the late medieval period are
exposed, not only by the foregoing objections, but most clearly by the fact that
the economies of those most highly urbanised countries with high levels of
technology and centuries long involvement in international trade such as Italy
actually *declined* in this period. Epstein himself is obliged to concede as much.
For Epstein to say that this was perhaps due to structural barriers to growth is
a conveniently vague tautology. In fact, Epstein's subsequent conclusions on
the transition to capitalism also amount to a tautology. We are not treated to
a detailed account of the transition of the structural change from one specific
type of society to another, as Brenner has felt obliged to demonstrate, even

49   Harriss 2005, p. 131.
50   Harriss 2005, pp. 58–61, 94–8.

though Epstein, unlike earlier historians of the rise of markets, recognises that this is what the transition must entail. Epstein knows that in capitalism the majority of producers are compelled to seek work for a wage, and yet he refuses to describe how this majority happened to become landless in the first place.[51]

He dismisses any notion of England's exceptionalism characterised by the expropriation of the peasantry in the fifteenth and sixteenth centuries. He assumes continuity in peasant landholding in England through the early modern period. He cites Robert Allen's work as an example of English peasants creating a revolution in productivity in the seventeenth century. However, what Allen assumes are traditional peasants with traditional holdings, were in fact a combination of freeholders, lessees and copyholders with large farms. The expropriation of much of the peasantry had already taken place.[52] What Epstein does provide us with is speculation about 'some of the institutional prerequisites' for the transition. These are the establishment of capitalist markets and security of absolute property rights, both of which required the centralisation of political sovereignty: 'These crucial changes were achieved in England from the latter part of the seventeenth century and elsewhere in the course of the eighteenth and early nineteenth'.[53] The problem for Epstein's thesis is that secure property rights on a constitutional basis were only achieved in seventeenth-century England after the majority of the peasant land had been expropriated: the development of capitalist markets was dependent upon that expropriation. Constitutional developments after the failure of two attempts at absolutism by English kings in the seventeenth century simply set the seal on what already had come to pass. Epstein does not explain the transition from feudalism to capitalism beyond the observation that politically centralised polities, like modern capitalist nations, even modern 'communist' ones like China, are better for capitalism than fragmented non-capitalist ones.

iv   H.R. French and R.W. Hoyle: Market Determinism

Most of the criticism of Brenner's prime mover in the evolution of feudal economy and the origin of capitalism has come from medieval historians, although Epstein has taken his thesis to its logical conclusion in the early modern period. To finish off this section on critics of Brenner's prime mover and its implications for the development of capitalism in England we can examine

---

51   Epstein 2000, p. 51 n. 34.

52   See the discussion on this point below and in Chapters Five and Six.

53   Epstein 2000, pp. 172–4.

the recent critique of Brenner by early modern historians H.R. French and R.W. Hoyle.[54] They focus on developments between 1550 and 1750, a period that they regard as the most formative in the origin of capitalism.

In concert with Hatcher and Bailey and others, Hoyle and French chide Brenner for aiming to replace the objective variables of commerce and demography with another exclusive one, agrarian class relations, 'rather than acknowledging that a particular outcome could be due to the impact of a number of variables – including population, access to markets and the possibilities for agrarian capitalism, the balance of class and tenurial relations in the countryside and the attitude of the state to agrarian change'. Following certain suggestions as to the number of levels on which Brenner's thesis can be criticised – Marxist theology, no empirical basis, possibly illegitimate comparative nature of his study – the superior tone continues with, 'Even so, it has to be asked whether it is possible to write an account of English agrarian change in which the class dimension of agrarian history is the exclusive motor. With some reluctance, we conclude that it is not'. Moreover, 'If we see the outcome as being determined by interacting forces rather than a single "underlying" force, then it also raises the possibility that the character of agrarian class relations might be determined by the character of agrarian capitalism rather than vice-versa'.[55]

Clearly, French and Hoyle portray Brenner as advocating class as an exclusive, autonomous prime mover in determining social change. Brenner's incorporation of demographic and commercial forces in historical causation has somehow eluded them. Second, although the last statement appears wonderfully vague, what French and Hoyle appear to be saying when they say that agrarian capitalism might be determined by an agrarian capitalist class structure, is that agrarian capitalism equates to the 'determination of market forces'. But this of course begs the question as to how these (agrarian capitalist) market forces were generated in the first place, and how market forces determine *new* class structures or *new* social-property relations. Their explanation is as follows:

> Whilst we do not see agrarian change being dictated by any single factor, agrarian capitalism emerged because in turn markets existed for farmers to sell into. If these offered opportunities, they also made farmers vulnerable to low prices and forced them into increasing their productivity and so acreage. Agrarian class structure is, in essence, about the competition between landlord and tenants for the farmers' surplus and the success

54   French and Hoyle 2007.
55   French and Hoyle 2007, p. 4.

(or failure) of farmers in retaining their income. Hence, *of all the forces acting on peasants and farmers, we privilege the market above others.*[56]

So in stark contradiction to their earlier pronouncements, this confirms that French and Hoyle do advocate a prime mover – market forces – although according to them not an exclusive, autonomous one. And for them, somehow agrarian capitalism emerged 'because markets existed for farmers to sell into'. Given what we know of the development of markets throughout the whole of ancient and feudal Europe, one is struck by the bold innocence of this statement. Their explanation of how this works in the early modern period, as opposed to say in ancient Greece, seems to be that for farmers to be able to retain their income in the face of landlord pressure to increase leasehold rents, farmers had to innovate and compete and increase their acreage at the expense of other farmers. The first point to make is that this is Brenner's thesis, given certain developed conditions. The second related point is that this situation of winners and losers in competition on the market requires not only the *existence* of markets, which after all have existed since time immemorial, but capitalist social-property relations. And the latter could only exist following on from and subsequently exacerbating the processes of expropriation of the majority of the peasantry. French and Hoyle think that during the sixteenth century the apparently undifferentiated peasantry of the fifteenth century became differentiated as the market got to work on them, leading to the emergence of the competitive yeomen with large farms.[57] As we shall see in later chapters, the yeomen were already prominent by the turn of the sixteenth century at latest. Furthermore, their assumption that the market naturally led to peasant differentiation and polarisation from the sixteenth century leaves one wondering how this follows given that the unprecedented growth of markets and commerce in the thirteenth century led to the fragmentation of holdings.

French and Hoyle prefer to concentrate on the second half of the sixteenth century and beyond. In that period 'small farms whatever their tenure did not pay, and because they did not pay they disappeared'.[58] But again this is a statement that can only be broadly applicable with the institutionalising of capitalist social-property relations based upon a competitive leaseholding tenantry. If peasant owner-occupier land with freehold rights secured the subsistence of peasant households, then those households would not have been subjected to market forces; they were shielded from the market for their necessities, and were no doubt helped further in doing so in those communities that

---

56   French and Hoyle 2007, p. 41. My emphasis.
57   French and Hoyle 2007, p. 12.
58   French and Hoyle 2007, pp. 40–1.

maintained unenclosed commons. In the absence of force or overtaxation –
such as occurred in France for example – what was there to compel them to
compete in a losing battle with bigger farmers if they owned their own property, and if the produce from that property was sufficient to provide them
with their necessities? They might choose to specialise temporarily, and to
grow market crops as they did in the medieval period if prices were favourable. If prices were not favourable, they could return to diversifying their produce. Unlike holders of leaseholds and copyholds they were not subject to
fixed terms of years or lives, and so were not in the position of being forced to
compete for the possession of their holding when these terms ran out. If their
holdings failed it was for reasons other than that the holdings did not pay in a
commercial sense. Small owner-occupier farms cannot compete on a capitalist market with large concerns manned by those with social and networking
power; but then again they do not need to. Severe fragmentation of small farms
through partible inheritance and lack of options for temporary modest accumulation on a generational, family-cycle basis was one way to failure. This was
even more likely to cause failure once there had already been a breakdown of
customary rights locally and capitalist farms and capitalist accumulators were
already well-established. Another way to failure was the continuity of forced
eviction. Neeson shows that a still significant subsistence-based English peasantry in the eighteenth century – comprised of smallholders as well as artisans
with rural industrial sidelines and common rights – had to be forced off the
land. This was achieved by acts of parliament in what can only be seen as one
of the more blatant examples of class robbery at home by the same people
who were directing atrocities abroad during the development and defence of
the British Empire.[59]

In conclusion, social-property relations should be treated as central to any
explanation of economic and social change. Brenner has demonstrated that
when these relations are specified for particular countries or polities in medieval and early modern Europe, it can be shown with remarkable clarity how
they produced divergent historical outcomes in the face of the same demographic and economic pressures. The source of the most recent flood of criticisms against Brenner's work is derived from either crude misinterpretations
of his thesis of social-property relations as prime mover, or from reading his
thesis through the prism of techno-determinist forms of Marxism. The lapse
by English historians into so-called pluralist approaches to economic and
social change which have limited explanatory worth has often been the result.

---

59   Neeson 1993; Gott 2011.

CHAPTER 3

Feudalism, Serfdom and Extra-Economic Surplus Extraction

One of Marx's most important contributions to historical materialism has been his thesis that the essential difference between different economic forms of society is the specific way in which the surplus product is extracted by the ruling class of non-producers from the producers.[1] In line with Marx, Brenner characterised feudalism as a form of society or a system of social relations in which the surplus product was extracted by extra-economic coercion or, in other words, the means of extraction was political. By contrast, the extraction of the surplus in capitalism is fundamentally, although not entirely, achieved by the economic coercion of the market. In feudalism, peasant possession and peasant forms of production meant that peasants were largely shielded from the market, and so lords could only extract a surplus from the peasants and maintain themselves through political and military domination. In capitalism, wage workers are compelled to sell their labour power as a commodity on the market in order to survive: political coercion is still involved, but it is *fundamentally* an economic, rather than an *extra*-economic, force that compels. In other words, it is the threat of unemployment in capitalism, in contrast to the threat of the point of the sword and legal retribution in feudalism that compels producers to submit themselves for exploitation by non-producers, whether or not they perceive it in this way.

It is the social relations of serfdom (unfreedom) that provide the clearest representation of extra-economic coercion in feudalism. By the early thirteenth century in England, peasants were subjected to various dues in addition to the rent for their holdings. Those peasants who were depressed into 'villeinage', an English legal term for serfdom, were also entirely subjected to their lord's jurisdiction and had no legal right to challenge their lord's decisions against them in a higher, royal court. Many dues to which 'villeins' were subjected were flexible – that is, they could be imposed arbitrarily at the will of lords. These included tallage or taxation, increases in fines on servile disabilities such as on the ability to marry or move away from the manor ('merchet' and 'chevage'), and increases in other fines on land transfers and seigneurial monopolies such as grain mills and bread ovens. Armed with these arbitrary powers, lords were

---

1 Marx 1991, p. 791.

able to increase the proportion of their income at the expense of the peasants, and this ability was backed by the threat of military force. Without this flexibility lords faced crisis because they would be unable to reproduce themselves in the face of inflation and the spiralling demands of political accumulation.[2]

Some historians have had problems with feudalism as defined by extra-economic surplus extraction and have been critical of Brenner's application of it. This definition has led Jane Whittle to assume that Brenner *equates* feudalism with the social relations of serfdom. She has argued that if serfdom had largely ended in England by 1420 then so must have feudalism, full stop. Indeed, she argues further that because capitalism did not develop fully until centuries later, there could not have been a transition from feudalism to capitalism: instead there was a long *gap* between the end of the feudal and the beginning of the capitalist modes of production. Her solution to this problem is to reject the concept of a transition from feudalism to capitalism in England after the destruction of serfdom in the early fifteenth century, and to replace it with the concept of a peasant society and economy without serfdom 'merging into capitalism' at a later date.[3] Aside from the lack of conceptual rigour that this thesis displays, her end date for feudalism in 1420 is achieved by failing to incorporate the broader structure of feudal social-property relations beyond the social relations of serfdom, including the continuing dominance of the feudal ruling class with its controls over landed property and its latent potential to re-enserf the peasantry.

This point can be developed more fully in response to Steve Rigby's objection to Brenner's thesis on the extra-economic character of surplus extraction in feudalism. Rigby points out that half of the peasants in medieval England were freeholders, and thus he argues that they were therefore not liable to extra-economic coercion: so feudalism in Brenner's sense, and more broadly in the Marxist sense, only applied to a limited section of social relations in English medieval society.[4] The first point to make against this objection is that, while freeholders were not subjected to certain flexible dues and the burdens that

---

2 For a useful introduction see Hilton 1990a.

3 Whittle 2000, pp. 10–12, 16.

4 Rigby 1995, pp. 49–52. Bruce Campbell has more recently calculated that about half of the peasants in England were freeholders by the end of the thirteenth century. This amounted to a substantial increase in the proportion between free and unfree since 1200. Peasants were given the carrot of free tenure as a means of encouraging them to clear previously marginal areas for cultivation and provide new rents for the lords in the context of a rapidly increasing population, rising demand for food and rising rents, and that accounts for the increase in freeholders. Freeholds covered substantially less than half of the acreage of available peasant landholdings however because freeholders were far more likely than unfree villeins to be

servile peasants were, they *were* subjected to extra-economic coercion in the form of private manorial and royal jurisdiction. These jurisdictions extracted manorial court fines, fines from seigneurial monopolies, in some cases tallage, state taxation and purveyance, all of which depended on extra-economic compulsion by feudal powers, and which formed part of the extra-economic take.[5] Freeholders, like the unfree, were also subjected to tithes which represented a fifth of total seigneurial income, although most of this was 'pocketed by the church'.[6] Second, because of the neighbourly and family interrelations as the result of intermarriage between villeins and freeholders, the impact and experience of villeinage or serfdom affected *all* peasants. It was also not the case that freeholders had higher status in the village than unfree villeins. It was in fact natural for smallholding freeholders to be employed at busy times of the year on the land of an unfree villein who held a larger virgate holding (typically 25–30 acres). Freeholders were more likely to seek wage labour to supplement their production from the land than were villeins. The livelihoods of many small freeholders were therefore dependent upon villeins protecting their surplus from the encroachment of arbitrary lordship. It was therefore understandably in every peasant's interest to remove serfdom; hence free and unfree peasants fought and died together in 1381, and at other times, for the removal of lordship or for at least its severe attenuation. Both attacked lawyers and lords' manorial archives and destroyed records of their peasant tenures.[7]

---

small holders and cottagers whose main income was achieved through wage labour. See the discussion on Campbell in the following chapter.

5 Hilton 1991, p. 193.

6 Campbell 2005, p. 18.

7 By the end of the thirteenth century peasant tenures in France were overall much freer than those in England as a result of the successful struggles of peasant communities in France for chartered rights. However English peasants were, as we have seen, distinguished more clearly into two main groups, free and unfree. George Comninel has argued that the large proportion of freeholders in England, compared to France in the thirteenth century, was a legacy of the different forms feudalism took in England and France. Freeholders in England had access to the common law administered by the crown, whereas their unfree neighbours were subjected to the manorial courts of their lords with no access to appeals. For Comninel this access to royal courts was a legacy of a relatively centralised polity in England compared to its decentralised character in France. While English lords benefited from their cooperative relationship with the monarchy and state in terms of the greater power they wielded over the peasantry as a whole, in France they had to share their legal powers with the state: Comninel 2000. While this is a useful insight, Comninel's thesis ties him to an overly legal interpretation of freeholders in England which obscures important aspects of their practical lives. The strength of villeinage in England amongst their neighbours and family had a great impact on them and their communities. This legal approach also leads him to overstate the

This leads to the third point. The nature of freeholders within feudalism is as much a broader historical as a politico-legal, tenurial question. It was as much a question of class power as of the legal veracity of free tenure as to whether free peasants would *remain* free, or whether, as in the decades around 1200, they would be consigned to villeinage as many in England who did not have written proof of their free status were. That lords were always on the lookout for legal means to ratchet up the level of dues from the peasant tenants on their estates can hardly be doubted; and by the same token peasants always sought to reduce that level. Du Boulay has found evidence in Kent in the fourteenth century of lords being advised to pore through their records to look for any hint of evidence of freeholders who held lands that had been subject to arbitrary impositions or servile customs in the past; any evidence with which they could make a claim to increase the extra-economic take from freeholders.[8] It is little wonder therefore why there was so much variety in the level of servile disabilities experienced by peasant communities. Kent peasants were among the freest in England by 1300 although this was not always the case. In fact this freedom appears to have been a recent phenomenon, because in 1086 manors in Kent were typically comprised of 'villans, bordars, cottars and slaves', comparable in this respect with relatively unfree Somerset in the west of England.[9] Nevertheless, when one examines the situation in the neighbouring county of Sussex around 1300, even where peasants had the same manorial lords as those in Kent, one finds that the majority of tenures were unfree: 'Only about forty miles separated South Malling in East Sussex from the archbishop's Kentish manor of Aldington, but in making that journey over the Rother he passed from a countryside where bondage was known till the end of the Middle Ages

---

importance of freehold land for the origin of capitalism in England. His assumption that the lords' demesne leases were freehold is incorrect; as is his statement that the English lords 'achieved a remarkably complete dispossession of the mass of peasants from the customary manorial tenures through a variety of largely legal means': Comninel 2000, pp. 46–7. Before the emergence of agrarian capitalism in the fifteenth century, only approximately a third of the land at most was held by freehold, the rest by leases and copyholds, and the terms for all of the leases and the majority of the copyholds were temporary and non-heritable, and therefore insecure in contrast to freeholds. With regard to expropriation by 'largely' legal means, English lords and their farmers were often too impatient in the fifteenth and early sixteenth centuries to wait for expropriation in this way. See Chapter Five below, and the case study in Part II.

8   Du Boulay 1966, p. 184.
9   Du Boulay 1966, pp. 144–5, 180–8; Darby 1977, p. 338.

to one in which royal judges had admitted in Edward I's day that personal freedom was the rule'.[10]

Related to the latter point it is also a broader historical question as to why
freeholders, let alone serfs, should pay any rent *at all* to feudal lords. Freehold
rent in one sense in the medieval period was as much a feudal imposition as
were servile dues, because this 'feudal rent' resulted from the imposition of
manorial lordship by military force on a potentially free owner-occupying
peasantry during what Chris Wickham has aptly called 'the caging of the peasantry' in western Europe as a whole between the ninth and eleventh centuries.
In the absence of attacks and plundering by bands of lords from elsewhere,
peasants had no need for feudal lords in order to survive. The caging of the
English peasantry in these centuries, a process which probably became so
intense in France – especially in the generations around the year 1000 – that it
has been described as 'the feudal revolution', left free and unfree owing heavy
dues and rents. Freeholders in the early middle ages were more likely to owe
a periodical tribute to lords and kings rather than specific landowning rents.
The revolution in feudal tenures in England was the outcome of the turmoil
of the Scandinavian invasions between the eighth and early eleventh centuries: the Anglo-Saxon great estates were fragmented into village or part-village-
sized estates, and they were devolved to, or usurped by, an enlarged class
of knights. The specificity of the English experience, that is, the precocious
cohesiveness of the English aristocracy and royal control over political structures, is important here: 'England had ... moved from being the post-Roman
province with the least peasant subjection, in 700, to the land where peasant
subjection was the completest and most totalising in the whole of Europe, by
as early as 900 in much of the country, and by the eleventh century at the latest elsewhere'.[11] This took place before further controls and dues were introduced in the decades after the 'Norman Conquest', and then again around 1200.
Christopher Dyer has also commented on the processes of the caging of the
peasantry as a whole. Referring to the situation in the early eleventh century
England – before the Normans – he says that,

> [t]he manorial tenants owing labour services ... consisted partly of peo-
> ple who had come 'up from slavery', and partly of an older stratum of
> dependent tenants pressurised into doing more work for the lord, and
> perhaps peasants previously free of major obligations who had been

---

10   Du Boulay 1966, p. 181.
11   Wickham 2009, chapter 22. The quote is on pp. 469–70. For a recent discussion on the
      feudal revolution and the subsequent crisis of government across Europe see Bisson 2009.

caught in the manorial net. We will never know for certain which route
into dependence on the manor was more important, and indeed this must
have varied with the region or type of estate. Our view is partly obscured
by the versions which lords liked to believe. Just as they presented themselves as the friends and protectors of their tenants, they also justified
their dominance by claiming that peasants had been granted parcels of
the lords' land, together with livestock and equipment, in exchange for
heavy services, making the whole arrangement seem like a reciprocal
exchange. But very rarely were lords filling up an empty piece of countryside. A more common situation was that they took over an inhabited
territory, and then had to subject it, and above all its population, to their
control. In these circumstances they had not given their peasants their
holdings, but took away lands they already held, and granted them back
on more oppressive terms.[12]

In England, the decades around 1200 saw further servile impositions on those
who could not prove that they were free, and the withdrawal of royal justice
which entirely exposed them to the private law courts of their lords. Brenner
argued that for lords to maintain their income in the thirteenth century, much
depended on the surplus extraction relationship represented by serfdom, particularly the ability for lords to increase dues on a flexible basis from servile
tenants. By this means they could keep ahead of inflation, and the increasing
demands of political accumulation, at the expense of the peasantry. However,
as I have argued at length in the previous section on the prime mover, for
Brenner the class structure of feudalism or feudal social-property relations are
not constituted solely by the social relations of serfdom, however important
they were in certain countries and in certain periods, but should be seen in the
wider context of feudal property allocation and class power. For Brenner it was
the continuity of these relatively strong feudal powers in England that played
a part in the development of capitalism in England. He argued that in the first
half of the fifteenth century, when serfdom had largely disappeared:

> It was the English lords' inability either to re-enserf the peasants or to
> move in the direction of absolutism (as had their French counterparts)
> which forced them in the long run to seek novel ways out of their revenue
> crisis. With the decline of their own self-discipline and self-organisation

---

12   Dyer 2002, p. 37. John Hatcher in a footnote to one of his earlier critiques of Brenner
      touched on this point in passing, but deemed it not relevant to incorporate into the
      discussion: Hatcher 1981, p. 25, n. 58.

under the pressure of the later medieval crisis of seigneurial revenue, the English ruling class was impelled, for a time, to turn the instruments of political accumulation in upon itself. But the resulting zero-sum game *within the ruling class,* in the context of declining overall ruling class incomes, could not constitute a stable solution.[13] Lacking the ability to re-impose some system of extra-economic levy on the peasantry, the lords were obliged to use their remaining feudal powers to further what in the end turned out to be capitalist development. Their continuing control over the land – their maintenance of broad demesnes, as well as their ability to prevent the achievement of full property rights by their customary tenants and ultimately consign these tenants to the status of leaseholders – proved to be their trump card. This control of landed property was, above all, an expression of their feudal powers, the legacy of the position the lords had established and maintained throughout the medieval period on the basis of their precocious self-centralisation. They would consolidate these powers by carrying their self-centralisation to an even higher level, using somewhat different forms, in the subsequent era.[14]

With regard to serfdom in particular, Brenner argued that 'Serfdom can be said to end only when the lords' right and ability to control the peasantry, should they desire to do so, has been terminated'.[15] The decline of serfdom at a particular point in time did not necessarily mean that it could not rise again in a changed political and economic context.[16] Extra-economic surplus extraction by lords from a possessing peasantry was a goal of lordship analogous to political accumulation through warfare. Whether feudal lords were successful in either is another question, and one which needs to be examined historically over the feudal epoch. The decline of serfdom may severely weaken feudal lordship, but not necessarily destroy it permanently. For Brenner, the transition from feudalism to capitalism entails 'the collapse or breakdown of lordly surplus extraction by means of extra-economic compulsion as one side of a two-sided development of class relations, the other being the undermining

---

13   Brenner is doubtless referring here to the factional conflicts among the leading nobility and monarchy which led to the deposition of Richard II in 1399 by Henry Bollingbroke (Henry IV). These conflicts came to a head again and were played out in the Wars of the Roses (c. 1453–85) that ended with the military defeat and death of the Yorkist Richard III by Henry Tudor (Henry VII), a Lancastrian.

14   Brenner 1985b, p. 293.

15   Brenner 1985a, p. 27.

16   Brenner 1996.

of peasant possession or separation of direct producers from their means of subsistence'.[17] Serfdom can be undermined in a particular feudal society, and yet that society would either still remain feudal – if in an attenuated form – or lead to a new distinct form of extra-economic surplus extraction such as absolutism. It is only when peasants are finally dispossessed, and are transformed into wage workers or capitalist farmers subjected to market forces for their survival, that they can no longer be re-enserfed or subjected to surplus extraction by extra-economic coercion.[18] Hence we find not only eastern Europe but parts of western Europe such as Italy and possibly even parts of France experiencing renewed feudal controls and increases in servile dues during the early modern period: from the late fourteenth century in Italy and from the 1770s in France.[19]

In conclusion, the social relations of serfdom were a major aspect of political or extra-economic coercion within feudal society. Dependent upon the outcomes of struggles between lords and peasants within the broad framework of feudal social-property relations, the level of imposition of disabilities characteristic of serfdom, and the number of the population subjected to it varied over time and place within the feudal epoch. Nevertheless, these servile impositions on some members of rural – and urban – communities directly affected the other members of those communities, and coloured the relations of the whole of society. Those who were not directly subjected to servile impositions were still under the private manorial jurisdiction of the lord, the royal jurisdiction of the crown, and the spiritual jurisdiction of the church. All of these jurisdictions were imposed in new forms following territorial conquests between the ninth and eleventh centuries. Freeholders did not escape the direct extra-economic take in the form of various fines and taxation, and aside from the servile impositions on their friends, neighbours and family, they lived under the political threat that they too could be drawn into the servile net.

---

17   Brenner 1985b, pp. 214–15.

18   This is not to say that capitalist accumulation in the early modern period was incompatible with forms of extra-economic coercion: controls on the movement of the poor in England itself and the enslavement of populations in its New World colonies, for example.

19   Epstein 1998, pp. 79–80, 82; Duplessis 1997, pp. 166, 169–70. For the relationship between seigneurial exactions on the peasantry in the late eighteenth century, and the role of peasant mobilisation during the French revolution see Jones 1998, chapters two and three, and Markoff 1996, chapters two, five and six especially.

CHAPTER 4

Class Conflict and the Crisis of Feudalism

In the foregoing critiques of Robert Brenner, the theme of the relative strength of England's lords and peasantry – social classes viewed as organised political communities – has often been central. This is necessarily so given that, in Brenner's account, the feudal crisis of the early fourteenth century in England, and the unintended emergence of agrarian capitalism in the following century, were the outcomes of fundamental conflicting strategies for reproduction between lords and peasants, as determined by specific feudal social-property relations in England. One of the pillars of Brenner's thesis is the identification of a relatively stronger lordship and cohesive aristocracy and monarchy in England vis-à-vis the peasantry (compared to that in France between 1100 and the feudal crisis of the late thirteenth and early fourteenth centuries), and his conclusion that this relative strength and cohesion determined divergences in economic and political developments between these two countries in the fifteenth century and early modern period.

England emerged after the conquest by the Normans with one of the most centralised polities in Europe, and with a mutually supportive monarchy and aristocracy. This translated into relatively mature centralised parliamentary and legal systems by the end of the thirteenth century. Brenner argued that, as a consequence of this cohesion amongst the English ruling class, English lords were able to extract an increasingly greater proportion of income from the peasantry during the twelfth and thirteenth centuries following the tightening of dues during the conquest itself. He cited the well-known consignment of half of the peasantry to villeinage in a legal revolution around 1200 which removed their ability to appeal beyond their lord's manorial lordship to royal justice, and subjected them to relatively high rents and arbitrary exploitation.[1] He argued that it was the ability of English lords to continuously raise dues from a large section of the English peasantry which helped them to profit from the economic expansion and intensive commercialisation of the thirteenth century. Hence they were able to maintain their incomes during a century in which inflation trebled the prices of arable produce, and in which there was pressure on lords for increased expenditure on political accumulation, warfare and display. At the same time, lords resisted uncompromisingly any move on

---

1 Important statements on the depression of the status of the peasantry in this period are in Hilton 1976, pp. 174–91, but see also P.R. Hyams, 1980, and Dyer 1996, pp. 277–95.

the part of the peasantry towards chartered rights in their customary holdings, something that the peasants in France achieved. Brenner cited the well-known evidence of lordship victories in the spate of legal battles with their peasant tenants in England in the late thirteenth and early fourteenth centuries as evidence of their continuing strength relative to lords in France, a country which in the same period typically experienced *peasant* victories. The feudal crisis began from the middle of the thirteenth century in France as French lords experienced a reduction in their income because peasants managed to secure fixed rents in what was an inflationary era. By contrast, in England the problems for lords began only in the early fourteenth century, hence the more assertive nature of lords against peasants in the courts at this time.

For Brenner, this continuous reduction in the real income of peasant households in England undermined the ability of peasants to invest and improve their holdings. At the same time, it increased their liability to impoverishment and famine as holdings got smaller due to increasing population pressure on the land and declining labour productivity. To add weight to his case, Brenner pointed out that where tenures were freer, such as in parts of East Anglia, greater densities of the peasant population were achieved on very small holdings as peasants had more options to improve labour productivity, and had time for industrial sidelines before crisis ensued. In France the decline of lordship income led to improvements in the financial machinery of the French state by the late thirteenth century. The consequent increase in the state-imposed tax burden on the peasantry undermined the high density and freer customary peasant property there. The property of French peasants was further undermined by warfare which took place on French soil in the early fourteenth century, warfare which the extra taxation funded. Developments in state taxation in England at the same time, in order to fund warfare, also served to undermine the better-off peasants in England who were subjected to it.

So for Brenner it was the nature of feudal social-property relations and feudal rules for reproduction that led to specific forms of feudal evolution and feudal crisis. Lords were forced to extract a surplus from the peasantry thereby undermining production, and they were forced to expand laterally into new holdings rather than allow customary peasants the freedom to improve productive efficiency on the old. The strength of feudal lordship, namely the capacity of lords to coerce the peasantry into giving up a surplus, and the unequal allocation of property, determined the income distribution between lords and peasants in different regions and this led to feudal crisis in different ways and at different times. When the crisis was confirmed and exacerbated by the Great Famine and the Black Death, the land-labour ratio tipped in favour of the peasants in the long run. Yet unlike in France, the continuity of relative aristocratic cohesion in England into the early fifteenth century enabled English lords to retain their private control over customary property and their large demesnes.

As I mentioned in my earlier critique of S.R. Epstein's account of the feudal crisis, in recent years research has led to a more positive view of the feudal economy than Brenner and demographic historians had earlier outlined. The new research points to a greater use of technology by peasants under pressure from holding division than was hitherto recognised, and to a greater sensitivity of peasant production to price signals. All of this is acknowledged by Brenner in his recent 2007 paper. His point however is that given feudal social-property relations and the resulting strategies for reproduction of peasants and lords in conflict, this partial commercialisation and market dependence of peasant agriculture could not lead to capitalism, and was undertaken only under pressure as a second option to the usual safety-first approach in which production was typically diversified. Epstein's view that there was no feudal crisis, and that if it was not for the Black Death the feudal economy would have continued to grow on the basis of increased state-building and the reduction of transaction costs, has no empirical basis and will be taken no further here. There has also been a developing consensus in recent years among some historians such as Bruce Campbell and Richard Britnell, including some in the Marxist tradition such as Christopher Dyer, that villeinage or serfdom in England at the end of the thirteenth century was not as burdensome as was once thought; and this chimes in with the findings that peasants had more freedom to pursue technical improvements in the manorial context. This perspective is used to provide support for the view of Campbell and Britnell especially that the pre-crisis centuries of commercialisation were more important for the development of capitalism in England than the post-Black Death period, something which I discuss at length in Chapter Seven on the periodisation of the origin of capitalism.

For the purposes of this present discussion, it is important to make the point at the outset that, right from the first paper, Brenner was aware of complexities in the relations between lords and peasants. He conceded that labour services in some cases were relaxed or commuted at the end of the thirteenth century, and unfree peasants were in practice mobile and not always restricted to the manor. Given the increased numbers of tenants from two hundred years of relatively rapid and continuous population growth, and the heightened demand for land and very cheap labour which lords could attract to their large demesnes, lords could afford to be more relaxed with regards to controls on peasants. It was not always necessary to waste time and money chasing serfs when holdings could be filled by other peasants who perceived that they had no option, beyond outright rebellion, but to succumb to harsh terms.[2] It follows therefore that this evidence of a relaxation of serfdom was not a sign of weakness in this context. This was also a period in which in many places in England serfdom dues were commuted for high money rents, although this need not have been regarded as a permanent once-and-for-all change. Conditions only turned against the English lords after the Black Death: labour costs became high and rent rolls were reduced on manors which had previously been able to maintain peasants on the harshest terms and high rents. Lords went on the offensive to maintain earlier levels of rent and serfdom dues, and restrict the market in labour; and they were provided with royal statutes to that effect. For a while they succeeded, but they reaped the whirlwind of 1381 as a result.

i   B.M.S. Campbell: The English Peasantry and the Feudal Crisis

Bruce Campbell has recently given support to Brenner's thesis on the determining role of social-property relations, particularly the way in which tenures were 'redefined and renegotiated' during the evolution of feudalism, the generation of feudal crisis, and the transition from feudalism to capitalism in England.[3] However, leaving aside for now his narrow definition of social-property relations as confined to the vertical tenurial relationship between lords and peasants, Campbell is critical of a number of factors in Brenner's thesis, particularly regarding the causes of the feudal crisis. Campbell's assertion that the genesis of the early transition to capitalism in England lay well before the Black Death 'in the vigorously commercialising and expanding world of the twelfth and thirteenth centuries', rather than the post-Black Death period, or during that 'long era of retreat and retrenchment that then followed [which] created the opportunity for a fundamental rationalisation and reconfiguration of productive forces and a redefinition of social-property relationships', is borne out of a fundamental re-examination and re-interpretation of lord-peasant relationships and the balance of class forces in the pre-crisis centuries.[4] It is this thesis that will be addressed in this chapter.

On the question of the relative strength of lords and peasants, Campbell has produced a set of essays that argue the inverse to Brenner, and go further than anyone else in refuting the argument that the increasing relative strength of English lordship vis-à-vis the English peasantry during the thirteenth century

2   For example, Brenner 1985a, p. 27.
3   Campbell, 2006, p. 236.
4   Campbell, 2006, p. 237; Campbell 2005, pp. 3–70.

(peaking at the beginning of the fourteenth century), was a key aspect of the causes of feudal crisis and the subsequent economic changes. Against Brenner, Campbell argues that, in terms of the proportion of income derived from the land, English lords by the early fourteenth century were in a worse position than at any time before and after. For example, he states that around 1300 'on current best estimates' lords received between eighteen and twenty three percent of net revenues generated from the land, compared with between thirty and thirty five percent during the period between 1688 and 1803.[5] He therefore rejects the traditional view, also espoused by Brenner, that the thirteenth century was a period of growing strength for English lords, characterised by increasing dues and controls on the peasantry and the extraction of an increasing proportion of the peasants' production surplus. The traditional view of course argued that coupled with increasing population pressure on the land these new impositions led to declining labour productivity, peasant immiseration and feudal crisis. Campbell argues that in England it was the English *peasantry* which had the upper hand over lordship in the thirteenth century, and that it was the strength of the *peasantry* that led to the crisis of feudalism or 'the agrarian problem in the early fourteenth century'. It was the English peasantry exploiting the lords rather than the other way around.[6]

Unlike Epstein, Campbell, whose work has focused on the nature of commercialisation and technology in England in this period, recognises the existence of serious levels of poverty and malnutrition in the early fourteenth century, and he calculates a fall in labour productivity during the thirteenth century of as much as 60 percent.[7] He argues that rather than this 'scarcely controlled poverty' being the result of pressure for rents and dues by exploitative

---

5 Campbell 2005, pp. 16–17. He says himself however that these figures should not be pushed too far as they are 'hardly robust'.

6 Campbell 2005, p. 24.

7 Campbell 2005, pp. 62–5. Examining work done on the 'Hundred Rolls' of 1279 (Kosminsky 1956, and Kanzaka 2002), Campbell finds that 60 percent of the peasant population, both free and unfree, were crammed into only five percent of the land, and this does not take into account 'a large but unspecified number of minor subtenants'. Over the next 40 years 'conditions degenerated further as populations continued to grow and economic opportunities outside of agriculture contracted rather than expanded'. By 1327–32 at least two thirds of rural households lacked 12s (12 shillings) of moveable goods and were deemed too poor to pay tax. Underemployment and unemployment was rife. Land productivity was as high as it would be in 1800, but labour productivity fell by about sixty percent between 1209 and 1309 and was lower between 1270 and 1329 than at any other time between 1209 and 1869. Agricultural output per worker was half as much in 1300 as it would be in 1800. Holdings were far too small to make optimal use of available resources. A general failure of demand ensued

and increasingly prosperous lords, it was rather the result of the weak position of these lords vis-à-vis the peasantry, particularly the better-off stratum. Their weak position forced them to allow the division of villein tenures which were originally made up of yardlands and half yardlands, and the further morcellation of holdings through an extensive and damaging structure of subletting. Moreover, for Campbell, the period between 1100 and 1300 should not in fact be characterised by the increasing *un*freedom of the English peasantry, but by its increasing *freedom*. Where Brenner, those in the Marxist tradition such as Rodney Hilton and Christopher Dyer, and other leading non-Marxists such as Hatcher and Britnell, view the legal revolution around 1200 as a victory for lords over the peasantry through consigning the majority of the latter to the private arbitrary justice of their lords (villeinage or serfdom), Campbell views the remainder of the peasantry who were now recorded officially as freemen as the more worthy of comment, and as having greater implications for the feudal crisis. He goes on to point out that following what he appears to regard as a period of enfranchisement around 1200, the proportion of free peasants to unfree in England increased as lords were forced to grant favourable tenures to peasants as an incentive to create new holdings in previously uncultivated areas. This was of course – as Brenner had pointed out – one of the lords' feudal rules for reproduction. Indeed, by the end of the thirteenth century, freeholders formed about half of the population. In addition to this increasing number of freeholders paying fixed rents to the lord, and thereby gaining an unearned increment at the expense of the lord in this inflationary period, Campbell argues – in line with an increasing consensus among historians of English villeinage – that *certain* villein rents and dues became fixed by custom, and once fixed custom was virtually impregnable due to the strength of peasant organisation. It follows, and this is his main point, that during the thirteenth century most of these fixed villein rents were therefore sub-economic – that is, they were below the market value of the land that the lord might realise in an open market. So for Campbell this situation provided for 'a rent-seeker's charter' which incentivised the better-off peasantry to accumulate and to sublet increasingly tiny portions of land to their poorer neighbours as land became increasingly scarce and valuable. They were able to charge increasingly high economic or market rents due to the robust demand.[8] This wealthy peasant stratum therefore benefited at the expense of both the lords and their poorer neighbours. While Campbell concedes that not all peasant dues to the

---

along with a brake of further market-generated economic progress. He says that this was 'structural poverty of the most intractable kind'.

8   Campbell 2005, pp. 45, 54–5.

lord were fixed and some remained flexible and theoretically arbitrary at the will of the lord, in practice he argues that it was difficult for lords to realise their potential in the face of peasant organisation. These dues did not provide adequate compensation for the losses lords were taking from the increasing low fixed rents and customs. For Campbell then, it was the ruthlessness of the peasantry combined with its organisational ability to keep lords at arm's length that was the cause of the feudal crisis. In direct contrast to Brenner's thesis, he argues that lords only grew in strength after the crisis and Black Death because they were able to develop contractual market (leasehold) rents and dispossess the peasantry.[9] For the lords to oppose the trend in the thirteenth century which led to the fragmentation of holdings and the impoverishment of the majority of peasants', Campbell argues that 'radical action' would have been required by the lords:

> lords needed to evict, consolidate and enclose, but they rarely chose to do so. Acute as was the need for tenurial reform, its social cost was too high and as yet there was no clear concept of what was required or how to bring it about. In later centuries, as the merits of engrossment and enclosure became apparent, a new class of commercially minded lords would deal more harshly with their tenants.[10]

This is a bold and stimulating study and thesis from a prolific and influential historian. However, Campbell's problems begin with his lack of a comparative perspective between England and other European polities, and with his understanding of Brenner's social-property relations as realtions constituted solely by the struggle for rent between lord and peasant, rather than as the whole macro structure of feudal society and its vertical and horizontal class relations.

ii   A Critique of Campbell: English Lordship and the Feudal Crisis

Campbell's attempt to develop his thesis with reference to one country only, England, severely limits the impact of his case. He argues that the so-called rapacious, exploitative lords of thirteenth-century England took a smaller share

---

9   These economic rents brought them a greater return than the sub-economic rents characteristic of villeinage and freeholding. However Campbell recognises that these contractual leasehold rents and peasant dispossession was achieved at too high a social cost and was responsible for 'the agrarian problem of the sixteenth century'.

10   Campbell 2005, p. 66.

of the tenant's surplus than both their Norman predecessors and their capitalist successors. Indeed, rather than examine on a comparative basis aspects of different countries within the same medieval context which Brenner has done to such fruitful effect, Campbell prefers to seek transhistorical comparisons within British history alone. He compares the economic and social context of late thirteenth-century England with that of eighteenth-century Ireland, and seeks to understand the social causes of the famine in Ireland in the 1840s from conclusions on the causes of the crisis of the early fourteenth century. He therefore points to the subletting tenants as the main cause of famine in Ireland.[11] Campbell's underlying project appears to be to rescue the English aristocracy both from the ignominy of causing famine in medieval England, and also from the ignominy of causing it in Ireland in more recent times.

His transhistorical statistical comparison of the proportion of income lords derived from agriculture in England between 1300 and 1688 to show that lords in 1300 were not all powerful is also, as he says himself, 'faulty', because it involves a comparison between feudal and capitalist social-property relations.[12] A more persuasive approach would be a comparison of the proportion of income lords derived from agriculture in the same close chronological period within a broader European context. These transhistorical aspects of Campbell's thesis will not do as a serious challenge to Brenner. Brenner had of course gone to great lengths to point out that it was the *relative* strength of the English lords compared to France especially that was key to his thesis: for example the ability to maintain controls over customary property and their relatively large demesnes. How does Campbell otherwise explain how English lords after the Black Death were able to develop contractual rents and dispossess the peasantry towards what he calls the Smithian 'sequential dynamic' while in France the Malthusian 'cycle' was yet again set in motion?

In addition to Campbell's avoidance of the question of the comparative strength between English and French lordship, there are glaring empirical problems with his thesis and numerous contradictions. Campbell treats free and unfree peasants as if there was a system of apartheid separating them. In fact, as Zvi Razi has recently pointed out (in his own critique of Campbell, Hatcher and others), freeholders and villein peasants were neighbours and bound together through intermarriage. They were therefore highly integrated in the

---

11   Campbell 2005, pp. 54–5.
12   Campbell 2005, p. 17.

thirteenth century socially, productively and in their political organisations.[13] The unfreedom of one section of the peasantry naturally affected everybody.

It is also the case that Campbell does not factor in numerous other sources of new revenue which lords tapped. Lords were forced to expand their manorial jurisdictions and enterprises into new lands in order to maintain or improve their status. One aspect of this was the granting of free status to peasants who were prepared to undertake the clearing of new plots in either economically marginal or in politically contested areas. This feudal rule for reproduction arguably increased the relative numbers of freeholders in the peasant population during the thirteenth century. But Campbell's assertion that this proliferation of freeholders resulted in the declining income for the lord is a clear contradiction. These new assarts were just that, *new lands* brought into cultivation at no expense to the lord, and they brought in *additional* rents. That was the whole point. At the time they were created, the magnitude of these new rents represented the market value of the land. Using his own figures taken from studies of the 'Hundred Rolls' that were compiled in 1279, he says that free rents *overall* 'seem to have paid' half the market rate, that is, between 3.5 and 4.1d (4.1 pence) per acre. However, the newly created assarts around 1279, and the freeholds that were taken back into the hands of lords because the peasant tenants defaulted in their rent payments due to poverty or through lack of peasant heirs, and indeed those freeholds that were actively accumulated by lords in this period in order to extend their estates, *paid the market rate*, and these would have been a boon to the lords. Moreover, while this market rate in 1279 was twice the *average* freehold rent, it was only 'at least' 1d per acre more than the rent that the villeins paid, namely between 6.8d and 7.1d. If this is the case then villeins paid only around 1d per acre less than the market value of the land in 1279 at a time of high demand. Villeins therefore paid a high price for this barely 'sub-economic rent', namely serfdom fines and controls, labour services, arbitrary taxation and seigneurial prerogatives which using Campbell's figures from his own research amounted to an absolute minimum of thirteen percent of lords' total income. Somehow Campbell concludes that these impositions on villeins did not compensate the lords for low fixed free rents.[14]

Lords also derived great benefit in the thirteenth century with the change to direct exploitation of their demesnes by their own officials. The demesnes had earlier been leased wholesale to other knights. This change was a response

---

13   Razi 2007, pp. 182–7. See also the discussion in the previous chapter on the relationship between freeholders and feudalism.

14   Campbell 2005, pp. 22–3.

to increased demand for produce and land by the rapidly growing population which led to high prices and increasingly cheap labour. Indeed the increasingly low wages to which lords were able to subject smallholders during the thirteenth century were an important cause of immiseration in the fourteenth century. The importance of wage levels to lords is indicated by the lengths to which they were prepared to go after the Black Death to keep them at pre-plague levels. Indeed low wages affected freeholders disproportionately more than villeins as the former were more likely to be smallholders and cottagers than were the latter. Across a number of midland counties in 1279, 59 percent of freeholdings were smaller than six acres compared with 36 percent of villein, and 33 percent of freeholdings contained less than one acre compared to 22 percent of villein.[15]

Campbell has massively overstated the role of wealthy peasants in the feudal crisis. Christopher Dyer, a historian working in the British Marxist tradition of 'history from below', agrees to some extent with Campbell that wealthier peasants did benefit from subletting in the late and early fourteenth century. He argues, however, that they were certainly not the ruthless accumulators that Campbell describes. Dyer says they were not usually able or willing to maintain their accumulations and then go on to develop wealthy dynasties before the Black Death. This situation can be sharply contrasted with the farmers in and from the late fifteenth century. These thirteenth-century peasants did not display the ruthless mentality towards the accumulation of property and towards their families and neighbours that one detects in the later period of emerging agrarian capitalism: 'They were not ruthless economic men', and they had no overall strategy to accumulate and specialise *a la* Adam Smith. Their accumulations were fragile and were fragmented among their offspring at the end of their lives.[16]

The ability of the peasantry to organise against their lords in the thirteenth century, and indeed up until 1381 and beyond, something that Campbell sees as confirming his argument that lords were already weakened before the Black Death vis-à-vis the peasantry, would not have been possible if a wealthier stratum was able to behave as independently and individualistically as Campbell suggests. Indeed Campbell says himself that, '[a]lthough a few individuals were able to exploit the land market to build up their holdings, on many manors the net trend over time was one of attrition, as almost all holdings shrank in size'.[17] In the micro studies which he cites to prove his own case he finds

---

15   Campbell 2005, p. 51.
16   Dyer 2002, pp. 176–7; Dyer 2005, pp. 50–1.
17   Campbell 2005, p. 53.

that 'much freehold land [in the English midlands] was in the possession of gentry, ecclesiastics, craftsmen and tradesmen' who did not cultivate but acted as middlemen subletting it piecemeal for terms of years. These were not therefore ruthless wealthier peasants from the manors in question but gentry and urban investors who had made money in trade and urban property and used it to exploit the high demand for rural property.[18]

Campbell's assertion that lords became progressively weaker in the face of wealthier peasants who subdivided their holdings to sublet them at a high market rate than they were paying the lord, does not hold up against the evidence. Campbell says the wealthier peasants' desire to subdivide and sublet contrasts with the lords' desire to keep traditional holdings intact and keep a control on tenure and rents in this way. In fact, as Dyer has shown, and something which Campbell himself recognises, lords *did* encourage (and make money out of the) subdivision of villein tenures and subletting, firstly because new tenants had to pay an entry fine to enter the property – and these fines were rising, and secondly because the rents of two half-yardlands were usually higher than the rent for one full yardland. These entry fines were arbitrary and not fixed, and they remained burdensome to peasants, commonly rising to three times the rental value around 1300 when originally they were equivalent to a year's rent. Campbell says that the evidence of 'The Hundred Rolls' in 1279 which covered the English midlands and beyond reveals that the smallest freeholders, like the smallest villeins, paid the greatest rents per acre to lords. The crown also encouraged subdivision on its ancient demesne land as a means of raising its rental income to compensate for relatively light servile dues which were typical on its lands. Campbell concludes that 'as and when opportunities permitted, lords did what they could to raise the value of their freehold rents', although most had to rest content with far less than a full competitive market rent.[19] However, this statement masks of course the other compensatory revenue from the exploitation of cheap labour, entry fines and marriage fines that lords benefited from, aside from the political controls that villein tenure afforded them. Looking at the situation from the perspective of the majority of the peasantry, Campbell's point that lords lost out to sub-economic rents on villein holdings would not have been apparent to them at the time. The peasantry would not have benefited from the high market value of their lands. Their main priority was survival on the ones they had.[20]

---

18   Campbell 2005, p. 57.
19   Dyer 2005, pp. 138–43; Campbell 2005, pp. 22, 54.
20   Razi 2007, p. 184.

Underlying all of this is the question as to what extent in England peasant rents and dues both free and villein became fixed during the thirteenth
century. Campbell argues that lords had 'abdicated control' of tenure as early
as the mid-twelfth century, before the legal revolution between 1180 and 1220.
He says that in order for lords to derive a good income, 'coercive feudal rents'
were necessarily imposed on English peasants by the new breed of rapacious
and violent Normans in the eleventh and twelfth centuries. This was because
the context of low population and low demand for land meant it was difficult to extract high rents from the natural workings of the land market alone.
These rents were subsequently by degrees 'metamorphosed' into fixed customary rents 'probably' in the century after the conquest, when lords' powers had
been stronger. Campbell says that customs were set down in writing at this
time before any anticipation of the inflation of prices and land values due to
developing commercialisation.[21] Campbell's authority for this statement is
John Hatcher's article on villeinage which appeared in 1981.[22] Hatcher argued
that there was an improvement in peasant conditions along with the shrinking
of demesnes in the mid-twelfth century. This was doubtless the indirect result
of the heightened rivalry between lords ('anarchy') during King Stephen's reign
when, at the same time, Anglo-Norman lords suffered serious setbacks with
regard to their previously conquered lands in Wales. Lords could not maintain
controls over peasants or seek to extract more from their production while
they lacked cohesion as Brenner has argued. But while Hatcher did argue that
some villein dues became fixed by custom, and that its consignment to record
during the course of the thirteenth century was to the detriment of the lord in
an age of inflation, he also stated that '[i]t is indisputable that many, perhaps
most, lords succeeded in burdening their unfree tenants with increased and
additional payments and obligations of one sort or another in the course of the
later twelfth and thirteenth centuries'.[23] So Campbell misread his authority.

We cannot, however, leave this discussion in the hands of Campbell and
Hatcher alone. Rosamond Faith adds another dimension. She finds that before
the twelfth century labour services were not deemed to be the main mark of
servility because most 'villeins' did them. In this sense the term 'villein' or
more usually 'villan' need not in the eleventh century necessarily refer to an
unfree or servile person, but simply to a 'villager'. It was the terms under which
labour services were performed that characterised freedom or unfreedom,
such as whether they were fixed or arbitrary 'at the will of the lord', or what

21   Campbell 2005, pp. 65–6.
22   Hatcher 1981, p. 9.
23   Hatcher 1981, p. 15.

type of work was involved. Faith, like Hilton, points to servile customs such as marriage fines ('merchet') that were newly introduced in the late twelfth century, thus denoting an increase or rise in serfdom or villeinage in this period rather than its decline. These new customs were written down not by accident or because of lack of foresight by the lords, as Campbell suggests, but to provide lords with greater legal redress given the potential for disputes. Another important aspect of this rise in serfdom from the late twelfth century was the removal of access to royal courts for those villans who could not prove that they were 'free'. This subjected them to the political 'private' jurisdiction of their local lords and represented a serious disability.[24]

Dyer also points to the legal revolution around 1200 as a time when the 'powers of private justice were given a new lease of life'. Lords maintained income levels from the peasantry in the thirteenth century and stayed abreast of inflation through rents from an increasing number of new assarts and new acquisitions, the maintenance of some key flexible dues and entry fines, and the skilful and direct exploitation of large demesnes as the voluminous mass of manorial accounting and legal documentation which still survives in English archives today bears testimony: 'the overall impression must be that the aristocracy at all levels adjusted to the rapid changes in the period 1086–1300 and profited from them'.[25] Why else would these same archives be among the first targets of the rebels' anger in 1381? This is a clear vindication of Brenner's thesis and shows a clear contrast between what the English lords were able to achieve in comparison to their counterparts in France. Dyer finds that the increasingly direct confrontations between lords and peasants in the thirteenth or early fourteenth centuries 'almost always resulted in victory for the lord'.[26] These conflicts were partly the result of lords aiming to compensate for the declining income from their demesne production due to reduced prices during the crisis. Lords sought to extract more surplus from the peasantry even though peasants in 1320 were paying more than ever to the lords. Entry fines and marriage fines offered lords the best source for profit and these rose in the 1310s when peasants could least afford them.[27]

Finally, it is interesting to note that Campbell is keen to identify English lords as weak vis-à-vis the peasantry in the thirteenth century and early fourteenth century, and blame the peasantry for the feudal crisis, and yet he does not see a contradiction between this stance and his acknowledgement of the

24 Faith 1997, pp. 245–65; Hilton 1976, pp. 174–91.
25 Dyer 2002, pp. 141–2.
26 Dyer 2005, pp. 34–5.
27 Dyer 2002, p. 242.

serious effects of warfare and its finance on the peasantry and economy at this time. He says that taxation and the draw on manpower for the infantry came when peasant families were least able to suffer it. Add to that purveyance, or the forced purchase of food from small communities at arbitrary prices – if they were paid at all – to feed the troops.[28] In recent years there has been a greater emphasis by economic historians of medieval England on the role of warfare as a cause of the feudal crisis and yet they view it, like they view the Black Death, as a wholly exogenous factor – that is, external to the impact of relations between class and class. As such they have lacked awareness of the interconnectedness of feudal social-property relations, the drive to political accumulation and state formation and the inextricable links between these horizontal relations among the monarchy and aristocracy and the struggle for rent between lords and peasants. As Brenner said, the faltering of lordship revenue after room for extensive development and new assarts had run out led to more sophisticated ways of gaining a surplus. Lords and monarchies took property from one another and from their tenants and this policy inevitably led to a downward spiral of warfare and declining productivity. In fact Campbell asserts that what amounts to the new focus on the significance of exogenous warfare in this period as a key cause of the crisis forms part of a fuller understanding than Brenner's account!

In conclusion, Bruce Campbell's recent work provides support for Brenner's thesis on the role of social-property relations in the evolution of feudalism, the generation of feudal crisis, and the subsequent transition to capitalism in England. Campbell's approach is hampered however by his application of social-property relations which recognises only the vertical class struggle between lords and peasants. For Brenner the feudal crisis was not simply determined by the strength of lords vis-à-vis the peasantry in the immediate rent relationship, but by conflicting rules for reproduction within feudal social-property relations more broadly. Brenner had never felt the need to characterise the English lords as rapaciously exploitative between 1100 and 1300; indeed, he has always avoided moral judgments of this sort. His interest was in the mode of feudal exploitation and its levels of success in different regions. If he wished to emphasise aspects of the strength or cohesiveness of English lordship and English lords and monarchy as a class with relation to the English peasantry, it was to demonstrate reasons why it, in particular, fared comparatively well before the feudal crisis in contrast to the ruling class on the continent, and how the continuity of aspects of that strength proved crucial to the emergence of agrarian capitalism in the fifteenth century. By the

---

28   Campbell 2005, p. 63.

same token he never saw the English peasantry in the thirteenth century as some passive mass suffering from the imposition by lords of unlimited powers raining down on them from high, a position that Hatcher never tires of trying to attribute to him.[29] Brenner recognised that English peasants were no less rebellious than those on the continent in this period, and the increasing strength of their organisation and resistance before the Black Death would serve them well in the late fourteenth century.

Campbell's argument that the feudal crisis in England was largely caused by peasant enfranchisement and increasing peasant controls over tenure during the thirteenth century, rather than the lords' consolidation and extension of serfdom, verges on the outrageous. The number and proportion of freeholders may have increased as new lands were brought into cultivation – but these new lands were developed under the management of the lords, and like the rents and tolls from newly founded boroughs, they generated new and additional rental income. The number of peasants per lord also increased overall, including the number subjected to villeinage and to increased servile dues and controls since 1200; and increases in the level of servility imposed on villeins had an impact on their freeholding family and neighbours. English lords also benefited from the increasingly low wages which they were able to pay labourers to work their very large demesnes which they now directly managed. Wealthy peasants took advantage of land hunger by subletting at a profit, but the lords and crown also divided property to benefit from high land values. The relative political strength of the lords over the peasantry in England is above all revealed by the fact that when their income did finally begin to decline due to the crisis around 1300, a crisis caused by declining labour productivity and the reduction in the immiserated peasantry's demand for food and non-agrarian products, they were still able and willing to generate compensatory income through increasing servile dues at a time when the peasants were least able to comply; and their success is written in the legal victories over the peasants in the early fourteenth century. At the same time there were new developments in state taxation to pay for warfare. This political strength and will on behalf of lords and state only served to exacerbate and deepen the crisis. The tables were turned after the Black Death – only after immense struggle – but the basis of English lords' power of the peasantry in the thirteenth century, their control of property and tenure, would enable them to play a decisive role in the remodelling of social-property relations in the fifteenth century, and lead to their resurgence as a capitalist aristocracy in the sixteenth century.

29   Hatcher 1981, p. 4; Hatcher and Bailey 2001, p. 73.

CHAPTER 5

Insecure Property and the Origin of Capitalism

> To assert that capitalism throve on unjust expropriations is a monstrous
> and malicious slander. Security of property and tenure answered capital-
> ism's first and most heartfelt need. Where insecurity reigned, it was
> because of the absence, not of the advent or presence of capitalism.[1]

As Eric Kerridge's impassioned plea suggests, the question of the security of
property tenure during the transition from feudalism to capitalism has in the
past raised tempers among historians. The answer to the question has implications for the way we view the nature of capitalism. Was the transition to
capitalism facilitated and characterised by a progressive increase in the security of the holdings of peasants and farmers following the decline of serfdom
and the removal of arbitrary feudal prerogatives? If so can we therefore view
the transition as a healthy break from feudalism in which the polarisation of
landholdings and the removal of the vast majority of the people from the land
was the result of an innocuous process institutionalised by a fair land market
of legally secure individuals? Or was the transition to capitalism facilitated and
characterised by an increase in the insecurity of the holdings of peasants and
farmers following the decline of serfdom, an insecurity which was instrumental in a deliberate and even forceful process involving particular class interests in the dispossession or expropriation of landholdings from the majority
of the population?

i   Tenurial Security Versus Tenurial Insecurity

Kerridge, writing a few years before the beginning of the original Brenner
Debate, took it upon himself to ensure that the word 'capitalism' and the
phrase 'security of property' were inextricably coupled, and furthermore to
argue that the security of property was key to the transition to capitalism. In
order to do so he had to firmly rebut the work of R.H. Tawney whose major
study, *The Agrarian Problem in the Sixteenth Century*, had been very influential.[2]
Until recently, Kerridge's intervention seems to have been successful because

---

1 Kerridge 1969, p. 93.
2 Tawney 1912.

the majority of historians cited in this present work have either passed over Tawney or dismissed him.

To Kerridge's exasperation, Tawney had firmly identified the transition to capitalism with the *in*security of land tenure. Tawney saw villein tenure, even with its hated disabilities, as secure from eviction because it was in practice heritable and, in spite of what Bruce Campbell has argued about its sub-economic value to the lord, it played an important part in the reproduction of feudal lordship on the basis of controls on both people and land and the cultural and ideological aspects of class position and display that these controls represented. Tawney regarded those land tenures that developed after the decline of serfdom in England, namely leaseholds and copyholds which developed from villein tenures, as insecure tenures because, unlike villein tenure, they were generally *not* heritable. Even in the cases where they were heritable, aside from illegal, forcible evictions that are well known for the late fifteenth and early sixteenth centuries, he found that where customary tenure was strong this would induce evictions through more persistent persuasion, intimidation and manipulation of the law and its lawyers, and that this would have implications for freehold tenure as well.[3]

In addition to his evidence for the above Tawney argued that the transition, which required the development of consolidated capitalised farms and the binding of production to the market, would hardly have been possible without this insecurity, and he pointed to the rebellions against enclosure in the 1530s and 1540s which for him undoubtedly expressed the genuine grievances of those already dispossessed, and of those who perceived that their holdings and way of life were under threat. He demonstrated brilliantly, and at great length, how political divisions and policy contradictions in the state government ensured that while some institutions such as the court of requests at Westminster were set up to give peasants under threat of dispossession a hearing, and laws were passed at the end of the sixteenth century to provide customary or copyhold tenants with a chance to retain or pass on their holdings to their offspring when old terms ended, the tide was relentlessly on the side of the capitalist encloser, whether lord or farmer, and not on that of the traditional small and middling peasant. The great landowners in the government's leading body, the privy council, and, by the end of the sixteenth century, the monarchy itself, found their future interests too closely entwined with

---

3   Tawney 1912, pp. 231–310. As he says on page 250: 'We cannot, in fact, be content with a mere summary of the legal position, for the law is not always strong enough or elastic enough to cope with shifting economic forces. Or rather its arm is short, and can only grapple with those conflicts which are sufficiently violent to force their way to Westminster'.

the changes even while exhibiting disquiet at the great social cost and disorder these changes were inflicting on large sections of the population.[4]

Kerridge was more willing to focus on the legal veracity of tenure than he was on the role of social power and class interests in the changes. Kerridge argued that the security of copyhold tenants from wrongful eviction or trespass is *proven* by the well-known survival from around 1500 of the many cases of copyholders bringing grievances to the royal courts. In other words copyhold tenancies were, like freeholds, protected from manorial interference by the common law from this date. He agreed that lords in some cases committed illegal actions on both customary and free tenants, and used their position to obstruct justice against their opponents, but he countered by arguing that illegality worked both ways and that customary tenants had 'fraudulent intentions' as well. He went so far as to say that customary peasants 'who did that kind of thing deserved to forfeit all their holdings for infidelity'.[5] Having therefore proven the legal basis of the security of copyhold tenure Kerridge further moved to doubly prove it by grounding his argument in what for him was a tacit logic as demonstrated in the following two striking but curious statements:

> The security of copyhold has been legally proved, but even if it had not been, it would be fair inference from the well known fact that knights, esquires and other gentlemen took up copyholds both of inheritance and of lives; they would not have done so had these estates been indefensible.[6]
>
> Bondmen apart, everyone had security of tenure as befitted their estates, and nearly all were quite untroubled in their possessions, never needing even to defend them in law or equity. Had it been otherwise, had farmers not been secure in their farms, they would hardly have undertaken any improvement, let alone the agricultural revolution they actually achieved. Men will not travail long and risk all their capital in the nagging fear of sudden confiscation. Tenures arose in feudal society; the doctrine of estates evolved to meet the needs of the capitalist farmer and his landlord, both of whom imperatively required security of tenure.[7]

While making these statements Kerridge was only willing to address the written status of the plot of land rather than the representative of the social class who actually held or occupied it in practice. The differentiation in material

4   Tawney 1912, pp. 314–421.
5   Kerridge 1969, pp. 79–81.
6   Kerridge 1969, p. 76.
7   Kerridge 1969, p. 93.

resources and patronage or, in other words, social power available to, and employed by, different classes in order to protect or increase their property, forms no part of his perspective. Second, it was these capitalist farmers and landlords undertaking the agrarian capitalist revolution who as Tawney argued were doing the evicting and improving at the expense of the smaller peasant holders. One cannot legitimately lump these together in the same category as *all* holders. Such people, lords and their large lease holding farmers, would hardly be vulnerable to eviction by their own hands. Third, Kerridge's formulation of the transition to capitalism seems to have the estates system of commercial landlord and capitalist tenant farmer as already in place at the outset of the transition, with no mention of the processes involved in the origin of that system, namely the removal of the majority of peasants from the land. Fourth, and something that should also not be ignored, is the dissolution of the monasteries in the 1530s which serves as another example of expropriation in that period. When Kerridge states that 'everyone had security of tenure as befitted their estates', he does not include the third of the landed wealth of England that belonged to abbeys, priories, convents and chantries that was stolen virtually overnight by decree of the monarch.

Brenner's definition of 'security of tenure' is similar to Tawney's, although he was less concerned with Tawney's emphasis on the force of social power as key to the transition, and more concerned with a *comparison* of the level of tenurial security that peasants enjoyed in England and France. Brenner's definition of a secure customary tenure is, like Tawney's, tenure that has more or less the equivalent security of freehold. For Brenner, as Tawney, tenurial *in*security was characterised by competitive leaseholds and copyholds for lives and years; the latter acted as the equivalent of leasehold because copyholders could be evicted when their terms of lives or years ran out. Whether tenants were legally secure *within* their terms of years or lives was not his prime concern, and this is where he differs from Tawney who was very much concerned to demonstrate a culture of illegal eviction *within* copyholders' terms of years or lives. Tawney showed how these evictions were contrary to Tudor statutes, and he highlighted the problems peasants faced in trying to litigate and to sustain that litigation. He argued that the state was only able to deal with extreme circumstances, or those cases which were serious enough to get to London. It could not deal with persistent persuasion and threats at the local level where the real battle was fought.[8]

Brenner's crucial point that cannot be simply passed over was that, in contrast to France where the peasantry with the state's backing gained

---

8 Tawney 1912, pp. 79–81.

proprietorship of the vast majority of the land (approximately 85 to 90 percent), in England lords retained comparatively greater controls of the majority of the land (at least two thirds) in the form of their demesnes which they
leased out at competitive rents by early fifteenth century, and in the form of
copyhold tenure which developed from most of the earlier villein and bond
tenure by the 1440s. Lords were all the time increasing their proportion of
leasehold land by acquiring freeholds and customary tenures that had become
vacant during the population downturn and as the result of peasant mobility
away from harsh tenures. Lords attached this vacant land to their demesnes
and converted it to leasehold. This was something not possible for lords in
France because customary peasant land was protected by the state, and peasants returned to it during the new economic and demographic up-phase from
the middle of the fifteenth century. Brenner argued that these varying levels
of control of much of the land by English lords, demesne and customary, was
above all an expression of the continuity of their feudal powers.[9]

ii   Leasehold and Copyhold: The Trump Card of English Lordship?

So what form did these greater controls through leasehold and copyhold tenure in England take? Brenner argued that because they prevented the peasantry from gaining proprietorial or freehold rights in their holdings, these
controls were the 'trump card' for English lordship, following the serious
threat to their reproduction by the feudal crisis, the decline of serfdom, and
their struggles with the peasantry more generally. Beginning with leasehold,
although given their traditional class position English lords would have preferred not to have transferred their demesnes to peasants, they were in a much
better position than their counterparts in France because of the greater *size* of
their demesnes and thereby their control of a greater proportion of the land.
Brenner's figure of a third of the land in England as being in demesne is taken
from Kosminsky's sample of manors in the English midlands in the late thirteenth century. Dyer more recently has calculated that, in the early fifteenth
century, demesne leases made up between a quarter and a fifth of the land
in lowland England. If we use Dyer's estimates which cover a broader sample
this still amounted to between two and three times the amount of demesne in
France which was only around eight to ten percent of the land, and from the

---

9   Brenner 1985b, pp. 287–95.

early fifteenth century that proportion of demesne in England would steadily increase as lords attached vacant customary land to it.[10]

Christopher Dyer has shown that the monetary value placed on leases by lords was quite high in the early fifteenth century, even though negotiations over that value between lords and peasants took place in a period of declining serfdom and low population. This value was based upon calculations derived from records of earlier demesne management by the lords themselves.[11] In the first generations of peasant lessees of demesnes during the fifteenth century the terms of years applied to the leases were also generally short, between seven and ten years. These terms clearly still favoured the lords but they gave way in the mid-to-late fifteenth century to terms of 20, 30 or 40 years reflecting reduced demand during the so-called 'great' recession of these decades. Nevertheless the leases were still taken up and so there was still some measure of competition. These relatively long leases persisted after 1500 although by this time there is evidence of farmers competing over short leases again. Dyer adds that where demesnes were leased, lords' income rose, giving them a good return at between 6d and 8d per acre.[12]

Keith Wrightson has shown how market conditions started to increasingly favour lords due to the increased demand for land especially from the mid-sixteenth century. Indeed by the late sixteenth century, leases shortened again to between seven and twenty years as the earlier longer leases reached the end of their terms. From the late sixteenth century there was a renewed wave of enclosure and transference of freehold and copyhold to leasehold which extended and deepened the already intensely competitive nature of agriculture. These shorter leases were accompanied by rapidly increasing rents. At this stage, in the late sixteenth and early seventeenth centuries, these high rents and relatively short leases also paradoxically benefited large farmers in important respects because it meant that smaller peasants were ruled out of the bidding process for the renewal of leases and copyholds. This situation enabled farmers to expand and improve their production at the smaller peasants' expense. Indeed with the severe inflation of prices at the end of the

---

10   Brenner 1985b, p. 247; Dyer 2005, pp. 89, 195.

11   Dyer 2005, pp. 201–2. Brenner in fact assumed the values of demesnes would be low at this stage, but he argued that 'so long as there was potential for the increased competition for the land the market in leases provided the basic condition for both the restoration of landlord incomes and the economic differentiation of the tenants': Brenner 1985b, p. 296.

12   Dyer 2005, pp. 201–3.

sixteenth century, such larger farmers had an increased incentive to expand their production given the greater returns of marketed produce.[13]

Clearly the transfer of relatively large demesnes to insecure leasehold in the late fourteenth and fifteenth centuries, and further transfers of customary and freehold lands to leasehold in the sixteenth and early seventeenth centuries, benefited English lords to an increasingly great extent. Even in the recession years of the fifteenth century they still gained a good return.

Regarding the security of customary or copyhold tenures in England, Brenner recognised that there was a mixed picture with much variety in different parts of the country. Some copyholds were granted for the life of the tenant or for the lives of husbands and wives and one heir. Some were granted for a term of years. Brenner was prepared to assume, like Kerridge, that these copyholds were secure for the negotiated terms, but only for that period: there was no guarantee of a continuation of the family line, nor of its attached customary rights for fuel and common, nor of the collective social organisation of production of which it was part. Fines were variable and so the renewal of the holding was, like leasehold tenure, subject to a market rent, or in other words it was made available to the highest bidder whether from inside or outside the village, by peasant, merchant, or gentleman. Some copyholds, however, were heritable and at the same time were subject to fixed fines as new heirs entered them. These were the equivalent of freeholds.

Brenner recognised that copyholders could, like their freeholding neighbours and family, theoretically receive justice in the royal courts by the early sixteenth century.[14] Although heritable copyholds with fixed fines persisted in some areas such as Kent, Brenner generally saw copyholds as insecure for small peasants.[15] His main thesis is that in addition to the generation of competitive leasehold rents as outlined above, the copyholds that had not already been attached to demesne leasehold due to lack of occupiers during the population downturn were undermined by those with deeper pockets when the time for renewal came, and in this way they acted in a similar way to the leaseholds.

---

13 Wrightson 2001, pp. 184–90.

14 Brenner 1985b, p. 294.

15 See also Tawney 1912, p. 301: 'It will be seen that the degree of security enjoyed by copyholders varies very greatly. When the copyhold is one of inheritance, it is legally complete, unless the tenants incur forfeiture by breaking the custom. An estate for life with right of renewal is virtually as good as a copyhold of inheritance. Estates for life or lives are precarious. Copyholds for years without right of renewal are scarcely distinguishable from lease. On the whole, when these examples are added to those of Dr Savine, it would appear that copyholds for life or lives were more usual than copyholds of inheritance, while fixed fines were the exception and variable fines the general rule'.

The result was the gradual accumulation of large farms, their productive improvement by farmers compelled to compete on a market of shortening leases and increasing rents, and the break up of traditional agriculture.

iii   The Level of State Protection for Peasant Property

Brenner's thesis on tenure has come under sustained opposition by a number of historians for various reasons. Croot and Parker, in their contribution to the original 'Brenner Debate', argued that he underrated both the hold of the English peasantry on the land and correspondingly the level of security those copyholders enjoyed who were subjected to competitive entry fines when terms of lives or years in their contracts had finished. They argued that by the early years of the seventeenth century the royal courts began to require that these increases in entry fines be set at 'reasonable' rates – that is, at an affordable non-market rate.[16] French and Hoyle, who have recently taken up the mantle of Croot and Parker and make the same point, find a case where the latter condition was set as early as 1585. Like Tawney, however, the latter do recognise that peasants were put off attempting to seek redress against their lords in the royal courts: they argue that 'there is no doubt that many tenants were cajoled into surrendering customary tenancies and accepting leases'.[17]

Robert Allen takes the implications of these legal developments concerning copyhold tenure in the sixteenth century further than anyone else. He views them as a turning point for the English peasantry. He argues forcefully in an influential work that, during the sixteenth century, the customary tenure of small landowners was protected by the state in cumulative fashion as a direct response to the disruption caused by the early enclosure movement (before 1520). For Allen this protection of copyhold and the general sweep of state legislation against overspecialising enclosure and depopulation in the sixteenth century, was so important and so effective that the seventeenth century should be seen as a 'golden age' for a stable, secure and therefore productive English middling peasantry – which he calls the English yeomanry – and so one for English agriculture generally. Allen argues that this security of customary tenure would only be undermined in the eighteenth century along with beneficial leases as the state became the creature of a parliament of landlords. They no longer protected copyholds from rack rents, and through forced enclosure by Act of Parliament they induced the removal of the remaining customary

16   Croot and Parker 1985, p. 82.
17   French and Hoyle 2007, pp. 10–12.

tenants who were clinging on in large numbers in some areas by virtue of customary rights. In addition, state policy served to increase the landed wealth
of lords who by means of new mortgages bought up the remaining freeholds.
Allen argues that the most productive century for agriculture was in fact not
the eighteenth century and its agrarian capitalism and rack renting as has
been traditionally argued, but the seventeenth century with its secure owner-
occupying yeomen peasants.[18]

So where Tawney and Brenner viewed the insecurity of customary tenure as
playing a significant role in the development of capitalist farms, these historians argue the contrary: for them, customary tenure was protected by law from
economic or market-determined rents from the late sixteenth century for at
least a century.

In defence of Brenner (and Tawney), the first point to make about the argument that customary tenure was protected by the state – particularly in the seventeenth century – is that it ignores the fact that an enormous amount of land
had already been engrossed by that time, and agrarian capitalism was already
mature in many places. I will return to this point later. The second point, which
I will focus on here, is that the evidence for this protection relies inordinately
on the single source category of royal statutes against forced depopulation and
overspecialisation which crowd the statute book in the sixteenth century up
until the 1630s. The extremely shaky assumption is that these statutes were
implemented *in practice*, and yet those royal justices of the peace who were
responsible for their implementation were the very gentry who were benefiting from their *non*-implementation. Moreover, as Tawney has shown in a devastating indictment, those also benefiting from its non-implementation were
leading aristocracy or the greater lords who made up the privy council itself,
the leading executive body of the state under the monarch. Having demonstrated the difficulty of prosecuting people in the royal courts for infringing the
statutes in question, because they were riddled with loopholes, he adds:

> Much more serious was the fact that the traditional policy could be
> carried out only by disregarding the financial interests of the wealthier
> classes, who could most easily influence parliament and the council, and
> who were locally omnipotent. In the first half of the sixteenth century the
> high position of many of those who were most deeply implicated in cut-
> ting land free from communal restrictions made them almost unassail-
> able. The royal commission of 1517 returned among enclosers the names
> of the duke of Norfolk, the earl of Shrewsbury, the duke of Buckingham,

---

18   Allen 1992.

Sir William Bolen, Sir R. Sheffield, the speaker of the house of commons, Sir J. Witte, the under-treasurers of state, and Sir John Cotton who was himself one of the commissioners.[19]

In the 1540s the rebellions against enclosure included a telling clause in the Norfolk rebels' demands in 1549. This required that all good laws since the time of Henry VII (from 1485) be implemented – that is, those 'which hath been hidden by your justices of your peace, sheriffs, escheators, and other of your officers, from your poor commons'. The Duke of Somerset who, of all those in the government, seems to be the only one who aimed to implement the statutes in order to protect the peasantry, was subject to a coup d'etat:

> The angry unanimity with which Somerset's colleagues turned upon his land policy was not wonderful for they were nearly all directly interested in the maintenance of the status quo. Warwick, who led the coup d'etat, had enclosed on a large scale. Sir William Herbert had made extensive enclosures on the lands he had acquired from the abbey of Wilton. The St. John family, the Darcy family, the earl of Westmoreland, had all local troubles with their tenants; and there are some indications that Sir William Paget and the detested and detestable lord Rich were in the same position.

By comparing a list of privy councillors between 1548 and 1552 with the list of grantees of monastic estates, Tawney demonstrated that many of the privy council who opposed Somerset and his land policy greatly increased their estates through the dissolution of the monasteries. 14 of the 32 landowners who received grants of more than £200 a year were privy councillors in one or other of those years, excluding the Earl of Warwick and Sir William Herbert. For Tawney,

> this fact alone shows the impossibility of enforcing laws forbidding depopulation during years following death of Henry VIII and the despair of legal protection which seems to have settled upon the classes affected by this movement ... the distribution among the wealthier classes of land producing a net income of not less that £110,000, gave them an enormous vested interest in preventing and evading legislation to check the most

---

19   Tawney 1912, pp. 379–80.

profitable use of the new possessions which were to endow the aristocracy of the future.[20]

No doubt the famous commonwealth anti-enclosure rhetoric did receive a
sympathetic ear from the crown in this period, when enclosure was framed
as ungodly because 'against the natural order of things', as a depopulator of
coastal regions leaving the realm vulnerable to foreign invasion, and as causing
a reduction in cereal production for the growing population from the 1540s. It
may also have become less attractive to farmers themselves as high grain prices
meant enclosure for pasture which characterised the period before 1520s was
less desirable. In addition, there was the momentous resistance by peasants
themselves culminating in the widespread rebellions of the 1530s and 1540s
especially. These are the factors that are cited as responsible for a slow down
of the enclosure movement between 1530 and 1580. However the rebellions of
the 1530s and the 1540s were more likely to reflect the success of the enclosure
movement rather than an indication of a potential hiatus; and the period following the downfall of 'Protector' Somerset in 1549–50 would have been worse.
Tawney, as we have seen, argued that these years were probably the harshest
for the peasantry, as the enclosing oligarchy which ran England were the chief
opponents of the peasants in the rebellions.

Indeed, in the second half of the sixteenth century, attitudes began to
change favourably towards enclosure. Wrightson shows how, in this period,
the values of 'improvement' *officially* took over from those of custom, and
certain statutes were actually repealed in the early 1590s. The renewed enclosure movement that followed, especially in the midlands, led to the midland
revolt of 1607, and this movement intensified in the 1620s. What was significant about the 1620s movement – and earlier – was that, as the crown became
engaged in massive engineering projects, it became deeply implicated in the
enclosure movement itself. The district of Sedgemoor in the Somerset levels
in the south-west of England was drained in 1618 along with the well-known
draining of the fens in the east which dispossessed thousands. Wrightson says
that the state was by then encouraging gentry in the process of disafforestation
of royal forests for the purposes of economic expansion. It is true that in the
1630s 'renewed anxieties about grain supplies led to state commissions against
unlawful enclosure in which archbishop Laud demonstrated his personal hostility to enclosers', but we know Laud was a most unpopular politician. After
the 'English Revolution', the spurt of extensive enclosure which threatened the
common fields of Leicestershire (a county that was probably the least affected

---

20   Tawney 1912, pp. 380–81.

up until then), led to a bill for renewed restraint on enclosure, presented in 1657. Wrightson says that this found no sympathy among the general members of the 'Republic'.[21]

So Allen's assertion that customary tenants enjoyed a climate of state protection against depopulating enclosers, and that anti-enclosure legislation was efficiently implemented in the seventeenth century, does not match even with the state and the monarchy's own actions. At best, the state was ambivalent after 1580 and well before that privy council members had blocked enclosure commissioners' attempts to implement the law, an action which lit the touch-paper for widespread rebellion in 1549.

To return to the particular criticisms of Brenner over the protection the state afforded copyholders with regard to market-determined entry fines on renewals, Brenner's response to Croot and Parker was that this apparent state protection for customary tenants against so-called 'unreasonable' entry fines

> began to be established only very late in the day – after a century of rising prices and rents. During that time there appears to have been no legally established limit to which fines could be raised, and be supported in court on appeal. Those copyholders who had survived to this late date must very often have been rather substantial figures, capable of paying the rising rents (in the form of higher fines) or buying up the property themselves.[22]

Indeed by the late sixteenth century agrarian capitalism was already well established in many areas, and although the pace of depopulating enclosure may have slowed in some areas after 1520, in the late sixteenth and early seventeenth centuries its consolidation and extension had just entered another very important phase. This was the 'first great age of the estate surveyor'.[23] In response to the rapid rise in prices and rents at this time lords commissioned meticulous surveys of their estates which were 'undertaken primarily for the purpose of facilitating the efficient exploitation of its potential rental value' – in stark contrast to strategies in France, it should be added. Wrightson shows that lords' income from rents doubled or trebled between 1580 and 1640 and because peasant incomes could not keep pace this represented a massive distribution of wealth to the landlord class. In the light of such evidence, Wrightson argues that such so-called reasonable rent increases in the early seventeenth

---

21   Wrightson 2001, pp. 202–11.
22   Brenner 1985b, p. 296.
23   Wrightson 2000, p. 188

century 'cut deep into the precarious surplus of small husbandmen'.[24] Using Allen's own figures for the size of peasant holdings in midland open fields where smaller farms persisted, Brenner demonstrates that these villages were already dominated by large, non-peasant farms by the early seventeenth century. Allen's golden age was not experienced by small traditional peasants, but by capitalist farmers with significant accumulations. This finding will form a large part of the discussion in the next chapter on the rise of the yeomen.

Hoyle has also rejected Brenner's thesis that the route to larger farms was through the transference of insecure copyhold to leasehold. He suggests that lords who were 'unlucky enough' not to have transferred copyhold tenures to leasehold before what he sees as effective legal protection against unreasonable entry fines on copyholds from the late sixteenth century, found themselves in a weak position, and in need of ready cash to make investments in more competitive tenures that would bring in a greater income in a context of rapidly increasing rents and inflation. These unlucky lords raised cash from customary tenants by confirming in writing their secure customary status, or by enfranchising them as freeholders. Hoyle even suggests that the number of freeholders increased between 1580 and 1650 due to this process. In other cases lords actually paid their customary tenants to convert to leasehold and subsequently remodelled their estates on new lines – that is, on the lines of consolidated large commercial farms. But far from 'turning Brenner's views upside down', as Hoyle suggests, these findings merely present an inevitably more complex picture, and the movement was nevertheless relentlessly towards leasehold. Hoyle himself shows that large farmers bought up these freeholds and leased them out en bloc.[25] Furthermore, Wrightson is clear, contrary to Hoyle's protestations, that in the years between 1580 and 1650 copyhold was not being preserved but was 'in retreat'; and while Wrightson is aware that customary tenures were being converted to freehold in this period, as Hoyle says, he has very good evidence that this process of 'enfranchisement' was a calculated strategy by lords which enabled them to remove the traditional trappings of customary tenure such as customary rights on common lands and rights to collect firewood and fish before subsequently buying up the freeholds and then leasing them out.[26]

---

24   Wrightson 2000, pp. 182–3.

25   Hoyle 1990, pp. 1–20. See Hipkin 1998, p. 661. He shows how large owner-occupying freeholders on Romney Marsh in Kent increasingly leased out their estates in the seventeenth century, and became rentiers as the division between landlords and leaseholding tenants sharpened.

26   Wrightson 2001, p. 184.

iv   Rising Entry Fines on Copyholds

We can now turn to evidence for rising fines in this period and the implications for tenurial security. What is clear is that at least entry fines on copyholds without inheritance and those where fines had not been fixed *were* rising from as early as the late fifteenth century, and there is compelling evidence that this process induced eviction as Brenner argued. Dyer's substantial sample of the Bishop of Worcester's estates in the west midlands reveals that entry fines of copyholds moved in line with competitive leasehold. Entry fines were maintained at a quite high level before 1430; between 1430 and 1470 they declined but then rose thereafter, and 'had become a substantial burden on some manors by the early sixteenth century', increasing significantly by the 1530s.[27]

Mavis Mate in her important new study of south-eastern England found that in Surrey and Sussex entry fines recorded in manorial court rolls rose significantly during the period between 1450 and 1550. One of the major developments in the period which must have contributed to this rise was the movement of wealthy outsiders – merchants, yeomen and gentry – into the manorial holdings, and this is a common theme in other studies.[28] The fines rose most notably in line with the sharp rise in prices in and from the 1520s. They rose earlier but not on the same scale as Dyer found in the west midlands. However Mate makes an extremely valuable point which should serve as a note of caution to historians who may wish to read the level of fines recorded in manorial court rolls at face value. She says 'as complaints made to Chancery clearly indicate, payments could be demanded by local stewards or by overlords such as the Abbot of Battle, and not appear on the court rolls'. She cites a court case at Feltham in Surrey dated between 1547 and 1553 where a new lord taking over the manor aimed to subvert the previous terms of a copyhold. It had previously been granted for four lives, but when the last-named person on the grant sought admittance to the holding the new lord refused to allow it unless the claimant paid an extortionate £10 fine. The tenant argued that no fine was due as it was paid at the initial surrender and past entry fines had been no more than 30s. The pressed tenant offered to pay £3 which was double the alleged previous level of fine in order to keep the land and told the court he was afraid that it would not be accepted. The outcome is not known.

Mate says that in this period 'the right of heirs to take over family property became less secure'. In one case in 1521 the Abbot of Battle had allegedly not honoured the grant for three lives he had made to his tenant William Strong.

---

27   Dyer 1980, pp. 287–90.
28   See for example Campbell 2005; and Whittle 2000.

When William died his son John paid five nobles (that is, 5 × 6s 8d), and entered the premises as heir. However another tenant offered the lord two oxen worth £3 and the land was granted to him instead. Mate also speaks of the 'increasing disabilities' of customary tenure in Sussex. By the sixteenth century, because of the high rents offered by the influx of wealthy outsiders into the manorial land market, lords became more assertive with regard to their legal rights over the land. Tenants' holdings became vulnerable to forfeiture if they did not play by the letter of the law. One tenement of 60 acres was seized by the Bishop of Chichester because a tenant had sub-leased it for a longer term than the customary one year without the lord's licence. The entry fine was put up for the highest bidder. The current holder offered £3 but an incoming gentleman offered 20 marks or £13 6s 8d. What is clear is that by the early sixteenth century in some areas lords were treating copyhold like leasehold tenure.[29]

Tawney's evidence shows striking increases in entry fines on seven manors in Wiltshire and Somerset between 1520 and 1569. Between 1520 and 1539 the average fine per acre for a sample of 42 tenants was 1s 3d, and by 1560 to 1569 the average for 29 tenants was 11s. Overall fines per tenant on three manors in Northumberland rose from between £2 18s 6d and £4 6s 9d in 1567 – which was already high – to between £4 10s 2d and £7 4s in 1585. He says:

> It is not surprising that the programme of agrarian reform put forward by the Yorkshire insurgents in 1536, and by the rebels under Kett in 1549, should have contained a demand for copyhold lands 'to be charged with an easy fine, as a capon or a reasonable sum of money'. It is not surprising that the court of chancery should have been bombarded with petitions to declare or enforce customs limiting the demands which a lord might make of an incoming tenant.[30]

Jane Whittle, in her study of a small sample of manors in east Norfolk between 1440 and 1580, found that entry fines were either fixed according to agreed custom between lords and peasant tenants, or, if variable, did not change much throughout the whole period. On the basis of this she refuted Brenner's argument – and Tawney's before him – that the insecurity of customary tenure was a factor in the transition to capitalism in England.[31] More recently, in a paper that takes England as a whole, she paints a more mixed picture that significantly modifies her earlier forthright anti-Brenner position. She says that

---

29   Mate 2006, pp. 194–207.
30   Tawney 1912, pp. 305–7.
31   Whittle 2000, pp. 78–9.

on some manors tenurial traditions allowed lords to undermine the security of tenure in the sixteenth century, but on others this was denied to lords. This is as Brenner and Tawney said. However in conclusion to this theme she says 'the important point is that engrossment was a common experience in manors with very different types of tenure, and therefore it cannot be explained by tenure alone'.[32] Unfortunately she does not attempt an explanation. Historians such as Tawney, E.P. Thompson and Wrightson would point to the local 'field of force' of custom and social power.

French and Hoyle, citing evidence in contemporary literature and the demands in Kett's articles in 1549, acknowledged that entry fines on copyholds *for lives* were rising by the 1540s. But they say there is no compelling evidence of extortionate fines on entry to holdings held by copyhold *by inheritance* before the 1570s, which they say were generally notional, at one or two years' rent. This was the case in my own sample in Kent as I shall show in detail in Part II. The problem was that, as early as the 1460s, the lord and demesne farmer were not prepared to accept the consequences of static rents and fines rents and fragmented subsistent holdings which covered two thirds of the rest of the manor. In the absence of legal means, ways were found to forcibly remove tenants. In other words it was the very legal security of tenure on this manor that induced evictions and engrossment.

The forced removal of tenants with copyhold by inheritance tenures was something that Brenner did not explore at length. This was because his method and aim was to examine reasons why agrarian capitalism developed in England and not in France. It was the insecure hold English peasants had on the land by virtue of copyholds for lives, and the extensive leaseholds in contrast to the early broad proprietorship in France, that quite rightly exercised him given the questions he had set out to answer. However, one could argue against Brenner that given the possibility that peasants with secure tenures could often be removed by force, the security of customary tenure *on its own* in France did not necessarily prevent the development of engrossment and enclosure in France. But of course, security of tenure cannot be dealt with on its own as an independent variable. All aspects of peasant, lord and state relations need to be taken into account and, when they are, it is clear that they did not favour engrossment in France. First, peasant proprietorship was already well entrenched in France by the end of the thirteenth century. Second, the symbiotic centralisation of the state machine developed by protecting the entrenched peasantry in order to tax them. This was made easier and necessary because of the relatively decentralised nature of French lords and their limited land base.

---

32   Whittle 2004, p. 242.

In conclusion, from the early fifteenth century the change from villeinage to copyhold tenure in England was a change that had come about largely through the successful resistance of peasants to attempts to re-enserf them during the seigneurial offensive after the Black Death, and the movement of many villeins into newly vacant freehold lands. Lords' desires to attract and maintain tenants on manors as a function of feudalism continued until the second half of the fifteenth century, after which the benefits of market rents on large competitive farms became increasingly apparent. The disabilities, but corresponding security in practice, that characterised unfree tenure largely disappeared by the early fifteenth century. Copyhold, in the majority of cases, can therefore be seen as compromise: it was a transitional tenure in which English lords who were forced to relinquish servile controls and dues nevertheless maintained important controls over customary tenure alongside the demesne leases. These controls enabled them to treat these tenures as competitive market rents. The evidence for rising entry fines in line with prices and demand for land in the sixteenth century now seems generally, if perhaps grudgingly, accepted. In this respect the transition to capitalism was to some extent facilitated in England by the insecurity of this new tenure alongside the expansion of leasehold tenure. Moreover, where traditional tenures proved tenacious, force was applied. By the end of the sixteenth century, agrarian capitalism (and its values of improvement over custom) and capitalist social-property relations were already in the ascendancy. By then, copyhold tenure was still important in many counties but despite the belated legislation designed to control the level of rents and entry fines and thereby reduce depopulation and poverty, it was to retreat rapidly in the following decades by a number of means in which it was converted to leasehold. Attempts by the state to protect customary tenure proved ineffective in England, especially after the feeding frenzy which followed the dissolution of the monasteries. The protection of customary tenure contradicted the English state's own landed interests in the long run, just as it contradicted the landed interests of the majority of gentry and yeomen who dominated local officialdom and justice. The transition was not a fair, innocuous process, undertaken by legally secure proprietors, but one in which a legally insecure peasantry was deliberately uprooted by a class nexus with greater social and economic power.

CHAPTER 6

The Rise of Capitalist Yeomen and a Capitalist Aristocracy

i   **The Origin of Capitalism in the Shell of the Commercial Landlords' Estate System**

For Brenner the transition from feudalism to capitalism in England was generated crucially in the *shell* of the lords' developing capitalist estate system. The powers English lords had maintained into the fifteenth century over the majority of the land in the form of large leased demesnes and insecure copyholds were their 'trump card' in their struggles with the peasantry because they prevented the peasantry from gaining proprietorial or freehold rights in their holdings. The enforcement of this trump card had the unintended consequence of generating capitalism as capitalist farmers – who were also usually lordship officials – developed these leaseholds at the expense of the peasants' insecure copyholds.

Brenner also argued that the transition in the shell of the capitalist estate system of commercial landlords explains the causes and outcomes of the English revolution in the seventeenth century. The traditional social interpretation of the English revolution argued that it was the outcome of the growth of a bourgeois class in the 'interstices' of feudal society in the form of the rise of gentry and yeomen in countryside and merchants and traders in towns in the context of commercial expansion and the growth of the productive forces. These new economic and social forces grew in direct opposition to an old feudal lordship which was then defeated in the 'bourgeois revolution' of the mid- and late seventeenth centuries. Against this interpretation Brenner argued that instead of there being a fundamental conflict between feudal lordship and these new commercial or capitalist classes, feudal lordship became 'bourgeois' itself. As commercial landlords leasing land on market-sensitive leases, English lords were a fundamental part of the newly emerging capitalist estate system in its triad form of landlord, capitalist farmer and landless labourer, which it helped bring into being unintentionally. This capitalist aristocracy was therefore as responsible for breaking the remaining extra-economic prerogatives of monarchy and its allies as the capitalist bourgeoisie that grew up in its shell.[1] By the

---

1   Brenner 2003, pp. 638–716.

end of the seventeenth century, 'English development had distinguished itself from that in most places on the continent in two critical, interrelated aspects. It was marked by the rise of a capitalist aristocracy which was presiding over an agricultural revolution'.[2]

A number of historians and social scientists of all political colours have criticised what they perceive to be Brenner's lord-centred approach to the transition from feudalism to capitalism. A line frequently quoted to support this critique of Brenner is taken from his first paper on the role of agrarian class structure in the transition to capitalism where he argued that the continuity of feudal powers over property in England and 'the peasants' failure to establish essentially freehold control over the land' enabled the landlords to 'engross, consolidate and enclose, to create large farms and to lease them to capitalist tenants who could afford to make capitalist investments'.[3] In recent decades, medieval and early modern historians – Marxist and non-Marxist – have emphasised the economic and political activities of peasants and artisans and argued that they had room to manoeuvre and generate the transition without lordship interference. It has been a measure of the success of the largely Marxist-influenced perspective of 'history from below' that medieval lords are seen to be bystanders where innovation and change was concerned.

On the basis of analyses of the English medieval peasant land market, the evidence of which comes down to us in the form of manorial court roll transactions, some have argued in forthright terms against Brenner that lords were not the key directors of change in the fifteenth and sixteenth centuries. Jane Whittle sees the victory of the peasantry over lords with regard to the decline of serfdom by 1440 as key: the removal of the taint of serfdom meant the land market was free to all comers and that engrossment and enclosure, and the resulting social polarisation promoting capitalist development, was generated by the peasants themselves. The peasantry are said to have 'expropriated themselves' without any interference by lords.[4] Henry Heller, an orthodox Marxist who sees revolutionary change coming entirely from below – that is, from the peasantry whose social position and outlook was driven by changes and developments in the forces of production – has accused Brenner of arguing that the transition was carried out entirely by the lords in the face of a passive peasantry. He has Brenner saying that lords *imposed* leases on the farmers

---

2 Brenner 1985b, p. 299.

3 Brenner 1985a, p. 49.

4 Whittle 2000, pp. 305–13. She recognises that wealthy interlopers such as merchants and gentry invested extensively in local peasant land markets but she does not follow through with the implications of this finding.

apparently against their will.[5] Other historians such as French and Hoyle, and Mavis Mate, either directly or implicitly following Croot and Parker's contribution in the earlier 'Brenner Debate', have argued that Brenner's focus on the role of lords has led to his failure to account for 'the rise of the English yeoman' out of the medieval peasantry which, in similar fashion to Whittle, they see as the product of piecemeal developments in the peasant land market.[6] Hipkin adds that '[l]ike Tawney, Brenner was explicit in assigning landlords the crucial role in carrying out engrossment, enclosure and the organisation of leasing to capitalist tenants'. Hipkin believes that his own demonstration of how tenants used their own initiative to accumulate very large holdings on Romney Marsh in Kent proves them both wrong.[7]

Christopher Dyer and Bruce Campbell both recognise the role of lords in the transition, particularly their role in the eviction of tenants and the enclosing of villages from the end of the fifteenth century, as is evidenced most clearly in the commission into enclosures in 1517–18. However, in indirect critiques of Brenner – although unlike the foregoing historians they do not seek to polarise the debate – they stress the role of peasants and (yeoman) farmers as the most important drivers of the changes. It was the latter who were initiating the changes – sometimes violently – by accumulating and engrossing holdings into larger ventures, something that had been going on for most of the century. Dyer says lords were, for the peasants, shadowy figures: lords *managed* the changes that were driven from below in the fifteenth century, they did not direct them. For example Dyer argues that the many cases of lords evicting tenants at the end of the fifteenth and early sixteenth centuries were mostly in villages which had already severely shrunk due to the processes of engrossment that the peasants had been undertaking for decades. For Dyer lords were just finishing off a process initiated by the peasants.[8]

With respect to much of the good recent research on peasant and yeoman accumulations, I will argue in the rest of this chapter that the attribution to Brenner of a simple lord-centred approach to the transition is another unfortunate misreading of his thesis. While it is an important feature of his thesis that the transition occurred within the *shell* of lordship for the reasons given above, a feature representing English exceptionalism, this is not at all the same as saying the transition was driven largely or solely by the lords. For Brenner

---

5   Heller 2011, pp. 97–8. This Marxist critique will be addressed in more detail in Chapter Eight.

6   Croot and Parker 1995, p. 85; Mate 1993, p. 65. See also Mate 2006: in this more recent work on south-east England her views have been modified; French and Hoyle, 2007, p. 12.

7   Hipkin 2000, p. 646.

8   Campbell 2006, pp. 207–8; Dyer 2005, pp. 66–85.

it is the social-property relations taken as a whole which are key. No matter how important accumulating middling peasants were in breaking traditional communal bonds or how important the emerging yeomen were (who eventually took control of the accumulations of middling peasants), and no matter how much freedom yeomen and peasants had to drive the changes in the transition, they did so as part of the developing estates system which was ultimately under the management of the lords. In fact there is very little between Christopher Dyer, Bruce Campbell and Robert Brenner when one puts it like this. The significance of this management by landlords can be read in the subsequent history of English political institutions, which they dominated.

ii   The Rise of the Yeomen

The first point to make in Brenner's defence is that, in spite of some inexplicable formulations by historians since Croot and Parker, those of French and Hoyle in particular, Brenner is entirely aware of 'the rise of the yeoman' in England. He is also aware of the significance of the manorial land market following the decline of serfdom that enabled these farmers to increase their holdings at the expense of smaller tenants. But his fundamental point is that the most significant aspect of the differentiation of the peasantry through the land market in England and the consequent transition to capitalism, in contrast to the Continent, was predicated on the previous development of commercial farmers and the compulsion for them to compete on the market to survive. For Brenner, the English yeomanry 'did emerge out of a process of socio-economic differentiation, but that process was itself only made possible by the previous transcendence of peasant possession'. He argued that the increasing differentiation of the peasantry in fifteenth century England was the result of changing social-property relations and was critically conditioned by the fact that in these new conditions these 'yeomen' farmers were compelled to compete with each other when leases and copyholds for lives and terms of years fell in. In the process of binding their production entirely to the market these farmers separated themselves from the secure possession of the land. By contrast the peasant land market in France did not result in peasant differentiation in the fifteenth and sixteenth centuries but in the fragmentation of holdings, just as it had in both France and England in the late thirteenth and early fourteenth centuries (especially in freer counties such as Suffolk and Kent). These contrasting changes in England and France followed the initial generation of a broad middling peasantry in both France and England by the middle to late fifteenth century as peasants in these countries made small accumulations of vacant land following the population downturn.[9]

One of the problems some historians get themselves into regarding the subject of the rise of the yeoman in England – apparently relatively autonomously from lordship – is their definition of the yeomen themselves. Early modern historians such as Allen, French and Hoyle, understand yeomen to be largely independent owner-occupying freeholders or the equivalent, rather than as mostly large leaseholding farmers as Brenner and the medievalist Dyer conceive them.[10] In fact French and Hoyle go much further and argue that the 'freeholding yeomen' – of whom they say Brenner is unaware – 'emerged in the sixteenth century out of the undifferentiated peasantry of the fifteenth'. This formulation seems to derive from Hoyle's earlier incredulity at Brenner's assertion that peasants took up large leases at all in the fifteenth century. Hoyle explains:

> In Brenner's analysis, tenants could be evicted in two fashions. The first of these, the leasing of land left vacant in the late medieval collapse, is really only relevant in fifteenth-century circumstances. (Given what we know about conditions of the fifteenth century, his argument is nevertheless perverse. It assumes that lords were able to find tenants to take land on leases at a time when we also know that lords were granting land on increasingly favourable terms – without fines, with rent reductions – because of the overall shortage of tenants).[11]

And back to French and Hoyle together: 'What landlords could not do at any time was summon into existence the capitalised, skilled and entrepreneurial farmers needed to turn a profit from large and agriculturally advanced holding which Brenner saw as being characteristic of the English experience'.[12]

So French and Hoyle – more Hoyle than French I suspect given the content of Hoyle's earlier paper – view these yeomen as freeholders, or the equivalent emerging as late as the sixteenth century. For them, the yeomen could not have emerged earlier because they assume that the peasantry was undifferentiated in the fifteenth century. In any case they speculate that the peasants would not have taken up large leases in that recessionary century and to even think

---

9   Brenner 1985b, pp. 299–301.

10   French and Hoyle 2007, p. 12.

11   Hoyle 1990, p. 5.

12   French and Hoyle 2007, pp. 11–12.

so is 'perverse'. The inability of these historians to account for the origin of the processes they attempt to describe seriously undermines their project. Robert Allen, by contrast, is well aware of the rapid and profound changes in the fifteenth and early sixteenth centuries, and yet his definition of the English 'yeomen' – as he applies it to the period which followed, especially the seventeenth century – leads him into difficulties with regard to the class driving the changes. He argues that 'paradoxically' following the 'abrupt transition to capitalist relations' in the period between 1450 and 1525,

> The depopulation that followed enclosure so alarmed official opinion that the crown began protecting peasant farmers. Legislation, investigation and prosecution were tools, but the most effective response was the extension of property rights to peasants by the Tudor courts. Copyholds and beneficial leases became secure forms of tenure by which many small farmers held their land. This legal revolution ended the worst abuses and created the tenurial underpinning for the yeomen farmers who flourished under Elizabeth and the Stuarts. The yeomen were owner-occupying family farmers – true peasants. Their economic significance cannot be overstated, for they were responsible for much of the productivity growth in the early modern period.[13]

Allen defines a typical 'yeoman village' in the seventeenth century as an 'open field' village made up of half yardlands (12 to 15 acres), yardlands (25 to 30 acres) and cottages (one to two acres), and as a co-operative enterprise regulated by the peasants themselves. He is concerned to demonstrate that it was these 'true peasants', whom he describes as yeomen, who had the greatest part to play in the agricultural revolution which ushered in the transition to agrarian capitalism. He rejects the traditional idea, espoused by Brenner, that capitalist farmers, working on larger acreages on the basis of competition and the separation from their means of subsistence, were the ideal agents of agricultural revolution. He describes the proponents of this theory as 'agrarian fundamentalists' who have set out to justify the development of agrarian capitalism and the expropriation of the peasantry for a higher goal. When, Allen argues, this class of yeomen (who held by freehold, copyhold and 'beneficial lease') declined during the eighteenth century – due to the buying up of freeholds by lords, the running out of terms of the beneficial leases and of the copyholds for years and lives, the transference of the latter two tenures to capitalist farms held on annual rack rents, and the forceful eviction by Act of

---

13   Allen 1992, p. 14.

Parliament of those copyholders who were able to cling on, productivity was thereby reduced due to the insecurity of annual rack rents which reduced the incentive of farmers to invest and accumulate. In this way the yeomen, who he argues had a proprietary interest in the land on the basis of the security of these three tenures in the late seventeenth century – copyholds and leases making up two thirds of the land and freeholds the other third – disappeared by the late eighteenth.[14]

My response to Allen is that in the fourteenth century the term 'yeoman' traditionally defined someone undertaking feudal or aristocratic household service (a 'valet') who was not of (or had not achieved) gentle status; but it evolved and became more prominent in the records from the early fifteenth century to represent substantial peasants who were, indeed, usually the new demesne leaseholders, and distinguished from more modest 'husbandmen' who were nevertheless making small accumulations themselves in the open fields.[15] It is not surprising therefore that, as early as the 1430s, new status terminology was applied to take account of them. While yeomen may have held a portfolio of holdings, especially in the fifteenth century, their main holdings were leases.[16] These were typically the leaseholders of the demesnes, a role that saw the majority of them leap from a position in the village peasant elite into market-dependent competitive farmers between 1380 and 1420, although this process began earlier and continued later. From there they were in the best position to develop at the expense of others, slowly at first but more quickly in second half of the fifteenth century as domestic and foreign demand for woollen cloth grew.

A recent important synthesis of the economy and society of late medieval England by Christopher Dyer clarifies the situation in support of Brenner's thesis on this point. Dyer shows that already in the poll tax records of 1379, farmers of demesnes were recognised as a distinct social category. Most peasants and artisans were required to pay 4d tax but 'farmers of manors and rectories' were equated with lesser merchants, franklins and innkeepers, and they were expected to pay between 1s and 6s 8d, the upper figure representing the

---

14   Allen 1992.

15   Almond and Pollard 2001, pp. 52–3.

16   See Tawney 1912, pp. 27–8. As Tawney says, the practical definition of 'yeoman' was more elastic than the contemporary legal definition: the latter regarded a yeoman as 'a man who may dispend of his own free land in yearly revenue to the sum of 40s sterling'. This sum enabled him to vote for MPs and to sit on juries. In practice the term was used by the middle of the sixteenth century to describe any wealthy farmer beneath the rank of gentleman, even though he might not be a freeholder.

lower ranks of landed gentry. In practice they paid no more than 3s 4d. At that point they were thinly scattered on the ground, but by 1509, when Edmund Dudley wrote his social treatise *The Tree of Commonwealth*, they were regarded as prominent and well-established members of the commonwealth. Dudley regarded them as the wealthy and ruthless equivalents of substantial merchants. Dyer reminds us that peasant differentiation, the development of early farmers, and some transfer of peasant plots to leasehold, can be traced back to the late thirteenth century. But he places emphasis on the novelty of this new situation in the late fourteenth and early fifteenth century when thousands of demesnes containing between 100 and 500 acres, amounting to a quarter or fifth of lowland land in England, were leased to leading peasants. Those assets that had been run by lords for the previous two centuries were transferred mostly between 1380 and 1420 to new management. The decision making was transferred to those who came mostly from lower class origins. Lords at first sought familiar reeves – that is, wealthier peasants who had earlier helped run the manor for the lords and whose role was as mediator between lords and the village community – but they later looked to outsiders and wherever could get a higher price:

> All farmers were new men in the sense that, whether they came from the locality or from outside, taking on a lord's demesne transformed their whole way of life and economic behaviour. The peasants who made up the majority of the new generation of farmers had previous experience of managing a holding of perhaps 30 acres. Overnight they found themselves having to run an enterprise of 300 acres. Those who had recently acted as reeves would adapt more readily, but they were still taking on new challenges and responsibilities. The collective experiences of thousands of farmers at the beginning of the fifteenth century amounts to one of those periods in history when a combination of circumstances compelled people to take a step upwards in skills, talents, and achievements.[17]

As Dyer says, these new men were suddenly exposed to the full force of the market as they moved from a largely subsistence holding to one so large that at least three quarters of its produce would have to be sold. He also shows how more of them had become *entirely* specialised and market-dependent by the end of the fifteenth century.[18]

---

17   Dyer 2005, p. 197.

18   Dyer 2005, pp. 195–7. One does not need to be a medieval historian to recognise the extent of change before 1500. Wrightson, an early modernist, recognised that in the early

A regional study of Kent for the period 1540 to 1640 helps us put our finger on the nature of yeomen in England in the later Tudor and Stuart period as well. Zell finds that,

> at its simplest, a yeoman was a commercial famer, someone who farmed for the market rather than merely to feed his family, and someone whose farm was large enough to require help from non-family labour. A farmer was more likely to be called a yeoman if he owned some land, but tenants of large gentry owned farms were also considered yeomen without an acre of freehold property.

Fifty to seventy-five acres was the minimum size of a yeoman farm in mid- and east Kent, and if these are included, there were roughly between 1,000 and 2,000 of them in Kent alone in 1600. A small number farmed 200 to 300 acres and sometimes more (especially in marshland areas), and these were enterprises comparable to the home farms of substantial gentry. Their moveable goods were often on a par with gentry in this period: 'Only the ownership of several hundred acres distinguished the petty squire from the successful yeoman farmer in Kent', the difference being that the yeoman – like capitalist farmers today – held his hundreds of acres by lease.[19]

We can therefore inform French and Hoyle that the English yeomen had emerged in revolutionary fashion by the early fifteenth century, and they were already a prominent element in English society by its end. Their main holdings were usually leases and they were compelled to compete on the market and undermine their previous rules of reproduction towards subsistence immediately upon taking up these holdings as Brenner has always argued, and this can hardly be clearer. Brenner did not argue that lords could 'summon up' these

---

sixteenth century 'peasant inequality was not in itself a novelty; it had existed from the earliest times. The degree of differentiation observable by 1500, however, was a relatively recent development, and one of considerable significance'. This was, he says, partly a consequence of leasing demesnes in large blocks which led to 'a radical differentiation between large-scale demesne farmers and the tenants of conventional customary holdings', and partly due to the gradual redistribution of customary land through the operation of peasant land markets. A disproportionate share of land went to those who combined ambition with relatively deep purses. Average holding sizes increased, but so did the range of holding sizes, especially in the more commercialised areas. He cites an example in Cheshunt, Hertfordshire, where by 1484 a third of the manorial tenantry held seventy percent of the land, and he concluded that by that date 'The English yeoman had emerged': Wrightson 2001, pp. 99–100.

19   Zell 2000, pp. 70–1.

tenants, as French and Hoyle suggest in their dismissal of him, nor were the leases imposed by lords on the wealthier peasants against their will *a la* Heller. To reproduce themselves, lords were *compelled* under duress of circumstances to make this revolutionary transfer of property to peasants. Seen in the light of a revolutionary transfer it is perhaps less surprising that lords usually found little difficulty recruiting tenants to take up this unprecedented opportunity. While these wealthy peasants were forced to become market-dependent and to undermine their previous safety-first strategy, the extent of the property placed at their own disposal must have made the decision easier. At this stage they may well have calculated that they could fall back on available subsistence lands if things went wrong. Lords themselves received a good return although as we have seen in an earlier chapter rents were reduced and leasehold terms lengthened temporarily between 1430 and 1470.[20]

As Dyer says, this transference of decision-making on the large English demesnes to peasants after 200 years of the direct exploitation of these large acreages by the lords (with the help of labour services characteristic of serfdom) was momentous. Brenner was also aware that the transfer of the demesnes to the peasants in this *unprecedented* fashion entailed a weakening of lords' class power, in spite of their continuing controls of the land. For Brenner, therefore, the changes were certainly not solely about the rise of an all-powerful capitalist aristocracy determining the changes at will, as his thesis has been portrayed. In fact, he sees this process as involving a developing mutuality between lords and these emerging capitalist farmers or yeomen. He remarked that for the lords to transfer these demesnes to the peasantry and thereby turn their back (temporarily at least) on serfdom and extra-economic surplus extraction, it

> would have required at least an approach toward a somewhat collaborative relationship between lords and a section of the peasantry. The lords would have had to give up precisely some of the advantage built into their class position which allowed them to extract a given level of surplus.

---

20   Du Boulay found that the income of the Archbishop of Canterbury's estates in Kent and
      Sussex in the last twenty years of the fifteenth century recovered from the mid-century
      slump. This was largely due to the demesne farmers who were contributing 40 percent of
      the Archbishop's landed revenue. Of Archbishop Warham's farmers (c. 1503–32), a third
      were described as gentlemen, half as yeomen and husbandmen, and there were also a few
      London merchants. Most notably for our purposes, however, *the biggest and most valuable
      leases were held by yeomen*: Du Boulay 1966, pp. 226–32.

This was a development running directly counter to the inherently antag-
onistic dynamic built into the lord-serf structure.[21]

Brenner shows how, as a result of these developing new social-property relations, these new farmers were compelled to compete, specialise and innovate,
and lords had to compete for good farmers working in their interests: hence
increases in productivity were generated through *systematic* specialisation, the
accumulation of surpluses and their re-investment in innovations in order to
cut costs.[22]

The first point to make in defence of Brenner against Allen's argument that
peasant (yeomen) farms in the seventeenth century were secure as a result of
protection granted to them by state legislation in the sixteenth century is that
the ability of the lords to simply let seventeenth-century copyholds and leases
run out their terms (and convert them to annual rack rents during the eighteenth century) demonstrates exactly the insecurity which these tenures represented, in direct contradiction to Allen's assertion. They were only secure to
a relative extent if one compares them to annual rack rent leasehold in which
case the farm rent was tendered out to the highest bid at the end of each *yearly*
term; they were not in themselves secure. Those who held them were certainly
not 'owner-occupiers'. The second point concerns the 'yeomen' village that
Allen describes as typical in the seventeenth century. For him it contained
half yardlands, yardlands and cottages, and was characterised by a form of co-
operative organisation that Allen says generated more labour productivity than
the capitalist farms of the eighteenth century. Such a statement will mystify
medieval economic historians because such villages are in fact typical of villages in the *thirteenth* century, well before the emergence of the yeomen. The
third point is that the latter description of seventeenth century villages and the
size of their holdings is contradicted by Allen's own figures on the sizes of landholding in the seventeenth century based on his sample of midland counties.
Brenner dealt with this point in his paper on comparative developments in the
Low Countries. He pointed to Allen's assessment of the size of an arable farm
that could be worked with family labour: this amounted to a farm of up to 56
acres with minimal seasonal assistance. Farms containing over 60 acres would
rely on larger supplies of wage labour. Peasant holdings of yardlands and half
yardlands in medieval England were generally much smaller, a quarter to a half
of this acreage, and these disguised a huge amount of underemployment and
unemployment and were therefore typically oversupplied with labour. So for

---

21   Brenner 1977, p. 43.
22   Brenner 1977 pp. 42–3; Brenner 1985a, p. 49; Brenner 1985b, p. 301.

Brenner the transcendence of peasant property was required for *systematic* growth in labour productivity in production of food grains and this trancendence was 'the *sine qua non* for industrialisation':

> In this context, it is entirely inappropriate to term the farmers who undertook an agricultural revolution in seventeenth century England either 'peasants' or 'small', as do respectively Allen (1992) and Croot and Parker (1985). On the contrary, the emergence of such farmers obviously represented precisely the rise of large farms and the transcendence of the small and peasant farming that had dominated English agriculture in the medieval period. By the early seventeenth century, the *average* farm size in the south midlands region studied by Allen was 59 acres. Even more to the point, farms of 60 acres or more occupied no less than 71 percent of the farmland, and farms of 100 acres or more 51 percent. The pattern found by Allen was, moreover, quite typical of English grain producing regions in this era. The break from small and peasant agriculture could hardly have been more definitive or self-evident. Indeed, my argument is decisively confirmed by the fact that part and parcel with the emergence of these farms came not only the predominance of capitalist social-property relations dominated by landlords and their commercial tenants, but a major increase in the long term growth of agricultural labour productivity. The burden of Allen's work on the English yeomen is thus the very opposite of what he contends: it confirms the fundamental role of large non-peasant farms, not small peasant farms, in the English agricultural revolution.[23]

The 'open field villages' that Allen describes could only be described as 'open field' if one wanted to make an analytical contrast with those villages that had been *entirely* enclosed into large farms. The average farm size in these so-called open fields was 59 acres in Allen's seventeenth-century English midlands sample, but at the same time the average was 210 acres in 'villages' that had been entirely 'enclosed'. The average size of farms in these surviving 'open field villages' suggests that the holdings within them had gone a long way towards the qualitative changes brought on by outright enclosure elsewhere. This was due to an earlier transformation within them caused by engrossment and specialised production for the market by large farmers and outside investors. So using his own figures Allen should have concluded with Brenner that the yeomen were large farmers in the seventeenth century.

---

23   Brenner 1997, pp. 298–9.

To press home this point we can turn again to Zell's evidence of Kentish yeomen. Zell finds that probate inventories between the 1560s and 1620 reveal scores of yeomen whom he describes as 'grain barons' and 'large-scale sheep-masters' in Kent, especially in east Kent, Romney Marsh and the north Kent marshlands. Comparing a sample of these inventories registered between 1565 and 1579, with those between 1600 and 1620, he finds that the number of large farms increased substantially between the two periods:

> In the first sample there were thirteen farms with a 100 or more acres of sown arable, thirty-one farms with 300 or more sheep, and twenty with 50 head of cattle or more (excluding calves). In the early seventeenth century there were forty-two farms with 100 or more acres of cereals, thirty-six farms carrying 300 or more sheep, and fifteen with 50 head of cattle or more.

The increasing accumulation of property by farmers in Kent not surprisingly corresponded to the increase in food that was supplied to the capital in the same period. In 1579–80, Kent shipped 14,500 quarters of cereals to London, 42,000 in 1615 and over 100,000 in 1638.[24]

iii   Lords and Yeomen: A Relationship of Mutual Interests?

Next I want to address the point made by critics of Brenner about the distinction between the role of the lords on the one hand, and that of the farmers on the other, in evicting peasants and engrossing and enclosing their holdings. Given what has been said about the mutual relationship between the two, this is a false distinction. It may well be true that in most cases the initiative for change came from the farmers; and no doubt Brenner would agree with this given that for him it was the farmers who were compelled to compete and as a consequence their mentalities changed to facilitate this often ruthless process. But farmers, as demesne lessees and moreover as the office holders of lords, usually would have had the backing of the lords and hence were supported by the latter's social power and connections.

For example, Christopher Dyer, on the basis of decades of research into this area, found that 'the farmer was in most cases a free man who developed a relationship with the lord on the basis of the mutual advantages of the contract'. He uses the example of Roger Heritage of Burton Dasset in the English west

---

24   Zell 2000, pp. 71–2.

midlands, a man who ran a mixed farm with a strong pastoral bias and died in 1495. His son John took over and within three years he cooperated with the new youthful lord Sir Edward Belknap to enclose land, force out the remaining tenants (at least 12 houses and 360 acres, the acreage having previously been divided into 12 peasant virgates or yardlands) and convert the whole township to a specialised sheep pasture.[25] Mavis Mate found that in the county of East Sussex between 1450 and 1550, '[m]any lessees had at one time or another served lords as reeves or rent collectors on the manor where the demesne was situated', and those who had not worked for the lord before required a letter of recommendation from another lord, particularly when demand for the leases increased by the sixteenth century.[26] Paul Glennie found in his study of the Lea Valley, just to the north of London, that by the 1530s 'a relatively small group of . . . families had come to dominate tenant land holding and in the next thirty years their prominence increased still further'. They all acted as officials and rent collectors for their London landlords.[27] More detailed examples of this relationship will be provided in my own study in Part II.

Capitalist development depended upon a mutual relationship between lords and their large demesne tenants, and yet there was an inherent element of conflict between these two classes over the level of rent. This does not represent a contradiction in the historical analysis; the contradiction lies in the historical relationship itself, and it played itself out in relation to the interests of both of these classes in the expropriation of the peasantry and the driving down of wages. The relationship between lords and their farmers changed over time, usually to the benefit of the lords as land became more valuable and competition for leases more intense. Some of the more successful tenant farmers became substantial landlords themselves through the wealth and influence they accumulated, and this is another indication of their shared sphere of operations with the aristocracy. Without a mutual relationship with lords and their effective backing in the changes, I do not see how otherwise these farmers who were often isolated individuals or a small minority in each village, although more concentrated in small town communities, could have driven through the changes as they did, not only in depopulated areas but in populated ones too. This is the question that needs to be asked of those historians who want to see an autonomous or simply a major role granted to yeomen and yeomen clothiers in the changes. It is clear that when the state sought to restrict evictions and over-specialisation, it required the co-operation of the lords to

---

25   Dyer 2005, pp. 199, 206–7; Dyer 2010, p. 34.

26   Mate 2006, pp. 214, 224.

27   Glennie 1988, pp. 26–7, 30–3.

rein in their enclosing tenants. The lords did not co-operate because the newly enlarged leaseholds were economically more profitable, and in political terms they also reduced the broad peasant resistance to lords' attempts to maintain or increase their income. I will have more to say on this point in the following chapter on the chronology and methods of expropriation.

The most forthright critic of the idea that there was a mutuality of inter-ests between lords and yeomen or emerging capitalist farmers in the transition to capitalism has been Jane Whittle. On the basis of her study of the mano-rial records of a small sample of rural settlements in north Norfolk in eastern England she argues, as I have said above, that the transition was an innocuous process of buying and selling on the land market following the decline of serf-dom. This was done without interference from the lord and it was the peasants themselves who expropriated each other. She categorically rejects the notion promulgated by Brenner, and Thirsk, Tawney and Beresford before him, that engrossing and enclosure were facilitated by the mutual interests between lords and their farmers. Aside from the narrow focus of her study, Whittle's analysis is in many respects contradictory. With what we know of the activi-ties of gentry in her sample they interfered a great deal. A close examination of her evidence reveals that gentry were the biggest engrossing tenants as well as deliberate depopulators of villages. She says herself that 'there was no sharp dividing line between the policies of lords and their larger, more powerful ten-ants who sought to engross holdings'.[28] More than just rejecting the idea of a mutual relationship between lords and their farmers that set them in conflict with smaller peasant tenants, she argues the contrary, which is that lords often sided with their smaller peasant tenants against their engrossing farmers. She only provides one example to support this view (and in fact even this serves to undermine her case). In this instance the ecclesiastical lord sided with peas-ant tenants against the engrosser because the engrosser, who also as we would expect held the demesne lease, enclosed part of the common fields. The pecu-liarities of landholding in Norfolk enabled lords to own rights to graze their sheep on the commons and this explains why in such unique circumstances the lord was upset at his rights being infringed. What is significant is that the engrosser, who was one of the largest tenants on the manor, and someone who had recourse to official manorial posts, was granted a warrant of good con-duct by Roger Townshend, knight, and Edmund Wyndham, esquire, indicating he had patronage from powerful lay lords outside of the manor in question.[29] The Townshends were in fact major sheep farmers adjacent to the west of

28   Whittle 2000, p. 200.
29   Whittle 2000, pp. 60–3.

Whittle's sample by the end of the fifteenth century, and they supplied the expanding cloth industry in Suffolk to the south.[30]

iv   Lords, Yeomen and the 'English Rising' of 1549

Since Whittle's research some very important new work has appeared on the widespread rebellions of 1549 which throws light on the relationship between lords and tenants and on the periodisation of the transition to capitalism. The relationship between 1549 and the periodisation of the transition will be examined in the next chapter. Here we will continue to focus on the relationship between lords and their capitalist tenants.

In his analysis of these rebellions, Andy Wood has entirely rejected Whittle's argument about the non-interference of lords in the transforming East Anglian economy. For him her analysis,

> flies in the face of a large body of evidence: of often ferocious riot and litigation between lord and tenant; of the attempted rebellions in the country in 1537, which as we have seen targeted the gentry; and of actual insurrection in 1549. Within early sixteenth-century Norfolk, a seigneurial offensive was underway, as lords increased rents, exploited copyhold customs, emparked land in order to create deer parks and enclosed commons ... In particular, lords were driven to expand their sheep flocks and manipulated customary foldcourse arrangements so as to ensure that they could graze their ever expanding sheep flocks on tenants' fields. Similarly, lords also overstocked common land. Kett's rebel demands were designed to curtail such lordly exactions. As Bindoff observed, if the Norfolk rebels had succeeded they would have 'clipped the wings of rural capitalism'. Certainly it is true of the likely impact of the rebel programme upon fiscal seigneurialism; but ... rebel demands would not have hindered the slower, steadier micro-economic changes within village communities from which the wealthy yeoman class was benefiting.[31]

Wood's critique of Whittle's views on the passive nature of landlords in Norfolk during the transition to capitalism is welcome; however he contradicts himself in his final point by stating (with Whittle) that accumulations into the hands of wealthier farmers in an autonomous peasant land market would have

30   Moreton 1992.
31   Wood 2007, p. 14.

continued locally anyway, even if the threat of enclosure by the lords would have been successfully resisted. This fails to acknowledge the mutual political relationship between lords and farmers and assumes that wealthier farmers had always acted on their own, and had always had the power to do so. The rebels' demands not only targeted gentry but yeomen as well, and if the rebellion would have been successful it is more likely that both would have been stopped in their tracks. Referring to the demands by Norfolk rebels in 1549, Wood says himself that the 'authors of the Mousehold articles envisaged the freezing of the long-term processes of social and economic change that were fissuring village communities'. The exclusion of the gentry from village society and economy was one aspect of the rebels' desires, another being the halting of the accumulation of copyhold lands by the yeomen.[32] Yeomen accumulations were not innocuous micro-changes, they were as visible and extensive as those of the lords, and carried out with the protection of lords. The rebels wanted rents and fines to return to the levels of the late fifteenth century and, if this desire would have been fulfilled, tenants would have been able to keep their copyhold tenancies and arguably there would also have been a movement towards a redistribution of enclosed estates at the expense of the yeomen. I have already indicated the nature of this relationship above and I examine it in more detail in Part II.

Wood suggests that, with regard to lord-tenant relations, there was continuity between the rebellions of 1381 and 1549. He argues that there was a class dichotomy between villagers and gentry in both, but that in 1549 the alliance between the wealthy villagers and the broader commons was now far more fragile than it had been in earlier rebellions in 1381 and 1450 due to the polarisation in landholdings and the rise of the yeomen that had taken place by the early sixteenth century. The conflicts in 1549 were different because 'they were the result of the complicated, uneven emergence of early agrarian capitalism'. Indeed the relationship between the yeomen and their village neighbours on the one hand and between the yeomen and the lords who were usually their lessors on the other was complex, not least because of the official roles yeomen carried out in the manorial context. In fact Wood suggests that 'relations of production and exploitation became the site of a messy, three-way conflict between an aggressive lordly class, an entrepreneurial group of wealthy yeomen farmers and a body of semi-proletarianised labourers'.[33] However, he goes

---

32   Wood 2007, p. 163.

33   Wood 2007, pp. 1, 11, 16. Whittle has recently responded to Wood's criticism. She maintains that lords were not driving the changes through engrossment and by raising rents and fines but that 'like many of their tenants, they were using their land and common rights

on to argue that the wealthy yeomen and smaller gentry, who often formed the leadership of the rebellion across England in 1549, moved closer to the lords in economic, political and cultural terms *after* the failure of the 1549 rebellions, and he suggests that this explains the decline in insurrection from the late sixteenth century as the smaller peasants lost their leaders. He says that rebellious words spoken by peasants were, from the late sixteenth century, no longer expressing visceral hatred of the gentry in particular as they were in the 1530s and 1540s, but targeting a more broader class of 'rich churls' which included gentry *and* yeomen whom they viewed as a common enemy.[34]

My own sense of the changing class structure at this time is that Wood's chronology is inaccurate, and that the yeomen were already close to the lords by the *early* sixteenth century if not much earlier in some areas. I do not see a dichotomy between village and gentry in 1549 even if, as Wood says, it was a messy rebellion due to fragile relationships within villages caused by engrossment and enclosure. Anti-enclosure protesters in the 1530s and 1540, mostly made up of peasants, rural and urban artisans, petty traders and the poor, were not simply targeting gentry, they were targeting seigneurial authority as a whole, and not only that but urban magistracies who typically held rural farms outside of their towns as well as having other trading and industrial interests. Seigneurial authority was responsible for enclosure in Norfolk, and this authority by the middle of the sixteenth century was also wielded by rich farmers, yeomen and many of whom had grown into small gentry themselves as the lord's estate officials as well as their main lessees.

As Wood says, the wealthier rural yeomen, and their counterparts in towns and rural industrial districts (clothiers), were regarded by the lords and by the rebels as 'the honest men' or 'the substantial inhabitants' of the village or town.

---

to engage in commercial farming'. This is certainly an advance on her earlier position that lords did not interfere at all in the land market. She has Wood saying that the rebellion was in response to 'a seigneurial reaction' similar to the one in the fourteenth century which attempted to turn the clock back to the high rents and unfree tenures which characterized the period before the Black Death. In fact Wood said that the rebellion was in response to 'a seigneurial offensive' which sought to enclose and engross in the manner of agrarian capitalists. This of course is something quite different. Lords in the sixteenth century were not dealing with or 'reacting' to a resurgent peasantry aiming to destroy serfdom as in the post-Black Death period. Lords were now resurgent and on the offensive themselves. Whittle concludes that the rebellion was a much 'messier' affair, 'a complicated three-way conflict between lords, wealthy tenants, and the rural poor, born out of Norfolk's highly commercialised society and economy', and 'a symptom of agrarian capitalism'. This is exactly Wood's conclusion: Whittle 2010, pp. 47–8.

34   Wood 2007, p. 204.

The honest men were essential to the functioning of the Tudor state. Thus in the crisis of October 1536, the duke of Norfolk placed his trust in the clothiers of Suffolk to maintain order in that county; likewise he wrote of the importance of maintaining the loyalties of the 'substantial yeomen'. Similarly, the honest men represented an important conduit of popular political opinion: when Sir John Russell and Sir William Parr wanted 'to know the certainty of the state of... [the] commons hearts', they asked 'the most discrete and substantial persons'.[35]

By the 1540s those whom the Duke of Norfolk described as the 'substantial yeo-men' were relied upon by the gentry to ally with them in order to put down the disturbances. In 1549 Sir Thomas Smith proposed that the rebels destroying enclosures in the Thames Valley counties immediately to the west of London were to be defeated, and he stated that the gentry 'and other leading and trust-worthy yeomen' should carry it out. Following widespread coordinated distur-bances in south-east Kent, Smith wrote to William Cecil that the rebels should be put down with armed force, 'proposing that the gentry and leading yeomen should be gathered into cavalry forces'. When on 5 May 1549, among other riots, 200 weavers, tinkers and artisans broke down enclosures at the cloth town of Frome in east Somerset in the south-west of England, 'The gentry expressed confidence that they were "strong enough for the repression of the worst sort"; together with the "honest yeomen and farmers", they intended to put down any further gatherings'.[36]

Now this dependence by the gentry on the wealthier yeomen could only be derived from the local official positions the latter held overseeing the local administration of both state and manor, and from a sense of mutual interest in the new status quo. It is true that the same could be said of the reeves in the thirteenth and fourteenth centuries. These reeves were manorial officials and intermediaries between lords and the rest of the villagers, but they were usu-ally unfree yardlanders, and never the significant landed and industrial inter-ests that characterised such intermediaries in the sixteenth century, many of whom were on the cusp of gentry status themselves. None of the leaders of 1381 were wealthy men, far from it; they were peasant artisans and poor priests.

If we take on board the foregoing argument that the interests of lords and their leaseholding yeomen were broadly mutual, we are left with the task of explaining why so many of these wealthy yeomen took on leadership roles in the rebellions against the lords. Many, like Kett, were weeded out and made

---

35   Wood 2007, pp. 16–17.
36   Wood 2007, pp. 17, 48, 53.

examples of by the greater county gentry who had become hysterical over their disloyalty. The Norfolk gentry wanted the rebels hung in much larger numbers than they actually were, but an intervention of the Earl of Warwick suggests this would have been impractical. He wrote to his colleagues drily that as a result of mass executions the gentry would have to plough the fields themselves. Sir Thomas Woodhouse said 'that my lord of Warwicke does the execution of many men at Norwich. And the gentry crave at his hand the gift of the richest of them, and do daily bring in men by accusation'. One Ellis Griffith recorded that 'following the battle of Dussingdale "many honest men were hanged, many of them without deserving it for the harm they had done, and some who had not even raised a stick to go to the field" '.[37]

The first point to make is that the rebellions across England were driven fundamentally and in terms of numbers by the *anti*-enclosure, *anti*-capitalist imperatives of ordinary peasants (husbandmen), artisans and poor in towns and countryside. Where leaders are known, many of the riots had leaders drawn from these groups. When historians speak of capitalism being driven from below, they must recognise that the majority of the commons in both towns and countryside were opposed to capitalism. Second, there may have been many local reasons for wealthier capitalist yeomen to take on leadership roles in the rebellions. They were after all in competition with each other, and there is evidence that they directed rebels against their rivals. Third, lords were also becoming more aggressive in this period and raising rents and accumulating more estates at the expense of their leaseholding farmers. Fourth, some farmers also had common cause with their poorer neighbours against lordship encroachments on common land. Finally, many wealthy yeomen were forced into leadership positions by the broader peasantry, including the artisans and poor. Many had no choice but to throw in their lot with the peasantry, many fearing they would be robbed or killed if they did not. Others may have joined in knowing that their positions in leadership roles gave them the opportunity to limit the impact of the actions of the peasants. Peasants saw their actions as legitimised by the monarchy under the Duke of Somerset and they maintained this legitimacy by mobilising themselves locally through the official (royal) mustering institution of 'the hundred'. This required the mobilisation of the officials as well, the wealthy 'honest men'.[38] This tradition of mustering through royal local government institutions was natural to the peasantry, and went back to at least 1381.

---

37   Wood 2007, pp. 72–3.
38   Wood 2007, pp. 172–5.

It does not follow to say, as Wood does, that the decline in insurrection in the late sixteenth century and after was due to the move in economic and cultural terms of the wealthy yeomen or 'honest men' towards the gentry, thereby leaving peasants, artisans and poor without leaders. These 'leaders' were employed for a specific legitimising purpose during the rebellion, they were not its initiators and organisers, and their leadership was not typical in any case. The implication that the wealthy were necessary for leading the rebellions is highly misleading: it echoes contemporary elite prejudices and the prejudices of modern conservative historians that those of lesser means could not have organised themselves. This is a perspective that one would not normally attribute to Wood, and I have no doubt the inference was unintended.

Wood's main evidence for his argument for the causes of the decline of insurrection is what he sees as a change in the targets of popular political language during the second half of the sixteenth century. He says that, while in the mid-sixteenth century popular speech 'had tended to identify the gentry as the "enemies" of the commons, seditious speech in the later Elizabethan period tended to define the "enemies" of the poor as a rather more vague social group: "the rich men" '. Capitalist farmers later on were often described as 'rich churls'.[39] However the term 'rich churl' formed part of popular speech as early as the end of the fifteenth century at latest, rather than the end of the sixteenth, and so I do not therefore find Wood's proposal that it was a new form of political language in the latter period convincing.[40]

It is true to say that further polarisation had taken place in rural society by the later sixteenth century and increased rapidly from the 1580s. But the decline of anti-enclosure insurrection from the late sixteenth century was not a matter of the yeomen and smaller gentry leadership moving away or becoming detached from the rest of the peasantry and their village neighbours, so that deprived of this leadership peasants could no longer protest. The decline of anti-enclosure insurrection, if this point does have some validity given the important midland revolt of 1607, the fenland riots of the 1620s and 1630s, and widespread anti-enclosure riots of the 1640s, has in my view more to do with the victory of seigneurial authority over the peasants in the enclosure movement in most places by the late sixteenth century. The crown would follow suit

---

39   Wood 2007, pp. 204–7.
40   Harris 1907–8, p. 556. Laurence Saunders, a dyer from Coventry, was a central figure in the mobilisation of the whole commonalty against the merchant-dominated magistracy of Coventry which between the 1470s and 1490s sought to enclose common land. He is quoted to have said: 'Sirs, here me! We shall never have our rights until we have struck off the heads of three or four of these churls that rule us'.

in the early seventeenth century, although there were still many battles to win. The commonwealth republic instituted under Oliver Cromwell would be even more ruthless. As Wood shows in the following quote taken from the 1590s, the gentry and farmers were not always identified in peasant political language as simply 'the rich': they were still distinguished from each other, while their mutual interests were recognised:

> One Essex man in 1591 was of the opinion that England was governed by a social alliance from which the poor were excluded, arguing that 'the noblemen and gentlemen were all one and the gentlemen and farmers would hold together one with another so that poor men could get nothing among them'.[41]

Such a sentiment would not have been out of place forty years earlier, and I return to this point in my own study in Part II.

In conclusion, Brenner's thesis is that capitalism originated in the 'shell' of the developing estates system of landlords in England, but not that it was a top-down imposition solely by the lords. His critics have misread his thesis in this respect, and this has largely been the result of a misunderstanding of the origin and subsequent development of yeomen farmers. The latter were large lessees in the fifteenth and sixteenth centuries and they were not usually independent agents. They gained crucial social power from their positions as officials of state and seigneurial institutions, and from their large leasehold properties. Without the former the latter would have been precarious or would not have developed as they did. The rise of a capitalist aristocracy and that of a capitalist yeomanry began blindly or unintentionally through the leasing of the demesnes in the late fourteenth and early fifteenth centuries. During the price rises of the sixteenth century from the 1520s and the dissolution of the monasteries, the benefits of accumulation and leasing to both the lords and the farmers became acknowledged and the steps towards capitalism more deliberate. The origin of capitalism was nevertheless essentially a top-down imposition on the vast majority of the population who opposed it: it was driven by seigneurial authority, an authority which featured farmers as well as lords. While there were local battles over engrossment and enclosure across England from the middle third of the fifteenth century, the top-down imposition came to a head in the 1530s and 1540s when co-ordinated resistance to the changes was met with overwhelming military force and the usual demand for a 'harvest of heads' by a hysterical aristocracy fearful for its property.

---

41   Wood 2007, p. 204.

Capitalist farmers originated from free and unfree peasant farmers with sub-sistence holdings during what was a revolutionary period in social-property relations in the decades around 1400, following the rebellion of 1381. But, given what has been said above about the mutuality between them and the lords, one cannot regard enclosure by these leaseholding farmers in the fifteenth and first half of the sixteenth century as amounting to the transition to capitalism from below. It is also a mistake to say that piecemeal accumulations among a broad small to middling peasantry in the fifteenth century amounted to the origin of capitalism. The same happened in France. This broad limited accu-mulation was the basis for the temporary golden age that peasants experienced before seigneurial intervention. *Anti*-enclosure and *anti*-capitalist rebellions were generated from below by the subsistence-based peasantry and artisans in town and countryside. These had to be defeated by lords and their tenant farmers for capitalism to develop.

CHAPTER 7

Periodising the Origin of Capitalism in England

The aim of this chapter is to locate the period in which capitalism originated in England. This is important because it has clear implications for causation. Brenner of course views capitalism as emerging in England after the crisis of feudalism in the early fourteenth century: more specifically after the decline of serfdom from the latter part of that century and the transference of the lords demesnes into the hands of the wealthier peasantry in the early fifteenth century. While these changes were significant they were not enough to create a rupture in feudal social-property relations in themselves. It was only with the process of expropriation that can be traced thereafter from these changes, especially from the late fifteenth century, that capitalism emerged in the countryside and in rural industry. In recent years attempts have been made by historians, either in direct or indirect criticism of Brenner's thesis, and of what amounts to a traditional periodisation stemming from Marx, to locate the key period of the transition to capitalism either earlier or later, and some have questioned the validity of peasant expropriation as the fundamental indicator of capitalist origins. Most historians place the key period for the transition to capitalism beyond the post-Black Death period, although they argue over which period proved the most formative or the most decisive. To begin with it is necessary to address accounts which locate it *before* the Black Death.

i   The Significance of Medieval Economic Expansion c. 1100–1300

Richard Britnell and Bruce Campbell, two of the most influential economic historians of medieval England in recent decades, both point to the period of rapid commercialisation between 1100 and 1300 as the most important for the origin of capitalism in England rather than the post-Black Death or early modern period. However they have contrasting reasons for doing so.[1]

In the famous chapter of the first volume of *Capital* entitled 'The Expropriation of the Agricultural Population', Marx argued that in England, 'The prelude to the revolution that laid the foundation of the capitalist mode of production was played out in the last third of the fifteenth century and the first few decades of the sixteenth century'. Lords in England achieved this by,

---

[1] Britnell 1993, pp. 359–69; Britnell 1996, pp. 233–4; Campbell 2006, p. 237.

forcibly driving the peasantry from the land, to which the latter had the same feudal title as the lords themselves, and by usurpation of the common lands. The rapid expansion of wool manufacture in Flanders and the corresponding rise in the price of wool in England provided the direct impulse for these evictions... The process of forcible expropriation of the people received a new and terrible impulse in the sixteenth century from the Reformation and the consequent colossal spoliation of church property... The estates of the church were to a large extent given away to rapacious royal favourites, or sold at a nominal price to speculating farmers and townsmen, who drove out the old established hereditary subtenants in great numbers, and threw their holdings together.[2]

Britnell takes issue with Marx's periodisation of the origin of capitalism. He argues that *on Marx's own terms* the period between 1100 and 1300 was more important and that 'the emphasis that has long been placed upon the late Middle Ages as a period of transition from feudalism to capitalism lacks adequate foundations, and seriously misrepresents the magnitude of earlier change'. Britnell points to greater wage dependency by 1300 than after; to larger units of production in the thirteenth century in the form of demesnes, units that he says were being broken up in fifteenth century; to key elements of the marketing structure of late medieval trade which were already in place by the late thirteenth century; to increasing market growth and orientation between 1100 and 1300 (that is, hundreds of new foundations of markets and fairs) compared to a contraction between 1300 and 1500; and finally he argues that towns had a greater impact on agriculture in terms of demand for its produce before 1300 than later.[3]

The Marxist thesis, from which Britnell derives his perspective, is drawn from Marx's pre-*Capital* studies where the emphasis is on the development of the productive forces rather than social-property relations and the mode in which the surplus labour or product is pumped out of the direct producers.[4] As such Britnell's focus is on elements of quantitative rather than qualitative change. At face value the remarkable expansion of markets and fairs and urbanisation between 1100 and 1300, and the contraction of these developments in the fifteenth century, appear to provide the basis for a powerful argument with regard to the origin of capitalism. This was capitalism developing

---

2 Marx 1990, pp. 878–82.
3 Britnell 1996, pp. 233–4.
4 While not a Marxist, Britnell's thesis in this respect is closely aligned to an orthodox Marxist perspective as we shall see in the following chapter.

'in the interstices' of feudal society as Marx memorably (although mistakenly) put it in his *Communist Manifesto*. Certainly the origin of capitalism does not make sense without this earlier commercial development and market integration. But the key point here is that this commercial (and demographic) expansion developed with at least the same intensity across Europe at this time, and from a more advanced starting point in many regions, without generating the necessary qualitative changes experienced in England during the fifteenth and early sixteenth centuries. In fifteenth-century England the numbers of markets and fairs did contract, and there was a good deal of urban decline in terms of demography. However in spite of this, or perhaps even stimulated by it, there was a qualitative restructuring or remodelling of social-property relations.

Britnell points to the level of wage dependency among English peasants and labourers as an important indicator of the origin of capitalism, and argues that it was greater in 1300 than in 1500. But wage dependency in 1300 was born out of overpopulation on politically constituted, densely populated peasant holdings; it was not the product of the expropriation of large numbers of peasants from the land. This situation had every chance of leading to feudal crisis, and was going nowhere in terms of a transition to capitalism. As will be described in more detail below, Christopher Dyer argues that the level of wage dependency in 1300 was about the same as it was in the late fifteenth and early sixteenth centuries. However in the late fifteenth century the population was half of what it was in 1300, and instead of being a broad phenomenon across rural society due to the fragmentation of holdings and underemployment as it was in 1300, in the fifteenth century it was concentrated in pockets of rural industry which was increasingly organised on the capitalist putting-out system. In the latter system, clothiers with capital controlled all processes of production – carding, spinning, dying, weaving, shearing (finishing) – from the purchase of raw materials to the selling of the finished cloth. In the 1520s artisans in these rural industrial areas paid the same taxation subsidy as ordinary labourers, and this finding should be taken seriously as indicating early proletarianisation among skilled peasant-artisans.

Britnell's reference to the existence of relatively large units of production in the form of lords' demesnes in the thirteenth century, and their fragmentation in the fifteenth century, cannot be taken very far. It is true that there is evidence for demesnes being broken up here and there in the fifteenth century, and leased in small parcels to a broad range of villagers. Indeed in such examples one can see possibilities for an alternative future for the English peasantry. But the major tendency in the fifteenth century was for demesnes to be leased wholesale, and also for substantial accumulations within the customary holdings themselves. This, as Tawney says, was the *only* tendency in the sixteenth century.[5] In addition to the demesnes, although some wealthy peasants did accumulate holdings in the thirteenth century, these larger holdings did not see continuity in the post-Black Death period; they were typically divided upon the death of the accumulator for the benefit of all heirs.[6]

Moreover, in the thirteenth century, demesnes were managed by lords' officials for the lords' own table and profit, most of which was allocated for non-profitable expenditure on display and warfare. The profits from the produce from demesnes can only be seen to have been invested profitably in feudal terms – that is, in the ability to further extra-economic ends. In the fifteenth century the demesnes were farmed by wealthy peasants producing in competition, an unprecedented step. So when the demesnes were leased to wealthier peasants in the fifteenth century, a novel dynamic of competitive production was set in train.

Unlike Britnell, and other economic historians such as Epstein, Bruce Campbell recognises that the developments between 1100 and 1300 were not going anywhere without the transformation of tenure and the expropriation processes that would ultimately be the outcome of struggle. Nevertheless, Campbell argues that the genesis of the origin of capitalism in England lay well before the Black Death, 'in the vigorously commercialising and expanding world of the twelfth and thirteenth centuries', rather than in the post-Black Death period or that 'long era of retreat and retrenchment that then followed [which] created the opportunity for a fundamental rationalisation and reconfiguration of productive forces and a redefinition of social-property relationships'.[7] As we have seen in Chapter Four above, Campbell focuses his argument on landholding tenure, and argues that the weakening of lordship, usually attributed to the post-1381 and post-Black Death period generally, and something that many historians see as important for the transition to capitalism, actually began between 1150 and 1300. He argues that this weakening of lordship in the earlier period was the result of the lords' loss of control over tenure in association with the process of commercialisation, inflation, technological developments in agriculture, and peasant involvement in markets, including land markets. According to Campbell, this situation led to crisis because of peasant tenacity in resisting lords' impositions of villein tenure, the ruthlessness of a wealthy peasant stratum in subletting at competitive rents, the growth of free tenures, and the overall inefficiencies built into a system of tenure which encouraged the fragmentation of holdings into small plots that

---

5   Tawney 1912, pp. 204–10.
6   See Chapter Three.
7   Campbell 2006, p. 237.

were not sufficient for subsistence. He argues that at this time the alternative to fragmentation, which was the development of competitive rents on substantial holdings and which required the dispossession of peasantry by the lords, was as unimaginable given the social cost as it was impractical given the certain overwhelming resistance.

Against this perspective I will simply reiterate here my earlier critique of Campbell. To begin with, there are problems with his empirical evidence for the weakening of lordship in thirteenth century England – the lords' so-called inadvertent abdication of their controls on tenure – and with his perspective on the progressive liberation of the peasantry during that century. Even more importantly, the issue of a weakened lordship in the thirteenth century is not one that is critical to the origin of capitalism. For example, in regions of France where the weakening controls over peasants in the thirteenth century are clearly documented, there was no transition to capitalism, but rather a transition to a more efficient extra-economic extractor of the peasants' surplus, the absolutist state. English lords were clearly weakened due to population downturn and peasant resistance by the end of the fourteenth century, but in contrast to those in France they retained the ability to control large demesnes and the terms of the new tenures that appeared in the fifteenth century.

Accounts and analyses which place the period between 1100 and 1300 as the most important for the transition from feudalism to capitalism can only take us so far. We can recognise the extent and importance of commercialisation in this period, the developments of a mature marketing and urban system, elements of medieval society routinely overlooked by early modern historians. But these accounts confuse qualitative capitalist development with quantitative commercial development, and fail to address the causes of diverging paths of development in different countries in the post-Black Death period. For an introduction to the periodisation of the origin of capitalism in the post-Black Death and early modern periods we can turn to two important overviews.

ii   The Early Modern Transition

Locating the chronology and context of the expropriation of the peasantry can help us to explain the origin of capitalism and the sustained development of capitalism within the extended transition. One method for examining this chronology is to calculate – from whatever sources different periods throw up – the extent of the land area of England that is known to have been 'enclosed' in each century and, with some rule of thumb calculations, compare these figures with the known square mileage of the whole extent of the land mass of

England. J.R. Wordie tackles this problem by a process of elimination. Enclosure by Act of Parliament in the eighteenth and nineteenth centuries generated historical sources of a very high quality, and these provide us with reasonably accurate figures of the extent of England that was enclosed by this means and at this time. Wordie argues that at least 75 percent of England was already enclosed at the outset of the main waves of enclosure by act of parliament from 1760, and as much as 70 percent already by 1700. Second, on the basis of what is known of medieval tenures in different regions and counties of England, he assumes that 45 percent of the land was already enclosed by 1500 or 1550. Importantly however for his purposes he argues that this so-called 'old medieval enclosure' in certain counties of the south-east and south-west, had nothing to do with the chronology of enclosure that changed England from an open field to an enclosed agrarian capitalist countryside, and so he dismisses it from his calculations of new enclosure. Third, he says that in spite of all the rancour against enclosures by Tudor commonwealthmen, and the widespread expression of anti-enclosure and anti-capitalist sentiments in 1549, he detects only two percent of newly enclosed land in the sixteenth century, a figure that he derives from extrapolating from the returns of the inquiries into enclosure in 1517 and 1518. This leaves the seventeenth century as the most important period for enclosure with 24 percent of the land enclosed in that century, compared to 13 percent in the eighteenth century as a whole, and 11.4 percent for the nineteenth century. 4.6 percent of England still remained in common in 1914. He concludes that it was the period between 1600 and 1760 that was most significant for England's transformation from an open field to an enclosed country.[8]

While this is a useful overview and starting point for discussion, there are obvious flaws with this approach, and Wordie would no doubt concur with much of the following critique. To begin with, the *quantitative* extent of enclosure as Wordie defines it must be distinguished from the context of the origin of capitalism. It is surely the period that is most important for the qualitative origin of the transition that is key, rather than the period when the most acreage was enclosed. Taking Wordie's figures at face value, the implication is that capitalist origins are really found in the seventeenth century. For him the late medieval period and the sixteenth century were insignificant with regard to the chronology of enclosure and the expropriation of the peasantry. However, what his calculation that most enclosure in England took place in the seventeenth century might actually indicate is that the structural basis of capitalist

---

8   Wordie 1983.

development – that is, the emergence of capitalist social-property relations – had already been irreversibly instantiated by 1600, leading to its further consolidation and extension. What also needs to be identified for our purposes is the relationship between enclosure and depopulation. If a large percentage of England's surface that was enclosed in the seventeenth century was made up of marginal areas with low densities of population, then its impact on the origin of capitalism will be lessened in contrast to the enclosure of a small percentage of land with high densities of population. Perhaps even more importantly, with regard to the fifteenth and early sixteenth centuries, because Wordie regards the 'old enclosed counties' of the south-east and south-west as already enclosed in 1500 as the result of their peculiar medieval tenurial character, he does not take into account the nature and extent of the precocious *engrossment* of small plots in these counties into larger farms in the fifteenth and sixteenth centuries, and hence the development of capitalist production in these areas. Medieval agricultural production in the so-called 'old enclosed counties' took the form of peasant communities largely producing for subsistence in severalty before 1450. Therefore enclosure does not imply either dispossession or the increase in the size of productive units here before 1450. 'Old enclosure' in these areas was as compatible as unenclosed open fields in the midlands with densely populated villages and customary practices in line with subsistence-based farming. It is enclosure as dispossession, either directly by eviction, or indirectly by the generation of large farms out of vacant land in the post-Black Death period which restricted the supply of land when the population rose in the sixteenth century, that is key for the origin of capitalism. By not including these areas in his calculations, Wordie has missed some of the most precocious regions for *new enclosure* and capitalist development. The changes within these 'old enclosed counties' and their importance for capitalist origins will be examined below, and analysed in more detail in the case study in Part II.

Furthermore, the engrossment of holdings in the open fields in areas *outside* of 'the old enclosed counties' does not come into Wordie's calculations of the extent of enclosure at all if these areas retained common rights, and yet the old enclosed ones are still treated as enclosed even though they did have at least some customary rights. Hence it is not surprising that the sixteenth century does not feature in his calculations, because the retention of customary practices coexistent with a significant measure of engrossment and enclosure – of the kind we see in the midland villages for example – most likely took place in a sixteenth-century context before being extinguished thereafter.

Although clearly influenced by the work of Tawney and Brenner, Keith Wrightson's recent work largely takes on board Wordie's figures for the chronology of enclosure. Nevertheless, Wrightson provides a brilliant, detailed overview of the changes, their causes and significance at particular times across the transitional epoch. In contrast to Wordie he stresses the importance of late medieval social differentiation among the peasantry, enclosure and the emergence of yeomen farmers well before the price and population rises in England from the 1520s worked their stimuli:

> In 1500 an estimated 45 percent of cultivable area of England was already enclosed and farmed in severalty. Much of this land had probably never been cultivated in open fields. A good deal however had been enclosed and converted to pasture in the late middle ages – an early enclosure movement which was particularly evident in the late fifteenth century and continued up to the 1520s.

While not seeking to minimise the importance of these early changes which he also ties in with rural industrial development, the expansion of overseas trade and urban restructuring, Wrightson, an early modernist, suggests that in 1520 farming was still predominantly subsistent. From his perspective there was neither a 'burgeoning agrarian capitalist mentality' nor an agricultural revolution because the changes were a blind response by lords, a second-best adaptation, to conditions of recession and population stagnation. Nor, he argues, was this a commercialised society with a mature urban system. However, he concludes that these late medieval developments nevertheless 'created the context of response' to conditions after the 1520s, and had a 'profound significance' for later developments in the sixteenth century.[9] We will return to these crucial points later.

Wrightson identifies the following period between 1530 and 1580 as one of economic consolidation and enhancement. It was stimulated by rising prices, rapid population rise and the massive transfer of church property to gentry and yeomen following the dissolution of the monasteries and chantries. But, as with the late fifteenth and early sixteenth centuries, the question of the *extent* of enclosure is a difficult one for this period also. He argues that, in spite of the economic and demographic context which produced the stimulation for lords and farmers to enclose and specialise, this period witnessed a hiatus in the enclosure movement. He says that newly enclosed land in the sixteenth

---

9 Wrightson 2000, pp. 99–104.

century *as a whole* only amounted to two to three percent, and this figure seems to have been derived from Wordie. Wrightson recognises that this over-all figure masks high levels of enclosure in certain areas, remembering that these statistics refer to the whole landed area of England (including vast areas of lightly inhabited forest, wold and moor). He says that the pace of enclosure slowed 'in part because of the statutes prohibiting enclosure involving the con-version of tillage to pasture, in part because rising grain prices rendered such conversion less attractive to landowners', and also because of peasant resis-tance. However, he argues that the previous period defined as one of depopu-lating enclosure was over. Between 1530 and 1580 the form enclosure took was different, and was mainly concerned with waste lands and peasants' and arti-sans' common lands. The changes were however no longer what he calls second-best blind adaptations or what Brenner calls unintended consequences of the post-Black Death context of declining rents and rising wages. Lords became more aggressive than hitherto having now recognised the potential for raising rents in this new context; and while peasant and yeomen tenants were increasingly squeezed as a result, the yeomen benefited from higher prices for their produce and the greater availability of increasingly cheap labour. The period sees the return of significant levels of poverty not seen since before the Black Death due to the increasing reduction in access to land for the rapidly rising population. Because of the pre-1520 structural changes in land holding, the subsequent rapid population rises from 1540 were not absorbed by land division as they were in France. So, unlike the thirteenth century, English peas-ants were in effect expropriated at birth. Already by 1540, they no longer had a *de facto* birthright to the possession of a holding.[10]

While developments in the fifteenth and early sixteenth centuries 'created the context for response' and were of 'profound significance' for the changes in the sixteenth century, for Wrightson, to some extent following Wordie's conclusions, after the so-called hiatus in enclosure between 1530 and 1580, it is the subsequent periods of the late sixteenth to the early seventeenth centuries and the late seventeenth to the early eighteenth centuries that are the 'turning points' in the transition to capitalist agriculture and a capitalist economy. Between 1580 and 1650 prices continuously rose and inflation in the late six-teenth century was more severe than that of the 1520s, so real wages declined further. Population growth also accelerated from 2.98 million in 1561 to 4 mil-lion in 1601 and to 5.23 million in 1651, although it had slowed and had stopped by the latter date.[11] By the 1580s lords renewed the earlier late medieval trend

10   Wrightson 2000, pp. 132–49.
11   Wrightson 2000, pp. 159–60.

of depopulating enclosure, but Wrightson argues that it should be distinguished from the earlier period in that it was less likely to involve conversion of arable to pasture, and more likely to ensure the continuity of arable production and the introduction of a revolutionary convertible husbandry. He says that change was usually carried out by agreement between landlords and principal tenants – confirming the conclusions of the previous chapter – and involved the restructuring of holdings into compact farms. This new enclosure movement facilitated the expansion of production: it included the drawing in of wastes including massive inning and draining projects; royal deforestation; the intensification of cultivation and the related development of convertible husbandry; and regional and intra-regional specialisation.[12]

In 1593 parliament discontinued the statutes against the conversion of tillage, apparently in view of the 'great plenty and cheapness of grain', and consequently 'a flurry of enclosures followed in midland counties'. However the relaxation of the anti-enclosure laws was ill timed for it immediately preceded the long dearth of the later 1590s and so the statutes were rehabilitated in 1597. This time however they were full of exemptions and the debate in parliament over this issue, particularly the contribution of the pro-enclosure Sir Walter Raleigh, reveals the extent to which the values of laissez-faire had already developed. By the early seventeenth century, support for Raleigh's view had gathered strength. Hence the government's response to the 'midland revolt' of peasants against enclosures in 1607 was ambivalent, and there was a growing disinclination to enforce even the exemption-ridden measures of 1597. As a consequence, the '1620s witnessed a rash of new enclosures throughout the kingdom, an acceleration of change in which the crown itself was by now deeply implicated in response to the energetic attempts of its surveyors to raise the revenues of the crown estates by the improvement of commons'. This included the drainage and enclosure of Sedgmoor in the Somerset levels in 1618, and the fens in the east. Such projects were carefully justified by the crown, and now 'improvement' received greater priority than 'habitation', a complete turn around from the policy of a century earlier. Thousands of fenlanders were overlooked and formidable resistance to the drainage which was sustained for three decades was gradually defeated by successive governments. Much the same was witnessed with the deforestation of royal forests in the west of England where the crown encouraged gentlemen and yeomen to make the clearances. There was local resistance from smaller subsistence-orientated tenants and cottagers who had most to lose from the consequent extinction of common rights, and earlier attitudes against enclosure remained. In the 1630s

---

12   Wrightson 2000, pp. 162–74.

there were renewed anxieties about grain supplies and this led to commissions against unlawful enclosure in which Archbishop Laud demonstrated his personal hostility to enclosers. Wrightson also points to the well-known pamphlet conflict between Moore and Lee in Leicestershire over the burst of enclosure which threatened the common fields of south Leicestershire in the 1650s. However between 1597 and 1657 assumptions regarding the disastrous effects of enclosure had changed and a bill for renewed restraint on enclosure presented in 1657 found no sympathy. Nevertheless, opposition lived on among defenders of village commons and among those prepared to help their cause.[13]

Urban artisans faced the same problem as the squeezed husbandmen due to overstocked labour markets in an increasingly capitalistically structured industry. However the situation is more graphically documented in England's *rural* industrial districts. Wrightson provides examples of the *complete* proletarianisation of many of these areas. In the 1620s conditions were desperate with wage levels not keeping up with prices. At the same time clothiers (rural industrial equivalents to farmers, who were nevertheless also farmers) benefited from the same conditions: 'In town and country alike, the final quarter of the sixteenth century and the early decades of the seventeenth century witnessed the emergence of a larger and more wholly wage dependent labouring population, which probably constituted at least half of the English population by the mid-seventeenth century'. A new *structural* poverty was witnessed by the mid-seventeenth century where poverty had become an inevitable experience for growing numbers from birth, no longer simply the result of accident, misfortune or old age. This was as Wrightson says 'a polarising society' now firmly based on the agrarian capitalist triad model of social relations.[14]

The late seventeenth century to the early eighteenth century was a period of huge commercial expansion in trade and industry: the colonial and slave trade that developed rapidly from the early seventeenth century flourished, making Britain the leading power among the sea-borne empires; old industries expanded, and new industries developed. Yet interestingly (like the fifteenth-century restructuring) there was a very new context of stagnant or declining population for much of the period and a related decline in grain prices. In 1651 the population was about 5.23 million. By 1701 it had actually fallen slightly to about 5.06 million. From here there was modest growth to the 1740s when it still only reached 5.63 million, a figure comparable to levels achieved in 1300. The key prices of wheat and rye fell gradually from the 1650s to the 1680s and, apart from the bad harvest years of the 1690s, they fluctuated at 20 percent

---

13   Wrightson 2000, pp. 209–12. See also Wood 2002, p. 90.
14   Wrightson 2000, pp. 194–201.

below the early seventeenth-century levels, and were particularly low in the early eighteenth century. Prices of livestock became stable in the late seventeenth century and rose modestly thereafter. Industrial products were stable in the late seventeenth century but then fell after the 1710s by ten percent. So, Wrightson points out, the purchasing power of a broad section of population was raised by 25 percent in real terms creating a new domestic context of broad social and geographical demand. Regarding the enclosure movement, it was a vital period of consolidation and the completion of the transformation to capitalist agrarian relations. 70 percent of cultivable land was enclosed by 1700. Much of the enclosure in this period was led by landlords and their stewards, in a process of attrition which was gradual but vital for the consolidation of the capitalist estate system. Wrightson describes well the fully commercialised or capitalist aristocracy that Brenner referred to that dominated this estate system. However he makes the point that these lords nevertheless maintained a traditional aura, and cultivated an authoritative paternalism which was necessary to attract large farmers at a time that was more difficult for the latter. By the early eighteenth century Wrightson calculates that three fifths of the English population were primarily wage workers, and yet the population was still comparable to its level in 1300.[15]

In summary, for Wrightson, the well documented depopulating enclosure movement of the period between c. 1470 and 1520 which was set in motion blindly, created the context of response to conditions after 1520. Then a process

---

15   Wrightson 2000, pp. 209–45. The distinctiveness of England's colonies in the New World which emerged in the early seventeenth century was that (outside of the Caribbean) the racial make-up of their populations was predominantly white. In contrast to the colonies of countries such as Spain, France and Holland, the dispossession of the peasantry leading to the development of agrarian capitalism in England produced a surplus population of unemployed or underemployed landless labourers by this time. Before industrialisation, the North American colonies absorbed increasing numbers of dispossessed English people and their children, because following the very difficult early years of indentured servitude there were possibilities for them to hold or own land. This emigration also reduced the potential within the dispossessed for discontent and disorder in England itself: see Wood 2003, chapter 4; Blackburn 1997, chapter 6. See also Rollison 2010, chapter 7, for a useful recent discussion on the already widespread problem of the dependent unemployed in late sixteenth-century England, and the consequent drive to conquer foreign and New World markets (and countries) in order to stimulate the expansion of industry in the metropolis, and thereby avoid insurrection through the provision of jobs. It should be noted, however, that the role of enclosure in this increasing dependency that was experienced by the English population in the fifteenth and sixteenth centuries is sidelined by Rollison in favour of an autonomous expansion of rural industry.

of more deliberate commercialisation built on these earlier structural changes. However for Wrightson the transition was not yet decisive before 1580 and commonwealthmen still thought themselves able to prevent detrimental change to the traditional peasant economy. The period between the 1580s and the 1620s was the first turning point. It witnessed a new rash of enclosures and of rural industrialisation, massive new crown projects, and these led to transformations in economy, society and attitudes. The late seventeenth century to the early eighteenth century was a 'vital' period in which the British economy (which was inordinately stimulated by super profits and cheap imports derived from the slave trade and slave plantations in North America and the Caribbean) witnessed the consolidation and completion of the transformation to a capitalist agricultural estate system and of a capitalistically organised trade and industry.[16]

iii   The Origin of Capitalism in the Long Fifteenth Century

Other historians have also pointed to the post-1550 or post-1580 period as key to the transition. Jane Whittle, on the basis of her study of manors in Norfolk between 1440 and 1580 argued, in her critique of Brenner, that there was no major structural change in the nature of the rural economy and society in England between 1440 and 1580. Using levels of proletarianisation and wage dependency as a key indicator of the progression of capitalist relations she concluded that change came before 1440 with the dissolution of serfdom, and after 1580 with the large-scale transference of land to competitive leasehold.[17] Mavis Mate, in her important recent study of the south-eastern counties of Surrey, Sussex and Kent between 1450 and 1550, found significant structural changes, but concluded that '[r]ather than pivotal, this period should be seen as displaying considerable economic vitality that provided the base for future developments'.[18] In the rest of this chapter I draw close attention to the significance of the period between the late fourteenth and early sixteenth centuries

---

16   Neeson demonstrates however that in the early eighteenth century, although confined to a few counties only, there still remained a widespread and partially independent English peasantry which fiercely guarded its customary values and common lands. These were mainly smallholding artisans with links to rural industry before the parliamentary enclosures were introduced. There was still a major chapter to undergo which led to the final disciplining of the English workforce: Neeson 1993.

17   Whittle 2000, pp. 305–13.

18   Mate 2006, p. 237.

for the transition to capitalism in England, not least because, in my view, it marked the origin of the transition. I will argue that the structural changes in property holding through the leasing of demesnes, engrossment and enclosure of open fields and traditional fields held 'in severalty' more typical of the eastern and south-eastern counties, related social structural changes and changing class strategies represent, more than any other period, the transition to capitalist social-property relations. What came after these structural changes, which, granted, were extremely variable over the country but advanced in the east and south east as they interacted with London was, as Wrightson has so well described, the consolidation, enhancement and extension of the fundamental earlier changes.

Any discussion of the significance of what can be described as the long fifteenth century should begin with the work of Maurice Beresford, which has been mostly overlooked, and the work of Christopher Dyer. Writing in the 1950s, Beresford was concerned to locate hundreds of deserted rural settlements in England and to identify the causes for their desertion. For him the petition of John Rous (d. 1491) as early as 1459 to parliament asking for legislation against depopulating enclosure, and his (Rous's) list of 58 depopulated villages in Warwickshire which he compiled in a book written between 1485 and 1491 are important chronological benchmarks.[19] The other benchmarks for Beresford are the first statute against depopulating enclosure in 1489, the bills of 1515 that led to the famous first government inquiries into depopulating enclosure in 1517 and 1518, the evidence of the latter returns, and the conclusions of John Hales in his *Discourse* which was written in 1548 in the midst of the mid-sixteenth century anti-enclosure movement. Hales was a commissioner of enclosures in 1548–9 and had first-hand knowledge and experience of the changes and of public opinion at the time. From this knowledge Hales concluded that most of the serious depopulating enclosure had already taken place before 1485.[20] Using taxation material to support Rous's contention that the villages on his list had been depopulated in his lifetime, and his petition of 1459, Beresford found that those to-be-depopulated villages were still well inhabited in the mid-fifteenth century. He concluded that the main flood of enclosure in England therefore took place between 1440 and 1520.[21]

---

19   Rous compared these mid-to-late fifteenth-century developments to the devastation
      caused by William the Conqueror's harrying of the provinces in the eleventh century in
      the aftermath of the Norman Conquest.
20   Beresford 1998, pp. 81–8, 102.
21   Beresford 1998, p. 165.

Beresford argued that the latter chronology rings true because the great majority of cases stemming from the inquiries into depopulating enclosure that began in 1517, and continued throughout the sixteenth century, involved only a few holdings or houses in a particular village: only a minority were concerned with the depopulation of whole or nearly whole settlements. 583 cases of depopulation were heard in the royal court of exchequer between 1518 and 1565. There was an early burst of activity from 1518 to 1530, then a lull, renewed interest in 1539 which was maintained until 1556, and after this date even the enclosure commissions failed to bring a great deal of business to court. Virtually all of the cases were from 13 midland counties and yet, as we shall see, serious depopulating enclosure had been going on all over the south east and east. In Beresford's sample from four of these midland counties which returned the most numerous cases, out of 482 cases between 1518 and 1565, 340 involved the destruction of only one house. There were 47 cases where six or more houses had been destroyed, and the rest accounted for figures somewhere in between.[22]

Beresford argued that the commissioners of 1517–18 were only picking up on the tail-end of a depopulating enclosure movement that had peaked before 1485; they found lords removing the final remnants of village communities that had either moved away or been evicted earlier. It is telling, as Beresford points out, that only a handful of villages on John Rous's list drawn up between 1486 and 1491 appear in the 1517 returns and, where they do, it is 'for the decay of the single house and the enclosure of a few odd acres, the last stage in the evictions'. The problem was that the remit of the commissioners could not go back before 1488 because depopulating enclosure was not against statute law before this, although it did infringe crucial customary rights within the manorial legal context. Indeed many big fish escaped the net simply by pointing out that the enclosure being investigated by the 1517–18 commission occurred before 1488. For example, the defence plea of Magdalen College, Oxford, before the judges of king's bench to the accusation that it had undertaken illegal enclosure in the manor of Golder against the statute, was that Sir Thomas Danvers, the previous lord, had enclosed the manor three or more years before 1488, and before the College took possession.[23]

This is not to minimise the importance of significant numbers of villages that were still being entirely depopulated in the decades directly after 1489. When one looks at these events on a case-by-case basis we gain an alternative perspective to that achieved by Wordie with his statistical calculations of the

22   Beresford 1998, pp. 115–16.
23   Beresford 1998, pp. 116–17.

percentage of England's land mass that was enclosed in different periods, and we can grasp more clearly the essence of what was happening. Beresford cites the 18 people from Wretchwick (Bicester) in Oxfordshire whose messuages were destroyed by the late prior of the monastery of Bicester in 1489 and who, according to the commissioners' report, 'have gone away to take to the roads in their misery, and to seek their bread elsewhere'. In Barcheston, Warwickshire, the jury accused the lord William Willington of enclosing 530 acres and destroying four houses and a cottage in 1508 so that almost all of the hamlet was laid waste and 24 people were 'expelled from their houses and tearfully seek food and work elsewhere'. Among the juries' returns for Northamptonshire in 1517–18 were the depopulations of Catesby where 60 were evicted, of Thorpe in Norton parish with 72 people evicted and in Glendon where 62 people were evicted.[24] In Buckinghamshire, the 1517–18 inquiry found complaints of houses being ruined or abandoned, or people forced to leave in 79 places going back to 1489. In eight of these places the record of the number of these tenants expelled, or the reference to the enclosure or devastation of the village, sug-gests a complete or near complete forced depopulation. Here is a flavour: in Burston seven houses had decayed and 60 people were evicted, so that the vil-lage is 'totally used for pasture'; at Doddershall 24 messuages were put down and 120 people gone; at Hogshaw and Fulbrook 11 messuages were either pulled down or used to house shepherds, and 60 people left the village and hamlet as a result; at Lillingstone Dayrell seven messuages and four cottages were demol-ished, 40 people were forced to leave and 'the whole vill was put down and remains totally devastated'; at Castle Thorpe seven messuages were destroyed and 88 people had to leave.[25] In Leicestershire in 1494 the Earl of Shrewsbury evicted 60 people from Bittesby. The following year Sir Ralph Shirley evicted 30 people from Willowes who the jurors said 'departed weeping and probably per-ished'. The following year Sir Robert Brudenell, the new owner of Holyoak and later chief justice, evicted 30 people who were said to have been 'killed or per-ished'. Sir John Villiers was accused of evicting 24 people from Brookby a few years earlier in 1492, but this was denied by his successors in 1545. Many of the depositions from inquiries were vague, but some were not, and the following gives another indication of the periodisation of these evictions. Beresford cites the case of Pendley (Hertfordshire) where in 1506 it was remembered that about 80 years earlier (that is, in the 1420s) Pendley was a village with more than 13 ploughs and diverse artisans. It was laid to pasture by Sir Robert Whittingham who built his manor place where the village once stood. To

---

24   Beresford 1998, p. 108.
25   Dyer 2005, p. 67 n. 60.

support this evidence Beresford finds that in 1440 a license had been obtained to empark 200 acres there and this may have been the beginning of the end for that village.[26] Surely one can be left in no doubt even on the basis of limited evidence such as this that momentous changes had been taking place before the early sixteenth century. As Rous said, forced depopulation on this scale had not been seen in England since the aftermath of the Norman Conquest.[27]

Fryde supports Beresford's view of John Rous as a serious and meticulous investigator. He describes these proceedings as 'brutal' and 'inhuman' and although they may or may not have been exceptional cases after 1489 there has been a tendency by historians to minimise their significance. Fryde finds that these mass evictions took place in the autumn or early winter 'after the last harvest had been cleared and in good time to prepare the conversion to pasture, in utter disregard of the dangers threatening the hapless victims during the most inhospitable part of the year'. In support of Rous's periodisation of the evictions he also makes the point that the civil wars known as the Wars of the Roses in the second half of the fifteenth century in England led to the confiscations of numerous estates, and these would have been granted to new owners who were more likely to radically innovate on taking possession of their new property. This was also most likely to be the case following the dissolution of the monasteries. In Warwickshire, Wormleighton was confiscated in 1495 and the leading official of Henry VII to whom it was re-granted (no doubt as a favour) depopulated it in 1499 evicting 60 people. Even an encloser's personal attachment to a certain village did not save it. Following a career as a London draper and sheriff, one man returned enriched to his native village of Cestover in Warwickshire which was granted to him by Edward IV between 1462 and 1467 and enclosed 500 acres of it turning most to pasture. Like Tawney, Fryde also questions the weight given to dubious statistics on acreage enclosed when we can point to these events that 'must have sent shudders of fear and insecurity through the entire countryside of the midland counties most affected'.[28]

For Beresford another key problem was that the 1489 statute was entirely ineffective. The main problem was that before 1536 the prosecution of depopulating enclosers relied on manorial lords reporting the illegal enclosures and actions of their farmer lessees. Lords were provided with the carrot that they would receive half of the profits of the fines received from a successful conviction. However Beresford points out that lords and their lessees had similar

26   Beresford 1998, p. 147.
27   Fryde 1988, pp. 810–11.
28   Fryde 1988, pp. 810–13.

interests – as we discussed at length in the previous chapter – and he knows of not one case in these returns where a depopulating farmer was reported to the authorities by his own lord. Citing Tawney, who had much earlier argued that the land-owning interests acted as a brake on the ability to implement anti-enclosure statutes, Beresford said that these interests are 'illustrated by the dumb defiance of the lords who did not take the opportunity which the act of 1489 allowed them, and failed to proceed against their depopulating tenantry. It is the failure of the lords to implement this act that seems to have led to the inquiries of 1517–18'. It was not until 1536 that the crown could get (or wanted to get) the opportunity to proceed against enclosing farmers in default of the lords doing so. Beresford also argued that the grazing interests were strongly entrenched at court and, referring to the difficult position of Cardinal Wolsey who had set up the commission of 1517, he pointed out that 'the commission was remembered as a grievance against the cardinal at his fall, just as in the next century Archbishop Laud was to have it remembered in the hour of his impeachment that "he did a little too much countenance the Commission for Depopulation" '.[29]

Beresford qualifies the impression that there was a simple top-down military style attack by farmers and lords on their villages between the mid- and late fifteenth century for the purposes of turning arable over to more profitable pasture. He says that depopulation was usually a process over time: 'Only a would-be encloser with great political strength, a strong and loyal body of retainers, a deaf ear to local protests and a firm grip on local juries could hope to evict scores of people in one sweep. We do hear of such cases in the returns of 1517: but more commonly the story is of the eviction of the last survivors'. He says that the departure of the other villagers often began with a voluntary movement by peasants who saw better opportunities in freer tenure elsewhere: 'The depopulation of a village would be the last act in a chain of circumstances'.[30] We need to remember however that in the context of the decline of serfdom migration from unfree tenures seriously infringed lords' jurisdiction and it was therefore a challenge to the power lords had over peasants. Migration may also not be as voluntary as it appears on paper in the evidence of deserted holdings and the apparent innocuous process of buying and selling land on the peasant land market as evidenced in manorial court rolls. It may have resulted from pressure and intimidation. Mavis Mate demonstrated this point in her evidence for Kent and I provide clearer evidence for it in Part II. Also the significance of lords removing the remnants of villages for

---

29   Beresford 1998, pp. 102–6, 118.
30   Beresford 1998, p. 138.

the purpose of leasing them out as large farms should not be underestimated. Once the last households were removed they were removed forever, and the opportunity for these villages to be resettled and to grow again, as they did in France, was foreclosed.

Christopher Dyer's work over the last three decades has culminated in a profound statement on what he describes as 'an age of transition'. He argues that while England did not have a wholesale capitalist economy in 1520, there were strong moves in that direction by that date. In the period between 1350 and 1520 which he coined as the 'long fifteenth century', while recognising the importance of growth in marketing and commercial mentality before 1300, he states that 'social structures and methods of production were remodelled'. It was certainly no longer a subsistent economy in 1520 as Wrightson assumes – perhaps from his perspective as an early modernist. Like Brenner, for Dyer it is the modification of the social-property relations in this period in large and key areas of England that should be our focus when it comes to the transition. In the decades and centuries that followed 1520 there were big changes, but the *logic* for these changes originated in the long fifteenth century. Change may not have been decisive until the late sixteenth century and arguably changes could have been reversed if the rebellions of 1549 had been successful, but the degree of structural change towards agrarian capitalism by 1549 made such a reversal increasingly unlikely.

For the first of the key changes between 1350 and 1520 we can recall Dyer's analysis of the revolutionary changes mentioned in earlier chapters that occurred in the decades around 1400. These were namely the transference of 25 percent of the cultivated area of English manors in the form of leases to thousands of peasants from the wealthiest stratum. These thousands of 'new men', usually referred to as yeomen, had become prominent by the end of the fifteenth century. By the time of the tax subsidy in 1525 these farmers were dominating figures, separate from their neighbours both in wealth and culturally in that they no longer adhered to the traditional values of neighbourhood and custom. Their assessments for taxation were in the £20 to £100 bracket while in most villages the majority of taxpayers had goods or wages valued at only £1 or £2. The most substantial villagers were assessed at £3 to £12, well below the farmers. This situation could only have occurred through the expansion of demesnes and the development of holdings by engrossing others.

Dyer demonstrates that lords deliberately enclosed common lands and evicted villagers. This was 'a significant strand of rural conflict in this period', but he argues that it was probably not the central tendency because removing peasants was not a straightforward task as Beresford had earlier pointed out. Nevertheless, lords who wanted to extend their pastures in this period had a number of other strategies *to the same disruptive effect*, such as overstocking commons and fencing the demesne to prevent common grazing (or encouraging ambitious demesne farmers to do so), or turning a blind eye to their farmers' disruption of the traditional agrarian routine. He says that when lords were *directly* involved they were usually just clearing up the remnants of sickly villages. Most of the enclosure was carried out by the peasants themselves, the leading villagers who used their positions in local government to facilitate the changes.[31]

One indication of developments towards a capitalist economy is a rise in labour productivity, and Dyer shows that farmers in the fifteenth and early sixteenth century generally specialised most strikingly in the case of pastures. They used the land in massive contrast to the previous direct management of the lords, the production of which was diversified. Indeed lords sometimes tried to limit overspecialisation. However farmers sought the best means of profit and typically responded to the market in the fifteenth century by increasing the area under grass. Dyer provides examples of very large-scale sheep farming on the Sussex coast in 1486, where there were 4,366 sheep grazing over two abandoned village sites. As Dyer says this farmer must have had a huge surplus over and above his £20 annual rent that he paid for the parish of Hangleton. In most cases farmers took over fixed assets only and so had to make a considerable capital investment if they wanted to introduce livestock and equipment and improvements such as enclosure and marling, and they also had to renovate buildings. Farmers used the labour of their families but also employed their own workers full-time and part-time. Dyer also shows how farmers were able to get themselves into such a position: 'The farmer was in most cases a free man who developed a relationship with the lord on the basis of the mutual advantages of the contract', and the engrossment and enclosure of such large farms 'could only be contemplated in collaboration with the lord'.[32]

Dyer also addresses directly the question of whether there was an increase in the number or proportion of wage earners in this age of transition, something that Whittle had very much discounted. Jane Whittle's main criticism of Brenner relates to his periodisation of the transition to an agrarian capitalist social-property structure. From her evidence of rural manors in north Norfolk she concludes that there was limited structural change in England by 1580 because limited proletarianisation had taken place in terms of a free wage labour force employed in agriculture. Landlessness had increased, but small-

31   Dyer 2005, pp. 67–72.
32   Dyer 2005, pp. 199, 206–7.

holding was still strong and it was combined with other subsidiary occupations and extensive common rights of pasture.[33] She does however recognise that the social structure in her sample in the early sixteenth century 'exhibited a strong polarisation, both in the possession of land, and in moveable wealth. The fuller the picture that can be obtained, the stronger the polarisation appears to be'. As early as 1515 'at least' 21 percent of the customary land of one manor – aside from the demesne – was already enclosed.[34] What appears to be happening is that while the countryside in her sample in the sixteenth century had not been entirely polarised into farmers and dependent wage labourers, dependence had certainly increased markedly creating smaller landholders and increasing numbers of servants. Dyer compares the poll tax evidence surviving between 1377 and 1381 with the muster of 1522 and the tax subsidy of 1524–5. He demonstrates that there was, during this time, a great extension of dependency within the putting-out system which was increasingly focussed in small industrial towns and expanding rural industrial districts. Industry which was previously unorchestrated and organised by artisans in the late fourteenth century became by the late fifteenth century controlled by (yeoman and gentry) clothiers, and wages became limited along with increased dependency. Artisans' wages in industrial districts were the same as labourers in the 1520s assessments, thus revealing an ominous stage in the proletarianisation of skilled workers. Dyer also points out that the very high proportions of workers assessed on wages in industrial districts in the early sixteenth century shows that land was already by this date no longer available as an alternative source of production for increasing numbers of people.[35] The stark implication of this is that the land had been enclosed into the hands of a few large interests, usually those of the very clothiers who employed the wage workers. It needs to be remembered that this large increase in the numbers of those who lacked the ability to gain access to land by the 1520s took place while the population stagnated in England as a whole, and it had stagnated at half the level it had reached in 1300. Outside of the expanding rural industrial districts Dyer examines the changed social structures in the areas of significant enclosure by the 1520s. His examples reveal a complete social polarisation in these areas. The assessments in some villages show one or a few large sheep farmers and the only others assessed were a few wage labourers or herders who worked for them.[36] So while there was no overall increase in the proportion of wage

33   Whittle 2000, pp. 305–13.
34   Whittle 2000, pp. 59, 224.
35   Dyer 2005, pp. 229–32.
36   Dyer 2005, pp. 231–2.

earning workforce since 1300, workers were crucially by the early sixteenth century distributed unevenly in the new economies of pasture farming and rural cloth and metal industries rather than spread over the countryside as underemployed workers in a period of general overpopulation like the decades around 1300.

A key pillar of Brenner's argument about the diverging economies of England and France from the later fifteenth century rests on the logic that the removal of peasants from the land in England created by this date an enlarged proportion of workers in non-agrarian occupations: the expansion of the cloth industry in rural small town districts which was stimulated by the great rise of cloth production for export from the late fifteenth century occurred in symbiosis with this expropriation. The rising proportion of workers in industrial occupations increasingly stimulated changes in agriculture due to domestic demand for agricultural products and cloth. Hence 'continuing English industrial expansion was founded upon a growing domestic market, rooted ultimately in the continuing transformation of agricultural production'.[37] In an important discussion on new sources of domestic demand and consumption in England in the fifteenth century, Dyer modifies the assumption that the fifteenth century was one of economic stagnation in England due to a stagnant population and modest levels of economic expansion before the end of the century. He argues that if we focus on levels and patterns of consumption per head rather than on levels of production output, the picture is far less pessimistic. Indeed with increased labourers' wages in the fifteenth century, and new demand from a wealthier farmer clothier stratum (as evidenced in will bequests which increasingly proliferate during the fifteenth century), one can point to domestic demand for clothing as driving the changes rather than the changes being export led. Add to this the demand for clothing, the expansion of new housing in the second half of the fifteenth century by the wealthier peasant stratum, and increasingly large units of production in the brewing of ale, a different picture emerges.[38] Overseas demand for English woollen cloth had expanded during the second half of the fifteenth century, and this demand increased rapidly by the 1520s. It is usually thought that this overseas demand stimulated the production of cloth in England and therefore stimulated enclosure for sheep farming, high-quality English wool, and the expansion of rural industry. It is true that the value of exports of English cloth was a third higher than domestic sales, and yet twice as much cloth was sold domestically than

---

37   Brenner 1985b, p. 325.
38   Dyer 2005, pp. 128–55.

exported. The difference was that domestic sales consisted largely of cheaper cloth varieties.[39]

Dyer very much concurs with Brenner's periodisation that the economies of France and England may have diverged from the late fifteenth century and strengthens further this position. Dyer points to Wrigley's estimate that 40 percent of the English population in 1688 were in non-agricultural occupations, and that figure rose to 50 percent in 1760, a much higher proportion than that found in France. Wrigley's suggestion on the basis of these calculations is that there must have been a divergence with France in the late sixteenth century. However Dyer says that the high proportions of non-agricultural occupations in industrialised areas, for example as much as 34 percent in Babergh Hundred in Suffolk in 1522, and in counties with large towns as well as numerous small towns and rural industry such as Devon and Staffordshire, the proportion could have been nearer to the 1688 figure: 'The divergence between England and the continent could be located in the late fifteenth century, as population growth after the Black Death and subsequent epidemics resumed in France and Italy while the English population remained at the same level until the mid-sixteenth century'.[40]

Other recent studies, in addition to those numerous classic studies on which Brenner based his earlier work, can be cited to support the foregoing periodisation of the changes. Marjorie McIntosh in her studies of the Essex manor of Havering, which included the town of Romford just to the east of London, shows that by the late fifteenth century many patterns and attitudes usually associated with 1600 were already present. She says that 'the community continued to change between 1500 and 1620' so that the 'shared outlook of the medieval years was disrupted and the willingness to work together for common goals weakened. Economic power and influence over religion and local government, formerly distributed among more than a hundred families of yeomen, husbandmen, and craftsmen-traders were by 1620 concentrated into the hands of just a few gentlemen and nobles with great landed estates'. Very significant changes had already occurred in the fifteenth century. During the 1450s and 1460s migration into the manor caused a rapid rise in the population, presumably driven by enclosure of rural districts where they had lived. This increase was made up of a few 'extremely wealthy' intrants but mostly of poor people. In the 1460s these intrants included a draper and lord mayor of London, a wealthy merchant of the west country who was an MP for Cornwall and also served as esquire to the crown, and a successful lawyer, recorder and MP of

39   Dyer 2005, pp. 149–50.
40   Dyer 2005, pp. 156–7.

London. These men accumulated 900 acres, 1200 acres and 500 acres respectively in the 1460s, although McIntosh is not able to say how such massive accumulation was possible. Between them they held 11 of the 25 estates in Havering, and these were becoming manors in their own right: these 'new tenants were in a position to develop the combined economic potential of extensive acreages, focused production for the market, readily available labour, resources for investment in agricultural stock and equipment, and the continuing demand of London'.[41]

Mavis Mate's conclusions that the period 1450–1550 saw important structural changes but was not pivotal for the transition to capitalism contrast with her findings and analysis (at least with regard to expropriation). She shows that accumulation was widespread before the 1520s:

> South-east England was largely immune from the prosecutions engendered by Cardinal Wolsey's commissions of enquiry into illegal enclosures, since much of the land had been engaged in pastoral activities and enclosed long before the end of the fifteenth century. Nonetheless, the complaints about the decay of tillage on both the Romney and Pevensey marshes does suggest that by 1550 some kind of permanent shift from arable to pastoral activity had taken place there.[42]

She argues that the increase in wage dependency as a direct result of the reduction in the number of subsistent smallholdings from the mid-fifteenth century was partly to blame for the increase in prices in the 1520s. This was because the increase in demand which led to the price rises came from a population still only half the size that it had been in 1300. She calculates from the taxation material of the 1520s that 53 percent of the population of the whole south-east region of Sussex, Surrey and Kent, rural and urban, was reliant on wages and yet with the stress again that the population was half its peak in 1300. She shows from rentals how increased polarisation had taken place by the 1520s with many yeomen producing for the market and using their positions as estate officials to facilitate their enterprises. She also shows how lords' interventions in the land market became more aggressive even before the stimulus of the price rises of the 1520s. Another feature was the movement into the land market of wealthy outsiders, clothiers, merchants and gentry. Massive investment in land holding in Kent took the form of inning or drainage projects on

---

41   McIntosh 1991, pp. 1–5. See also McIntosh 1986.
42   Mate 2006, p. 191.

the coastal marshes from the mid-fifteenth century, and these new lands were given over to grazing interests.[43]

In a later paper dealing largely with the post-Black Death century she provides examples revealing the development of inequality among Kentish landholders even earlier in the fifteenth century. Between the Black Death and 1447 the number of tenants in Gillingham in eastern Kent had reduced by two thirds since the Black Death but the accumulation of land was not universal, and land holding was not spread evenly. Former holdings were accumulated by some individuals and by newcomers: a comparison of a rental of 1288 with one of 1447 reveals that while some holdings were enlarged others got smaller. In fact a quarter of all holdings contained two acres or less. She says that a simultaneous process of consolidation and fragmentation had gone on 'everywhere' in Kent, 'leading to considerable inequality in holding size'. For example at Otford in 1440, eight percent of the population held 100 acres or more while 40 percent held between one and five acres.[44]

If by stating that the changes before 1550 were not 'pivotal' Mate means that the changes could still be reversed after 1550 then she may well have a point, but we should be in no doubt about the challenge facing those wishing to go back to 1450. However, it appears that Mate is rather more circumspect than this on the significance of the earlier changes, because in her conclusion on the state of landholding in south-eastern England by 1550, she states that 'The land, however, was not yet divided into large capitalist farms worked by wage labour. Small holdings and farms of 7–10 acres still existed over much of the area and on some manors made up a quarter of the holdings. What had disappeared by 1550 were the tiny farms of half an acre that had been absorbed into large units. Moreover the gap between the larger and smaller units was growing and would become even wider in the century to come'.[45] Yet from her analysis and this conclusion one should surely derive the alternative conclusion that if holdings between seven and ten acres made up only a quarter of the holdings in 'some' areas, and the tiny holdings typical of relatively free medieval Kent gavelkind country had completely disappeared, then the larger capitalist farms worked by wage labour *were* certainly widespread by 1550. My own study of Kent in Part II will reinforce this alternative conclusion.

Jane Whittle's statement that there was no significant structural change between 1440 and 1580 in England has already been criticised by Wood and myself in the previous chapter. This aside it is worth noting that a few years

---

43   Mate 2006.

44   Mate 2010, p. 18.

45   Mate 2006, p. 213.

later Whittle substantially modified this influential thesis although without reference to these problems in her earlier work. She now concedes that *there were fundamental changes before 1580*. She says that the social structure of the late sixteenth century was fundamentally different to that of the fourteenth century:

> In the fourteenth century there was a gulf between manorial lords and everyone else, be they poor freeholders or servile tenants. By the late sixteenth century a new gulf had emerged between lords and large tenants on the one hand, and the landless and near landless on the other ... By the late sixteenth century ... we can say that some parts of England already looked more capitalist than peasant, in that farming was primarily profit rather than subsistence-orientated. The unusual situation of a substantial tenantry, unburdened by serfdom, and lightly burdened by rents and taxes, had allowed a substantial capitalist farming sector to develop away from the direct control of the gentry and aristocracy. Typically these capitalist farmers or yeomen held a mixture of freehold, customary and leasehold land, their farms were large but rarely greater than 150 acres, and they relied chiefly on the labour of family and servants rather than day labourers. It was the emergence of these men which led to a polarisation of rural society below the level of the gentry, between those with land and those without, transforming the nature of village communities.[46]

Also as we have seen in the previous chapter she more recently stated that the conflicts of 1549 were 'a symptom of agrarian capitalism', thereby conceding in even more stark fashion that profound structural change must indeed have taken place before the 1540s.[47]

iv   Resistance and Periodising the Origin of Capitalism

In the previous chapter I examined the anti-enclosure rebellions of 1549 in terms of changing relationships between lords and peasants, in particular in terms of the mutual relationship between increasingly wealthy yeomen and increasingly commercially minded landlords. I discussed arguments by Wood and Whittle concluding that because of the latter changes, which were

---

46   Whittle 2004, p. 246.

47   Whittle 2010, pp. 47–8.

fundamental to the transition to capitalism, the rebellion of 1549 was 'a messy three-way conflict' between lords, yeomen and the peasant and poor commons. This was in contrast to the rebellions of 1381 and 1450 that were more clearly defined as a conflict between lords and peasants (and their urban counterparts). It remains here to remark more broadly on the significance of the rebellions of the first half of the sixteenth century up until 1549 as indicators of the periodisation of the origin to capitalism.

The rebellion of 1549 has traditionally been regarded as 'Kett's rebellion' and as a result attention is usually focused on a limited geographical area, that of Norfolk. Remarkable new work has placed more emphasis on there being a broadly based *national* rebellion that took place across southern and eastern England, and one that did not have a single figurehead. Even in Norfolk itself Robert Kett was only one of a number of the 'leaders' of the rising in that county, his name being preserved for posterity by a hysterical gentry that aimed to vent its spleen on a particular symbol. From Somerset and Wiltshire in the south-west, through the Thames Valley area of Oxfordshire, Buckinghamshire and Berkshire to Norfolk, Suffolk, Surrey and Kent in the east, the targets of the rebellions were enclosing and emparking landlords and farmers. A huge anti-monarchy and anti-gentry rising also took place at the same time in Yorkshire, and another known as the 'Western Rising' took place in Cornwall and Devon which was largely against radical Protestant reforms, but also involved tenurial disputes.

The rebellions of 1549 were foreshadowed in the 1530s which witnessed other major rebellions. Recent work on popular attitudes to the Reformation and the dissolution of the monasteries reveals that the English peasantry and artisans in town and countryside viewed these so-called religious changes as a wider movement of expropriation. When the Catholic queen Mary was placed on the English throne on a tide of popular support in 1553 this had less to do with religious preference than with the desire to remove the members of the incumbent regime who had supported widespread illegal enclosure and who had brutally put down the rebellion of 1549 and executed the duke of Somerset ('Protector Somerset') whose commissions almost all of the enclosers in the privy council had opposed.

The insurrections by the commons in both towns and countryside in 1548 and 1549 were coordinated over large regions. The timing of the insurrections is significant. They were a response to three declarations by Protector Somerset to send enclosure commissioners around the country to look into illegal enclosures. While some commissioners like John Hales were allies of Somerset, most of them were the very gentry that had been committing the enclosures. For the commons – that is, ordinary peasants and poor in town and countryside across southern and eastern England – the declarations leading to these commissions provided them with the legal and political authority to rebel against those gentry who had been destroying villages and replacing them with parks, and against those who had overstocked or encroached on the peasants' common land. It seems to have been the attack on common land and its relationship with the increasing exclusiveness of power locally and in the counties that was at the forefront of grievances. As mentioned earlier, common grazing land and common rights over fuel for smaller landholders were crucial pillars of their household economies and their very survival as peasants. The local polity that was built around their organisation was also very important.

The rapid coordination, the genocidal anti-gentry rhetoric, and the intention to fight to the death that many of these peasant-artisan militias displayed and expressed are indications that grievances were long-standing. The increasing seigneurial offensive against common lands and common rights, and the racking of rents and entry fines, was fuelled by the dissolution of the monasteries and the transference to gentry and wealthy yeomen of properties that they had only a speculative interest in. This offensive left small tenants, and sometimes larger tenants, with little choice but rebel. The decline of such widespread insurrection thereafter that Wood points to and that we have discussed in the previous chapter was less to do with some of the yeomen leaders moving closer to the lords than with the defeat of this desperate rebellion which resulted in the slaughter of thousands of rebels and execution of many of the survivors.[48]

In conclusion, the origin of capitalism in England can be firmly located in the long fifteenth century, the period in which social-property relations were remodelled. By 1600 the first two elements of the agrarian capitalist social-property relations triad were the dominant economic, political and ideological force. The orthodox Marxist and Smithian perspectives which view the key capitalist social structural changes as driven by continuous developments in the forces of production cannot be sustained. As Brenner has argued, and as is now virtually incontestable, unprecedented commercial and demographic growth in the up-phase of the feudal economy between 1100 and 1300, and within the framework of feudal social-property relations, led to a serious decline in labour productivity and feudal crisis. Historians who point to the consolidation and extension of enclosure, the widespread application of available techniques of agrarian production, developments in overseas trade, New World colonisation and super profits from slavery, industrialisation, profound

---

48 For the foregoing discussion on 1549 see Wood 2007. For new work on popular attitudes to the Reformation in England see Shagan 2003.

social polarisation and changes in political attitudes in the period between 1550 and 1750 as the most decisive or pivotal for the transition to capitalism, can say that these developments were important elements and stages in the transition from feudalism to capitalism. And yet while they were important – perhaps with regard to the consolidation and extension of enclosure even decisive – they were by no means formative. These post-1550 developments took the form of the consolidation and extension of an economic and political logic that had been created by a historic rupture in social-property relations in the previous period, a new logic that was the exception among regions and polities in Europe.

Capitalism did not originate in a period of demographic and commercial expansion breaking through the fetters of the old system having grown up in its instices. It originated in the aftermath of demographic collapse and subsequent stagnation, and during a period of relative economic recession in terms of output for the most part. In the face of peasant mobility and resulting stagnating rents and increasing wages, lords were forced to transfer their demesne property by lease to the upper stratum of a broadly prosperous peasantry. With the unprecedented co-opting of these yeomen into a new political nexus of mutual interests between lord and farmer the scales of the class struggle increasingly tipped in favour of the latter from the 1440s, against the broader peasantry, and it is from here that we see the emergence of agrarian capitalism growing up in the shell of the lords' estate system.

CHAPTER 8

Orthodox Marxism versus Political Marxism

Robert Brenner and political Marxists have come under fierce criticism in recent studies by orthodox Marxists such as Chris Harman, Henry Heller and Neil Davidson. Material production – the imperative for human beings to produce the means with which to reproduce themselves – lies at the heart of historical materialism. Political Marxists prioritise the established social-property relations of a particular society, and they therefore focus on how these relations, *both within and between the main classes*, determine access to the means of production, subsistence and the distribution and use of the surplus product. Orthodox Marxists locate the immediate processes of production at the *forefront* of their perspective and they therefore prioritise the productive forces – that is, the means, methods and techniques in the immediate production process and its social organisation. The extent of the differences in approach can be gauged by a recent deliberately provocative statement by Neil Davidson:

> Perhaps more than any other Marxist tendency since Althusserianism ... political Marxism claims to have discovered a unique insight into the meaning of Marx's writings, a meaning undisclosed to previous generations of Marxists and perhaps even to Marx himself. I regard these claims as wholly illusionary, but they have been accepted by people who fail to understand the extremity of what is implied. If the Brenner thesis – and certainly the version associated with Wood – is correct, then any aspirations we may have for a socialist future are solely dependent on the outcome of the voluntarist clash of wills ... and that if Marx had held the position that political Marxism ascribes to him, then he would effectively have abandoned not merely the less precise early formulations found in, for example, *The German Ideology*, but the entire theoretical basis of historical materialism.[1]

This recent orthodox Marxist critique against Brenner and political Marxists often falls into the same category as the non-Marxist critiques that have been presented in earlier chapters, not in the least because the latter have often provided the historical authority for the former: for example, the charges include the so-called detachment of social relations from economic and demographic

---

1 Davidson 2012, pp. 398–9.

forces, the lack of an endogenous source of change, and a top-down, ruling-class centred approach to the transition from feudalism to capitalism. But, as the above quote indicates, rather than generate a plausible, objective historical analysis which has the potential to persuade those who do not hold orthodox Marxist views, the critique is entirely driven by the requirement to protect and promote a vision of revolutionary socialist transformation in the future. As we shall see, the accusation of voluntarism – among other things – against Robert Brenner and Ellen Meiksins Wood (the Wood referred to in the above quote) stems from a total misreading of Brenner's thesis and its application by Wood and other political Marxists such as George Comninel, Benno Teschke and Charles Post. Far from abandoning historical materialism, Brenner's social-property relations perspective has sought to bring it to life by rejecting the tendency to teleology and techno-determinism in earlier orthodox accounts. This tendency leads to easy dismissals of Marxism by historians such as Steve Rigby who otherwise recognise the fruitfulness of a historical materialist approach in generating historical knowledge. Unfortunately, by also reading Brenner through the prism of orthodox Marxism, he has understandably resorted to a liberal pluralism as the most plausible way forward.[2]

The aim of this chapter is to address this recent challenge to political Marxism by the orthodox Marxist perspective, particularly the work of Davidson. I aim to demonstrate that Davidson's work, both historical and theoretical, repeats the teleology and techno-determinism found throughout Marx's work and the subsequent orthodox tradition and that, moreover, its flaws are further exposed in Davidson's misreading of every aspect of Brenner's thesis. At the same time, given the tendency for historians to read Brenner's thesis through the prism of orthodox Marxism, the contrast will hopefully further illuminate Brenner's distinctive approach, and lead historians such as Rigby to re-examine their preference for a pluralist approach over Brenner's class-centred thesis.

i   The Theoretical Foundations and Project of Orthodox Marxism

Historical materialism is an ambitious totalising theory which claims to account for the whole social process of history or, in other words, the economic, social, political and ideological interrelations of a particular society, its historical development and transition to another form of society. Historical materialism as theorised by orthodox Marxism achieves this interrelated

---

2 Rigby 1998; Chapter Two above.

totality in the following way: gradual cumulative changes in the forces of production (means of production, methods and techniques of labour) determine
or shape the social relations of production (that is, the class relations and division of labour around the immediate process of production) and these in turn
determine the nature of wider relations (legal, political, ideological 'superstructure'). The determination, it is argued, is not all one way, and the determinants are themselves determined in complex ways. Regarding transitions from
one society to another, the proposal of this thesis is that in all class societies
the direct producers will, where possible, always aim to increase their wealth
by seeking gains from trade through changes in productive organisation, in
other words by specialising production in response to price changes for particular commodities. This results in improvements in technology and therefore
improvements in labour productivity and economic development. At a certain
stage in the development of the productive forces within *any* form of society or
mode of production, the old social relations of production present an obstacle
to the further development of these forces. An era of social revolution therefore begins because the development of the productive forces brings into being
a new class or classes from below which are better able to develop the productive forces and economy that formed them in the first place. If the old ruling
class resists its impending obsolescence in the face of new economic and social
forces it will either be defeated in violent (bourgeois or proletarian) revolution,
or the society will collapse under the weight of its fetters.[3]

This outline is based on Chris Harman's interpretation of Marx's 'Preface' to
A Contribution to the Critique of Political Economy in his recent *Marxism and*

---

3 Probably all Marxist historians began with this model at one time and had it in mind while
doing research. In a work on English towns and the transition published in 2007, although
written in 2002, I was still struggling with the theoretical relationship between the immediate process of production and wider relations. I had not entirely grasped the implications of
Brenner's perspective on social-property relations, particularly the importance of the link
between vertical and horizontal class relations within a particular society. Although for a
number of years I had been deeply influenced by Brenner's comparative social-property relations perspective and his and Ellen Meiksins Wood's insistence on the specificity and internal solidity of particular societies or modes of production such as feudalism and capitalism,
my interest in the perspective of 'history from below', in 'peoples' history', led me to prioritise
the vertical relationship between lords and peasants, and the way peasants' and artisans
make a living, to the conscious neglect of the study of the preoccupations of monarchies and
aristocracies beyond the limited vertical surplus extraction relationship with the peasantry.
The study of conquest, battles and state and legal constitutions forms a separate discipline to
social and economic history in most British academies. Bringing the two disciplines together
has been one of the most interesting and hopefully fruitful aspects of my research since then.

History.[4] As it is presented here the theory is transhistorical and therefore ahis-torical because it claims to account for the historical process in all historical societies and for transitions from both feudalism and capitalism. It is teleologi-cal because an analogous historical precedent for a desired future proletarian revolution and transition to socialism is read backwards into earlier so-called bourgeois revolutions and their role in the transition to capitalism. In other words the historical process leading to a future socialist revolution which will overturn capitalism is prefigured in the earlier historical process leading to bourgeois revolution which supposedly overturned feudalism. There is also a sense that class struggle is confined to the 'era of social revolution', which sup-posedly takes place when the forces become incompatible with the relations, rather than being embedded within the structure of everyday life. Also, as Brenner says of the orthodox approach generally, social relations are seen only in terms of the vertical relationship between exploiters and direct producers. *Above all* it appears as if historical change is determined by the techniques and organisation of the immediate productive process itself, hence the tendency to technological determinism.

In order to avoid oversimplifying or caricaturing this recent orthodox Marxist position by discussing the plausibility of abstract models, its theoreti-cal foundation can be more usefully and informatively examined by looking at how it is applied in historical analysis. Throughout this chapter, I will take Davidson as the main representative of this recent orthodox perspective and refer to the others in order to highlight similarities and differences in approach and emphasis. Davidson's recent work is the most thorough and extended of the works, and is set up as the most radical challenge to political Marxism. I begin with a critical appraisal of his work and its relationship to Marx's thought. Then, once the foundations of his theoretical approach have been established, I examine in detail his critique of Brenner and political Marxism.

Davidson has produced a set of studies on the origin of capitalism in Scotland in which he has sought to locate that country within what he believes was the transitional context of Europe more generally. He sets out his approach in the following way:

> Important changes occurred in the feudal mode of production in Europe between the eleventh and seventeenth centuries, but over two distinct periods, each with a different significance. The first period, between the eleventh and thirteenth centuries saw increases in productivity, measur-able by increased crop yields, through the application of technological innovation and direct seigniorial supervision of the labour process. The

4   Marx 1970; Harman 1998, pp. 7–28.

evidence of these centuries demonstrates that feudalism was capable of developing the productive forces, to a degree, without the relations of production posing an obstacle – the capitalist elements in the European economy were in any case of minor importance at the time, except in parts of northern Italy and Flanders. Then the onset of general crisis early in the fourteenth century indicated that the epoch in which feudalism represented an economically progressive stage in human development had come to an end, but that capitalism was not yet in a position to replace it. In the second period, between the resumption of economic growth in the mid-fifteenth century and the late seventeenth century, increases in productivity ceased to be generated by the feudal system itself, but instead by those still subordinate but by now expanding sectors based on commodity production, and consequently on money as a medium of exchange.

In response to these developments the feudal system began to display two new characteristics, both of which however left the central exploitative process unchanged. One was the form in which the surplus was appropriated. The general commutation of servile dues and the attendant shifts from labour rent through rent in kind to money rent refined the system without bringing about the domination of capitalist relations of production – the existence of money being a necessary, but insufficient condition for this to take place. The other was in the nature of the state. By the middle of the fifteenth century absolutism had begun to replace the estates monarchies of military feudalism as the typical state for across most of Europe. The two were linked. One of the conditions for the emergence of absolutism was the increasing social weight of those classes – particularly the mercantile bourgeoisie – for whom money played an increasingly important role as a means of exchange. Neither characteristic developed very far in Scotland. The effect of the Glorious Revolution in 1688, in Scotland and England, was the destruction of the absolutist state of James VII and II, but the meaning of this act was different in each country. England had virtually completed the transition from feudalism to capitalism by 1688 and the Revolution therefore consolidated the rise to power of the agrarian and mercantile bourgeoisie which had begun centuries before under the Tudors. Scotland had hardly begun the transition from feudalism to capitalism by 1688 and the revolution therefore merely restored to power the feudal landowning classes whose authority had been temporarily displaced by the Stuart experiment.[5]

---

5   Davidson 2004a, pp. 231–2: paraphrased in Davidson 2012, p. 513.

This passage is clearly a reiteration of Harman's interpretation of Marx's 'Preface'. For Davidson, between 1100 and 1300 'feudalism' developed the productive forces through technological innovation, and the increased productivity levels can be measured by improved crop yields. The level of the development of the productive forces achieved at this stage did not pose a threat to existing feudal relations of production because these existing relations corresponded to, and functioned with, this level of development; they were not 'an obstacle' to further development. Forms of capitalist production can be identified at this stage and they reflected developments in the productive forces, but generally 'capitalist elements' were of minor importance and were not capable of developing the productive forces beyond that already achieved within feudalism. So the positive development of the productive forces within feudalism in these pre-crisis centuries 'represented an economically progressive stage in human development'. However, the general crisis of the fourteenth century indicates that feudalism had exhausted itself and was no longer able to develop the productive forces in order to increase productivity beyond the current level. Development of the productive forces could only resume with the 'resumption of economic growth' (developing trade and population) from the mid-fifteenth century by new social relations developing from below – that is, by those that were 'still subordinate'. These new social relations were linked to developing commodity production and money as a medium of exchange – by the latter Davidson appears to mean emerging capitalism. By ending the period under examination at the end of the seventeenth century, Davidson appears to refer to what he views as a bourgeois revolution in England in which these new capitalist relations growing in the womb of the old society destroyed the fetters (the absolutist state) that were holding back continued development of the productive forces. The development of the agrarian and mercantile bourgeoisie or capitalists, along with the development of money rents and trade accompanies, or is a condition of, the development of a new centralised form of state, absolutism, across most of Europe, which he therefore appears to identify as a European-wide process of transition from feudalism to capitalism. These capitalists were better able to develop the productive forces than was hitherto possible by the old feudal relations, although the old form of exploitation remained in place in the form of the central absolutist state. England represented the most advanced case of this transition by the late seventeenth century and these new classes from below destroyed the absolutist state which posed an obstacle to the further development of the productive forces.

There are many problems with this account of the transition to capitalism: for example, the contention that it was driven from below and the related bourgeois-capitalist nature of the revolution of 1688; the so-called capitalist nature of absolutism – minus the king and state apparatus; and the transition as a parallel development across western Europe. These problems will be addressed below in the analysis of Davidson's critique of Brenner. For now we can recognise the orthodox Marxist techno-determinism and teleology in Davidson's approach to the transition that I identified above with Harman. It is techno-determinist because of the central or prime focus on the development of the productive forces, and teleological because the development of the productive forces within feudalism is viewed as a progressive stage in 'human social development', to be superseded by the next progressive stage – capitalism. A serious, and closely related, problem for Davidson is that his trans-historical approach, his lack of recognition of the highly specific economic processes in historical societies such as feudalism, leads him to the assumption that the productive forces were developed between 1100 and 1300 following the establishment of feudal social (property) relations to such an extent as to lead to feudal crisis. Davidson recognises elsewhere that it is increases in the social-productivity of labour that is all-important for genuine economic growth and 'human social development' and it is this that technological developments are geared towards. And yet here he unaccountably confuses land productivity, or output from the land, with labour productivity, or output by each labourer. Land productivity increased significantly between 1200 and 1300 but this was due to an increasing number of inputs from labourers, the result of overpopulation on jurisdictionally defined resources or politically constituted property. As Bruce Campbell calculated, and as I have discussed in an earlier chapter, labour productivity in England fell by 60 percent in the same period. In other words, this increase in *land* productivity was achieved at the expense of *labour* productivity. The key purpose of technological application is to cut costs, and it does this by increasing labour productivity, or the amount of productive output an individual labour is able to produce in the same amount of time as before, without destroying the labourer's capacity to labour by overwork. Only ongoing, systematic improvements in labour productivity will generate sustained growth.[6]

---

6   Davidson's assertion that improved yields took place 'through the application of technological innovation and direct seigniorial supervision of the labour process' is highly misleading. To begin with, as his colleague Chris Harman recognised, improvements in agricultural technology in this period were 'scant': Harman 1988, pp. 79–81. Second, there was no direct seigniorial supervision of the labour process, outside the lords' demesnes at least. Peasant possession, a key aspect of the internal solidity of non-capitalist societies ensured that it was the peasants who were the skilled agriculturalists, and carried on production independently of the lord within their communal productive organisations. Lords could only interfere by political means from outside.

Feudal society was dynamic in this period if we examine it in terms of its ability to develop trade, increase rapidly the number of village and small town markets, and urbanise – that is, increase the proportion of town dwellers to rural dwellers. But that dynamism had little to do with increases in the productivity of *labour* on the land, which would have allowed an increasingly greater proportion of people to move or be moved out of agriculture and into industry, and the continuous development of larger capitalised units of production. Overseas commerce and its tributaries were largely the product of a luxury trade dependent on aristocratic demand, and the founding of small towns and village markets were the product of the lords' extensive development at a time of population expansion. These were strategies that the lords employed to improve their income channels (through tolls, customs and market court profits) in order to maintain their economic and political position in relation to other lords, as well as to satiate increased demands for non-productive expenditure on warfare and display. Indeed, towns were agents of conquest and were founded around castles as a means of supplying the armies and officials that maintained them. For example they were essential in the conquests undertaken by the English crown and nobility in Wales and Gascony in France in the twelfth and thirteenth centuries. Even after serfdom was thrown off, without the development of leasehold farmers producing in competition there was no systematic impulse to improve labour productivity. It cannot be doubted however, as I have stressed in previous chapters, that developments in commerce and market integration in this period were very significant, and the development of capitalism does not make sense without these prior developments. However there was no necessary or even logical step from here to specifically capitalist social-property relations. The same commercial developments occurred throughout Europe, in many parts of Europe more advanced compared to England, without generating capitalism, even if pockets of capitalist *production* can be identified in some places. States or polities on the continent became increasingly centralised on the model of absolutist monarchies which retained and depended upon a mass peasantry on the land.

This non-development of the productive forces, that is, specifically the lack of increase and even marked cyclical decline in labour productivity in feudal and absolutist societies based on mass peasant production more generally was recognised by Marx. Indeed increasingly in *Capital* one sees Marx moving towards a perspective which points to the specificity of modes of production and their internal solidity in the face of developing commerce. And yet in contradiction he still sought to apply the transhistorical model of his earlier theory. This can be demonstrated by examining how Marx justifies his theory historically. At the end of the first volume of *Capital*, Marx explained how the theory could be applied both historically and for a future transition to social-ism. Not surprisingly he was unable to explain how the productive forces were developed within feudalism and absolutism thereby generating capitalism. For peasant society, Marx took as his model 'the petty mode of production' of small free proprietors – without serfdom – and this clearly reflected his knowledge of the French peasantry of the first half of the nineteenth century which he had so much to say about in his *Eighteenth Brumaire of Louis Bonaparte* and in the third volume of *Capital*:

> This mode of production pre-supposes the fragmentation of holdings, and the dispersal of the other means of production. As it excludes the concentration of these means of production, so it also excludes co-operation, division of labour within each separate process of production, the social control and regulation of the forces of nature, and the free development of the productive forces of society. It is compatible only with a system of production and a society moving within narrow limits which are of natural origin. To perpetuate it would be, as Pecqueur rightly says, "to decree universal mediocrity".[7]

As a preliminary to this statement Marx recognised that 'this [petty] mode of production also exists under slavery, serfdom, and other situations of depen-dence. But it flourishes, unleashes the whole of its energy, attains its adequate classical form, only where the worker is the free proprietor of the conditions of his labour, and sets them in motion himself: where the peasant owns the land he cultivates, or the artisan owns the tool with which he is an accomplished performer'.[8] So, even with this unleashing of its whole energy after the throw-ing off of serfdom, Marx is saying that this petty mode of production 'excludes ... the free development of the productive forces of society' or, in other words, that the productive forces are not developed within this mode beyond 'narrow limits and which are of natural origin'; how much less so would that be the case where the peasant labour and peasant surplus product was coerced through serfdom. Nevertheless to fit the transhistorical model, and in stark contradiction, Marx states that somehow, '[a]t a certain stage of development it [the petty/feudal mode of production] brings into the world

---

7 Marx 1990, pp. 927–8. By 'co-operation', Marx is referring to the specific way production is organised in capitalist industry. Of course co-operation in the more general sense of sharing tasks and resources took place in medieval villages as agricultural production was commu-nally organised.

8 Marx 1990, p. 927.

the material means for its own destruction. From that moment, new forces and new passions spring up in the bosom of society, forces and passions which feel themselves to be fettered by society. It has to be annihilated; it is annihilated'.[9]

Marx's evident teleological distaste for this mediocre, natural way of life, its non-progressive tendencies, its disallowance of a transition to capitalism and hence also of the desired future transition to socialism which requires capitalism to precede it, is only surpassed by his revulsion towards the processes of its dissolution which amount to the forcible removal of the mass of the peasantry:

> Its annihilation, the transformation of the individualised and scattered means of production into socially concentrated means of production, the transformation, therefore, of the dwarf-like property of the many into the giant property of the few, and the expropriation the great mass of the people from the soil, from the means of subsistence, and from the instruments of labour, this terrible and arduously accomplished expropriation of the mass of the people forms the pre-history of capital. It comprises a whole series of forcible methods, and we have passed in review those that have been epoch-making as methods of the primitive accumulation of capital. The expropriation of the direct producers was accomplished by means of the most merciless barbarism, and under the stimulus of the most infamous, the most sordid, the most petty and the most odious of passions.[10]

So to recap, Marx is acutely aware that the removal of the peasantry is required as the prelude for the history of capitalism, but his own analysis of the nature of that mode of production, and the forms of economic development applicable to it, reveals that it is incompatible with the transhistorical Marxist theory. While significant peasant economic development was possible either with or without serfdom, which Brenner and Marx recognised, there was no systematic or even significant sustained development of the productive forces in agriculture in a mode of production overwhelmingly based on a mass peasantry and a feudal or absolutist style ruling class coercing it. So the development of the productive forces cannot and most demonstrably has not created the material agencies or social forces which could lead to the dissolution of this mode. The dissolution only occurs with the expropriation of the peasantry.

---

9   Marx 1990, p. 928.
10 Marx 1990, p. 928.

However, after the expropriation of the peasantry has reached a certain point, it is here that Marx's theory becomes plausible and powerful: it is what happens next, the development of capitalism and the theoretical transition from capitalism to socialism to which it is most suited and for which it was surely generated. It is necessarily quoted in full:

> Private property which is personally earned, in other words that which is based, as it were, on the fusing together of the isolated, independent working individual with the conditions of his labour, is supplanted by capitalist private property, which rests on the exploitation of alien, but formally free labour.
>
> As soon as this metamorphosis has sufficiently decomposed the old society throughout its depth and breadth, as soon as the workers have been turned into proletarians, and their means of labour into capital, as soon as the capitalist mode of production stands on its own feet, the further socialisation of labour and the further transformation of the soil and other means of production into socially exploited and therefore communal means of production takes on a new form. What is now to be expropriated is not the self-employed worker, but the capitalist who exploits a large number of workers.[11]
>
> This expropriation is accomplished through the action of the immanent laws of capitalist production itself, through the centralisation of capitals. One capitalist always strikes down many others. Hand in hand with this centralisation, or this expropriation of many capitalists by a few, other developments take place on an ever increasing scale, such as the growth of the co-operative form of the labour-process, the conscious technical application of science, the planned exploitation of the soil, the transformation of the means of labour into forms in which they can only be used in common, the economising of all means of production by their use as the means of production of combined socialised labour, the entanglement of all peoples in the net of the world market, and with this, the growth of the international character of the capitalist regime. Along with the constant decrease in the number of capitalist magnates, who usurp and monopolise all the advantages of this process of transformation, the mass of misery, oppression, slavery, degradation grows; but with this there also grows the revolt of the working class, a class constantly

---

11   By 'self-employed worker' Marx is referring to a peasant or artisan. By the 'socialisation of labour' Marx is referring to the concentration of labourers into towns and factories in capitalism, following their removal from the land.

increasing in numbers, and trained, united and organised by the very mechanism of the capitalist process of capitalist production. The monopoly of capital becomes a fetter upon the mode of production which has flourished alongside and under it. The centralisation of the means of production and the socialisation of labour reach a point at which they become incompatible with their capitalist integument. This integument is burst asunder. The knell of capitalist private property sounds. The expropriators are expropriated.

The capitalist mode of appropriation, which springs from the capitalist mode of production, produces capitalist private property. This is the first negation of individual private property, as founded on the labour of its proprietor.[12] But capitalist production begets, with the inexorability of a natural process, its own negation. This is the negation of the negation. It does not re-establish private property, but it does indeed establish individual property on the basis of the achievements of the capitalist era: namely co-operation and the possession in common of the land and the means of production produced by labour itself.

The transformation of scattered private property resting on the personal labour of the individuals themselves into capitalist private property is naturally an incomparably more protracted, violent and difficult process than the transformation of capitalistic private property, which in fact already rests on the carrying on of production by society into socialised property. In the former case, it was a matter of the expropriation of the mass of the people by a few usurpers; in the latter, we have the expropriation of a few usurpers by the mass of the people.[13]

Marx recognises here that the absolute development of the productive forces occurs only 'once capitalism stands on its own feet' through competition between capitalists, cost cutting through technical application, making economies of scale through further centralisation of production and thereby the socialisation of the now free labour force, detached from its own means of labour, its means of subsistence. This centralising of production and socialising of labour is in direct contrast to, and the negation of, the scattering of production and producers on the land in feudalism and the 'petty mode of production' generally. As capitalists buy each other up in the competitive process (expropriate each other), for Marx, it is the over-monopolisation of production into few hands and the integration of the whole earth within this

---

12   For example, peasant proprietorship.
13   Marx 1990, pp. 929–30.

monopoly that causes capitalism's dissolution, presumably because capitalist units can no longer expand and without competition there is no imperative to develop the productive forces. But capitalism is dissolved by 'the mode of production, which has flourished along with and under it', based upon the centralisation of production and the socialisation of labour, especially in towns and factories: this occurs as the specific result of capitalist development itself.

The different, highly specific, 'laws of motion' that distinguish feudalism and capitalism could not be more starkly put. Moreover, agency in the dissolution of the respective modes of feudalism and capitalism is entirely different, and turned upside down. For Marx, the capitalist transition from feudalism was driven from above, 'by a few usurpers', while the projected transition from capitalism to socialism is driven from below, 'by the mass of people'. There would appear to be little scope for Marx's transhistorical theory here, except in stark contradiction to the historical analysis and narrative. More will be said about the agency of the 'few usurpers' in the transition to capitalism below.

It turns out that, for Davidson, Marx's theory is not as applicable to both bourgeois and socialist revolutions as he would like, but not for the same reasons that we have identified in the foregoing. Although, as we have seen, Marx was unable to demonstrate how the forces of production are developed within the petty mode of production or feudalism, and that forcible expropriation from above was required for a transition to capitalism, Davidson suggests that Marx in the 'Preface' 'is taking the transition *from feudalism to capitalism* as his model for transitions and revolutions more generally'.[14] In other words, Marx's transhistorical model was based on the earlier bourgeois transition, not the later socialist one. Regarding the model's applicability to the transition *from capitalism to socialism*, Davidson states that, 'there are problems with [Marx's] generalisation since the working class, unlike the bourgeoisie, cannot become the bearer of new social relations prior to actually seizing political power'. Following Georg Lukàcs, one of the post-Leninist thinkers in the 1920s, he argues that, 'Because the working class is non-exploitative there is no prior development of an alternative socialist or communist mode of production' and that to think otherwise would be 'utopian fantasy'. For Davidson it follows that, with the transition to socialism, 'The process of transition therefore *begins* with the destruction of capitalist states and the substitution of transitional soviet "states that are not states" – but only as prelude to their ultimate self-dissolution, as capitalist (and in some cases residual pre-capitalist) productive relations are replaced by socialist ones'.[15]

---

14   Davidson 2012, p. 156.
15   Davidson 2012, p. 498.

Davidson, despite his insistence on the importance of revolutions from below in Marx's earlier transhistorical theory, repeats the pessimism shown by Marxist intellectuals in the early twentieth century towards working people as potential agents of radical historical change along the lines that Marx predicted.[16] All the elements for revolution predicted by Marx following the development of the productive forces under capitalism appear to be present in much of the world, and have been longstanding particularly in western Europe and the USA: the centralisation of productive units, the socialisation of labour and massive capitalist monopolies. But quite understandably the working class, and wage workers more generally, will not show any tendency or interest in socialist revolution or radical change of any sort while the vast majority still have the most rational option of doing what they have always done to maintain themselves and their families – their immediate challenge – and that is to seek capitalist employment. This tests the patience of orthodox Marxists, and hence Davidson has opted to retain all that was unworkable and suspect in Marx's theory, the techno-determinism and the teleology, and then proceeded to distort its most fruitful, powerful and demonstrably accurate aspect. Davidson's thinking is closer to the preoccupations of Lenin and Trotsky during the revolutionary period in Russia in the early twentieth century than to Marx, and as such it is geared to justify a particular and potentially disastrous revolutionary approach to political activism in the present. Marx, as we have seen, was clear that a new mode of production develops within capitalism eventually leading to its dissolution. The revolutionary precedent Davidson really wants to invoke is what took place in Russia in 1917 rather than in England in 1688 and in France in 1789. For him, socialism will need to be built from scratch after a violent global revolutionary event. This will no doubt be led top down by a revolutionary vanguard of charismatic orthodox Marxists.

Rather than reject Marx's thesis that socialism as a mode of production develops within capitalism, and leads to its dissolution, it is possible to demonstrate how this works, and point to ways forward that are far more plausible and desirable than violent revolution. Such speculation should not be the preoccupation of Marxists alone but that of any responsible citizen who is prepared to consider alternatives to capitalism should the latter prove unfit for purpose. Because of its specific 'laws of motion' capitalist development leads to the centralisation of production, the socialisation of labour and business

---

16   This is of course the attitude that the British Marxist tradition sought to counteract by showing both the potential of working class movements historically and the powerful forces with which they have had to contend: see for example Thompson 1991, and Saville 1987.

monopolies. But these developments in themselves do not represent a socialist mode of production developing within capitalism, no more than commercial expansion and urbanisation represent a capitalist mode of production developing within feudalism. However, with these prior developments within capitalism, alternatives to violent revolution present themselves. For example, if, due to a chronic crisis of capitalism, wage workers no longer had the option of seeking capitalist employment, concessions born out of necessity in industrial and agrarian production may be drawn from big business and the state in the form of co-operative, non-market ventures, following perhaps the election of a party given a mandate for necessary radical change. If these ventures were successful they would expand from there and require a further piecemeal reformation in the state over time. This is how a more socialised, co-operative, democratic mode of production could develop in a potentially, relatively non-violent way within capitalism, and genuinely from the bottom up. It is, arguably, only in a way such as this that any alternative to capitalism could be generated on any solid foundations, acceptable to the vast majority. As we shall see, because of their misreading of social-property relations, or relations of reproduction, orthodox Marxists describe Brenner's use of class struggle as voluntarist, and yet the orthodox Marxist perspective on socialist revolution displays a voluntarism of the most dangerous sort.

Davidson's contrast between the Scottish path to capitalism and the English path is also revealing of this orthodox approach. In the section on primitive accumulation in *Capital*, Marx pointed to the expropriation of the peasantry in the Highlands of Scotland which took place at the time he was writing, as a current example of what happened in England in the late medieval and Tudor period. However, Davidson argues that these belated clearances in the Highlands of Scotland, that is, the expropriation of the peasantry, largely in a short space of time during the 1840s and 1850s, did not form part of the transition to capitalism in Britain, and had nothing to do with Marx's 'primitive accumulation' or expropriation of the peasantry, because capitalism was already established elsewhere in Britain and was already under threat by socialised wage labour in the form of the Chartist movement. In fact the expropriators of the Scottish Highland peasants were,

> members of an existing, and thoroughly rapacious, capitalist landowning class seeking to increase their income as efficiently as possible; a class whose disregard for human life (and, indeed, 'development') marked it as having long passed the stage of contributing to social progress. Precisely because these events were not a consequence of the transition to capitalism, but of its established laws of motion, the successful displacement of

the Highlanders should not be seen as inevitable, let alone 'progressive', but as an unnecessary political defeat for the exploited and oppressed.[17]

Davidson is implying here that those lords who expropriated peasants *during* the transition from feudalism to capitalism *were* contributing to social progress, *did* have a regard for human life and human 'development', and their actions were by some measure inevitable presumably given the historical necessity to develop the productive forces. And, unlike in Scotland where the expropriation of the Scottish Highland peasantry was 'an unnecessary political defeat for the exploited and oppressed', by implication, the expropriation which amounted to the defeat of the mass of peasantry in England from the late fifteenth century was for Davidson therefore a *necessary* political defeat historically because these peasants were no longer able to develop the productive forces. I wonder if Davidson recognises the implications of what he has written. The inference appears to be that he is as easy with human life in the past as he is with it in the future given the nature of his revolutionary perspective. During his theoretical critique of Brenner, and other political Marxists, Davidson states that '[o]ne does not have to accept, in Second International or Stalinist style, that human social development has gone through a succession of inevitable stages to reject the ascription of absolute randomness to key historical turning points as a viable alternative'.[18] The latter position is what Davidson completely incorrectly attributes to Brenner as we shall see; and his application of what he asserts is Marx's once and for all time undeveloped and fixed theoretical approach in his own historical work closely resembles the former ahistorical, stagist position that he says he finds unacceptable.

Having examined the nature of current orthodox Marxism in terms of its theoretical foundations and its applicability, we can now examine more profitably orthodox Marxist critiques of Brenner and political Marxists. In these critiques they, like the non-Marxists, not only reveal their entire lack of grasp of Brenner's thesis but also expose the severe limitations of their own approaches.

ii   Feudal Social-Property Relations

Davidson believes Brenner's application of class as social-property relations to be too narrowly conceived as a historical materialist theory because it is, he asserts, unable to encompass the totality of relations in a particular society.

---

17   Davidson 2004a, p. 229.
18   Davidson 2012, p. 420.

He says that Brenner and the political Marxists have no terms to explain events that lie outside of social-property relationships and that when they do address wider aspects of a particular society they are therefore subject to Rigby's charge of pluralism. I will argue that it is not the application of class as social-property relations that is narrowly conceived, just Davidson's own presentation of it. For example, Davidson says that the application of social-property relations treats 'non-human aspects of nature as an extraneous factor', and that political Marxism 'has difficulty explaining aspects of human society that are not reducible to "social-property relations"'.[19] Readers who have followed this far will see that this interpretation fails to recognise the dialectical integration of vertical and horizontal relations within social-property relations which encompass all decision-making and strategies for reproduction within a particular society and economy. Orthodox Marxists like Davidson, in common with many non-Marxist critics, essentially view class only in terms of vertical exploitative relations between producers and non-producers. Davidson declines to take on board the crucial difference between the traditional formulation of relations of production and Brenner's relations of *re*production. Relations of production usually refer to the vertical class relations involved in the immediate process of production, the nature of which is usually seen as determined by the means and techniques applied in the latter. The term 'relations of *re*production' refers to a *process* in which the two main classes within a particular society reproduce themselves. This involves horizontal competition and collaboration within these classes as well as the vertical class relationship in the immediate process of production. In other words relations of *re*production express the whole structure of relationships within a particular society, and how particular social classes within that structure *make a living*. Davidson in fact acknowledges that he is aware of the broader meaning of social-property relations in contrast to social relations of production. Refusing to use the political Marxist term, he says, 'Brenner is clearly right to emphasise the multiple levels of oppression, cooperation, and competition involved in social relations of production', and yet Davidson proceeds to overlook the significance of this for understanding the political Marxist approach to specific systems of social relations, and transitions from one to another.[20] It cannot be over-stressed that horizontal class relations are not included in Brenner's thesis as a passing matter of emphasis, they are as crucial for an adequate historical account as vertical class relations. As such they have to be specified at *every stage* of the analysis.

---

19   Davidson 2012, pp. 408–9.
20   Davidson 2012, p. 398.

Like many recent interpretations based upon a certain reading of the work of Adam Smith, Davidson's unilineal view of history as the progressive development of the productive forces ignores the significance of demographic cycles within feudalism and absolutism, and the specificity of social-property relations in these societies which causes them to occur. Given his teleological, stagist perspective, he assumes that a system of wage labour – capitalism – would inevitably emerge out of feudalism due to developments in productivity in town and countryside. Hence he has great problems with Brenner's feudal rules for reproduction based on peasant possession, extra-economic surplus extraction, extensive rather than intensive economic development, and non-productive expenditure on warfare and display, which when taken together lead to a decline in labour productivity, to crisis and cyclical economic non-development. For example, the significance of peasant possession of property and the means of production for understanding relations within feudalism is not grasped. As we saw earlier, Davidson assumes that production was under the supervision of the lords, and Harman too sees the lords driving all the major technical changes within feudalism.[21] This is entirely misleading. It was the peasants who were the expert cultivators, and the peasants who held the vast majority of land in the medieval period. Some lords, usually monastic, developed techniques on their own home farms, but the lord's main productive strategy was generally to extract the surplus through mediators by means of political and military pressure.

Given these substantial blind spots in his interpretation of Brenner's thesis, Davidson finds himself able to describe this cyclical process of feudal economic non-development – which naturally he caricatures – as 'a closed circuit'; and he is exasperated at the thought, given his assumption (or desire) that feudalism *must* develop into capitalism, that 'if Brenner is right, peasant small production could have carried on almost indefinitely beneath pre-capitalist social structures'.[22] Davidson can only conclude that Brenner's thesis, based upon social-property relations, 'conceives of feudalism as a self-enclosed, self-perpetuating system that cannot be undermined by its own internal contradictions'.[23] As we have seen in Chapter One, Brenner argues that the development of capitalism in late medieval and early modern polities within Europe was not the rule but the *exception*; an unintended consequence of specific conflicting feudal rules for reproduction. For Brenner the only cases where capitalism developed were England and the northern Netherlands,

---

21   Harman 1998, p. 77.
22   Davidson 2012, pp. 400–1.
23   Davidson 2012, p. 409.

although sustained continuous development only occurred in England beyond the middle of the eighteenth century. Pressures from these developments then exerted their influence on the other countries as countries and polities in France and Germany sought to compete economically and militarily. Hence Marx's attribution to England of the classic transition to capitalism.

Davidson, Heller and Harman reject Brenner's contention that capitalist social-property relations were so specific to England. Given their unilineal approach they assume that developments in productivity and commerce in medieval Europe and beyond amounted to a developing capitalist *world system*, and therefore must have occurred more broadly across Europe simultaneously. I will examine this argument in more detail below. Here we can address Davidson's scepticism as to how capitalism developed in England out of Brenner's feudal social-property relations. Because, given Brenner's theory that there is no inevitable or even probable development of capitalism from feudalism, and that capitalism is the *least* likely outgrowth of feudalism, Davidson can only assume that on Brenner's terms feudalism had no internal contradiction or endogenous source of change enabling breakdown and a transition to capitalism. Davidson therefore suggests that Brenner is forced to use class struggle as an 'exogenous shock mechanism' by which means he has capitalism emerge out of feudalism in England. And Davidson reinforces this suggestion by applying the same logic to the only other transition to capitalism Brenner recognises in the medieval and early modern period, that of the northern Netherlands. He quips that in England Brenner's exogenous shock is class struggle, in the northern Netherlands it is ecological crisis.[24]

All feudal societies in Europe changed across the medieval period but they generally did not develop capitalism, most developed absolutism. Absolutist states driven by centralised monarchical dictatorship and large bureaucracies generated mercantile capital and expanded world trade through colonisation of the New World, Africa and Asia, but they did not lead to or equate with capitalist development or a transition to capitalism. For Brenner, the internal contradiction within feudalism is not the simple oppositional interests generated between lords and peasants, but conflicting reproductive strategies based upon broader feudal social-property relations stemming from their establishment in the tenth and eleventh centuries. One can see divergent outcomes of class struggle as they were engendered by the conflicting reproductive strategies of specific social-property relations, based on different allocations of property and internal organisation within the two main classes. In England the *unintended* outcome of class struggle, given also broader dialectical relations

24   Davidson 2012, pp. 410–11.

within the main classes, was the transference by leasehold, under duress, of the lords' home farms (very large by European standards) to the wealthier peasantry, which subsequently although not inevitably, led to capitalist expansion through the accumulation and centralisation of previously scattered land-holdings. In the northern Netherlands where the reclamation of peatlands was undertaken by peasants, increasingly free from lordship, this had the unintended consequence of turning the peasants into market-dependent capitalist farmers, because over time the rise in sea levels and the subsidence of the peat due to its exposure made the land too wet to grow bread grains. The peasants' means of subsistence was thereby undermined and they were forced to specialise and innovate in competitive production. This transformation was not caused by an exogenous shock, it was the result of peasant interaction with a particular environment in the Netherlands, engaging in feudal rules for reproduction within a specific set of social-property relations.

Given Davidson's stance on Brenner's feudal social-property relations in his recent more theoretical work, it is all the more remarkable that in his own historical research on the transition in Scotland he has come up with one of the clearest examples so far of the persistence of specific feudal social-property relations and their inability to develop into capitalism.[25] He describes Scotland in the late seventeenth and most of the eighteenth – even the early nineteenth in the Highlands – as a partly feudal, partly tribal society, with highly decentralised sovereignty and, as a consequence, chronically feuding lordships. Most of the peasant rent was still paid in kind and in labour services, and lords enjoyed feudal monopolies over ovens and mills. Davidson says there was *no possibility of change towards capitalism* because there was no development of the productive forces, and change in that direction suited neither the lords nor the peasants, *even though* there was in the seventeenth century, for the first time, a capitalist model south of the border which could be followed. The peasants did not want to starve by becoming market-dependent, and the lords were forced to maintain their status amongst other lords. The maintenance of status and livelihood required the ability to super-exploit the peasantry, the means to retain a military following made up of vassals and sub-vassals, and large numbers of peasant tenants renting their lands on whom they could also draw to fight. For Davidson, while the famine of 1695 revealed to many Scottish lords the limitations of their way of life, it was only after the defeat of the Scottish lords who were opposed to the Union with England at Culloden in 1745, and their pacification that followed through various measures (including de-militarisation), that they decided to impose capitalist

---

25   Davidson 2004a, and 2004b.

social-property relations in Scotland. They did this on the basis of the already existing English model – as far as they could adapt to it – through their own self-transformation from feudal military lords to commercial landlords, and through the eviction and differentiation of the Scottish peasantry, first in the Lowlands and later in the Highlands. For Davidson, in contrast to what he says happened in England, capitalist social-property relations were imposed entirely from above, and the Scottish model formed the prototype for the transition in the rest of Europe during the nineteenth century. We will come to the nature of bottom-up or top-down transitions below. For now we can thank Davidson for his example of feudal social-property relations in Scotland, a country that was only forced to adopt capitalism following pressure from England, the only capitalist nation existing, because like other European nations Scotland was unable to, or did not desire to, generate capitalism endogenously.

Davidson attempts to get around this fundamental contradiction in his work by stating that Brenner's thesis corresponds more closely to the Scottish transition rather than to the actual English transition, and the real origin of capitalism for which it was developed. As just mentioned, the Scottish case 'inadvertently' became the prototype for the other top-down transitions in the more backward countries across Europe, especially post-1848. This began in Prussia where feudal lords supposedly gave up their less lucrative extra-economic powers by transforming themselves into commercial landlords and then imposing differentiation on the peasantry, for instance evicting them, although he does not say how this was possible. He supplements this assertion with a classic Marxist thesis namely the process of 'combined and uneven development' where more backward nations are brought up to date by those more advanced.[26]

Leaving aside for now the fundamental contradiction in Davidson's work, given what he has said about Brenner's thesis the latter should not logically be applicable to *any* transition. It seems that in his historical work, in contrast with his purely theoretical work, the only thing Davidson can find wrong with Brenner's thesis is that in contrast to Scotland where he (Davidson) says the transition was mostly top-down, the English transition was both top-down and bottom-up but probably more bottom-up along with the early bourgeois revolutions. This point will be examined in more detail below. First we need to continue to examine Davidson's critique of social-property relations.

---

26   Davidson 2004b, pp. 415–16.

iii   The Causes of Diverging Outcomes of Class Struggles in Europe

Davidson's assertion that Brenner uses class struggle as an exogenous shock mechanism enables him to conclude that Brenner cannot therefore explain why class struggle in the late medieval period resulted in different outcomes from the crisis of feudalism in different polities and regions across Europe:

> [Brenner's] attempts to deal with this problem are among the least convincing aspects of the entire thesis. Brenner points to the different capacities deployed by the classes involved: these lords had better organisation, those peasants displayed less solidarity; but without an explanation for the prior processes by which these classes acquired their organisational or solidaristic qualities, these are descriptions which, to borrow a favourite expression of Wood's, 'assume precisely what has to be explained'.[27]

This charge that Brenner does not account for the origin of, or prior processes determining, the ability of particular peasant communities in different countries and regions of medieval Europe to resist seigneurial power, as opposed to the outcome of this resistance, is one of the most striking misrepresentations of Brenner's work that I have had to address in this book. It is central to Brenner's thesis that the origin of the strength and organisation of communities of lords and peasants in late medieval Europe can be traced back to the establishment of specific feudal social-property relations within particular polities in the tenth and eleventh centuries. Subsequently, '[i]t was the various property settlements which emerged, in different places, from the later medieval seigneurial reaction and the class conflicts which accompanied that reaction which laid the basis for the dramatic regional divergences which were to characterise economic evolution in the subsequent epoch'.[28] An understanding of the origin of the different levels of class power between lords and peasants in different regions naturally stems from an analysis of the historically specific processes of class formation in different regions.

To repeat, excessively decentralised lordships in competition with monarchy in western Europe following the break up of the Carolingian Empire contrasts with a greater cooperation between monarchy and aristocracy in England. The cooperation and cohesiveness of the latter was the result of the precocious centralisation of power in Anglo-Saxon period, and it was

---

27   Davidson 2012, p. 412.
28   Brenner 1985b, p. 215.

confirmed and taken to another level with the Norman invasion, the Normans having been the most centralised and organised duchy in France. Polities in eastern Europe were conditioned by extensive colonial development. The relatively decentralised polities in continental western Europe resulted in relatively high levels of competition between lords, a relatively small proportion of personal property in relation to that held by the peasantry, and therefore in weaker controls by lords over long-standing, organised peasant communities. This was in contrast to the situation in England where relative cohesiveness between lords as a result of their relatively close relationship with the monarchy, ensured the retention of a much higher proportion of property in relation to the peasantry, and stronger controls over the peasantry. In eastern Europe the early freedoms enjoyed by colonising peasants were overturned due to the weakness of peasant organisation: the undeveloped and individualistic nature of peasant organisation was conditioned by the form of earlier colonial settlement. After the feudal crisis and the subsequent famines and Black Death, the specific differences in feudal social-property relations across Europe – the competition and cohesiveness within the main classes, and the corresponding relationship between the main classes – determined different outcomes which are entirely consistent with those differences. This is one of the most remarkable and powerful aspects of Brenner's comparative approach. The origin and outcome of class struggles can be linked closely and in detail to particular social-property relations within specific polities and traced back to the nature of their establishment in the tenth and eleventh centuries. This is not to go completely the other way and say that the outcomes of these class struggles were predetermined by the different established structures of class relations in Europe. It is to say that the balance of class forces generated by these established structures favoured one side or the other, and that certain outcomes could be expected.

The miscomprehension by orthodox Marxists of this fundamental aspect of Brenner's thesis is further exposed in Harman's work. For the same reason as Davidson, Harman also says that Brenner cannot explain 'why the anti-feudal forces were more successful in the west than the east and, in the west itself, more successful in England than in France'. Harman simply assumes that for Brenner, the different outcomes were a voluntarist clash of wills between different classes. Harman's explanation for the differences comes down to more pronounced urban and rural industrial development in the west compared to the east, because in the west 'the towns represented centres of power independent of the feudal lords which made it more difficult for the latter to impose their interests on the whole society or ... to always bend the bureaucracy to their will'.[29] This conclusion which misconceives the relationship between feudal lords and towns, and overemphasises the impact of towns on agriculture in medieval and early modern Europe, reflects the central role Harman assigns to towns and the commercialisation process in the origin of capitalism and we shall examine this in a later section.

iv   The Origin of Capitalism and Bourgeois Revolution:
        From Above or Below?

Robert Brenner has addressed the prominent role given by orthodox Marxists to 'bourgeois revolution' in the transition from feudalism to capitalism in England. He argued that agrarian capitalism was already dominant in the English countryside by the middle of the seventeenth century, and he questioned whether the role of the English 'revolution', which can be traced from its beginnings in 1642 to its final completion in 1688, was of great significance. For Brenner, all it did was block attempts by the Stuart dynasty to impose an absolutist political system on the English population which would have made English kings and queens, rather than the current 'crown in parliament system', the central if not sole executive power. Moreover, the chief opposition to the crown was the broad aristocracy, the broad ruling class who were having their position and property threatened, rather than a capitalist bourgeoisie made up of smaller producers in town and countryside. The lords became divided during the conflict and took sides following the mobilisation of popular forces against crown and parliamentary monopolies, and against capitalist enclosure.[30]

    Henry Heller, an orthodox Marxist who rejects this thesis, argues that,

> jettisoning the idea of bourgeois revolution meant throwing out the most revolutionary component of the Marxist theory of history, or the element most intimately linked with the expectation of future proletarian revolution. The conception of bourgeois as well as proletarian revolution assumes that underclasses can acquire sufficient economic and political power to overthrow the ruling class. Political Marxism suggests that the economic and political initiative in the advance of history remains with the ruling class.[31]

---

29   Harman 1998, p. 101.
30   Brenner 1993, especially the 'Postscript'.
31   Heller 2011, p. 116.

Heller invokes the 'really revolutionary way' proposed by Marx's theory of history, which necessitated transformation from below: small producers come into conflict with the old ruling class and overthrow it, and set up capitalism – this is how bourgeois revolutions are supposed to happen.[32] Davidson concedes that feudal lords had a role in the transition from feudalism to capitalism by transforming themselves into commercial landlords; but for him, like for Heller, most important is the prior development of capitalist farmers out of earlier differentiation due to the development of the productive forces.[33]

These are clear examples of how orthodox Marxists feel they have to promote revolutionary transitions from feudalism to capitalism from below in order to justify the potential for, and expectation of, a revolutionary transition from capitalism to 'socialism from below' in the future. This is teleology of the crudest kind. It follows from this that if Brenner and other political Marxists argue that the transition from feudalism to capitalism was essentially driven by lords and their farmers, or in other words that it was top-down, then they have foreclosed any expectation of a socialist transition from below in the future. This conclusion is a fundamental mistake, as are its theoretical and empirical underpinnings. Political Marxists recognise that, unlike in feudalism where peasants were shielded from the full implications of the market and so had to be removed from their holdings against their will, it is precisely the specific social-property relations in capitalism, where wage workers are already entirely exposed to the market, that there is a potential to generate transformation from below. So the suggestion of a potential transition to a more co-operative, classless society in the future can therefore be retained, without having to *justify* it by promoting the idea and precedent of a bourgeois capitalist revolution *from below* in the past. Nevertheless orthodox Marxists generally cannot entertain or even acknowledge this argument, because they reject the empirical as well as the theoretical basis of a top-down origin of capitalism during its first break in England.

Readers should refer to the discussion in Chapter Six above for a detailed analysis of the empirical evidence for the top-down nature of the transition to capitalism, and yet, given its importance for the present discussion, it will also be necessary to discuss this theme here at some length informed by Marxist debates.

While I argue that the origin of capitalism in England was not the result of a revolutionary process driven from below, it was more complex than a top-down imposition as Brenner himself clearly recognised. It was certainly not

---

32   Heller 2011, p. 80.
33   Davidson 2004b, p. 417.

solely driven by lords, the ruling class, as orthodox Marxists have him saying, and for the debate to continue productively they will need to cease doing so. For Brenner, in England the lords oversaw an agricultural revolution driven by capitalist farmers with whom the lords had a mutual relationship.

The evidence for the direct evictions of peasants by lords in the late fifteenth and early sixteenth century comes from royal statutes beginning in 1489 which aimed to halt depopulating enclosure and damaging overspecialisation, and from the royal enclosure commissions of 1517–18. This evidence reveals that widespread evictions of peasant tenants by their lords had taken place across the English midlands since 1485 at latest. Many other local studies where evidence is available, including that presented in Part II of this book, reveal that it certainly had occurred earlier and was far more widespread. The direct forcible eviction of peasants by lords in the second half of the fifteenth and early sixteenth centuries was an important stage in the expropriation of the English peasantry. This involvement of the lords is incontestable, and Marx picked up on it because it is the most visible aspect in the state records of the profound early processes of that expropriation. However it had a crucial and distinct prelude in England. This was the historically unprecedented transference by lease of the lords' home farms or demesnes, amounting to twenty to thirty percent of the best land in lowland England, to the wealthiest of the peasantry a century earlier, mostly between 1380 and 1420.

Borrowing uncritically from Terence Byres' recent article on peasant differentiation, Heller and Davidson have Brenner saying that these leases were forced upon peasants against their will as part of the top-down imposition by an all-powerful class of lords in the face of a passive peasantry.[34] Byres' justification for this curious interpretation is that Brenner does not view the peasantry as socially and economically differentiated before a section of them took up these transforming leases. Apparently, for Brenner, because of their common approach towards feudal rules for reproduction, the peasantry must have been a homogenous mass with similar property. In fact, Byres says that because of his perspective on feudal rules of production, Brenner is forced to present the peasantry in this way, because if Brenner acknowledged that a wealthy elite existed he would have to concede that there was a stratum that was prepared to become market-dependent as early as the thirteenth century. Byres says, quite rightly, that the peasantry in England had always been differentiated, although more controversially he adds that, as a result of this differentiation, by the end of the thirteenth century there was a peasant elite on the boundaries of these feudal rules for reproduction who might potentially risk

34   Byres 2006, p. 57; Davidson 2012, p. 403; Heller 2011, p. 49.

becoming market-dependent to further improve their wealth and status. Moreover he suggests, on this basis, that the elite were proto-capitalist *before* the transference of the leases to them. Hence the driving force for capitalism was the peasant elite, without which lords would have had no one to trust with the ability to farm the much larger acreages. Byres goes even further to suggest that it was this aggressive peasant elite in England in the late medieval period who caused capitalism to be generated from below, in contrast to a much more docile, flattened peasantry in Prussia which made capitalism from above in the nineteenth century necessary there.[35]

It is true that Brenner was not as explicit as he could have been about peasant differentiation in medieval England, and this is a minor lacuna in his work that has led to these serious charges. But to say that he deliberately refused to acknowledge peasant differentiation in order to get his thesis to work is untrue, and really a non-argument. What Brenner wished to show was that *the differentiation that mattered,* namely that which turned peasants using mostly family labour and largely producing for subsistence into capitalist farmers during the early modern period, was the large leases which gave their holders a new set of problems, a new imperative to compete and innovate. In response to similar arguments in the earlier debate, Brenner pointed out quite rightly that a strong middling peasantry with quite a large acreage had developed in the fifteenth century in both France and England and yet, subsequently from between about 1450 and 1550, polarisation of tenancies in England, based on leases and the enclosure movement, contrasted with the fragmentation of tenancies in France in the same period. So accumulation was not hidden in Brenner's thesis.[36] In fact it has long been known that in the century after the Black Death the vacant holdings served to increase and strengthen a middling peasantry in England rather that generate increasing social polarisation and differentiation. They also served to provide free holdings for those who had previously been serfs. Rodney Hilton, as Byres says, has done as much as anybody to bring to our attention the inequalities among peasants, and he paid particular attention to the significance of the wealthier stratum for capitalist development from the second half of the fifteenth century. However, Hilton argued that the period after the Black Death, which included the major peasant rebellion of 1381, was not one in which rich proto-capitalist peasants were suddenly let off the leash. He found that between 1350 and 1450 'the number of smallholders was considerably reduced; the middle stratum was strengthened; the rich peasants also improved their position but not so consistently as did

---

35   Byres 2006, especially pp. 60–1.
36   Brenner 1985b, pp. 290, 300. See also Hilton 1990b, pp. 76–7.

the middle peasants'. He concluded that 'it is possible that the century after the Black Death was the golden age of the middle rather than of the rich peasantry (the yeomen)'.[37] The yeomen had their leases but in general it was only in the second half of the fifteenth century that the wealthy leaseholders and the lords began to eat into the modest holdings of the broad middle peasantry if not directly evict them outright.

Brenner's thesis is entirely compatible with a differentiated peasantry in English feudal society, and, in the late fourteenth century, with a section of the wealthier end of the peasantry experienced and willing to take on the momentous transference by lords of the leases of their demesnes. It is telling that the peasants from the wealthier stratum of their class did not choose to become market-dependent a century earlier in the late thirteenth century even though, as has been said in a previous chapter, they made significant accumulations. From a rational point of view this was not in their best interests. This is what Brenner says. Besides the uncertainties of the market, the peasants in the late thirteenth century were subject to heightened extra-economic controls and the customs in common were under attack by the lords in the decades around 1300 as the bargaining power of the lords over the peasants peaked. But given the opportunity to farm hundreds of acres from the late fourteenth century, this was clearly enough incentive for a section of the peasantry to take rational steps towards market dependency, even if that meant cutting themselves off from the community solidarities that had traditionally protected them from encroachments by feudal lordship. Feudal controls were of course weakened and modified from the late fourteenth century as serfdom declined due to peasant resistance and mobility to freer tenures and industrial opportunities. At this stage the taking up of leases was tentative and the new lessees probably still had their own lands to fall back on if things went wrong. But with the backing of lords, further engrossment of the customary lands was possible and many had successfully made the transition to full market dependency by the end of the fifteenth century.

Davidson's and Heller's contention that English lords forced passive peasants to take up the leases is therefore an entirely incorrect interpretation of what Brenner said. From Brenner's perspective, lords were forced to *offer* these resources to wealthier peasants in the decades around 1400 in order to maintain pre-Black Death levels of income and power. That income was under serious threat due to the reduction or fixing of rent levels following the demographic downturn and the decline of serfdom after widespread peasant resistance to the post-Black Death seigneurial reaction which culminated in the class war of

---

37   Hilton 1990b, pp. 75–6.

1381. This transfer of resources was a historic and unprecedented *concession* by the lords to the peasants, and as such was in itself a revolutionary development. But it did not represent the beginning of a revolution from below to install capitalism. Peasants exhibited a strong class consciousness in this period, as witnessed especially in the rebellion of 1381; but while their goal as a class was to remove serfdom, arbitrary royal taxation and even lordship altogether, their motivations were by no means proto-capitalist. These highly skilled, resourceful, commercial and increasingly literate people had a vision of an alternative to both feudalism *and* capitalism which was subsistence-based and democratic, and at the very least a realisable goal of self-governing communities. They should be given more credit by historians for their potential at this point to see this vision through, even though that potential was unfulfilled. Focus on the preoccupations and assumed mentality of a tiny peasant elite misreads the dominant processes and activities of the peasantry as a whole in this period, one which is best characterised by a strengthened and increased middle peasantry with a non-capitalist outlook. It is all the more remarkable therefore how capitalism developed in England from this situation.

The leaseholders were recruited from a wide range of people: both middling and wealthy peasants, artisans, merchants, clothiers, clergy and gentry. The peasantry, often in the form of the manorial reeve or bailiff, dominated the earlier phase of leasing in the decades around 1400. Gentry became increasingly involved from the late fifteenth century, although depending on the size of their estates they usually sub-leased these farms for a profit. This was particularly the case after the mass of dissolved monastic property came on to the market in the 1530s and 1540s. Many of the peasants who took up this concession by the lords had previously farmed about 30 acres. They were previously subsistence-based farmers at the wealthier end of the peasantry and able to market small surpluses. They were not however a proto-capitalist elite. By contrast, the new farmers were now, overnight, farming hundreds of acres, and instead of consuming the vast majority of their produce, they would now be forced to sell three quarters of it.[38] Contrary to assumptions made by orthodox Marxists, Heller, Harman and Davidson, while there was economic differentiation, *there was no prior development of of a class of capitalist farmers in England* before the transference of these leases in the decades around 1400.

The English peasantry had always been highly differentiated for a number of reasons, some of these stemming from pre-feudal times.[39] One need only

---

38   Dyer 2005, pp. 196–7.

39   Hilton 1990b.

glance at the lists of slaves, cottagers, smallholders ('bordars') and more substantial villagers ('villans') in the Domesday Book that was drawn up in 1086.
Peasant land-market activity and the sensitivity of peasants to market price
signals during the economic up-phase that followed between 1100 and 1300 led
to accumulation by some, but before the second half of the fifteenth century
this generally took the form of life-cycle accumulation – that is, it was dispersed among heirs on the death of the accumulator. In his studies on peasant
differentiation, Hilton concluded that while we can point to significant differentiation among medieval peasants in England, 'it would nevertheless be a
mistake to exaggerate the capacity for large scale land accumulation by already
well-to-do peasants'. Regarding the processes involved in the accumulations of
wealthier peasants in the thirteenth century, he found that land transactions
in the court rolls dealt with very small quantities of land and there were certain
limits placed on accumulations by the norms and customs of peasant communities, and by the calculations of lords' who sought to control the land market
in order to avoid social polarisation, maintain stability and ensure there were
enough solid middling peasants – the backbone of peasant communities – to
pay the rents and carry out the obligations that lords required.

> [The peasant land market in the thirteenth century] was a market which
> acted as an agency for adjusting the relationship between the landed
> families of peasant communities according to norms which were also
> mirrored in inheritance and other customs, namely the maintenance of
> traditional property divisions between the peasant strata. It is quite pos-
> sible that customary prejudices against accumulation, which are cer-
> tainly found later, were in existence at this period. The production of
> agricultural commodities for the market, with the object of making a
> monetary profit, which in turn would be reinvested for expanded repro-
> duction, was not yet a driving force within peasant society.[40]

So, as Brenner says, it was the leasing of the lords' farms from the late fourteenth century and the differentiation consequent on the revolutionary transference of resources from lords to peasants which was key to the origin of
capitalism in England. The peasants who took up these leases and became
wealthy yeomen as a result, and their counterparts that controlled the rapidly
expanding rural cloth industry, were by the early sixteenth century a prominent class across England, clearly distinct from the rest of the peasantry, artisans and petty traders.

---

40   Hilton 1990b, p. 74.

Returning to the question of who was responsible for the expropriations of the small and middling peasantry, while leading late medieval historians such as Christopher Dyer and Bruce Campbell recognise the significance of direct evictions by lords at the end of the fifteenth century at least, they point out that while large inhabited villages were frequently evicted, the vast majority of cases of evictions uncovered by the 1517–18 commissions took the form of clearing away the last few houses of already depopulated villages and hamlets. For these historians, serious depopulation had already occurred and along with the plagues, it was the new men, the yeomen that were responsible for this during the course of the fifteenth century. It is a valid point that initiatives for change usually or often came from the farmers. But what needs to be highlighted is that these demesne farmers were usually manorial officials and as such they were not only close to the lords politically but their success was increasingly linked to that of the lords. In study after study, from R.H. Tawney through to Joan Thirsk, and through to many recent studies including my own, this is found to be the case. During the royal commissions into enclosures in 1517–18, lords were charged with delivering to the royal courts their leading tenants who enclosed illegally, and they were given the incentive to do so with the offer of half the fines of successful convictions. And yet not one case has arisen where a lord actually did this, and this explains why the commissions were so unsuccessful. So although lords and farmers had conflicting interests which were built into the class relationships of agrarian capitalism, there was much that was mutual between them, particularly during this early process of remodelling social-property relations during the long fifteenth century, a period of relative economic stagnation and low land values. Lords would improve the terms on which they leased their property at the expense of the farmers from the end of the sixteenth century when land values and competition increased in their favour.[41]

In this context it cannot be argued that the origin of capitalism in England was driven from below, nor that capitalism was deliberately installed from above. The remodelling of feudal social-property relations around 1400 began as a response by English lords to the loss of extra-economic controls through serfdom, declining rents and rising wages, and the wealthiest strata of the peasantry were drawn towards the lords' political interests as resources were transferred to them. The whole process of expropriation and the historic rupture in feudalism that followed was disastrous for the vast majority of English peasants. A systematically increasing proportion of them would never inherit a subsistence plot and would be forced to search for work as labourers in a

---

41   See the discussions in Chapter Six and Chapter Seven.

context of a rapidly rising population and declining real wages in the sixteenth century. Bitterness and hatred by the majority of the peasantry towards these farmers and lords would present itself in the widespread rebellion of 1549. Defeat in 1549 represented the final defeat of the peasantry's resistance to expropriation and what turned out to be capitalism although there would be many more local battles. The profound remodelling of social-property relations that took place in the fifteenth and first half of the sixteenth centuries was consolidated and extended during the rest of the sixteenth and seventeenth centuries. In the eighteenth and early nineteenth centuries the parliament of capitalist landlords passed many Acts to remove what was still a significant peasant artisan element in England clinging to the margins. This was not a new model of expropriation directed from above, which would soon be imitated in Scotland and Prussia. It was merely the logical extension of an already existing model. A true history from below in England in this period would be of local and widespread resistance by the vast majority of peasants to enclosure and capitalist imperatives, rather than one emphasising the drive of a small elite to impose those imperatives on the vast majority. The peasantry were unable to resist capitalism, and yet their resistance doubtless shaped the course of capitalist development, capitalist political institutions and modern working-class traditions.

During this remodelling of social-property relations, it was not the case that English lords simply transformed themselves into commercial landlords which is what Davidson asserts happened in England, Scotland and the rest of Europe. That may have been the case elsewhere as lords sought to follow the already existing model in England, although it could not have been a straightforward process. In England, lords were forced to transform against their will by pressure for liberty from peasants and artisans. The process of removing their extra-economic powers began with lords giving up their large home farms on lease and thereby relinquishing their need for enforced labour services. Subsequent lordship rivalry in the Wars of the Roses that followed the loss of territory in France, the outcome of these conflicts and the development of Tudor centralisation, led to the demilitarisation of the feudal class, the removal of its need for private retinues of knights, and a stake in state sovereignty. All of this occurred as the outcome of struggle, it was not what the lords suddenly *preferred* as a better alternative to their decentralised feudal power.

Davidson does not appear to recognise the role lords had in evicting peasants in the late fifteenth and sixteenth centuries, something which exercised Marx so much. Instead he patches together work from other historians (from Hoyle and Whittle especially) to paint a picture of peaceful piecemeal accumulation within the peasantry based on the innocuous transfer of plots on a local land market, something that I criticised in an earlier chapter.[42] Davidson's aim of course is not to argue for an entirely peaceful, innocuous transition to capitalism. For him, there was violence, but that is reserved for the seventeenth century when the mandatory revolutionary act bursts through the old relations that acted as a fetter on the new bourgeois society. He misses the significance of the mass anti-capitalist peasant rebellions of the 1530s and 1540s, and miscomprehends the class relationship between lords and peasants in English medieval society. For example he asserts that:

> The wish to better the circumstances in which we live has been one of the main impulses behind the attempts to develop the productive forces and it is intimately bound up with class society, not least because in a situation where the direct producers have to hand over part of what they have produced to someone else, there is a very real motive – one might also say, an imperative – to increase their output, a motive that need have initially nothing to do with market compulsion.[43]

Here we have the Smithian ahistorical perspective in which 'one of the main impulses' of 'we' human beings in *any* historical context including pre-class societies is to improve ourselves by seeking the gains from trade.

---

42   Davidson 2012, pp. 524–8. Whittle argued that in this way 'the peasants expropriated themselves'. A similar thesis was commented on over fifty years ago by Kosminsky when he criticised an earlier historian with a similar perspective to Whittle. For this historian, 'there is no forcible expropriation from the land. The peasants expropriated themselves because it was advantageous to do so'. Kosminsky said that this approach had the appearance of 'an unsuccessful attempt to make primitive accumulation respectable. The expropriation of the peasants is lifted from the consciences of the landlords': Kosminsky 1956, p. 210. Davidson also apparently wishes to lift the consciences of the landlords. For instance, he quotes Mark Overton: 'In general, economic differentiation was a process which took place among the tenantry. Moreover landlords, especially in the sixteenth century, showed little interest in developing their estates for capitalist tenant farming, and as a rule they were not very adventurous in promoting innovation in agriculture: Davidson 2012, p. 528. One need just refer Davidson to two far more impressive authorities on the subject, Wrightson and Tawney, who were discussed in the Chapter Seven. They both point to the late sixteenth and early seventeenth centuries, for example, as the 'great age of the surveyor' in which lords employed professionals in order to maximise the productivity of their estates before leasing them more profitably to capitalist farmers. Whittle also recognises that in the last decades of the sixteenth century the county of Norfolk witnessed 'the creation of large and very large farms' by landlords to the same effect: Whittle 2000, p. 195 n. 38.

43   Davidson 2012, p. 524.

But while it is true that people in all forms of society may seek to improve themselves, the question is whether they have the option or capability to do so. As Brenner has always argued:

> Peasants for their part sought as much as possible to exploit the gains from trade through involvement in the market, but found themselves significantly thwarted in doing so because full specialisation leading to dependence upon the market was incompatible with the pursuit of other highly valued goals – security from bad harvests via production for subsistence, social insurance via having many children, the endowment of children with the wherewithal to form a family by means of subdivision of holdings.[44]

However, Davidson is saying something more: that capitalist social-property relations are not the only relations that determine a systematic development of the productive forces. For him, feudal extra-economic exploitation provided 'a very real motive' or even 'an imperative' for peasants to increase their output through developing the productive forces, that is, by specialising and thereby rendering themselves market-dependent, and Davidson is not just talking about an elite here but *all* peasants. Davidson quotes the following passage from Wedderburn's *The Complaynt of Scotland* published in 1549 – interestingly the year of mass anti-capitalist peasant rebellion across England – as an example of the outlook of an oppressed Scottish labourer in the sixteenth century in this respect: 'I labour day and night with my hands to feed lazy and useless men, and they repay me with hunger and the sword. I sustain their life and with toil and sweat of my body, and they persecute my body with hardship, until I am become a beggar. They live through me and I die through them'.[45] Davidson assumes that the most likely response for this labourer to this hardship and oppression meted out by the ruling class, even though reduced to beggary and death, is to improve the productive forces! This seems particularly inappropriate given that he has demonstrated that Scotland continued to remain a feudal-tribal society well into the eighteenth century, and there had been very little if any development of the productive forces in Scotland even 200 years after this passage was written.

Davidson refuses to accept the point made not just by Brenner, but by specialist medieval historians such as Rodney Hilton, that peasants in thirteenth century England lived in what Hilton calls 'organic' *communities* with 'a common agricultural routine' and, even though significantly differentiated

---

44   Brenner 2001, p. 296.
45   Davidson 2012, pp. 523–4.

economically, they relied on each other for both political and economic support. In other words, there was much more to hold them together than to draw them apart.[46] Not only did peasants possess the land which provided their subsistence, they were organised in political communities that helped them protect it against their adversaries, the lords. When lords attempted to encroach on peasants' surpluses or even on their ability to subsist, the first priority for peasants was to defend themselves. If lords managed to be successful in their encroachment by increasing the level of surplus extraction, either through removing customary rights, increasing taxes arbitrarily or adding new serfdom dues, peasants did not respond by seeking out ways to cope by improving the productive forces. What they did do was refuse to accept these encroachments and *fight back*.[47] Sometimes disputes were passed down from generation to generation for hundreds of years by peasant communities. It is typical that the victories that lords achieved against peasants in the late thirteenth and early fourteenth century were readdressed by those peasants' successors after the Black Death and during the rebellion of 1381.[48] As we will see in Part II, the peasant commitment to ancient customs that were no longer recognised by lords could continue well into the fifteenth century. Davidson ignores this reality for peasants in medieval England (and Scotland) in favour of a productive forces model in which peasants are curiously passive for the most part of the medieval and Tudor period until the violent revolutionary explosion in the seventeenth century. On the contrary, extra-economic exploitation had the effect of *reducing* the motivation and means to improvement, not increasing it. It had the effect of drawing peasant communities together, not of turning them into individualistic proto-capitalists. This was the essence of feudal social-property relations.

Byres' article was designed as a defence of Rodney Hilton's work on peasant differentiation and the origin of capitalism *against* Brenner's thesis. While there are ambiguities in Hilton's approach – his greater emphasis on the decline of serfdom rather than the expropriation of the peasantry as key in creating the context for the emergence of the capitalist entrepreneur being a case in point – his work generally supports Brenner.[49] It is significant for this

---

46   Note that 'organic' does not mean 'natural'.

47   Hilton 1990a.

48   See Faith 1981.

49   At the outset of his contribution to the original 'Brenner Debate', in reference to Brenner's first paper in 1976 Hilton said that 'while I agree with Brenner's emphasis on the overall determining role of social relationships in the evolution of feudal society, I think there are complexities that he has ignored': Hilton 1985, p. 119 n. 4. Those complexities were addressed in Brenner's second paper in 1982 that was three times as long.

discussion that Hilton's important collection of essays on medieval England and France was entitled *Class Conflict and the Crisis of Feudalism*,[50] and not *Peasant Differentiation and the Crisis of Feudalism*, or worse.

We can now examine more particularly the implications of this discussion of top-down or bottom-up transitions for the 'bourgeois revolution'. Heller and Davidson need not take on board my perspective on the top-down nature of the transition in England; they can get their authority from Marx. As we have seen above it is one of the contradictions of Marx's transhistorical theory that the key 'epoch-making' process in the transition from feudalism to capitalism in England, namely the expropriation of the mass of the people, was undertaken 'by a few usurpers', while the transition from capitalism to socialism will take the very opposite form, namely the expropriation 'of a few usurpers by the mass of the people'. Moreover, Marx was well aware of this situation in an earlier essay:

> The great puzzle of the conservative character of the English revolution, to which M. Guizot can solve only by attributing it to the superior intelligence of the English, is in fact explained by the lasting alliance of the bourgeoisie with the great landowners, an alliance which fundamentally distinguishes the English from the French revolution, the latter having destroyed large landed property by dividing it up into smallholdings. This class of large landowners allied with the bourgeoisie, which it may be added, had already risen under Henry VIII, was not, as were the French feudal landowners of 1789, in conflict with the vital interests of the bourgeoisie but rather in complete harmony with them. Their estates were indeed not feudal but bourgeois property. On the one hand, they provided the industrial bourgeoisie with the population necessary to operate the manufacturing system, and, on the other hand, they were in a position to raise agricultural development to the level corresponding to that of industry and commerce. Hence their common interests with the bourgeoisie; hence their alliance.[51]

Even though Marx points to the broad ruling class, the great landowners, as key to the English revolution in the seventeenth century, Davidson, who uses this quote, still considers that revolution as amounting to a bourgeois revolution driven from below. This is because of 'the nature of the enemy that had to be overthrown: absolutism that had become a fetter and a hindrance to the new

---

50   Hilton 1990a and 1990b.
51   Marx 1992, p. 252.

bourgeois society'.[52] This revolution from below driven in large part by the aristocratic ruling class would seem to overstretch Heller's concept of revolutionary underclasses. Using a transhistorical analogy Heller would no doubt be disappointed to learn from a fellow revolutionary that his expectation of a future socialist revolution might take the form of big business and the banks overthrowing parliament.

For orthodox Marxists, it is not enough of course for the *English* revolution in the mid-seventeenth century to be bourgeois (capitalist), and driven from below in order to set free the new bourgeois (capitalist) society growing in the womb of the old. The other classical 'bourgeois revolution', namely the French revolution which began in 1789, is required to be the same. Even though Marx argued, as we have seen, that the English and French revolutions were fundamentally different, Davidson argues that in both cases the enemy was the same and that 'above all' the outcome was the same. But in spite of Davidson's selective quotations from Marx with the purpose of demonstrating the development after 1789 of an already existing capitalism as a result of the revolution from below, we are still left with a picture of France, as Marx wrote as late as 1852 in his *Eighteenth Brumaire of Louis Bonaparte*, as a nation of millions (sixteen million) of impoverished, subsistence-based, peasants tied to the land alongside, but separate from, large scale international commerce and substantial industrial development in many towns. Moreover, these peasants were represented politically by the emperor Louis Bonaparte as they were by Napoleon Bonaparte earlier. This is the picture of the small peasant proprietor in the petty mode of production that we met earlier, one which excludes the development of the productive forces in agriculture. But if anything the peasants' situation was even worse in 1852 than in 1789 due to mortgages which represented 'their enslavement by capital', as well as state taxation, 'the source of life for the bureaucracy, the army, the priests and the court':

> After the first revolution [1789] had transformed the peasants from a state of semi-serfdom into free landed proprietors, Napoleon confirmed and regulated the conditions under which they could exploit undisturbed the soil of France, which had now devolved on them for the first time, and satisfy their new found passion for property. But the French peasant is now succumbing to his smallholding itself, to the division of the land, the form of property consolidated in France by Napoleon. It was the material conditions which made the feudal peasant a small proprietor and Napoleon an emperor. Two generations have been sufficient to

---

52   Davidson 2012, p. 136.

produce the inevitable consequence: a progressive deterioration of agriculture and a progressive increase in peasant indebtedness. The
'Napoleonic' form of property, which was the condition for the liberation
and enrichment of the French rural population at the beginning of the
nineteenth century, has developed in the course of that century into
the legal foundation of their enslavement and their poverty. And precisely this law is the first of the 'Napoleonic ideas' which the second
Bonaparte has to uphold.[53]

The French 'bourgeois revolution' under the Bonaparte dynasty protected
rather than expropriated peasant property, just as earlier dynasties had protected it in order to preserve it for taxation. While certain feudal prerogatives
and seigneurial impositions on peasants were removed – and only after pressure from mass and widespread peasant uprisings which were in fact responsible for the revolutionary turn of the National Assembly in 1789 – there was no
unleashing of agrarian capitalist accumulation in the countryside. Indeed the
widespread uprisings led to the smashing of the enclosures of seigneurs and
gros fermiers. Instead, peasant property was strengthened as common rights
were protected and the poor peasantry benefited from the redistribution of the
church lands and the property of the émigré aristocracy who opposed the revolution, thereby creating an even broader base of peasant ownership: in Marx's
words there still remained 'the petty mode of production based upon a mass
peasantry'.[54]

   To support his thesis that the French bourgeois revolution was a capitalist
revolution, Davidson quotes another passage in the same section of Marx's
Eighteenth Brumaire: 'In the course of the nineteenth century [before this passage was written in 1852] the urban usurer replaced the feudal lord; the mort-
gage of the land replaced feudal obligations; bourgeois capital replaced
aristocratic landed property'.[55] But first of all this reveals that French society
was not capitalist before the revolution in 1789; and second that Davidson confuses the existence of usurers and mortgages with capitalism. Usurers and
mortgages seem to have served to make the condition of the mass of the population worse rather than to have generated agrarian capitalism: even in the

---

53   Marx 1992a, pp. 238–43.

54   For the role of the peasantry in the French revolution including the abolition of seigneur-
      ial exactions see Markoff 1996. For analyses on the strengthening of peasant property in
      France after the revolution and until the second half of the nineteenth century see
      Rosenthal 1992; Price 1983.

55   Marx 1992a, p. 242, cited in Davidson 2012, p. 137.

middle of the nineteenth century a large majority of the population remained subsistence-based. As we shall see below, and as Brenner recognised, hereditary peasant property was undermined in the seventeenth and eighteenth centuries and large commercial farms were developed employing wage labour, particularly in the Paris basin, but the vast majority of the population remained on the land. In many areas they survived on tiny holdings as smallholding labourers supported where possible by rural industry. There was even a seigneurial 'reaction' or offensive in many regions after 1760 in which feudal labour services and other dues were either increased, or at least re-introduced having earlier lapsed.[56]

Orthodox Marxists follow what they deem to be consistent with Marx's transhistorical theory of revolution from below on the back of the development of the productive forces because, for them, without the latter there can be no successful revolution. Yet Marx, not only in his mature work, but as early as 1852, recognised the prominence of the lords in the English revolution. He saw that its 'conservative character' confirmed the already prominent role of the lords in the further development of capitalism. Davidson, instead of asserting that Brenner's top-down thesis applies more to Scotland than England, should, following Marx, and the historical evidence, have asserted that it applies to both, with the former country being transformed in an even more radical fashion following pressure from the latter.

v   Peasants, Markets and the Role of English Towns

As we have discussed, one of the reasons that the transition from feudalism to capitalism has been driven from above is the nature of peasant possession, peasant political communities and peasant attitudes towards the market, particularly the preference to avoid market dependence, and hence the tendency to limit specialisation. While this important observation by Marx from the *Grundrisse* onwards, which developed alongside but in contradiction to his transhistorical theory, accords with the political Marxist perspective on the specificity of social-property relations in feudalism, it is not generally accepted by orthodox Marxists who find it difficult to reconcile with their model of the progressive development of the productive forces leading to the emergence of capitalists out of the differentiation of the peasantry.

Hence, as indicated earlier, a key dispute between political and orthodox Marxists centres on peasants' relationship with the market; whether peasants

---

56   Duplessis 1997, pp. 169–70; Jones 1998, pp. 45, 51, 54, 57.

will generally seek to increase their wealth by specialising or changing their relations of production in order to seek the gains from trade, deliberately making themselves market-dependent. Davidson in his critique of Brenner and other political Marxists goes further than any other critic with regard to the question of the so-called market aversion of peasants. Because Brenner argues that as a reproduction strategy peasants in pre-capitalist societies generally choose or tend to diversify their produce and not become market-dependent, Davidson concludes that for political Marxists capitalism is 'intrinsically alien to human nature'. He adds, '[w]hat I am suggesting therefore is that the entire elaborate edifice of the Brenner thesis is based upon a conception of human nature in which it is seen as innately opposed to capitalism – indeed, in which it is seen as innately opposed to economic development as such – and will only be induced to accept capitalist relations under duress'.[57]

As has been explained in the foregoing critique of Davidson, and in an earlier discussion of Epstein, Brenner has not argued that peasants are innately opposed to the market, capitalism or economic development. This extreme accusation reveals again how Davidson and orthodox Marxists fail or refuse to recognise the specificity of feudal social-property relations. Having said that, Davidson *can* recognise it where it applies to 'backward societies' such as in Scotland and eastern Europe in the nineteenth centuries, but apparently not in the 'advanced' areas of Europe in the medieval period.

Peasants diversify production and avoid market dependence as a rational means of avoiding famine due to bad harvests and market uncertainty. *Because they possessed land they had this option.* Even in the context of severe overpopulation in the late thirteenth century, while many became increasingly market-dependent due to the fragmentation of their holdings and were forced under duress as a second option to undertake market-dependent side lines in rural industry to support their increasingly limited subsistence base, they did not generally choose to separate themselves from their subsistence base either physically by migrating to towns or by specialising their production. Even the wealthiest that Byres refers to did not. That is not to say that there are no conditions in which peasants may choose to either specialise or leave the land voluntarily. Brenner pointed out that while the peasant strategy towards production prioritised a safety-first approach rather than specialisation in the late medieval and early modern periods, he qualified this by acknowledging that this 'cannot be taken to hold good in all times and places'.[58] In his critique of

57   Davidson 2012, p. 419.
58   Brenner 1985b, pp. 322–3.

Neo-Smithian Marxism, Brenner listed a number of conditions for capitalist development. The first is as follows:

> Thus the emergence of the possibilities for profitable production thanks to the establishment of commerce, classically in urban manufacturing, does not necessarily mean the movement of producers to take advantage of them. For this to occur, in the countryside there must be no substantial barriers to leaving agriculture, such as serfdom or slavery. In other words, any direct forceful controls over the movement of the direct producers, arising from the social relations by which the ruling class extracts a surplus from them, must be eliminated. Concomitantly, *either the advantages to entering urban production must outweigh the incentives of the agricultural producers to remain in the countryside*, or they must be subject to forcible ejection from the land. In other words, the property of the direct producers in the means of agricultural production must be broken, or else they will not move towards growing industrial opportunities.[59]

Here we can see that Brenner allows that peasants may choose to leave the land in favour of opportunities in the towns or industry, but only if the advantages outweigh the incentives of peasants to stay. One could see how established peasants' younger sons and daughters, unable to benefit sufficiently from inherited land, may have had this incentive to move, particularly at the end of the thirteenth century at a time of severe overpopulation when even favoured inheritances were dwindling due to fragmentation of holdings. But, in feudal Europe, the advantages of industry and its concomitant market dependence were never going to significantly outweigh the incentives of peasants to stay. This was in fact, paradoxically, particularly the case at the end of the thirteenth century at the height of population and pressure on the land, because increasing impoverishment due to the fragmentation of holdings led to reduced discretionary expenditure and therefore reduced demand for urban products. Hence the opportunities in the towns diminished rather than improved overall in contexts of overpopulation. The opportunities of urban employment would only arise therefore through ongoing urban and industrial development in feudal Europe, and for this to happen there would have to be ongoing developments in labour productivity in agriculture in order to enable fewer and fewer agricultural producers to feed a growing population without a subsistence base in towns and industry. However, ongoing improvements in

---

59 Brenner 1977, p. 35. My emphasis.

agricultural labour productivity presuppose the existence of agrarian capitalist social-property relations.

In twenty-first-century China huge towns and industries are being built from scratch, directed by a communist dictatorship in the context of an already advanced world capitalist economy. If the wages paid in these brand-new industries represent a large increase in the ability for the very poorest of the peasants to survive, one can potentially see their incentives to move off of the land and render themselves market-dependent as the most rational choice available. But even in this extreme transition scenario one has serious doubts that whole families of peasants would generally desire to take up this very uncertain opportunity, and cut off their traditional subsistence base. Although it is difficult to gain a full picture, it is clear that peasants are being displaced by enforced expropriation or its threat in time-honoured fashion and opposition is growing to it.[60]

Moving more specifically to the role of towns and industry in the transition to capitalism, given their emphasis on commercialisation as part of the development of the productive forces, orthodox Marxists are very critical of what they see as a lack of engagement on Brenner's part with towns and cities in his analysis of developing agrarian capitalism. For them peasant expropriation is a secondary, dependent aspect of a largely urban-centred transition. Chris Harman says that Brenner ignores the role of towns in the transition, and makes no attempt to link agriculture with industry. He says Brenner's thesis has no coherence, because without acknowledging urban and commercial development he cannot explain why the outcome of the crisis in fourteenth century in England was different to those in previous agrarian crises such as that in the period following the collapse of the Roman Empire. Harman says that the all-important productive forces developed more quickly in the towns compared to the countryside, and so towns had a greater impact on agriculture than vice-versa. Because every town contained butchers and merchants dealing in agricultural products in the thirteenth century, he concludes that agriculture was being transformed at that early stage, long before Brenner's unintended outcome in the fifteenth century. Commercialisation centred on the towns caused peasant differentiation and led some peasants to employ others. As mentioned above, for Harman it is the weaker prominence of towns in eastern Europe in contrast to western Europe that enabled the enserfment of peasants in the east, while capitalism developed in the west.[61] So for Harman, whose thesis is closely related to the classic 'commercialisation thesis', the

60   Andreas 2012, pp. 128–35.
61   Harman 2007, pp. 188–93; Harman 1998, pp. 69–73, 92–6.

transition from feudalism to capitalism entails a general process of urbanisation and marketisation which is organised and stimulated by town based merchants. This all occurs from below and without lordship involvement hence:

> Capitalism began to emerge not as merchant capitalism (the Pirenne-Sweezy version) or as agrarian capitalism (the Brenner version) but as a network of productive units in both handicrafts (in town and country) and agricultural production using free labour separated to varying degrees from real control over the means and materials of production, a network bound together by the activity of a section of merchant capital which itself was centred on the towns.[62]

Like Harman, Davidson is also bemused by the lack of urban involvement in the transition in Brenner's thesis. He states that in Brenner's thesis the urban economy was untouched by capitalist social property relations, and that political Marxists, with their focus on expropriation in the countryside, 'have no explanation at all for urban capitalist development, other than by osmosis'.[63]

These arguments and observations are largely spurious. Brenner regards towns and non-agrarian industry as a crucial though dependent, secondary sector in feudal societies because feudal social-property relations were dominated by rural relations between lords and peasants. Any transformation of rural society would be determined by the latter rather than the former. In his paper on the Low Countries in 2001, he did recognise however the earlier neglect of towns in his thesis, and sought to remedy this deficiency by demonstrating how even in the most highly urbanised and overseas trade-orientated polities in late medieval Europe, 'the incomparably powerful demand for agricultural goods could by itself in no way determine the nature and extent of the supply response of agriculture'.[64] Capitalist development, he argues, took place in the northern Netherlands (maritime Holland), one region of the Low Countries, but this was the result of peculiar social-property relations in that polity rather than an automatically determined stimulus from the towns. For example, in the most urbanised region of the Low Countries and one of the most urbanised regions in Europe in and from the late medieval period, namely the inland southern Low Countries, economic evolution continued to be peasant-orientated.[65]

---

62   Harman 1998, p. 98.
63   Davidson 2012, pp. 412–14.
64   Brenner 2001, pp. 279–80, 302.
65   Brenner 2001, pp. 304–15.

With regard to the role of towns in capitalist development in England, this is all well-known, and I can briefly fill in some of the gaps left by Brenner. Before we begin it should be mentioned that continental historians, particularly those of the Low Countries, understandably find England a relatively non-urbanised country in the late medieval period. If towns are defined as settlements with over 10,000 inhabitants, then England in the fifteenth century would probably only have London, and a handful of provincial towns that did not greatly exceed that size. Southern Wales, where agrarian capitalism developed simultaneously to England in the shell of English lordly estates, would not be on the map, given only a handful of towns there achieved over 2,000 inhabitants in the medieval period, and the numbers were reduced in the fifteenth century. In fact it could be suggested that England's relative *backwardness* with respect to urbanisation and powerful urban jurisdictions was a contributive factor in the precocious transition in that country, particularly given the further fragmentation of sovereignty large and powerful towns represented on the Continent and the parasitic nature of those towns on rural surpluses either through direct monopolistic controls or through supplying luxury products to lords, products paid for by peasant rents and dues.[66] Nevertheless, England was a commercialised country by 1300, even though that commercialisation was typically based on dense networks of small towns. These small towns were closely integrated into rural society but were nevertheless functionally separated from the latter by higher population densities and a much greater range of non-agrarian occupations, artisanal and mercantile, than could be found in villages and rural industrial districts.[67]

During the transition to capitalism in England, the relationship between the towns and the countryside is fairly clear. Before the fifteenth century, manufacture of cloth – the industry that took the lead in early capitalist development in England – was largely undertaken in London and provincial towns such as Bristol, Coventry, York and Norwich under the auspices of trade guilds and companies, mercantile and artisanal. The larger town governments were monopolised by oligarchies of merchant guilds which restricted competition by preventing artisans from taking on mercantile functions. Restrictions were also placed on those wishing to set up as traders and artisans within a

---

66   Guy Bois made such a suggestion in his contribution to the earlier 'Brenner Debate': Bois 1985, pp. 112–13.

67   For this paragraph and what follows see the collections of urban studies in Palliser 2000, and Clark 2000; for industry see Zell 1994; see also Dimmock 2007, and the case study in Part II below.

particular town. Guild membership, apprenticeship and the wages of journey-men were strictly controlled. During the fifteenth century mercantile controls over the artisan guilds in the larger provincial towns and London increased, along with the tightening up of government oligarchies by merchants. At the same time, the proportion of cloth manufactured in rural and small town districts in relation to its traditional base in the larger towns increased. The decline of serfdom in the decades around 1400 led to increasing peasant mobility from harsh tenures and enabled peasants to take up industrial opportunities free from guild restrictions and freer land tenures. Engrossment and enclosure from the middle third of the fifteenth century gave this process more momentum, but this time by political force from above. Larger towns such as Exeter and Salisbury flourished as cloth centres, but it was rural districts in Gloucestershire, Devon, east Somerset, Suffolk, the Weald of Kent, Berkshire, Essex and Wiltshire that generated the early capitalist cloth industry in fifteenth-century England. They increasingly traded directly with London and cloth production from the larger towns was lost to these competing districts as a result. The organisers of the industry were capitalist clothiers who dominated the governments of small towns from which they administered a putting-out system in the surrounding rural districts, and they increasingly controlled all aspects of production. These clothiers were the industrial counterparts of the capitalist yeomen and like the latter they leased demesnes, accumulated land and rented it out, and became increasingly powerful within village and small town assemblies during the second half of the fifteenth century and the first half of the sixteenth century. With profits from industry they accumulated land, and with the profits from rents invested further in industry.

During the sixteenth century, the larger provincial towns were forced to change their function, and so became largely internal distribution or import and export centres, run by cliques of gentry and overseas merchants. The populations of London and the rural industrial districts were increasingly fed by expropriations in the countryside. London expanded exponentially during the sixteenth century as a result and increasingly formed the single urban trading hub of the transition to capitalism in England. As such it became the largest city in Europe. However, monopolies of overseas merchants in London meant that trade was still tied to the extra-economic prerogatives of a patrimonial monarchy, even though their exports were produced in rural industrial districts on an increasingly capitalist basis. The future metropolises of the British industrial revolution were developed from agglomerations of small towns and rural industry rather than expanding medieval cities: for example, Manchester, Liverpool, Bradford, Birmingham and Leeds in England – Swansea and Cardiff in southern Wales.

The town-centred approach to the transition from feudalism to capitalism
of orthodox Marxists such as Davidson is at least partly derived from a certain
understanding of the relationship between capitalism and wage labour and of
the perceived origin of wage labour in urban and industrial society. It is this
understanding that leads Davidson and orthodox Marxists to question the
focus of political Marxists on the agrarian origin of capitalism and the expropriation of the peasantry and, moreover, to question their actual definition of
capitalism. Davidson says that political Marxists define capitalism as 'a system
of market compulsion', whereas, following Marx, *he* defines it as a system of
'competitive accumulation based on wage labor'.[68] The curt definition that he
attributes to political Marxists enables him to state that they 'do not even
accept that wage labor . . . is necessary for capitalism'.[69] He complains:

> If capitalism is based upon a particular form of exploitation, on the
> extraction of surplus value from the direct producers through wage
> labour, then I fail to see how capitalism can exist in the absence of wage
> labourers. How is surplus value produced in a model that contains only
> capitalist landlords and capitalist farmers?[70]

My response to this is to say that a system of market compulsion, one requiring
both capitalists and labourers to compete on the market to sell their products
and labour power, and a system of competitive accumulation based on wage
labour, are not necessarily alternative definitions. Political Marxists define
capitalism – when fully developed – as a system of social relations in which
both the main classes are dependent on, or compelled by, the market to make
a living. This system pre-supposes the detachment of workers from their means
of subsistence so that they are compelled to sell their labour power as a commodity on the market. 'Competitive accumulation', by which Davidson presumably means 'competition in production' – something that is only present
in a system where the economic actors are market-dependent – is one of the
system's attributes, not its fundamental definition. The political Marxist who
finds herself under attack from Davidson in this respect, charged with the
unlikely offence of not recognising the relationship between capitalism and
wage labour, is Ellen Meiksins Wood. What she in fact says, which is both
demonstrably true and entirely logical, is that an increasing proportion of
wage labour is the *result* of the proletarianisation process, *consequent* on the

---

68   Davidson 2012, pp. 414–15.
69   Davidson 2012, p. 416.
70   Davidson 2012, p. 417.

processes of the transition from feudalism to capitalism. The origin of capitalism does not require a proletarianised workforce at the outset; such a workforce is developed *during* the transition to capitalism through agrarian capitalist expropriation and development.[71] As Brenner said in an early paper, the origin of capitalism is the origin of free labour; the origin of *the process* by which labour power and the means of production become commodities.[72] As capitalist development through 'primitive accumulation' or expropriation of the peasantry proceeds, so a proletarianised workforce is produced from which surplus value can *then* be extracted.

The origin of capitalism in England was generated at first in the fifteenth century by pastoral farming – sheep grazing – which did not require a large or new type of workforce. Peasants were expropriated by farmers and lords, and the lands were given over to sheep to supply wool for a growing rural cloth industry. The relationship between expropriation and the growth of industry in this way was symbiotic. As peasants left harsh tenures and expropriated plots they aimed to find work in rural industry and in the towns, especially London. As the population rose from the 1520s, noticeably rapidly from 1540, in concert with further expropriations, the increasing proportion of landless proletarians in town and rural industries increased the demand for urban products and food which they could no longer produce themselves. The resulting price increases generated by this demand provided further incentives for farmers to expropriate, as land and produce became increasingly valuable. This led to a further increase in the proportion of landless proletarians, more demand and so on. Hence the emigration of hundreds of thousands of landless English people to the colonies as early as the seventeenth century, and the industrial

---

71   See the quotes from Wood that Davidson uses which are quite clear on this, in Davidson, 2012, pp. 416–17; but especially Wood 2002, pp. 129–34. Here Wood acknowledges the reluctance of some to view agrarian capitalism in its developmental stages as capitalist in the absence of a fully developed wage labour force. She concedes: 'That reluctance is fair enough, as long as we recognise that, whatever we call it, the English economy in the early modern period, driven by the logic of its basic productive sector, agriculture, was already operating according to principles and "laws of motion" different from those prevailing in any other society since the dawn of history. Those laws of motion were the preconditions – which existed nowhere else – for the development of a mature capitalism that would indeed be based on the mass exploitation of wage labour': Wood 2002, p. 131. I would not make the same concession because the processes involved in agrarian capitalist development and the consequent generation of a proletariat are clearly capitalist. We could call it 'petty commodity production', but then what would we call what medievalists recognise as non-capitalist petty commodity production in the thirteenth century?

72   Brenner 1977, p. 33.

revolution in the following century, is made possible in England because of the process, begun in the fifteenth century, in which the majority of the population had become landless, and thus dependent on the market for work with all the implications this had for domestic demand for food and clothes. This is the whole point of focusing on the development of *agrarian* capitalism, the precondition for ongoing sustainable industrial development based to a great extent on domestic demand and not simply reliant on imports from feudal and absolutist economies with their own non-capitalist cyclical patterns.

Davidson does not grasp the origin of this fundamental process, and this is why his accusations against Wood appear fanciful. For him, a predominantly wage-based labour force must have been present at the outset for emerging capitalists to exploit; otherwise there would have been no capitalism. It follows that the origin of capitalism therefore just occurs as the extension of an ongoing commercialisation process, the division of labour between town and countryside, developing commerce, and improvements in the productive forces in classic Smithian fashion. For Davidson and Harman, the expropriation of peasants is just part of the process which is stimulated by urban and commercial development. A wage-labour force develops in towns throughout the medieval period thanks to the development of the productive forces, and this occurs alongside capitalist farmers and labourers who are generated in the countryside by the same process. This occurs *prior* to the origin of capitalism and is responsible for it.

Against Davidson and Harman, I have already argued that there was no class of capitalist farmers in England before the transference of the lords' demesnes by leasehold to the wealthier peasants, especially between 1380 and 1420, and even then they could only become capitalist if they were able to expand further into the rest of the peasant holdings. Regarding a developing wage-labour force in the towns, there had been no increase in urbanisation and the proportion of wage labourers in England between as early as 1300 and as late as 1520. There was, however, a restructuring of wage labour into pockets of rural industry in symbiosis with the development of capitalist farms in the countryside. Following the large scale expropriations of peasants in the second half of the fifteenth century and early sixteenth century, the production of cloth from rural industry took off as domestic and foreign demand increased rapidly. It is important to note that domestic demand in England increased before the population began to rise in any significant way from about 1540, and this was because of the already large proportion that had been cut off from subsistence. Commercialisation and the stimulation of trade and industry in towns cannot be simply cited to assume a concerted response in agricultural production. As we shall see below, the evidence for the lack of genuine and sustained economic growth in rural society across Europe in the late medieval and early modern period makes this clear.

vi   The Origin of Capitalism: England or Europe?

Brenner argues that capitalism originated and developed only in England and parts of the northern Netherlands and maritime Flanders in the late medieval and early modern periods. Only England sustained that development continuously through the eighteenth century, and it is only when it had largely developed in England that competitive and military pressure from this more dynamic and self-sustaining economy caused changes elsewhere. This argument is roundly dismissed by orthodox Marxists such as Davidson and Heller. Although they view England as the dominant capitalist country by the seventeenth century, they argue that capitalism developed first elsewhere in Europe and spread later to England. However, I argue in this section that this view stems firstly from misinterpretations of Marx's discussions of primitive accumulation, and secondly from confusing isolated forms of merchant capitalist organised *production* with integrated and sustained capitalist *development*. Of course if the orthodox Marxist focus on the development of the productive forces is to have any relevance to history, then we should expect to see capitalist development occurring more or less simultaneously across Europe given similar commercialising pressures everywhere. The core of the Marxist debate on this stems from Marx's statements in the first volume of *Capital*:

> In the history of primitive accumulation, all revolutions are epoch-making that act as levers for the capitalist class in the course of its formation; but this is true above all for those moments when great masses of men are suddenly and forcibly torn from their means of subsistence, and hurled onto the labour-market as free, unprotected and rightless proletarians. The expropriation of the agricultural producer, of the peasant, from the soil is the basis of the whole process. The expropriation assumes different aspects in different countries, and runs through its various stages in different orders of succession, and at different historical epochs. Only in England, which we therefore take as our example has it the classic form.[73]

---

73   Marx 1990, p. 876.

Heller and Davidson both attempt to limit the impact of the last sentence. Rather than take on board the first couple of sentences as representing the 'classic form' of expropriation as the basis of the whole process of the development of capitalism in England – the sudden and forcible removal of the peasantry which Marx states took place at the end of the fifteenth century and beginning of the sixteenth century, and that *only in England* has it the classic form, they say that England takes *only* the classic form.[74] Without revealing to us what they think this classic form is, and whether being 'classic' has any significance, they prefer to focus on Marx's point that expropriation took place at different times in different places, although not *after* England but *before*. In the footnote to the above quote Marx pointed out that 'capitalist production developed earliest in Italy', but was not sustained. So Heller and Davidson take this as their cue that capitalism did not originate in England. In fact Heller states that '[c]apitalism – from the start a single system – actually began in Italy, spread to Germany and then to Holland and France. England was the last stop in this progress'.[75] His evidence for this begins with a quote from Marx taken from the introduction of his chapter on 'The genesis of the industrial capitalist' in the first volume of *Capital*, although rather than Italy, the process in this respect begins with Spain and Portugal:

> The different moments of primitive accumulation can be assigned in particular to Spain, Portugal, Holland, France and England, in more or less chronological order. These different moments are systematically combined together at the end of the seventeenth century in England; the combination embraces the colonies, the modern tax system and the system of protection.[76]

What Marx is referring to here is 'primitive accumulation' as the wider dispossession and slavery of people in the Americas, Africa and India, the discovery of gold and silver in America by the Spanish at the end of the fifteenth century, and the consequent commercial-mercantilist wars between European nations over the fruits of new colonies 'which has the globe as its battlefield', and which was still going on while Marx was writing with England's 'opium wars' against

---

74   Heller 2011, p. 53; Davidson 2012, p. 157.
75   Heller 2011, p. 52. See Wood and Teschke's critiques of Perry Anderson's similar 'value-added' approach to European capitalist development: Wood 2002, pp. 47–9; Teschke 2003, pp. 158–65.
76   Marx 1990, p. 915.

China.[77] While Marx describes Holland as 'the model capitalist nation of the seventeenth century' the colonial administration of which 'is one of the most extraordinary relations of treachery, bribery, massacre and meanness',[78] there is no sense that this colonial dispossession and commercial warfare reflects the development of a capitalist mode of production in Spain, Portugal and France as the result of the expropriation of the peasantries in those countries. The conquest of countries, the development of new colonies, and global trade wars within particular European countries cannot be equated with the sustained development of a capitalist mode of production. What Marx is saying here is that England emerged as the dominant commercial-mercantilist power from the end of the seventeenth century, something that is generally recognised.[79] But this would surely have not been possible without the development of agrarian capitalism in the previous two centuries as a result of the expropriation of the English peasantry. For English lords and farmers, agrarian capitalism paid dividends. With the rationalising of estates and important innovations in convertible husbandry in the sixteenth and seventeenth centuries, systematic innovations in both agrarian and rapidly developing and epoch-making industrial sectors of the economy in the eighteenth and nineteenth centuries, and increasing demand from a population removed from its subsistence base, its ongoing development was largely self-sustaining in symbiosis with industrial development. In this way, and with the help of a new national bank in the late seventeenth century, investment in a centralised warfare machine and empire following the revolutionary settlement of 1688 was also massively increased and sustained through the eighteenth and nineteenth centuries, and without disrupting production through excessive taxation of the producers who were increasingly producing more per capita than their continental counterparts.

The orthodox Marxist understanding of the term 'primitive accumulation' in the above quote is derived from Adam Smith. It assumes that for capitalist development to occur a 'prior' accumulation of capital was required in order to invest in and kick start that development. Gold and silver from the New World from the sixteenth century onwards and the super profits from the slave trade and plantations from the seventeenth century onwards would suffice. Marx

---

77   Marx 1990, p. 915.

78   Marx 1990, p. 916.

79   See for example Brewer 1998, p. xiii: 'From its modest beginnings as a peripheral power – a minor, infrequent, almost inconsequential participant in the great wars that ravaged sixteenth and seventeenth century Europe – Britain emerged in the late seventeenth and early eighteenth centuries as the military *Wunderkind* of the age'.

rejected this view and was more explicit and categorical about his own meaning of 'so-called' primitive or prior accumulation in another part of the chapter
in *Capital* on this topic which serves as a direct criticism of Smith's use of that
term. For capitalist development a transformation in social relations had to
take place:

> The capital-relation presupposes a complete separation between the
> workers and the ownership of the conditions for the realisation of their
> labour. As soon as capitalist production stands on its own feet, it not only
> maintains this separation, but reproduces it on a continually extended
> scale. The process, therefore, which creates the capital-relation can be
> *nothing other than* the process which divorces the worker from the own-
> ership of the conditions of his own labour; it is a process which operates
> two transformations, whereby the social means of subsistence and pro-
> duction are turned into capital, and the immediate producers are turned
> into wage labourers. So-called primitive accumulation, therefore, *is noth-
> ing else than* the historical process of divorcing the producer from the
> means of production. It appears as 'primitive' because it forms the pre-
> history of capital, and of the mode of production corresponding to
> capital.[80]

We can maintain that the origin of capitalism and the classic form of the
expropriation of the peasantry leading to sustained capitalist *development*
took place in England in and from the fifteenth century while recognising that
isolated forms of early capitalist *production* in the shape of the merchant capitalist putting-out system took place first, or at least on a greater scale and
intensity, in other countries, namely Italy and the Low Countries; and an
expanded world economic system was initiated from parts of Europe other
than England, namely Portugal, Spain and Holland.[81] This is by no means the

---

80   Marx 1990, pp. 874–5. My emphasis.
81   In the putting-out system merchant capitalists owned and controlled the whole produc-
     tion and marketing process. Raw materials such as wool were distributed to artisans in
     their homes or workshops and the merchants collected the finished articles such as cloth.
     In its purest form the artisans did not even own the tools such as looms and spinning
     wheels and were paid for what they produced as in piece work. This system represents a
     process of proletarianisation from an earlier domestic system in which the artisans did
     own the tools and had much greater control therefore over the production process and
     terms and conditions.

same as saying – as do Heller and Davidson – that capitalism developed earlier in other countries and then spread to England.

The orthodox Marxist argument is weakened further by Heller's conclusion that in the early modern period, capitalism did *not* develop in continental Europe as 'Italy failed to consolidate a territorial state because of the too great strength of merchant capital, while in Germany and France feudalism proved too strong'.[82] He therefore presents us with the tautology that capitalism did not develop in these countries because they remained feudal. What we can say is that England was influenced by *commercial* developments on the continent with which it had been integrated for centuries, but England would not have developed capitalism either if its feudal social-property relations would have been similar to those in Italy and Germany. Hence it is the peculiarity of English feudal social-property relations that are central to understanding why capitalism developed in England.

Again, the purpose of this exercise for orthodox Marxists appears to be to promote a future socialist revolution based on extremely doubtful speculations about the earlier bourgeois precedent. Heller views these arrested or limited developments in Italy and Germany as 'more or less successful experiments' in capitalism that eventually 'flowered' in England. He goes on: 'This in itself has important implications for understanding a possible transition to socialism. While nothing is predetermined, we can suggest at least that socialism is developing historically through a succession of trials and errors based on an analogous underlying and general tendency'.[83] The teleology expressed in this statement is remarkable.

I will not subject readers any further to this orthodox Marxist political strategy. However, questions concerning capitalist development in comparative perspective across medieval and early modern Europe need to be addressed, and Brenner's comparative thesis constantly tested against up-to-date knowledge. Brenner did not use Italy within his systematic comparative framework, but given its significance in this debate I will begin with an outline of current knowledge on that country, then proceed with brief outlines on Germany and France, and finish with some observations on the Low Countries.

All medieval and early modern countries had their peculiarities but none so much perhaps as Italy. The rise of city states in Italy from about the year 1000 was, more than any other European country, the legacy of ancient Roman city-dominated society and economy. Between 1100 and 1300 urban centres ruled by oligarchies of merchants and landlords, and sometimes by single overlords,

---

82   Heller 2001, p. 52.
83   Heller 2011, p. 75.

increasingly dominated their surrounding territory known as the *contado*, and to a lesser extent the region beyond known as the *distretto*. As these territories expanded, ruling urban oligarchies and overlords in different city states came into conflict with each other and with rural magnates within the *contado*. The horizontal aspect of social-property relations in Italy was particularly prone therefore to division and conflict. Power and sovereignty in the peninsula was highly fragmented and decentralised both territorially between city states, and between power centres in town and countryside within city-state territories. Additionally, inherent conflicts between the papacy and the Holy Roman Empire (ruled by post-Roman German kings) over political supremacy were played out in the form of rivalries between cities and within oligarchies.

The conflicting interests between urban oligarchies and rural magnates led to the emancipation of the serfs in rural Italy as early as the the thirteenth century, the development or consolidation of large and more efficient commercial farms, and a mobile labour force. But it appears that this emancipation was not won through peasant struggles from below; it was a means by which the urban oligarchs could detach the peasantry from their rural magnate rivals who had previously been the peasants' lords. By doing so the oligarchs were firstly able to subject the peasantry to disproportionately heavy taxation – in the style of absolutism – and secondly they were able to secure a rural labour force in order to feed the fast-growing cities. The emancipation was therefore limited. Moreover, peasant immigration into the cities was restricted in order for the countryside to remain populated for this purpose, and the law courts that were based in the cities upheld statutes that favoured citizen's rights over those of the peasants', and upheld landlords' claims over their peasant tenants. The commercial farms of the thirteenth century in the *contado* were likewise dominated by urban-based lords, and their production was managed on the basis either of intensive labour in a period of abundant population or by sharecropping arrangements (*mezzadria*). In the latter system, which was dominated by the investments and interests of the lord, the lord rented the farm to peasant communities and the peasants gave him or her half of the crop. Clearly the relationship between the cities and the countryside was extra-economic: even given the peasantry's emancipation from serfdom, the political and the economic were inextricable tied.

With regard to industry in the thirteenth century, the major urban centres in Italy and the Low Countries were the major industrial centres of medieval Europe, especially before 1350. In Italy forms of an early merchant capitalist putting-out system in the important textile industry can be identified on a large scale in centres such as Florence and Verona. But here again production and access to raw materials was controlled by the merchant oligarchs of the city states. There were no ongoing developments in industrial production in symbiosis with expropriation in the countryside. Instead a highly mobile, youthful labour force of artisans moved from city to city as the latter became more or less successful. Profits were not reinvested in production but in typical feudal fashion were allocated to non-productive spending on warfare and war-driven trade which was necessary for the maintenance and extension of territorial power.[84] This situation in Italy has been described as 'an urban and commercial feudalism', although *rural* lords remained important, particularly in the *distretto* or regions at the furthest distance from the reach of the cities.[85]

In the later medieval and early modern periods the destructive conflicts in the century after the Black Death, and invasions from the late fifteenth century – particularly by France – led to wider territorial consolidation into fewer territorial states which subsumed the city states. Concessions of jurisdictional rights were given to rural elites and a rapid process of re-feudalisation in the countryside took place between the late fourteenth and the mid-sixteenth centuries. There is little or no evidence for the relationship between peasants and lords in the north of Italy at this stage, but Epstein suggests that while peasants may have been subject to new extra-economic dues from new rural lords, they may have benefited from the removal of the fiscal demands of the urban monopolies.[86] In other words they swapped one form of feudalism for another, collective lordships for individual lords. The much less urban-dominated south of Italy and Sicily had always been more seigneurialised than the north, and between twenty percent and fifty percent of the lords' incomes came from their seigneurial dues drawn from peasants, although as in the north there were striking variations in different regions. Not surprisingly the various social-property relations in different regions and the consequent level of lords' extra-economic controls and exactions over the peasantry in different manors and regions determined the lords' responses to the seventeenth-century depression:

> Where strong seigneurial rights survived, exactions increased in line with population, rising sharply during the sixteenth century and tapering off after the demographic and economic downturn of the 1630s and 1640s; by contrast, lords in more commercialised regions responded to declining

---

84   For the foregoing summary, see Scott 2012, pp. 5–63; Pounds 1994, pp. 312–14; Du Plessis 1997, pp. 55–9. See also Jones 1997, for greater detail.

85   Wood 2012, p. 42.

86   Epstein 1998, pp. 79–80.

rents by attempting to reintroduce the exactions they had previously allowed to lapse.[87]

Increasing exactions on the peasantry were coupled with declining real wages during the sixteenth century rise in population. The picture is of increasing peasant indebtedness and declining output. While investment improved productivity in some areas, the landlord strategy was for extensive rather than intensive growth and so the *mezzadria* system was extended as lords benefited from land hunger and high rents.[88]

In spite of greater territorial centralisation in Italy, sovereignty remained fragmented until unification in the late nineteenth century. The weakening of urban governments that had earlier dominated Italy is reflected in the increasingly informal mafia-like control of political and economic activities of extended families that were linked to and patronised by feudal lords.[89]

Regarding property rights to land, the picture is one of urban encroachment into rural landholding. Epstein suggests that the seigneurial reaction in central and northern Italy in response to the demographic downturn after the Black Death was manifested in fiscal and military pressure as princes and city states competed in feudal fashion. Peasants were forced to sell up or migrate. In the late fifteenth century, commons were eroded and some peasants were subjected to forced evictions by lords, especially in the south. In 1647 the state of Venice systematically sold its commons to rich townspeople to pay for its war with the Ottomans. Nevertheless rural landownership by peasants and rural commons remained resilient. In much of central Italy, and in parts of the north, the most significant development in the early modern period according to Epstein was the consolidation of land from highly fragmented and dispersed plots into consolidated farms of 10 to 30 hectares. These farms were however labour intensive, crops were diversified rather than specialised, and they were designed for family subsistence. Sharecropping (the *mezzadria* system) also remained important and was extended. Much larger farms (50–130 hectares) were developed in the north in the fifteenth and sixteenth centuries across much of the Po valley for cereal production (although it is not clear on what tenure this was based beyond cash rents paid by rural entrepreneurs to the urban owners). Contrary to Heller, who assumes that these large farms represent examples of burgeoning agrarian capitalism in Italy that then spread elsewhere and finally to England, *all* agrarian production in early modern Italy,

---

87   Epstein 1998, p. 82.
88   Duplessis 1997, pp. 55–9.
89   Epstein 1998, pp. 85–7.

whether on consolidated farms or smallholdings, differed fundamentally from that in England in that it was increasingly labour intensive, with labour productivity declining as a result. The overall tendency in the long run was holding fragmentation stimulated by land hunger from the increasing and underemployed rural population. As a corollary, rather than large-scale urban industrial development, the picture is one of *rural* industrial expansion from the late seventeenth century, but one highly integrated into peasant production as a support for peasant incomes.[90] The urban Italian textile industry that had previously been so important had collapsed by the middle of the seventeenth century. This was the result of a slump in domestic demand given the heavy levies on peasants, a significant decline in population due to repeated plagues, and inroads made into traditional Italian markets by Dutch, French and English producers.[91]

Epstein concludes that this agrarian system represented a 'dead end' for Italian economic development. He argues that 'The reason for this failure ... was neither a lack of developed markets nor a too entrenched peasantry, but the absence of sufficient sources of non-agricultural employment for the men and women who crowded the fields'.[92] This conclusion is curious because the lack of sources of non-agricultural employment is perfectly compatible with an entrenched peasantry. Nevertheless, we can conclude that, although the economy was commercial and fairly dynamic, and peasants and lords were able to respond to market opportunities, it is clear that it was the persistence and even strengthening of feudal social-property relations in the early modern period that determined this outcome of cyclical non-development. The origin of these institutional limitations on economic growth in Italy can be identified in the specific form of feudal social-property relations that were established in that country in the tenth and eleventh centuries, namely the rise of the city states.

Heller argues that western Germany took the baton of capitalist development in Europe from Italy in the late fifteenth and early sixteenth century on the basis of its expansion of mining and metallurgical industries and investment of merchant capital in a diverse range of textile industries. This new economic dynamism 'made possible the strengthening of not only capitalism but also feudal reaction'. The outcome of this contradiction was, as he sees it, the German peasant war of 1524–6, an 'early bourgeois revolution' which if successful would 'have meant the initiation of the process of primitive

---

90   Epstein 1998, pp. 88–93, 105–6.
91   Duplessis 1997, pp. 95–6.
92   Epstein 1998, pp. 107–8.

accumulation on the land'.[93] However, as Tom Scott, a leading historian of medieval and early modern Germany, has argued, implicitly following Brenner, without the expropriation of the peasantry and the commodification of landed property, the mere existence of markets and manufacturing, even with large numbers of wage workers and merchant capitalist forms of putting out – industrial systems linking town and countryside – does not necessarily lead to ongoing capitalist development.[94] Without the transformation in rural social-property relations, manufactures based on merchant capital simply form an attribute of a feudal or absolutist economy, even if that economy is interconnected internationally and develops New World colonies.

The mining industries in Germany, which Heller views as most important because of the large numbers of wage workers employed, were particularly volatile and not sustainable due to the exhaustion of ore seams and competition from the Americas. Many of the miners were transient squatters.[95] Western German cities and their merchants were often 'vassals of the emperor' whose close co-operation with the latter ensured extra-economic trading privileges, monopolies, concessions, and political influence in exchange for loans: 'they developed no civic or "bourgeois" culture of their own; their ideals and values remained those of the feudal-aristocratic world in which they were embedded'.[96] Developments in manufacturing in Germany from the mid-fifteenth century, while impressive, did not stimulate widespread transformations in the countryside which would have led to an ongoing proportion of the German population dependent on the market, including the nobility who would have had to transform themselves into mere rentiers to large capitalist farmers. This dynamism formed part of a cyclical up-phase in feudal economies across Europe which was to be followed by a down-phase from the late sixteenth century due to declining productivity in agriculture in the context of overexploitation and overpopulation, resulting in declining revenues, declining demand for non-agricultural products, and increases in non-productive expenditure on warfare and display. If we are talking about production for the world market from the late fifteenth and sixteenth centuries as key to capitalist development in Europe, which orthodox Marxists like Heller wish to do, then we might as well call eastern Germany and eastern Europe capitalist given that its agriculture was, in the same period, increasingly geared to international export, in contrast with western Germany. The fact that this commercialisation of agriculture in the east was based upon the caging of a previously relatively

---

93   Heller 2011, pp. 62, 70.
94   Heller 2011, p. 69.
95   Scott 2002, p. 106.
96   Scott 2002, pp. 21–2. See also pp. 35–6 for the aristocratic origin of urban elites.

free peasantry with only light feudal dues through the imposition of a neo- or second serfdom in the same period would, given Heller's perspective on capitalist development, seem of little consequence.

As in Italy, while forms of merchant and aristocratic capitalist organised *production* can be identified, there was no already existing capitalism to be strengthened by a new economic dynamism, no ongoing systematic capitalist *development* in Germany, and, as we shall see, there was nothing bourgeois (capitalist) about the German peasant war. This was because the transformation of feudal social-property relations on the land did not take place in late medieval and early modern Germany. Early modern western German rural society was characterised by the development of strong village communities after the late medieval feudal agrarian crisis in the fourteenth century, and by the long-term stability of peasant household farms and communal agriculture in the rest of the early modern period. The weakening of seigneurial lordship in the late fourteenth and early fifteenth century in the aftermath of the feudal agrarian crisis led to attempts to consolidate lordship jurisdictions into compact territorial units where they had previously been fragmented. Lords sought to raise the level of feudal dues on peasants and increase their jurisdictional power over them between 1450 and 1525.[97] However, the strengthening of village communes and the broadening of their political scope from the late fourteenth century ensured widespread rebellion and successful resistance to these seigneurial strategies, although not everywhere, and the territorial consolidation of seigneurial jurisdictions was left incomplete. The German peasants' war of 1524–6 largely represented a continuity and the culmination of seventy-five years of resistance, and although it was defeated it checked aggressive attempts at seigneurial encroachments on peasant rights and incomes in the centuries to come.[98]

Princely 'states' were 'a welter of claims and rights', secular and ecclesiastical, rather than clearly defined territories. From 1550 at latest, in the competition for the peasant product between these 'states' and lesser aristocratic and seigneurial lordships (including collective urban lordships) – the administration of which was little different from their larger princely rivals,[99] Robineaux argues that the princes of western Germany became increasingly successful at

---

97   Robisheaux 1998, pp. 132–4; Scott 2002, pp. 236, 239. Scott argues that the motivation to
      reintroduce serfdom in western Germany was largely to restrict the movement of the
      peasantry. As lords built up their territorial 'states in miniature' they exchanged peasants
      and sought to render them immobile in order to control access, in extra-economic fashion, to labour power: Scott 2002, pp. 171–6.
98   Robisheaux 1998, p. 137; Scott 2002, pp. 48–50, 178–82, 233–4.
99   Scott 2002, pp. 13–23.

protecting peasant property against rival seigneurial encroachments, and this development became 'irrevocable' after the mid-seventeenth century. The princes supported hereditary peasant proprietorship, prohibited excessive rent increases and forcible expropriation, and aimed to halt plot fragmentation by instituting impartible inheritance laws. These measures helped to provide for stability in peasant holdings and ensured the peasantry would retain a firm hold on the land. However these 'peasant protection policies' (*Bauernshutzpolitik*) were a means for the princes to protect their tax base to pay for wars, and so peasants would pay a price for the retention of their holdings. After the mid-seventeenth century, and the highly destructive and expensive Thirty Years War, princely governments successfully ensured regular exactions from the peasantry.[100] Duplessis argues that landlords nevertheless managed to take advantage of land hunger to considerably raise ground rents, entry fines and feudal dues, and that before the end of the sixteenth century peasants owed at least a third of their gross yield to state and lord.[101]

As a result of these exactions any economic development was hampered. Little of this money was re-invested in the land, but instead used by princes to build armies, state office-holding bureaucracies and royal courts – often in imitation of French monarchs – and invested in other items of conspicuous consumption such as spectacular renaissance castles. There were no improvements in labour productivity and the great majority remained subsistence based and increasingly poor as they survived on increasingly smaller holdings in many regions. As in France social stratification was marked among the peasantry and a wealthy peasant elite developed by the mid-seventeenth century. However, the increasing princely state and seigneurial levy made them unwilling or unable to improve productivity on their holdings through capital investment. Instead they typically benefited from subletting the problem to smallholders and money lending.[102] Aside from the heavy feudal levy, in periods of overpopulation and high demand for land by semi-landless peasants due to plot fragmentation these large tenants – like the lords – could make more money from renting small plots to peasants than from the returns of capital investment to improve productivity.[103]

100   Robisheaux 1998, pp. 134–6. See Scott for the tendency for fixed term leases and forms of copyhold tenure to be transformed into hereditary tenures, the leases and copyholds – like in England – having been originally developed from feudal tenures: Scott 2002, p. 85.
101   Duplessis 1997, p. 75.
102   Duplessis 1997, pp. 74–6, 162–4.
103   Brenner 2001, pp. 287–8.

The German peasant war of 1524–6 was no more a bourgeois revolution than was the rebellion of 1381 in England. Even if the most radical possible outcome of the German rebellions would have been achieved, namely the overthrow of feudal lordship, this would by no means 'have meant the initiation of the process of primitive accumulation on the land'.[104] Capitalism was not the only alternative to feudalism and one cannot simply assume that the removal of lordship would open the floodgates to capitalist development. The most likely outcome of a root-and-branch peasant victory in the 1520s would have been a more productive and prosperous peasant-based society.

Rural production in eighteenth-century western Germany was still run by peasant farms on the basis of various common field systems, the integrity and routine of which was reinforced by strong self-governing village communes.[105] What ultimately appears to have ensured the persistence of strong peasant communities is the excessively decentralised sovereignty among levels of aristocracy in western Germany as established in the tenth and eleventh centuries. As in Italy, this remained the situation until unification in the late nineteenth century. The resulting balance of reciprocity and competition between western German princes and aristocracy for the peasant product led to the continuity of non-capitalist landholding, and the peasant communities in western Germany were as a result of this balance probably the strongest in Europe. The relative cohesive organisation of the centralised English state and the English nobility appears in clear contrast with the territorial fragmentation and rivalries between the nobility and princes in western Germany.[106]

As with the latest evidence for Germany, recent studies and syntheses of work on France largely support and deepen Brenner's own earlier thesis and

---

104   Heller 2011, p. 70.

105   Robisheaux 1998, pp. 111–16. See Scott 2002, p. 82: Even in the eighteenth century 'there was no widespread enclosure movement along the lines of England'.

106   In the conclusion to his discussion on reasons for varying political and tenurial settlements between lords and peasants in west and east Germany in the aftermath of the 'crisis of feudalism', Scott argues that neither the Marxist nor neo-classical models 'accords sufficient weight to the play of high politics – the impact of territorialisation, both the mobilisation of landed estates in the service of the prince through mortgages, and the uneasy balance between the separate, though reciprocal, interests of the state and the interests of the aristocracy': Scott 2002, pp. 196–7. That is true of orthodox Marxism, but it is exactly these horizontal relationships between state and aristocracy that Robert Brenner has repeatedly tried to highlight as at least as important as the vertical relationships between the aristocractic state and the peasantry. What Brenner also does is to demonstrate the direct relationship *between* the two sets of relations.

analysis.[107] Dewald and Vardi begin their analysis of the French peasantry by stating the following:

> At all points between 1400 and 1789, the French peasantry constituted an enormous mass of population: 15 million people in 1500 (nearly three times the total population of contemporary England), almost 26 million in 1800. Throughout the period they made up about 90 percent of the French population. France only ceased to be a primarily rural society in the late nineteenth century, well after the onset of the industrial revolution.[108]

The figure of 90 percent is a significant overestimate because it refers to everyone living outside of towns containing 10,000 inhabitants or more.[109] If more modest-sized towns are included the figure would probably be nearer 80 percent, although modest towns, particularly the broad base of small towns with under 2,000 inhabitants, were very much integrated into peasant society. This figure can be reduced further because not everyone living in rural society was a peasant. Nevertheless a large majority of the French population on the eve of the French revolution were peasant cultivators. The picture is also one of little or no overall increase in urbanisation in France between the late medieval period and 1800, and the same was true in the rest of Europe outside England and the Netherlands. In England, by comparison, the percentage of the population living in towns of over 10,000 people quadrupled in the same period.[110]

While the French population remained primarily peasant between 1500 and the late nineteenth century, there were significant changes in all aspects of peasant property holding. As Brenner recognised, the peasantry in France generally held their lands by hereditary tenure until the mid-sixteenth century and this gave them effective ownership. However, increasingly subdivided plots due to overpopulation after 1550, harvest failures, highly disruptive warfare on French soil and excessive increases in taxation borne disproportionately by the peasantry – largely to pay for the ambitions of the French absolutist state – undermined this tenure as peasants were forced into debt and ultimately forced to sell up. At the same time demand for land increased from sections of the population outside the peasantry in line with the numbers and wealth of aristocratic royal officials in France's developing absolutist state, and

---

107   See for example Dewald and Vardi 1998; Duplessis 1997.

108   Dewald and Vardi 1998, p. 22.

109   Duplessis 1997, p. 165.

110   Wrigley 1985, p. 708; Jones 1988, p. 4.

urban lawyers and merchants from the same urban milieu also invested. Another key feature of the early modern period was the consolidation of property by seigneurial lords in an attempt to wrest control of the land from the peasantry who were only paying nominal fixed rents.[111] Historians have calculated that by the seventeenth century, in lower Brittany, peasants were proprietors of only eleven percent of the land, and in the grain growing regions around Paris and Toulouse the figure was twenty percent. Further away from these urban areas, and in places where the soil was less attractive, peasant proprietorship remained strong however. Overall estimates for the whole country suggest that in the eighteenth century peasants effectively owned a third of the land, fifty percent was owned by bourgeois and nobles, and ten percent by the church.[112]

Before the so-called Religious Wars (1562–98), French agriculture had already begun to show signs of stagnation and even decline in the 1540s due to plot fragmentation and declining labour productivity. This followed a century of expansion generated by a strong middling peasantry from the end of the Hundred Years' War in 1453.[113] The first wave of peasant sales took place in the late sixteenth century, and these are linked to the devastation and fiscal demands caused by the wars of the second half of the sixteenth century. After a short-lived recovery there was another major wave of peasant sales from 1625 with the onset of the Thirty Years' War.[114] The French peasantry carried a much higher proportion of the nation's tax burden than peasantries elsewhere, and demands from the French state were higher than elsewhere. In England the nobility taxed themselves to pay for wars while, in stark contrast, in France the nobility were largely exempt from taxes. So while French lords were massively increasing their share of land ownership in France vis-à-vis the peasantry, the peasantry had to shoulder the burden of rising taxation and from a decreasing land base. Hence taxation of the French peasantry quadrupled per capita between the 1560s and the 1630s, and from the 1630s 'a revolution in taxation' took place to pay for the full scale war with Spain and then the wars of Louis XIV.[115] Already by the middle of the seventeenth century it is calculated that the majority of the French peasantry held below the subsistence minimum of five hectares, and as many as ten percent became wandering beggars. But what is crucial in the French case is that *the majority of the peasantry who*

---

111   Dewald and Vardi 1998, pp. 27–8; Duplessis 1997, pp. 60–1.
112   Dewald and Vardi 1998, p. 28; Jones 1988, pp. 7–9.
113   Duplessis 1997, p. 59.
114   Dewald and Vardi 1998, pp. 25, 28; Duplessis 1997, pp. 60–1.
115   Dewald and Vardi 1998, p. 40; Duplessis, pp. 62–3.

sold up did not leave the land: 'Most continued to own small plots of land, and usually they rented additional plots', and supplemented their household economies by the waged work of the whole family, often migratory waged work.[116] While they no longer effectively owned the majority of the land, they still *occupied* it.

Despite the growth of absolutist government and the flight of many lords to royal office in Paris, before the late seventeenth century seigneurial lordship remained a significant burden on the peasantry, although this was highly variable throughout the country. Nevertheless, the great wave of peasant revolts from the middle of the sixteenth century to the early eighteenth century, especially before 1670, was targeted at the state and its excessive taxation. This was of course in striking contrast to England where the peasants targeted seigneurial lords and farmers in enclosure riots and mass rebellion in the sixteenth century.[117] Seigneurial dues, monopolies, tax exemptions and enclosed commons would increasingly come to the fore of peasant grievances in France during the eighteenth century and become a widespread national rebellion at the start of the French revolution following the tightening up of the seigneurial regime or 'feudal reaction' in the second half of that century.[118]

Larger peasants benefited from their neighbour's adversity and they accumulated large farms, mostly held by lease by the middle of the seventeenth century; this was a similar situation to their counterparts in western Germany. Economic power was translated into political power in local government and they managed the common lands and the burden of taxation in their own interests. They also innovated in commercial crops and adopted new rotation

---

116   Dewald and Vardi 1998, pp. 25, 28–9; Duplessis 1997, p. 170. The periodisation of 'expropriation' in France compared to England is telling, and reflects the continuing hold of the peasantry on the land. Many peasants in England were forcibly expropriated, thus ending their golden age in the fifteenth century. In France they were forced to sell their heritable lands only after they had become weakened from the late sixteenth century. Reflecting on his study of Normandy during the original 'Brenner Debate', Guy Bois stated that 'What I was able to observe in Normandy fully accords with his [Brenner's] analysis: from 1520–30 one can see the beginnings of a tendency towards the expulsion of tenant farmers (a faint echo of the British enclosure movement), which in the end encountered fierce peasant resistance and the complex development of which would need to be followed right through the wars of religion. This is the same class struggle as occurred in England, but the result is different because the peasantry in France proved to be very strong': Bois 1985, p. 109.
117   Dewald and Vardi 1998, pp. 34–5, 40–1.
118   Jones 1988, pp. 34–59. Peasant discontent with manorial lords was exacerbated by the increase in fiscal pressure from the absolutist state at the same time.

patterns. However, while these farmers may appear at first to represent the French version of the English yeomen, they in fact existed in a very different system of social-property relations. Escalating taxation, rising rents and other seigneurial dues drained capital from the countryside, discouraged innovation and were not compensated by landlord investment. Lords' investment was largely 'extensive' – that is, it was spent on the purchase of new lands in the context of increasingly high rents due to land hunger. The rest was spent on non-productive consumption. Most of the massive revenue from state taxation was squandered on military ambitions, and on building favours through offices in the bureaucracy.[119] As in western Germany, even as early as the late sixteenth and early seventeenth centuries, these farmers saw their best option in sub-leasing and usury, rather than in capital-intensive agriculture:

> Their considerable incomes came less from their land than from collect-ing rents and seigniorial dues, farming taxes and tithes, and extending mortgages and usurious loans to their more numerous poorer neigh-bours. Whenever possible, they sent their sons into commerce or the law, or married them into the lower nobility.[120]

Not only labour productivity, but even total output of French agriculture declined between the 1660s and the 1720s.[121] Conditions improved for the French peasantry in some respects during the eighteenth century as the state reduced restrictions on rural industry and its commercial networks enabling the peasantry to involve themselves in more profitable sidelines. In the six-teenth and seventeenth centuries the state had sought to protect the urban guilds from rural competition. The share of taxation was also spread more equitably on the nobility (although loopholes allowing tax exemptions for the latter remained a ripe issue leading up to the revolution in 1789), and the expansion of royal courts enabled the peasantry to seek justice outside of local private seigneurial courts.[122]

Brenner's assessment of French agriculture in the early modern period as non-capitalist in contrast to the agrarian capitalism of England remains undi-minished. The French rural economy was not immobile and its agricultural productivity in terms of yields per acre in some periods was similar to that in England. However, given French social-property relations in the early modern

---

119   Duplessis 1997, pp. 62–3; Dewald and Vardi 1998, pp. 26, 30–2.
120   Duplessis 1997, p. 63.
121   Duplessis 1997, p. 164.
122   Dewald and Vardi 1998, p. 41.

period, in the crucial factor of *labour* productivity there could be no growth in France, and hence no ongoing urbanisation and industrialisation. Even Philip Hoffman, whose approach to the productivity of French farming is more optimistic than most, recognised that in terms of *labour* productivity French growth was low, only 27 percent between 1500 and 1800, while at the same time it doubled in England. He places the blame mostly on warfare.[123] Warfare was certainly an important factor, but the key point in French development was the continuing hold the peasantry had on the land in symbiosis with the developing absolutist state. This ensured that the farming of small plots and even the larger commercial farms were based upon intensive labour methods rather than extensive labour-saving methods that would have led to growth in labour productivity with all its implications. The intensity and level of warfare and military taxation, which was particularly excessive and destructive in France, had a direct and damaging effect on output from peasant production within French absolutist social-property relations, as Brenner argued. However, even in the middle half of the eighteenth century, a period characterised by fewer, less damaging wars, most estimates only place growth in basic output (*land* productivity) at between 25 to 40 percent. Even the most optimistic estimates suggest that output only just matched population growth, and this small expansion virtually ceased after 1770 when the peasants in regions such as Normandy, the Auvergne and Burgundy, where seigneurial lords remained strong, were once again subjected to a seigneurial offensive which resulted in increased rents, more labour services and other fees.[124]

Davidson relies on a particularly curious part of Hoffman's work on France to argue against Brenner that capitalist agriculture developed in France in the early modern period, and that this development was driven from below by French peasants. Hoffman is at pains to demonstrate – against earlier pioneering French historians such as Bloch and Ladurie – that even small peasants were a driving force for capitalist development in France. Hoffman, in an attempt to portray French peasants as displaying overwhelmingly individualistic characteristics, asserts that French peasant villages in the early modern period were very uncooperative places, despite their communal organisation of common resources and open fields.[125] In England, in the sixteenth century, common fields were sites of early enclosure conflicts as small peasant landholders depended upon them to graze small numbers of animals and collect

---

123 Hoffman 1996, pp. 133–6.

124 Duplessis 1997, pp. 166, 169–70; Brenner 2007, p. 109: Brenner cites figures from Allen 2000, p. 20, and Clarke 1999, p. 211. See also Jones 1988, p. 16.

125 Hoffman 1996, pp. 24–5.

fuel. Peasants fought to preserve them against capitalist encroachment. When the common fields in England were usurped this made it very difficult if not impossible for smaller peasants to survive. However, Hoffman says that far from being reliant for their subsistence on common fields, the poor peasants in France 'often favoured the dissolution of the commons'. Hoffman's evidence for this is taken from a sample of villages in the Paris basin and south-eastern France during the French revolution. When villagers in these regions were asked if they wanted to divide their common pasture following legislation from the revolutionary National Assembly, the poor overwhelmingly voted for the division of the commons, while the rich peasants wished to preserve them. This is because the rich monopolised their use.[126]

Hoffman's evidence for an individualistic, uncooperative and thereby capitalistically disposed poor peasantry in France is ill-conceived and entirely misleading. Villagers did vote to divide the commons in some regions in the early 1790s (without necessarily waiting for legal sanction to do so). However, such division took place in only a handful of cases in each department, particularly in areas such as Paris where landless or near-landless villagers predominated who were desperate for even a small piece of land. Desperation became especially intense after the disastrous harvest of 1788, and shortages and spiralling prices of grain in the years that followed. In most cases peasants opposed division of the commons, because the commons were, as they had always been, a crucial support and asset to the balance of peasants' agricultural economy. It is telling in this respect that conditions of hardship were most keenly felt among the peasantry where there were no longer any commons. The lords and rich farmers opposed the division for difference reasons: for example in 1793 legislation was introduced for the land to be distributed on a 'par tete' basis – that is, through an equal distribution among its users, thereby benefiting the poorest at the expense of the rich. The lords also opposed it because, in earlier decades or centuries, many had appropriated either all or part of it, legally or otherwise. What also perhaps made division of the commons less necessary for the poorest peasantry was the revolutionary government's policy of the division of the property of the church and émigré aristocrats. In the short term, the outcome of competition for this land at auctions, among bourgeois and village communities, saw peasants as the chief beneficiaries in some departments, and the bourgeois in others, although the latter dominated the purchases overall. However, the bourgeoisie increasingly chose to invest in commerce and industry, and in the following two or three decades much of this land was transferred to the small peasantry. The landless agricultural

---

126   Davidson 2012, pp. 528–9; Hoffman 1996, p. 27.

labourers in many regions probably benefited more from large-scale illicit land clearances (*defrichement*) of rough wastes, following the removal of seigneurial controls.[127]

What mostly characterises the actions of the peasantry during the French revolution is the widespread mass anti-seigneurial uprisings from 1788 across France against seigneurial dues, seigneurial courts, seigneurial appropriations of common land and enclosures by *gros fermiers* who were often agents of the seigneurs, and attempts to remove common rights to grazing of the stubble of all lands after the harvest, gleaning, wood-cutting and haymaking on the meadows, etc.[128] It is clear that rather than ushering in capitalism, the revolution strengthened the subsistence-based agricultural economy, and this situation continued until the second half of the nineteenth century. The peasantry also emerged from the revolution stronger politically with the removal of the seigneurial regime and development of municipal government in every commune.[129]

For Davidson, following Hoffman, the evidence for small peasants preferring to divide the common waste reveals the true colours of the French peasantry as capitalist. And yet, while this conclusion is in itself inconceivable giving the empirical evidence of peasant actions and petitions (*cahiers*) during the revolutionary years of 1788 to 1793, in contradiction, he also states that the opposite scenario where peasants protected their commons against encroachment was also as a result of their capitalist motivations.[130] Hoffman found only one example of French peasants fighting to protect the commons, in Varades on the border of Brittany, and, according to his interpretation, they did so 'to protect their stake in what was clearly capitalist agriculture'. For a hundred years after 1639 the peasants resisted their lord's attempts to enclose the village commons. But he says:

> Although the poorer peasants of the parish did let their own cattle graze too, the common pasture was not the preserve of subsistence farming. Rather, it was the meeting place for nascent rural capitalism, the locus for

---

127 Jones 1988, chapter five, pp. 253–4. It is also the case that during the seventeenth century peasants had been willing to collectively sell their commons. However, this was not part of some individualistic commercial strategy, but the result of a desperate need to avoid famine. In other words, they sold their commons for the same reasons they were forced to sell their own plots during that century: Duplessis 1997, pp. 59–63, 166.

128 Jones 1988, chapters three and four; Markoff 1996, chapters five and six.

129 Jones 1988, chapter eight.

130 See especially Markoff 1996.

a curious alliance between modest peasants and the agents of commercial agriculture.[131]

How does Hoffman come to such a conclusion? In a case of 1661, part of the ongoing struggle, a number of villagers in Varades (near Nantes to the northwest) were accused of letting animals graze on the lord's portion of the commons. Of the 27 interrogated in detail, 15 were day labourers, boatmen, weavers or spinners. Of the 11 who were accused of pulling up what appear to have been enclosure markers and of threatening the lord's haywards, nine were of the same background. In other words these were smallholding artisans who needed the commons to pasture animals to supplement their diet and household economies. And yet Hoffman is exercised by the fact that a few peasants admitted to having 40 sheep, some of which had been leased to them for a share of the product by a local merchant: the peasants were therefore using the commons to raise livestock for sale. He concludes that 'the poor of Varades were in league with agricultural capitalists'.[132] Now what appears to be happening here is that some of the better off and yet clearly modest peasants aimed to make a bit of money in a share-cropping arrangement rather than use the commons for pure subsistence. This hardly made them capitalists and the commons 'a meeting place for nascent rural capitalism'. There may or may not have been an abuse of the commons in this case in French customary usage, but if so it was hardly on a great scale. In sixteenth-century England, typical capitalist farmers grazed many hundreds and even thousands of sheep, and I will demonstrate clear examples of this in Part II. Hoffman assumes that a subsistence farmer 'might pasture a cow or perhaps a horse, but not sheep, and certainly not forty of them'. On the contrary, the possession of 40 sheep would be easily compatible with a subsistence farmer, who was nevertheless involved in the market. Hoffman's definition of subsistence is more appropriate for a micro plot holder, or even a landless labourer. The key point here is that the majority of the villagers were typically part peasant and part artisan whose production was subsistence-based and their use of the commons was a crucial support for their survival. This is the general picture. Hoffman's analysis is a particularly extreme example of the confusion that exists for some historians distinguishing between capitalism and commerce, and Davidson's extensive coverage of this case – and the emphasis he places on it as 'full of interest' with regard to capitalist development in France – reveals his own misconceptions about capitalism.

---

131   Hoffman 1996, p. 23.
132   Hoffman 1996, p. 23.

For his next example, Davidson cites Henry Heller's work on France (which is geared to promoting the French revolution as a capitalist revolution following what he perceives as the development of capitalism in that country). Heller finds that in Languedoc and Normandy 'a differentiation – indeed, a polarisation – was already taking place by the first half of the sixteenth century', and furthermore – citing Kriedt – Davidson states that 'the expropriation of the peasantry began to intensify from the 1740s':[133]

> Whereas the peasants were more or less successful in defending the 'occupancy' of the land against outside attempts to take it away from them, the landlords also tried to enlarge their estates mainly at the expense of the common land. Thus, common rights were carved up, forests were closed and grazing rights superseded. Production on the estates became more rationalised, also in the sense that the landlords tended to rely on the *gros fermiers*. The latter in turn usually leased the land to the peasants, thus interposing themselves between the landlord and the mass of peasants.[134]

Davidson adds that '[c]learly this is not exactly the same as the process in England, since an element of both feudal rent and payment in kind was retained within the peasant relationship to the landowners or larger tenants'.[135] This is true because, to begin with, there is no basis in this quote for Davidson to argue that the expropriation of the peasantry intensified from the 1740s. Kriedt is saying that peasants were not generally expropriated from their means of production: they still occupied the land even if they no longer held it in hereditary tenure as before, something we have discussed above. Second, we have *lords* carving up the commons and removing the peasants' common rights, something which is in direct contradiction to Hoffman's earlier arguments which Davidson cites approvingly. Lords who had earlier appropriated common land would feel the force of determined peasant uprisings during the early years of the French revolution as we have just seen. And third, as in Germany, we have a situation where lords leased their consolidated demesnes to big farmers who, instead of investing in greater labour productivity and expanding their enterprises, saw their best option in sub-letting at market rates to the mass of small peasants suffering from severe land hunger. Fourth, feudal rents and payment in kind were also retained. This situation could not

---

133   Davidson 2012, p. 529.
134   Davidson 2012, p. 529. This quote is taken from Kriedt 1983, p. 111.
135   Davidson 2012, p. 529.

be more different from that experienced in England. When landlords in England rationalised their estates and leased them to 'big farmers', hundreds of years before this French example, this either involved the removal of the remaining peasant tenants or the tenants had already been removed in earlier waves of enclosure.

Apparently recognising the weakness of this example Davidson quickly moves on to another in the urbanised Toulousian and the Lauragais region where according to him dispossession of the peasantry really 'was a fact', and that '[t]he French peasants were considerably less secure than Brenner claims'.[136] According to David Parker the peasantry held only a fifth or less of the land there by the early eighteenth century. They did however represent between sixty and seventy percent of the population and survived on tiny plots, 84 percent holding less than 7.41 acres (3 hectares). Again, there is no contradiction here with Brenner's thesis. Brenner recognised that the French peasantry had their hereditary property undermined during the early modern period, as we have seen above (as Dewald and Vardi concluded), and yet the vast majority of peasants nevertheless remained on the land by leasing small plots, supplementing their household economies through labouring on the larger holdings. This is simply another example of a mass peasantry which was still tied to the land in France as late as the early eighteenth century, either through ownership or renting of small plots, and they would continue to do so well into the following century. Presumably the rest of the population were urban dwellers – non-capitalist bourgeois – who also had holdings in the surrounding territory, and lords who held the rest, and who sub-leased the lands to the peasantry. In this situation, there was going to be no endogenous self-sustaining capitalist development based on integrated domestic demand. As Hoffman recognised, there was no growth in labour productivity and urbanisation in France between 1500 and 1800. Even overall output barely matched population growth, even in periods of economic expansion.

Given their desire to see capitalism throughout early modern Europe, orthodox Marxists are pleased with Brenner's allowance that capitalism developed in Holland in the early modern period.[137] Opposition to this view comes however from a political Marxist, Ellen Meiksins Wood, a close colleague of Brenner.[138]

Wood agrees fundamentally with Brenner's thesis on the origin of capitalism in England, but she finds the Dutch case ambiguous to say the the very

136 Davidson 2012, p. 530.
137 For Brenner's position on the Low Countries see Chapter One in Part I.
138 Wood 2002a; Wood 2012, pp. 110–16.

least, and has strong doubts over whether there was a transition to capitalist social-property relations in the northern Netherlands in the same period. She recognises that as a result of the ecological degradation of the soil following earlier colonisation, Dutch farmers were forced to specialise in animal rearing and dairy products and sell these in order to buy in food grains from the Baltic in order to survive. However, she argues that Brenner places too much emphasis on ecological degradation as the means by which peasants became market-dependent and were forced to switch to dairy farming. She points to the rapid urbanisation in the region in the sixteenth century as a result of the growing domination of the cities of Holland in international trade, shipping and finance, and its capture of sources of cheap grain from eastern Europe in the fifteenth century through the Baltic ports. This followed the subjection of the eastern European peasantry to serfdom and the (non-capitalist) commercialisation of agriculture there. For Wood, it was the securing by *extra-economic* means of this supply of essential bread grain from the east that should be given greater emphasis in the analysis of the switch to dairying by the relatively small Dutch owner-occupiers on the peat lands.

Wood is particularly critical of Brenner's lack of incorporation of the broader social-property relations in his thesis on capitalism in the Dutch Republic, particularly the role of the state and its heavy taxation for non-productive purposes. She argues that the Dutch state remained essentially feudal if urban-centred: it was headless and multi-polar and its elites relied increasingly on extra-economic income rather than increased revenue through improving productivity.[139] More controversially, in line with her argument outlined above, she also argues that the overall logic of the Dutch economy remained pre-capitalist. For her, farmers' privileged access to cheap produce in the Baltic grain market was reliant on the extra-economic trade interventions of Dutch merchants rather than on competitive production within an integrated economic region. Unlike the English landlords, whose increasing wealth was dependent upon the competitive production of their tenants, the even greater wealth of Dutch elites was dependent upon commerce and its taxation, and – increasingly during and following the general crisis of the seventeenth century – on lucrative office holding in a state with motivations and characteristics very similar to the French tax/office or absolutist model. It was the latter

---

139   The early modern Dutch state was an assembly of political formations generated in the late medieval period, made up of 'independent, small lordships; federations of urban and rural communities; an autonomous city with its hinterland; ecclesiastical principalities; territorial principalities; and personal unions of principalities': Van Bavel 2010, pp. 74–5, pp. 263–70.

extra-economic course that Dutch elites took in response to this economic crisis, and during the eighteenth century much of their earlier investment in production dried up. In England by contrast the tenant farmers developed in a mutual relationship with the lords and responded to declining agricultural prices with increases in productive investment to enhance labour productivity and cost effectiveness, a response which unlike that of Dutch elites was symptomatic of capitalist social-property relations.

Brenner has in his most recent paper reaffirmed his earlier position that economic development in Holland took the same form as England during the early modern period 'despite the many major differences between Dutch and English agriculture in structure and operation'.[140] For him the similarities which are symptomatic of capitalist social-property relations and capitalist development are more compelling than the differences. With the help of recent statistics from Robert Allen, he argues that unlike everywhere else in Europe, in both countries the population continued to grow and did not hit a Malthusian ceiling, because in both countries there were ongoing improvements in agricultural productivity and the progressive movement of an increasing proportion of the population outside of agriculture which was sustained by those improvements. And, in a crucial related process, in both countries proto-industrial work was separated from the household economies and became specialised in industrial districts which quickly evolved into fast growing towns.[141] Brenner's statistical indicators of capitalist *development* in the two countries between 1500 and 1750 are compelling in this respect. However, the question that arises is why was that development significantly halted in Holland during the eighteenth century? Agricultural productivity in Holland saw a remarkably steep decline in comparison with England between 1750 and 1850, and this was not helped by the precipitous rise in the price of grain exported from the east from 1750.[142] Wood suspects that Brenner's argument that this was due to the close integration of the Dutch economy into the feudal economies of the rest of Europe is not sufficient explanation, and that much greater focus should be placed on the nature of the Dutch state.

A major problem with Wood's critique of Brenner is her focus on his analysis of the peasant, owner-occupied, peat lands, and yet Brenner also pointed to certain regions of the maritime northern Netherlands and maritime Flanders, where capitalist social-property relations appear to have existed in the form of landlords and large leaseholding tenants similar to those in

---

140   Brenner 2007, p. 106.

141   Brenner 2007, pp. 108–9.

142   Brenner 2007, p. 109; Brenner 1985a, p. 53.

England. Her critique should therefore be broadened and modified to include these regions beyond the peat lands. Indeed, Bas Van Bavel has drawn attention to the development of agrarian capitalist social-property relations in another area of the Low Countries, namely in parts of the inland Guelders river area which is located to the south-east of the maritime northern Netherlands. He argues that property relations in some parts of this area followed the English model of a strong lordship-dominated property structure. A highly manorialised regime from the early settlement of the region, lords continued to maintain controls over land holding in the fifteenth and sixteenth centuries following the decline of serfdom through the spread of competitive short term leasing. According to Van Bavel this led to sharp social polarisation among the peasantry, resulting in the triad capitalist model by 1580. He also argues that while for much of the late medieval period Holland's rural economy was peasant (owner-occupier)-orientated, it too succumbed to the ravages of competitive leaseholding from the end of the sixteenth century (bourgeois investors from the growing cities were particularly prominent in this process), and the triad structure had also emerged there as a result.[143]

The uniqueness and complexity of the origins and development of varying forms of social-property relations in the Low Countries certainly presents a challenge to historians. While, as Wood has pointed out, the Dutch state remained multi-polar in the early modern period, and much of its economy (if we can describe the Dutch Republic as having one economy) was deeply dependent upon overseas trade and sources of grain from the serf economy of the east, rather than on an integrated domestic market, agrarian capitalist social structural forms appear to have existed on the English model in certain areas and for certain periods, although stemming from different origins: from early aristocratic reclamation and settlement, taking the form of landlord lessors and large tenant lessees; from social polarisation following the expansion of short-term competitive leasehold during the fifteenth and sixteenth centuries in areas that had earlier been strongly manorialised; and from a similar process as the latter on owner-occupier lands in the late sixteenth and seventeenth centuries. And yet at the same time other major regions in the Low Countries, even under the influence of unprecedentedly large urban economies, saw holding fragmentation. There was no such diversity in England. Some regions in England developed the agrarian capitalist triad form earlier than others, but none reverted back to the Malthusian cycle in which peasant holdings re-fragmented in the early modern period as was clearly the case in the Low Countries.

---

143   Van Bavel 2007; Van Bavel 2010, pp. 176, 242–6, 259–60.

Whether one comes down on the side of Brenner or Wood, it is becoming increasingly clear that the central determining factor of economic and social development or non-development in the regions within the Low Countries was social-property relations and not self-propelling commercialisation. Van Bavel has repeatedly underscored this conclusion in his recent work, much of which is informed by new archival research.

Overall, recent research confirms Brenner's thesis that, outside of England the early modern period witnessed cyclical economic non-development in Europe. Even in the precociously highly urbanised Low Countries, economic development was halted in the eighteenth century. Sustained increases in labour productivity into the eighteenth and nineteenth century were only achieved in England following the systematic expropriation of the peasantry from their means of subsistence and means of production, much of which was achieved by direct eviction and intimidation from the second half of the fifteenth century. But this 'classic form of expropriation' occurred only in England and it laid the basis for the first modern industrial revolution. In France and Germany, much peasant property began to be undermined much later, from the late sixteenth century, especially in France, due to the excessive fragmentation of plots due to rapid population increases during the previous century, excessive state taxation, military destruction and the persistence and even increase in some regions of a significant seigneurial burden. As a result peasants were forced to sell up and a polarisation in landholding had taken place by the mid-seventeenth century. Generally, peasants could not be evicted in the English manner because peasant property was protected by the state, especially in Germany. However the mass of peasantry, while losing much of their means of subsistence, remained on the land by retaining their means of production through leasing small plots that had been accumulated by lords and their larger tenants. This contrasted with the systematic removal of the peasantry during the processes of accumulation in England. In Italy consolidated farms were developed in the territories of city states as early as the thirteenth century, and military and fiscal pressure after the Black Death forced many peasants to sell up and migrate, while common lands were eroded as they were sold off by city states from the late fifteenth century. As in France and Germany, however, Italian peasant villages and rural commons remained resilient and production was labour-intensive and saw declining labour productivity over the early modern period, even on the large consolidated farms. In Italy the countryside became 're-feudalised' as the old city states were subsumed under larger territorial powers. In France and Germany too, urbanisation could only go so far in the absence of increases in labour productivity, and industrialisation was mainly confined to rural areas as a support for peasant household economies. All periods of expansion and innovation were eventually stifled as capital was drained from the countryside by state and seigneury.

In conclusion, recent critiques of Brenner and political Marxism by orthodox Marxists have served to underscore the fundamental differences between the two approaches. Orthodox Marxists are hampered by their systematic misreading of Brenner and Wood especially, and by their commitment to the transhistorical elements in Marx's revolutionary theory which Marx himself could not justify historically, and which he clearly contradicted in *Capital*. The orthodox Marxist thesis on the transition to capitalism remains closely associated with the traditional commercialisation thesis: it is urban- and trade-centred and essentially views capitalism as the result of progressive developments in commerce and the techniques and organisation of production. It overlooks Marx's later emphasis on the internal solidity of particular societies such as feudal societies in the face of the potential dissolving effects of commerce, and contradicts his clear understanding of the origin of capitalism as essentially and primarily the result of rural expropriation: for Marx capitalism had an agrarian origin. As we have seen, political Marxism embraces these emphases in Marx's later work. It does so, fundamentally, by insisting on the primacy of specific social-property relations in any analysis of societies such as feudalism and capitalism and in the analysis of historical development from one to the other.

PART TWO

Economic and Social Transformations in Kent: A Case Study

∴

A case study on the origin of capitalism in Kent provides an opportunity to address the questions thrown up in earlier discussions to one of the most commercialised and free counties in late medieval and sixteenth-century England. The county was closely integrated commercially and politically with London and the crown, and situated between London and the continent:

> Trevelyan is unjust when he depicts medieval England as an island on the edge of the European world. Actually her south eastern corner, with London and Kent and its many harbours, extended into its very heart; London is closer to the coast of France than to Bristol, closer to Flanders than to Yorkshire, closer to Paris than to Durham. The Channel does not divide England from the continent so much as connect her with it ... the south east of England lay at a great crossroads where the trade routes from Scandinavia, the Baltic, the North sea, the Atlantic coast and the Mediterranean all met.[1]

By the early fourteenth century, most of the peasantry in the county held their lands by a relatively free customary tenure which was hereditary. These holdings were typically already enclosed rather than spread out in open or common fields, and as a result common land was much rarer in Kent than in regions such as the midlands where agricultural production was undertaken in open fields:

> The south east is well known as a land of early enclosure and several cultivation where, during the Middle Ages, a man's holdings were likely to lie scattered and hedged about, a field here, a piece of pasture there, a copse and an embanked tract of marshland beyond. But the country is large and various, and there is the evidence of one's eyes, let alone of the documents, that large and open fields existed too.[2]

By some definitions the county was already capitalist in the fourteenth century, or otherwise it certainly had all the ingredients to make it so if commerce was allowed to take its natural course. Kent and other counties in the south-east of England were indeed among the first regions to develop agrarian capitalism from the second half of the fifteenth century. The commercialisation perspective proposed by medieval economic historians such as Richard Britnell

---

1 Kosminsky 1956, p. 321.
2 Du Boulay 1966, p. 130.

and orthodox Marxists such as Neil Davidson who both view capitalist development as the result of the progressive development of the productive forces might therefore appear to be vindicated to some extent. However in Chapter Nine below I show that the attributes just described were entirely compatible with a traditional subsistence-based society. The peasantry was relatively free and holdings were occupied on a more individualistic basis in contrast to the midlands for example, but, as I hope to demonstrate in Chapter Ten, like everywhere else in England agrarian capitalism was generated and developed through the engrossment and enclosure of holdings of all forms of tenure and organisation, and this process was not by any means a natural extension of an already commercialised society. Chapters Eleven and Twelve are both concerned with the periodisation of the emergence of an agrarian capitalist social-property structure, the development of new mentalities, new political structures and, above all, a new economic logic. Chapter Thirteen explores how a cultural production grew out of these new developments and reflected changes in the preoccupations of both the centralising Tudor state and local government. This study goes beyond the usual accounts of the transition by integrating a small town into the analysis, and it thereby includes the political and commercial structures of agrarian society beyond village and manorial settlements in which inhabitants of the latter were closely involved.

The study is based on original primary research, and Lydd and its region were chosen as a focus because of the survival of a particularly extensive and rich archive for that area in the fifteenth and sixteenth centuries. The administration of the seigneurial lords survives in the form of manorial rentals, court rolls and accounts from the thirteenth century, and unusual and remarkable insights into the administration and organisation of those below the gentry can be derived from the particularly rich borough record. Another important source for understanding changing structures of property ownership, class relations, consumption, inheritance practices and mentalities is the voluminous testamentary record that survives for this region. For Lydd alone, approximately 500 wills survive for the period between 1450 and 1550. These provide insights into thousands of late medieval lives, including people of all backgrounds, even those too poor to require a will.[3]

---

3   To avoid over-referencing in the footnotes, all references to wills appear in the Appendix. The name and date of the will in the text is sufficient to find the archive reference in the Appendix.

CHAPTER 9

Economy and Society in Late Medieval Lydd and Its Region

The aim of this chapter is to provide insights into the economy and society of Lydd and its region from the late thirteenth century to the middle of the fifteenth century. The focus of interest is on the first half of the fifteenth century and the nature of this community or set of communities before the processes of engrossment and enclosure transformed it from a fundamentally peasant, feudal social-property structure, into a fundamentally capitalist social-property structure. What I hope to demonstrate is that in this precocious region for the emergence of agrarian capitalism, before the middle decades of the fifteenth century, there was little indication of the transformation to come. It is my contention that this community or set of communities remained robustly subsistence-based in the first half of the fifteenth century, part-peasant and part-artisan with petty commercial trading providing its dominant culture both in terms of production and government. Large farmers leasing demesnes were now present and, on the basis of those leases, they were the wealthiest in the region below the gentry. But if one examines the first half of the fifteenth century as a discrete period, in its own right, one does not sense that they could come to represent the dominant culture in the near or even far future. As Hilton pointed out, this was a period for the middle peasantry, not the yeomen capitalist farmers. Change could only come through a momentous economic and political rupture both from within and from outside of this community. In other words, there was no inexorable rise of capitalism after the decline of serfdom and the transfer of the lords' demesnes to the wealthier peasantry.

Lydd is located in the Romney Marshes on the southern coast of Kent in the south-eastern corner of England. In the medieval period the parish of Lydd contained a small town of the same name and several rural manors. At about three miles across in all directions it was the largest parish in Kent. To the south it faced northern France to which its inhabitants had easy access by boat. They also had easy coastal links with the southern and eastern ports of England and with London via the Thames estuary. Some eight miles to the north and west of Lydd the marsh land rises up into the Weald of Kent which in the late medieval period was a vast stretch of woodland and in the fifteenth century became densely settled as a result of the development of an important cloth industry and ironworks. Lydd had access to the Weald both by road and by estuary.

Some 60 miles distant by road lay northern Kent and London which Lydd's inhabitants frequented by horse as well as by boat along the coast.

i   Demographic Change and its Causes

Because of the importance of the question of demographic change in the earlier theoretical discussions, it will be given its due attention here. Research on state taxation in medieval Kent provides a clear introduction to demographic changes in this period. A comparison of taxation evidence in 1334–5 for eight 'hundreds' – that is, taxable units of settled territory – in Romney Marsh with that of another eight hundreds in the nearby Weald reveals that about fifteen years before the Black Death in 1348–9 the population density was considerably higher in the Marsh than in the Weald. The Marsh contained 55 people per 1,000 acres, and the Weald only eight people per 1,000 acres. In fact the population density in the Marsh was only marginally lower than that recorded for the fertile regions of the north-west of the county and its central and eastern lowlands. However, taxation subsidies in the 1520s reveal that by the early sixteenth century the contrast between the Weald and the Marsh had been reversed.[1]

The Marsh became depopulated in the late medieval period as its traditional mixed farming was increasingly replaced by rich grazing grounds for cattle and sheep by farmers who were increasingly based either in or not far from the Weald. The population of the Weald became increasingly dense from the middle third of the fifteenth century as it became an important region of rural industry in both cloth and iron. The cloth industry developed in symbiosis with increasing specialisation in the Marsh which was by the late fifteenth century the principal grazing region of Kent.

It is generally recognised that the widespread change to pastoral farming was the major factor in the permanent depopulation of the Marsh that took place in this period. But the timing and the causes of the change are assumed rather than demonstrated. Environmental factors are assumed by some to have been the key drivers of the change. The decay of ports bordering the Marsh such as New Romney and Hythe coincided with the silting up of their harbours in the fourteenth and fifteenth centuries, and this effect on the harbours and consequent decline in trade has been cited as a probable reason that

---

1   Hanley and Chalklin 1964, pp. 65–6; Killingray and Lawson 2010, p. 58. A 'hundred' was a unit of territory that was subjected to royal taxation and the local royal court. It originally represented a hundred farms in the Anglo-Saxon period, hence its name.

many left the Marsh. The silting of harbours of ports such as New Romney, Lydd's neighbour, had begun in the early fourteenth century, but as we shall see the extent of this process by the end of the fifteenth century suggests that it was most likely the result of the significant investment by Wealden gentry and major ecclesiastical lords in the inning of new land and reclaiming old land from the sea. This reclamation was done in order to lease valuable marsh land in large blocks to commercial farmers. Inning and reclamation changed the shape of the coastline and affected the natural scouring motion of the sea, and it was this artificial process in the context of particular economic changes in the fifteenth century which led to the silting up of places that previously had harbours rather than an accident of nature. Indeed contemporaries blamed the decay of harbours at Rye and Sandwich in the sixteenth century on earlier inning.[2] Another environmental cause, flooding by inundations from the sea, is also cited as an important factor in the depopulation of the Marsh in this period, or at least it is thought that flooding had a role in initiating or hastening the process. But flooding affected a few very small settlements at most, particularly in the west of the Marsh and over the border into Sussex.[3] In fact areas vulnerable to flooding in the fifteenth century actually stimulated investment in the Marsh in order to preserve old and create new valuable fertile marshland for grazing in the context of a renewed and sustained market demand for wool. In the 1470s there was talk of the risk of 'inestimable losses' of property if wall defences and drains were not properly constructed. There is however no evidence of any catastrophe caused by flooding at this time, and if there was it would have almost certainly been mentioned in the detailed town accounts. The blame for this risk was placed on small occupiers who had defaulted in their drainage tax, and this marked the beginning of a reorganisation of drainage maintenance in the area.[4] This tightening up of the drainage regime that had been in place for more than 200 years accompanied greater investment in the Marsh and the expansion of capitalist leasehold farming.

With regard to the timing of the changes, in a recent study of the economy of late medieval Kent, Mavis Mate argues that the depopulation of the Marsh occurred on a greater scale than elsewhere in Kent soon after the Black Death. She detects that in the aftermath of the Black Death, in spite of the well-known attempts by the state to pin back the level of wages, wage levels were extremely variable across the county. This was the case even where workers were subjected to the same lordship such as Battle Abbey or Canterbury Cathedral

---

2   Murray 1931, pp. 208–10; Hipkin 1995, pp. 138–47; Mate 2006, p. 171.
3   Hanley and Chalklin 1964, pp. 65–6; Mate 1991, pp. 130–6.
4   See below.

Priory, thus revealing that wages were negotiated according to local conditions. For example, between the 1350s and the 1370s a shepherd at Meopham in
north-west Kent could earn 5s 6d, compared to 6s to 7s in north-east Kent, and
10s to 12s on some Romney Marsh manors. Mate deduces from this evidence
that there was a greater contraction of population on Romney Marsh than
elsewhere in Kent in these decades, because in order to achieve these wage
levels workers must have had greater bargaining power there, probably due to
a relative scarcity of available labour. She argues that her contention is reinforced by the inclusion of six Romney Marsh parishes in Maurice Beresford's
list of 'lost villages' in England, namely Eastbridge, Orgaswick, Orlestone,
Blackmanstone, Hope All Saints and Midley.[5] She says that the Marshes were
already 'teeming with animals' in the early fifteenth century, an indication that
they had already replaced the people. Pastoral farming was stimulated early in
the century by the Hundred Years' War which led to demand for food and
clothing by English troops in France, especially in the fortress at nearby Calais.[6]

There is, however, no evidence to suggest that these settlements became
deserted immediately in the decades following the plagues in the fourteenth
century. In fact, as a general rule, substantial settlements throughout the Marsh
continued into the fifteenth. The village of Midley (which developed out of
Lydd parish into a separate parish) was about a mile and a half from Lydd
church. Poll tax evidence for 1377 records 43 people in Midley and 89 people in
nearby Old Romney in that year.[7] The poll tax targeted everyone over the age
of 14 years, and we can therefore assume that, bearing in mind possible tax eva-
sion, these numbers represented approximately sixty percent of the total population. On the basis of this evidence there is no doubt that rural settlement
near Lydd continued to be significant in the immediate post-Black Death
period. Midley became the base for large farmers such as William Brokhill in
the late fifteenth century, and this had implications for engrossment and
depopulation, but there is also evidence that a community of sorts remained
there in the first half of the sixteenth century.[8]

From an archaeological point of view, Mark Gardiner has pointed to the
ruins of the churches of Midley and Hope All Saints that survive today as

---

5   Mate 2010, pp. 11–12.

6   Mate 1987, pp. 523–5.

7   Fenwick 1998, p. 395.

8   References to the rector of Midley in William Butcher of Lydd's will of 1492 and John Holme's
    of 1496 reveal a functioning parish there at this time, as does a bequest by Vincent Daniel in
    1520 to finish the tabernacle of Midley church. In 1533 Simon Leche bequeathed to 'poor
    maidens' in Midley parish. For Brokhill, see Mate 1987, p. 533.

evidence that these settlements were not abandoned until after the mid-sixteenth century. If the ruins of churches belonging to settlements do not survive, Gardiner argues that this is because they were generally destroyed *before* the middle of the sixteenth century, and their materials were used for building by inhabitants still living in settlements nearby. He also argues that the crises over flooding in the Marsh in the fifteenth century were generally temporary, and, as I have said, investment in inning and drainage was the rule.[9]

Apart from Hope All Saints, which lay very close to New Romney, the other four vills on Mate's list of deserted villages were situated further inland in the north of the Marsh, adjacent to the Weald. This area was the ancient Marsh region called 'Romney Marsh proper', technically '[t]he Level of Romney Marsh'. It was situated above the ancient sea wall that is known as the Rhee Wall, and at 23,000 acres it was slightly larger than the area of the Marsh below the wall (which contained approximately 20,000 acres and Lydd parish). The poll tax returns of 1377 that survive record 58 people in Eastbridge and eight in Blackmanstone. The latter figure seems small but this was always a tiny vill. It is revealing that its larger neighbour, Dymchurch, returned a figure of 102 taxpayers. Other rural settlements spreading from east to west on the edge of the Level of Romney Marsh returned the following numbers of taxpayers in 1377: Burmarsh 72, Bilsington 81, Newchurch 202, Snave 70, Kennardington 175 and Appledore 269.[10] While there may have been a contraction in the immediate decades following the Black Death and subsequent plagues in the 1360s especially, these substantial populations of rural vills do not point to some special demographic change or depopulation on Romney Marsh before the fifteenth century which contrasts with elsewhere in Kent. There is, however, evidence that the population of the 'Level' may have contracted significantly later on, by the middle third of the *fifteenth* century. In 1462 its inhabitants or potential inhabitants were granted a charter by the crown providing them with similar privileges as those with the Cinque Ports franchise. This was an attempt by the state to attract and retain people and thereby ensure that the southern coast of Kent had settled communities and the human power necessary to defend the realm against a military invasion.[11] This was indeed one of the general concerns the crown had in the decades that followed with regard to depopulating enclosure in these areas.

Below the Rhee Wall in the manor of Appledore (mostly in Brookland parish) to the north and west of Lydd, there is evidence of a fairly dense peasant

---

9   Gardiner 1998, pp. 130–2.
10   Fenwick 1998, pp. 390–6.
11   Techman-Derville 1936, chapter 3.

population between 1400 and 1470. With little evidence of significant accumulations and consolidations of land for most of the period, these peasants held modest holdings and many supported these holdings with by-trades. Over half of the transactions in the land market in the period were of holdings containing less than five acres. There are signs of significant accumulation only towards the end of the period. For example, there was one holding of 73 acres, but more frequently holdings of between 15 and 30 acres.[12] There is evidence of accumulations of small plots in the west of Lydd parish in the late fourteenth and early fifteenth centuries and the deliberate formation of these plots into a substantial consolidated leasehold farm. However rental evidence for the largest rural manor in Lydd parish, that of Dengemarsh, reveals a density of population and land market in very small plots in the 1430s, similar to the evidence for Appledore (Dengemarsh will be examined in more detail below).

What appears to have happened on Romney Marsh as a whole in the post-Black Death period is that, rather than a broad contraction of population across the area immediately after the plagues in the 1340s and 1360s as Mate has argued, there was most likely a movement and resettling of population in the Marsh and adjacent Weald in the late fourteenth and first half of the fifteenth centuries as peasants and artisans sought better opportunities and freer conditions. It seems very unlikely that the area could be popular in the 1330s with the population density comparable to the highest densities elsewhere in the county and only 20 years later to witness a complete reversal in comparative fortunes in this respect; unless of course one resorts to assumptions about accidental environmental factors. Let us finally return to Mate's deduction from the evidence of high wages on Romney Marsh in the 1350s that these reflect the bargaining power and the scarcity of labour. The taxation evidence of 1334–5 reveals that, in addition to a high density of population on Romney Marsh, the inhabitants of the Marsh were comparatively prosperous returning an average of 4s each to the crown's coffers. This figure compares favourably to the taxable wealth derived by the crown from the fertile districts of north-central and north-eastern Kent. Relatively high densities of population corresponded to relatively high incomes and therefore presumably relatively high wages on Romney Marsh *before* the Black Death. Relatively high wages were therefore a feature of the region in the late medieval period as a whole, rather than a new feature caused by demographic downturn after the Black Death. I will argue that it was changes in production and demand, and the processes of enclosure and engrossment from the middle third of the fifteenth century

12   Sweetinburgh 2002, pp. 140–56.

especially, which were responsible for the sustained and permanent depopulation of the Marsh.

As a member of the Cinque Port federation Lydd's franchise, like that of the other ports along the Kent coast who were also members, ensured that it was not subject to standard royal taxation. This limits our ability to derive comparative population indices from the late thirteenth century to the early sixteenth century. The absence of evidence from the poll taxes of 1377 to 1381 and the subsidies of 1524–5 present a particular problem. Our knowledge of population in Lydd parish in this period is largely dependent upon manorial rentals and so some indication of the nature of the patchwork of the manorial landscape will be necessary here at the outset. In the mid-fifteenth century some seven manors and sub-manors claimed jurisdiction within Lydd. Aldington, the archbishop of Canterbury's enormous demesne manor, engulfed virtually the whole of the 'urban' area of Lydd and much surrounding land in the form of the 'half-hundred of Langport'. In addition were the Aldington sub-manors of Old Langport and New Langport alias Septvans which covered the west side of the parish from the town and overlapped with the small parishes of Old Romney in the north-west, Midley in the west, and Broomhill in the south-west. These were held by knight's fees. The Old Langport manor took in some of the properties on the north and west of the town as well as some of Old Langport village. Also to the south-west of the town was the manor of Scotney, a recent foundation of All Souls College, Oxford. To the south and east of the town was the important manor of Dengemarsh. This was a separate coastal limb of the large inland manor of Wye which was held by Battle Abbey. The other manors were Belgar to the north-west, which belonged to Bilsington Convent and Priory, and Jacques Court, the ancient seat of the Etchingham knights of Sussex, which lay close to the town on the north-east side. The church was a benefice of Tinterne Abbey which also owned a number of commercial properties in the town.[13]

So besides the town of Lydd, the parish contained numerous other rural settlements. The most significant manors were Aldington, which contained most of the town properties, and Dengemarsh which linked the town to the coast in the south and east. A survey in 1285 of the Aldington manor recorded 100 tenants in the densely packed few streets of the town.[14] If we apply a multiplier of 4.5 to 5 in order to include whole households in the calculation, this figure represented a population of approximately 450–500 people, and placed the town in terms of habitation on the lower rung of urbanised settlements in

13   Hasted 1972, pp. 420–39.
14   Whitney 2000.

England at this time. A rental of Dengemarsh from about the same time in 1310–15 records 56 tenants.[15] However, exactly half of these tenancies were held by 'co-parceners' (that is, shared by more than one holder). Some of these co-holders were named brothers or simply 'heirs of' earlier holders. So earlier tenancies on the manor had been divided or shared among a greater number of holders, and this is as one would expect given the general peak in population around 1300. If we therefore double the count of the 28 holdings with co-holders, the overall number of holders becomes 84, and probably more. We must however be wary of assuming that all of these holders actually lived in the manor, because, from what we know from later records, burgesses of Lydd also held plots in the manor and Dengemarsh was closely tied to the town with representation in the town government and common council. Indeed 28 people named in the rental occupied no land in the manor, but had sublet it to others. What we do know is that at least 49 messuages (that is, habitable tenements that may include more than one household) were recorded as paying rent on Dengemarsh in 1432, and in the 1460s during a dispute over recent engrossment it was stated that some 70 households had been removed from the north of the manor alone. It seems therefore that the population of Dengemarsh was comparable to that of the borough of Lydd around 1300 although spread over a much wider area. Given the other manors, the overall population of the parish and a little beyond (as the manors were not entirely coterminous with the parish boundary) must have amounted to well in excess of 1,000 people in 1300; and traders, shoppers and other visitors would have swelled this population a good deal more.

A greater degree of imagination is required for population estimates for the first half of the fifteenth century, particularly for the town. The town's administrative accounts begin in 1428 and as soon as they open they record extensive investment in the building of a 'Common Hall' or Town Hall, and in the following two decades the building of a new belfry and church tower.[16] All of this was paid for by local taxation and one might conclude that this is evidence of broad prosperity in the town, and an area attractive to migrants. There was also an increase in the number of freemen in the town in the first half of the fifteenth century – that is, in the number of people accepted as worthy of the franchise and who were willing to pay an entry fine for the privilege. The number of freemen fluctuated between 64 and 70 between 1432 and 1442, with an average of 67, and from there it jumped to 84 and 81 in the two surviving lists for 1446.[17]

---

15   Scargill-Bird 1887, pp. 42–52.

16   East Kent Archive Centre (EKAC), Ly/fac 1, or Finn 1911.

17   The National Archives (TNA), E 179, 226/57, 75, 84; 227/99; 228/114, 128, 138; 229/149.

It is the absence of vacancies and the density of holdings in the manor of Dengemarsh in 1432 that provides the most convincing evidence of a healthy density of population in Lydd parish in the first half of the fifteenth century.[18] There is evidence of some decay in the 1350s, but overall and quite remarkably there appears to have been an increase in population density between the 1360s and the 1430s. This process will be examined in more detail in the next chapter. The decay in the 1350s appears to have been temporary and the result of tenants moving away from less favourable tenures. The Dengemarsh rental and custumal of 1310–15 mentioned earlier reveals that a form of tenure called 'gavelmede' accounted for only 36 acres and yet at 3–4s per acre it comprised, in terms of monetary value to the lord, almost a third of the rental. Tenants holding this land were allowed to pasture 16 sheep 'on the stone' or on the scrub land and beach shingle. But, besides the very high rent, they owed carrying services for Battle Abbey and this obligation meant that these holdings had an attached taint of servility. This situation continued at least until 1337.[19] Five years after the Black Death the account of 1354–5 records the 'decay' of approximately 20 acres of land on Dengemarsh manor, and that these holdings were now tenantless and in the hands of the lord. The majority of the land in decay – the record of at least 13 acres can be deciphered from the original manuscript – was previously held by gavelmede tenure at 3–4s per acre plus services.[20] By 1432 the income from the tenants of Dengemarsh had dropped by a third from about £20 to about £13. No decay is recorded in 1432 and all of the rents were virtually the same at approximately 4d per acre. This drop in rental value can be accounted for by the removal of the very high gavelmede rents because there was not a reduction in population.

It appears that the tenants increasingly refused to take up this tenure and preferred to subdivide elsewhere in the manor. They also made things difficult for Battle Abbey's rent collectors to do their job. For example in the 1350s the Abbot of Battle complained to the king that the men of Lydd 'openly and in secret so threaten his men and servants at the manor of Dengemarsh ... with loss of life and limb ... that some dare not come to the manor for the direction of his business or stay there'.[21] It is worth noting that in 1432 every holder within one 'tenementum', an ancient holding that had been subdivided among many holders, held half an acre of land called 'littlegavelmede'. This suggests that there had been some reorganisation of the original gavelmede holdings.

---

18   TNA, E 315/56, pp. 226–41.
19   TNA, SC 6/889/14.
20   TNA, SC 8/889/15.
21   Calendar of Patent Rolls (CPR), 1354–8, p. 428.

The monks who wrote the rental perhaps kept the old name in case opportunities arose in the future to re-introduce its earlier benefits to the Abbey.

We can compare these population figures with those for the sixteenth century. On Dengemarsh there were only six messuages recorded in 1538 compared to the 49 in 1432; and of the 154 names (plus servants) recorded at the general muster of local militia in Lydd 10 years later in 1548, only 14 were from Dengemarsh.[22] The detailed Aldington rental of 1556 which covered most of the town recorded 152 named holders of 188 tenements and shops. So while in the mid-sixteenth century the population of the town appears to have increased from the 100 recorded tenants of 1300, the population of the parish as a whole, in stark contrast to the period between 1300 and 1430, was largely confined to the town.

ii   Communications and Trading Networks

When one is studying the origin of capitalism in late medieval England, one can presuppose the existence of mature commercial trading networks in place at the outset although, as I have argued in the earlier theoretical discussion, without assuming that the latter as productive forces will inevitably generate a fundamental remodelling of the social-property structure. There is now a broad consensus among medieval economic historians that, while relatively unstable and subject to significant modifications in the fifteenth century, a mature, enduring and substantially integrated trading network with a functioning urban hierarchy was in place in many parts of England by 1300. This was especially the case in the south-eastern counties which supplied London with grain and fuel.[23]

With regard to Lydd, there is very little sense that it was a localised and inward-looking political community or set of communities. As we shall see, in the fifteenth century, Lydd's political and legal business saw members of its government and other freemen or burgesses dealing with gentry and ship owners from all over Kent, London, and across the English Channel to France and the Low Countries. Looking more directly at trading networks we can examine a range of sources to corroborate an impression of Lydd's trading hinterland. Borough court records record the names and geographical origin of the debtors and creditors involved in various trading arrangements, sometimes stating the commodity at the centre of the dispute. This method has shown when

<hr>

22   See Chapter Two.
23   See the summary of this research in Dyer 2000, pp. 103–9.

applied in other studies of small towns that such trading links were mostly local within a five mile radius, and that the function of small towns in the medieval period was to provide services and a centre of exchange for their immediate hinterlands of villages and hamlets.[24] Borough court records survive for Lydd between 1501 and 1541, covering 18 years between these dates. This evidence appears rather late for a study which hopes to gain an impression of the area in the mid-fifteenth century, but it is likely that such trading networks to be found in this slightly later record would have been developed from an earlier period, and we can confirm this by corroborating other materials such as wills and deeds.

The court dealt in these years with men and women from 30 different towns and villages in Kent and beyond. It was mainly concerned with pleas between visitors and people from Lydd, but also with pleas made by visitors against each other. The latter reveal the hinterland for which Lydd in certain respects provided a marketing focus. Some pleas also reveal partnerships between Lydd men and others who lived outside the parish. Most of these places lay in the Marsh or strategically circled both the Marsh and Weald. They included towns and villages such as Tenterden and Halden which accommodated significant areas of rural industry.[25] By far the most numerous pleas involved people from New Romney, Old Romney and Rye which were the nearest towns and village. New Romney and Old Romney were three miles distant, and Rye was about 12 miles, although the latter could be quickly reached along the coast. The edge of the Marsh and Weald were a distance of eight miles. Not surprisingly, in addition to Rye, contacts spread along the coast with representatives of most of the other Cinque Ports from Hastings in Sussex to Faversham on the other side of Kent being recorded. Trading contacts also stretched to Canterbury and London, and in addition a Dutchman and four Frenchmen are recorded. As a coastal port and isolated to some extent in the Marsh, Lydd's small urban function would inevitably not conform to the standard inland model. However,

---

24   Hilton 1992, p. 55; Dyer 1992, p. 190.

25   For example in 1511 Henry Aucher, a gentleman of Westwell, just north-west of the Weald, and James Swan of Lydd, presumably as a result of business arrangements relating to land use on Dengemarsh, impounded eight horses belonging to John Bate of Lydd. In 1513 John Fright of Shadoxhurst in the Weald was subject to pleas of debt and trespass in Lydd court valued at the significant sums of £4 6s 8d and £10 by William Lambard and Thomas Sander who were from the same place. In 1514 Roger Harlakenden, a gentleman of Woodchurch in the Weald, brought a plea of account against Henry Broke of Lydd, perhaps the outcome of a breakdown in an ongoing business relationship. In 1515 a Lydd cleric, John Fisher, brought a plea of debt worth £10 against Robert Wylverden, a clothier from Halden in the Weald: EKAC, Ly/JB 1.

while it had a substantial fishing industry, Lydd's overseas trade was limited compared to that of its larger neighbours Rye and New Romney whose links to the continent were extensive and boosted in the early fifteenth century by renewed demand for the supply of food to English troops and garrisons in France.[26] Fishing boats could be launched and drawn up on the shingle at Dungeness on the coast at Dengemarsh but larger ocean-going trading ships could not be harboured there. Lydd's sea-going trade had to transport commodities up a river channel called the Wainway to the south-east of the parish in trows or small lighters where they were unloaded at an inland dock a few miles from the town and carted in wains or wagons from there. The bigger ships anchored at a place called the Camber which lay on the coast between Lydd and Rye and the town accounts are full of recorded expenses for people of Lydd there on business.[27]

The large testamentary record for Lydd in the fifteenth and first half of the sixteenth centuries also provides good evidence of the geographical horizons of Lydd's inhabitants. The approximately 500 wills consulted provide references to debtors and creditors, property, legal and financial affairs, gifts, tithes and money for spiritual services to other parish churches and their vicars and priests, will officials such as executors, supervisors and feoffees, and of course bequests to kin and others. These links largely reinforce the evidence in the court books revealing a mostly tight hinterland in the Marsh and Weald, while providing a much larger sample of places, 56 in all. Most of the geographical connections recorded in the wills are references to the ownership of property outside of Lydd's parish by people of Lydd, and to bequests to kin and land sales. These were closely followed by bequests to churches in the form of tithes, the maintenance of the churches' fabric, and requests for prayers. Some of these properties and connections with other churches were possibly an indication of the testator's origin. For example research on migrants to nearby New Romney has found that people who migrated their between 1433 and 1533 maintained property and contacts with the place of their birth in the Weald and on the other side of the Marsh. In their wills they bequeathed to churches and to relations whom they had earlier left behind.[28]

26   For New Romney see Butcher 1974; for Rye see Mayhew 1987, and Draper 2009. See also Mate 1987, pp. 523–5, for the impact of war with France in the early fifteenth century.
27   For the Camber or 'Camera' see Finn 1911, throughout. For the inland dock see TNA, Exchequer Depositions, Mich. 9, Kent and Sussex 1619. For transportation from the Weald: EKAC, Ly/ZS FA 2, 3 and 6.
28   Butcher 1974, pp. 22–6.

In addition to the court and testamentary record, numerous property deeds provide indications of trading horizons, interesting insights into the mobility or permanent migration of people *from* Lydd, and business partnerships that had developed as a result. Most of the interest comes in the form of women who had migrated from the town and alienated or sold part or all of their inherited property lying in Lydd parish. This record begins in the 1420s and it reveals similar links to the wills and court books, including connections with London as well as places such as Cranbrook and Tenterden which were the main markets and industrial centres in the southern Weald. There are also cases of joint landholding in these deeds between people from Lydd and those from Cranbrook, Tenterden and Halden again. These examples reinforce the other evidence pointing to strong bonds between these two areas in the first half of the fifteenth century. This was a period which witnessed the expansion of industry in the Weald and the beginning of an investment drive by ecclesiastical lords in the Marsh, soon followed by more serious depopulating engrossment and enclosure. The bonds between these two areas had important implications for the integration of expanding industrial production and the supply of raw materials from the middle of the fifteenth century.[29]

Movement between Lydd and the Weald went both ways as a result of these connections. For example, on two occasions in the early 1430s the government of Lydd hired a ship from William Broker and his co-owners from Reading (a small settlement near the inland shipbuilding port of Smallhythe in the Wealden parish of Tenterden) in order to fulfil their annual obligation as a Cinque Port to supply transport for the crown overseas. After this we no longer hear of Broker from Reading; however a William Broker appears as a local tax collector of Lydd in 1436 and as a jurat (a member of Lydd's government)

---

29 Here is a flavour of the 16 deeds that survive between 1428 and 1508. In 1428 Alice Adam, the wife of Stephen Adam of Tenterden, sold tenements in Lydd borough which had earlier belonged to Thomas Maket of Lydd, her father. In 1437 Joan Field, the wife of Peter Field of New Romney, released the main house of her recently deceased brother to two Lydd men, Richard William and John Lucas, and Thomas Lucas of Halden; the latter was the brother of John Lucas of Lydd. Other examples clearly show partnerships between men of Lydd and those of the Weald. In 1453 Alice Swan of Lydd, heir of Geoffrey Norrington of Lydd, granted two acres in Lydd to Robert Dunney of Tenterden and Thomas Norrington of Lydd, probably her brother. She was the wife of James Swan of Lydd who had partnerships with Laurence Mongeham of Stone on the edge of the Marsh and John Baker of Tenterden town. In 1472 Agnes Durham, the wife of John Durham of Lydd and daughter of the recently deceased William Smyth of Lydd, granted land to Robert Durham of Cranbrook, presumably a close relation to her husband, and Thomas Hall of Lydd: Finn 1911, pp. 61–2, 226, 237–8, 283.

representing Dengemarsh between 1440 and 1461.[30] Thomas Caxton, an important figure in Lydd's politics in the 1460s and 1470s as we shall see, also migrated to Lydd from Tenterden and was immediately appointed common clerk of the town in 1458 and jurat from 1468. He seems to have been head-hunted for his litigation skills.

In summary, by the middle of the fifteenth century communication between the small towns and villages of Marsh and Weald in the form of commercial and kinship networks was extensive. No sudden opening up of these networks was required for the origin of capitalism because they were already in place. This is important for our purposes because by 1450 the Weald had taken over Canterbury, Kent's main urban centre, as producer of most of the county's broad cloths, and from here production and population would steadily increase and then expand rapidly from the turn of the sixteenth century. This increase in the production of cloths in the Weald followed the contours of the expansion of the textile trade in the Low Countries where much of it was bound. It also followed the contours of large reclamation and inning projects on Romney Marsh by Wealden gentry and ecclesiastical lords, and of the conflicts generated by the lords and their farmers through the enclosure movement on the Marsh.[31]

iii   Social and Occupational Structures in the Fifteenth Century

In the first half of the fifteenth century Lydd still resembled a peasant society, albeit one with a small town market at its centre, a significant fishing station and fish market attached to it on the coast, and mature commercial networks as we have seen. The household economies of the general run of wealthier families at this time were solidly multi-occupational and multi-skilled. They combined artisan production and services with brewing and baking, and relatively small-scale peasant agrarian production. Fishing and shipping dominated the culture of the town and subsistent fishermen, mariners, and those with fellowships and partnerships in ships and boats were also supported by relatively small-scale landholding. At the wealthiest end of the social spectrum a few Lydd men held large demesne leases that had been made available since the 1420s at latest. These men and others also accumulated and sublet real property in the town that they held from the archbishop of Canterbury. Outside of a limited number of examples of concentrated property holding there was

---

30   Finn 1911, pp. 30–3, 41.
31   Zell 1994; Draper 1998; Hipkin 1995.

little competitive capital investment in specialist industry. Windfalls, however, were expected from frequent wrecks on the coast and from ransoms and the capture of foreign ships and their high status officials. Indeed, located on this part of the south-eastern coast of England facing France the culture of Lydd parish was both piratical and militaristic and there was an extra-economic outlook at the peasant level in such communities at this time.

The inhabitants of Lydd town in the fifteenth century pursued a range of occupations which distinguished this main settlement from the surrounding villages both within the parish of Lydd and in the Marsh beyond, and which would therefore have drawn the latter into the town for its products and services. We do not have the benefit of a census of occupations but deeds, wills and the town accounts provide a useful impression of the type of peasant settlement Lydd town was at that time.[32] In addition to large numbers of carpenters and blacksmiths, the artisans included a handful of tailors, shoemakers, cask and barrel makers, tanners, and building workers. The victuallers included many butchers, brewers and bakers, innkeepers and cooks. There were also barbers who sometimes acted as surgeons, and millers. A mercantile element was present with evidence for a vintner, a spicer and mercers. Some were simply styled as 'chapmen', another name for petty trader. There were no wealthy merchants in Lydd specialising in overseas trade.

The large numbers of carpenters and blacksmiths recorded may reflect the prominence of the building, repairing and wrecking of ships and boats in the area in the late medieval period. While boat building had probably transferred to specialist areas such as Smallhythe, an inland port linking the coast, Romney Marsh and the Weald, by 1400 there was still much work required for wrecks and repairs.[33] Dungeness (Denge Ness or Denge Point) on the coast of Dengemarsh manor was notorious for wrecked ships in the late medieval period. The lucrative nature of wrecks led to disputes between inhabitants of Lydd and Dengemarsh and Battle Abbey and these become apparent as soon as court records begin in the early fourteenth century. A dispute over common rights on wrecked ships in 1310 which ended in a victory for the Abbey was revisited in 1329. After they had been wrecked at Dungeness, ships of France, Portugal and Newcastle carrying wool, cloth, fruit and skins found their cargo

32   Finn 1911.

33   Draper 2010, p. 58. A shipwright appears in the Dengemarsh rental of early fourteenth century, and a boat wrecker ('wrekbot'), appears in a court roll of that manor in 1320: these are glimpses of the specialist work there: Scargill-Bird 1887, p. 46; TNA, SC 2/180/57.

distributed and sold by the locals before the Abbey's officials could get to them.[34]

It is mariners and fishermen who dominate the early fifteenth-century record of Lydd. They were in charge of ships capable of piracy, ship service in the wars of the crown, and routine use for coastal fishing. In the first two thirds of the fifteenth century such men were prominent in the government of Lydd. William Broker, Robert and Richard William, William and Richard Smith, William and Stephen Elys, and William Benet were said to have had shipping partnerships and fellowships, and it is likely that they had their own boats and probably shares in larger ships. In 1493 a ship called the Hayne of Lydd was requested for royal service. It was owned by Robert Cockeram and Robert Alwey of Lydd.[35]

The Cinque Ports had for centuries been notorious for piracy, and their role in this enterprise should not be underestimated. In 1412 a deal was struck by the 'masters and mariners' of Lydd and New Romney over best practice for gaining ransoms on the French coast. In 1455–6 an accord was made between the masters of the boats of Lydd and 'The Portuguese'.[36] In return for their Cinque Port franchise men from Lydd were obliged to provide one of the five ships allocated to New Romney for 15 days each year. This obligation fills the accounts of Lydd in the fifteenth century which record food and other supplies bought by the town either from Lydd traders or from other markets for the ships. The following examples provide an impression of what such ship service entailed. In 1471–2 William Benet and his fellowship were paid to organise a ship for the king's voyage to Calais, and this included payment for the wages of 37 men. In 1474 as well as those of the master of the ship and others, wages for 19 men, plus certain youths and one boy were paid for a voyage lasting 15 days. Men from Lydd were also expected to defend the coast militarily. In 1470 it was agreed by the 'masters of the boats and commons' that the masters and their crews should keep continual watch at Dungeness during festivals and other times, and each crew to have at least four bows, and four bills or staves. That year injured men were carried back from Dungeness to the town. Large guns or canons called serpentines were also kept there.[37]

From various sources we gain an impression of the extent to which fishing and shipping dominated occupations in Lydd. In the deal that was struck between Lydd and New Romney masters and mariners in 1412, 18 of them were

34   Daniel-Tysen and Lower, 1886, pp. 152–92; TNA, SC 2/180/57.
35   Finn 1911. For the Hayne see p. 325.
36   EKAC, Ly/4/12/1; Finn 1911, p. 170.
37   Finn 1911, pp. 149, 260, 271, 281, 293.

from Lydd and 13 were from New Romney. If these 18 men were all masters of fishing boats and they each controlled crews of usually between nine and 12 men, and all of these men had families, fishing and seafaring would account for the occupations of a quarter of Lydd's population in the early fifteenth century.[38] In 1448–9 the Lieutenant of the Cinque Ports requested 40 fishermen from Lydd for a voyage, and so he expected such a number from that town. If all of those 40 fishermen had families then these alone would produce a fifth of the population of Lydd.[39] Of 468 wills consulted between 1460 and 1558, 71 people bequeathed fishing equipment from a single net to boats, complex fishing machinery and cabins at Dungeness. These represented a fraction of those actually involved in fishing because many testators did not mention specific property in their wills, while many poor fishermen would not have made a will.

The fishing and seafaring population in the first half of the fifteenth century had a strong base on Dengemarsh, and those representing Dengemarsh in Lydd's government were mariners as often as not. For long periods fishermen dwelt in cabins or lodges at Dungeness, and it was here that there was located an important fish market.[40] The fish went far and wide. Fishmongers from London are recorded in the town accounts in 1470 and 1478, and fish was sent from Dungeness by packhorse to other inland markets and buyers as well as to London.[41] Evidence for these fish distributers, or 'ripiers', only appears in the Lydd record from the early sixteenth century when the court record begins, but there must have been ripiers in Lydd throughout the fourteenth and fifteenth centuries as there were in Rye.[42]

Although the town of Lydd was open and commercialised in the first half of the fifteenth century, its peasant credentials can be identified in the widespread landholding of its inhabitants which acted as a support to subsistent household economies. In addition to the vast majority of the houses and shops in the town, Aldington manor contained many small plots of land that would have supported these urban occupations. The 600 acres of land outside of the

---

38   See Dulley 1969, p. 55, for crew estimates.

39   Finn 1911, p. 134.

40   Finn 1911, pp. 245, 315; EKAC, Ly/fac 2, p. 134.

41   Finn 1911, pp. 220, 282.

42   For example, a plea of debt in 1513 against John Butcher, ripier of Lydd, by Edward Gyfford of London may well have been the result of a deal that went wrong with Butcher's expected delivery of fish to London from Dungeness. In 1518 Nicholas Lawder, a ripier from Bethersden in the Weald, owed debts to two Lydd men, and it is likely that these men were fishermen EKAC, Ly/JB 1, p. 35; EKAC Ly/JB 2, p. 3. See Dulley 1969 for Rye ripiers.

demesne in Dengemarsh manor in 1432 were fragmented into smallholdings and tiny plots, and these plots were held by a broad section of inhabitants in the town and the manor. For example 24 Lydd men who held land on Dengemarsh in 1432 had been or were to become jurats in the government. Another 10 performed scot or tax collection for Lydd. Small landholding was an important support for the households of petty traders and artisans. Equally, if not more importantly, it supported the livelihoods of fishermen and mariners whose incomes may often have been erratic.

A study examining bequests of landholdings from the surviving wills up to 1558 of both rural and urban parishes in Kent found that, in rural parishes, 71 percent bequeathed farmland and six percent bequeathed houses only. For the towns the percentages were 35 percent and 30 percent. In Ashford, a small town where the farming element was most evident, 49 percent left lands. The figures for Lydd are 39 and 19 percent. Given that many people from Lydd parish did not refer to property in their last testaments, especially in the decades around 1500, these figures show that land holding by a broad section of people living in small town parishes was normal in the late medieval period. There are, however, two caveats to make about these figures. The first is that Lydd's parish was larger than most and contained a number of rural settlements which would therefore significantly distort any figures indicating landholding activity in small towns alone, particularly in the first two-thirds of the fifteenth century before the onset of depopulating enclosure. Second, a much higher percentage of people from small towns would have left farmland in the first half of the fifteenth century in contrast to the first half of the sixteenth century because between the mid-fifteenth century (when wills begin to made in large numbers for the first time), and the mid-sixteenth century land in east Kent was being concentrated into fewer and fewer hands.[43] With regard to those people with the capacity to invest in land beyond their parishes, Dulley points out that much of the land owned by townspeople was marshland grazing: 'in Romney Marsh if they lived in Ashford or Hythe, in Sheppey or nearer home if they came from Milton or Sittingbourne'. Draper has found that of the lease-holders of All Souls College farms on Romney Marsh between 1443 and 1505, whose wills have been identified, 11 came from rural parishes and 14 from urban parishes. Of the 14, eight were from Lydd, five from New Romney and one from Sandwich.[44] One can therefore conclude that landholding was a very significant element in the economies of small towns in this region in the fifteenth century. There was a functional separation between small towns and

---

43   Dulley 1966, pp. 95–8.
44   Dulley 1966, pp. 96–7; Draper 1998, p. 118.

their rural hinterlands based on distinct occupations and services, and yet there was still a fundamental reliance by small town inhabitants on farmland for subsistence and prosperity.

It was, above all, the extent of land held by individuals that determined the social structure of Lydd, rather than wealth from mercantile or artisanal petty commodity trade. The subsidy or freemen's tax of 1446 provides us with a useful marker to the social structure in that year. 84 Lydd freemen were assessed that year. Henry Aleyn stands out with his assessment of 5s. The assessments of the next highest, John Bate senior and William Fermour alias Godfrey (or Godfrey alias Fermour), were significantly less at 3s 4d, and the next, Thomas Wynday, was assessed at 2s 4d. Below these four, 10 were assessed at 2s, 32 at between 1s and 1s 8d, and 38 at between 4d and 8d.

The four leading men were all jurats at some stage. In his will of 1457, Aleyn instructed his executors to sell 20 acres of his lands in the parish of Woodchurch in the Weald. Although this may not have accounted for all of his property there, what seems to have propelled him to the top of the taxation assessments in 1446 was his lease of the farm of the demesne of Scotney manor. This was situated in the south-west of Lydd parish and it also overlapped with Broomhill parish. Scotney demesne was the most valuable farm in Lydd parish and Aleyn leased it from at latest 1446 until 1457 when he most likely died. He had in fact contributed to the formation of the lease in the first place, and thereby helped to form part of the basis of the original foundation of All Souls College a decade prior. For example, he sold his own plots to the College and acted as a feoffee or trustee in its land transactions. The lease was worth £60 per annum to All Souls College in 1446, and this very large sum was derived from the large flock of sheep that formed part of its value.[45] This new foundation and the installation of a flock at this time would have been stimulated by developments in the cloth industry in the Weald. Aleyn's property connections with the latter have already been mentioned. Aleyn also seems to have held a swannery in Lydd parish. In the years of turmoil from 1446 up until Cade's rebellion in 1450, he sold swans to the town which the latter used on diplomatic missions to curry favour with the county gentry.[46] The fact that Aleyn stands out so clearly from the rest of the freemen has revealing implications for the social structure at this stage. Aleyn was typical of the new farmers on Romney Marsh with their close associations with wealthy ecclesiastical lordships. Nevertheless

---

45 Oxford Bodleian Library MS dd All Souls c 323: see Ralph Evans's unpublished transcripts and notes on the manuscript that are kept at the Romney Marsh Research Trust. I am grateful to Gill Draper for providing me with these; Draper 1998, pp. 113, 118 n. 57.

46 Finn 1911, pp. 122, 128–9.

compared to the wealthy farmers of the sixteenth century who cultivated the patronage of the county gentry, the patronage networks of these farmers within lay society were relatively limited. The executors that testators chose to look after their bequests reveals a good deal about power and influence. Aleyn chose as executors of his will, John Sarlis, Thomas Ayllewyn, Thomas Bate junior and Edward Elys. The first two were jurats, although not among the leading ones. Bate was still young and would not join the juratcy until 1470. Elys was part of a mariner farming family of relatively middling wealth and never held office.

John Bate senior, rated equal second in the subsidy, like Aleyn sold swans to the town in 1447, on this occasion to sweeten the relationship between the town and the archbishop of Canterbury. Indeed Bate and Aleyn began their office holding careers in the borough together as scot collectors in 1445, and so they may have had a close relationship. It is most likely that Bate was farming the 300 acre demesne of Dengemarsh in 1446, having been the farmer there since at least 1441 and probably much earlier, and it is this lease that attracted the high subsidy.[47] William Godfrey alias Fermour, who was assessed at the same level as Bate in 1446, may well have been from Westbrook, a village or hamlet within Lydd parish and close to the west of the town. It seems likely that he was the same man who with 37 acres held the fourth largest acreage on Dengemarsh manor in 1432, listed behind three gentry who were not associated with the town as freemen. The latter were the heirs of John Dering with 59 acres, Thomas de Etchingham with 55 acres and Henry Finch with 50 acres. William may have been the son of Thomas Godfrey who, like Aleyn, had accumulated holdings in the west of the parish and passed them on to All Souls College.[48] From Thomas's lands were generated the lease of the farm of Newland in 1443. He also held an unstated amount of property at Scotney and New Romney, and these were presumably extensive enough for him to be assessed at the same level as a large lease holder like Bate. Like Aleyn the executors of his will were from among the leading men of middling wealth in Lydd.

Many wills like those above are limited in detail. The following will of Henry Bate of Lydd in 1478 provides a good insight into the wealth and property of a leading man in Lydd parish in the fifteenth century. Henry Bate was a butcher and appears to have been in partnership with Andrew Bate, the latest Bate to

---

47   The Dengemarsh demesne was divided into two leases in the early sixteenth century, both valued at approximately £20 per annum. Only one of them was available in 1446, the other having developed following engrossment from the 1460s: see Chapter Eleven below for the development of leases in the region.

48   Draper 1998, p. 115.

hold the Dengemarsh lease in the 1460s, and he was probably the son of John Bate senior who we met earlier. Henry bequeathed a total of approximately £75 in ready money, including 20 marks each to his four daughters. He held his own lands 'in the parish of Lydd and elsewhere in Kent and Sussex'. His feoffees were instructed to sell messuages within the town that were held by a tailor and a vintner revealing his investments in urban property for subletting, and he also received back various small plots of land that he had probably sublet. He bequeathed his main tenement and various holdings amounting to approximately 25 acres to his wife plus 80 acres to be split between his four daughters. These holdings gave him a firm yeoman status. The 20 marks to his daughters was very high compared to the other wills in the fifteenth century and comparable to the bequests of some of the wealthy farmers of the sixteenth century. However, daughters were more likely to be given money than land, and the absence of male heirs undoubtedly contributed to the magnitude of this form of bequest. His wife was also given 80 sheep and half of his lambs, and other sheep were given to his six servants. He also cultivated cereals to a significant extent. He mentioned no executors, but the four feoffees he instructed to organise his property included three Bates from the town. He and his partner Andrew Bate did have wider connections and patronage however. In the year before Henry's will they were both chosen as head officers by the aristocratic royal sewer commissioners to develop a more complex marshland administration in the face of tenants defaulting in their land tax payments.[49] Henry Bate's will outshone all but a few wills in the fifteenth century, but it appears quite modest compared with those of the 1540s, as we shall see in Chapter Eleven.

Those of broadly middling wealth and status in the town in the fifteenth century engaged in a wide range of occupations. These were the fishermen-farmers of varying degrees of wealth, artisans and tradesmen who were often at the same time brewers and bakers with some land, and husbandmen or yeomen without substantial leases. Sometimes the range of occupational diversity undertaken by individuals is rather striking. John Serlis, an executor of Henry Aleyn's will, was one of the 10 men assessed at the rate of 2s in 1446 below the small handful of men referred to above. Together with his wife he was presented in the Aldington manor court in 1449 as a common baker and she a common brewer for breaking the rules of assize.[50] He was paid 20s by the town in part payment of seven 'bunys' or large casks of beer, and six barrels of beer,

49   Dugdale, 1662, pp. 47–55.
50   Lambeth Palace Library, Estate Documents, no. 136. This record survives for the years 1449 and 1488 only.

plus 6s 8d for bread to supply a ship in 1444–5.[51] He must have held a tenement and a shop in the town, and in addition he held six acres on Dengemarsh from 1432 and probably a range of small plots elsewhere in the parish. In his will of 1479 he paid tithes to the church of Broomhill, a small parish adjacent to Dengemarsh, revealing landholdings there, and he named four feoffees who were tasked to provide his wife with various scattered small plots. He bequeathed various fishing nets, and he had a cabin and a capstan at Dungeness, the latter possibly used for drawing up boats onto the shore, and this evidence reveals substantial involvement in that trade. He also bequeathed padded breeches, a helmet, gauntlets, a shield and a sword, possibly revealing an earlier career as a soldier. Like many other fishermen in Lydd he would have defended the coast from invading continental navies in his life time, as well as possibly fighting against English aristocratic armies during Cade's rebellion in 1450 and subsequent battles during the Wars of the Roses. Serlis was among those who attempted to resist, on the town's behalf as well as his own, epoch-making enclosure on Dengemarsh in the 1460s. When summoned to appear in court to testify during this resistance he was described as a 'yeoman'.[52] He held no large leases which increasingly came to define yeomen in the late fifteenth and sixteenth centuries. The term 'yeoman' still retained a technical definition of a 40s freeholder, and these men had been admitted to the franchise for electing MPs in 1429–30. He was given no such title in his will or elsewhere. Serlis was the kind of person Harvey had in mind when describing the leading social forces behind Cade's rising of 1450.[53]

William Gros worked for the town permanently as a common serjeant during the years of political turmoil between 1447 and 1454, after which he became a jurat. The accounts are full of references to his activities and errands in these years: he was in fact imprisoned in Canterbury Castle at one point in 1450, possibly during or in the lead-up to Cade's rebellion.[54] He was an innkeeper, a brewer and a baker. He passed his inn-brewery to his son in 1464. Like Serlis and his wife, Gros was presented as a common baker and his wife as a common brewer for breaking the Aldington assize in 1449. His will also records that he had lands but the extent of these is unstated. John Downe and Laurence Hamon were tailors, and the latter sublet his messuage-workshop from Henry Bate in the 1470s. However in 1488 they were also presented in court as

---

51   Finn 1911, p. 100.
52   Finn 1911, p. 322.
53   Harvey 1991, pp. 104–11.
54   Finn 1911, p. 147.

common brewers and bakers for breaking the assize.[55] They also held land. For example John Downe bequeathed two tenements, a barn and two small plots of land in his will of 1505. In 1488 alone, 19 brewers and six bakers were presented for breaking the assize. Most of them were either jurats at some point or from jurat families.

The Smiths, the Williams, the Benets and the Elyses were all mariner families, and all held plots of land on Dengemarsh in 1432 to support their trades. William Smith and Richard Smith held 33 acres and 21 acres respectively. Richard was assessed at 2s in 1446, the same level as Serlis, and William slightly lower on 1s 6d. William and Thomas Benet held 14 acres together as heirs of Richard, allowing their father to live in his messuage there. William was assessed at 1s 4d in 1446. These and the households of men like John Serlis and William Gros were typical of the middling groups in Lydd in the fifteenth century. They were, nevertheless, prominent among the broadly based jurats and they worked tirelessly for the commonality. There were very substantial farming interests as we have seen in the form of Aleyn, the Godfreys and the Bates, but these were in the minority and they were not the dominant force in the government and culture of the town and parish at this stage.

iv   Politics and Government

In recent years historians have done much to show that so-called high politics was not solely the domain of the higher echelons of medieval and early modern European society. Ordinary peasants and artisans recognised they had a stake in the outcome of the political struggles of monarchs and aristocrats, and their involvement was critical.[56] In this spirit, before looking at the nature of government in Lydd in the fifteenth and sixteenth centuries, I will examine political conflicts of the fifteenth century and the involvement of communities such as Lydd. The relationship between these conflicts and Lydd's defence of custom and traditional production in the context of capitalist enclosure is examined in more detail in the next chapter. What I want to convey at this point is the remarkable self-organisation that these small communities achieved, and their capacity for negotiating political and military upheavals in the first half of the fifteenth century. They were certainly not easy targets for would-be enclosers.

---

55   Lambeth Palace Library, Estate Documents, 136 and 137.
56   See for example Wood 2007, Shagan 2003, and Cohn 2006.

The Hundred Years' War between England and France in the first half of the fifteenth century made particular demands on the communities of south-eastern England, especially Kent. Soldiers were quartered locally before embarking for France and they imposed a significant burden on local finances. The forced purveyance of local goods and food to garrison English settlements in France was punitive. The Kent countryside and London experienced streams of settler families in misery and poverty returning from Normandy following the loss of English held territory in the late 1440s. They told stories of war mismanagement and accused leading English aristocrats of being traitors in ceding too much to the French in treaties. Like the rebellion of 1381, thousands of English farmers, peasants, artisans and labourers, led by people of the same background, took part in Cade's Rebellion in 1450, which was largely a response to oppression in the county and political mismanagement of the war. The rebels came mostly from the counties surrounding London and East Anglia, especially Kent, and they received support from the London poor. They mobilised armies which marched on London, took over the city, and made demands either to the king or his representatives there which threatened to undermine English aristocratic power. Besides grievances over war mismanagement and corrupt English government, the key to the economic background of the rebellion was a slump in cloth exports and a serious recession in the cloth industry. The cloth industry had developed since the late fourteenth century right across southern England and many had become dependent upon it to make ends meet. The slump was caused by a loss of trade with the German Hanse merchants and those of the Low Countries. This loss of trade was seen as a direct result of government failures in treaties, and by the lawless privateering of the English aristocracy who at one point captured a whole fleet of German ships during peace time. The blame was again targeted at the new regime. The so-called Wars of the Roses was at heart a civil war between aristocratic affinities in the context of declining aristocratic income through the loss of territory in France and the decline of rents in England. It began a few years after Cade's rebellion and the loss of Normandy and continued in the following three decades. The battles and political fallout were not confined to the aristocracy however: the people of Kent supported Richard Duke of York when he landed as a rebel at Sandwich in 1460.[57]

Our evidence for the involvement of Lydd in politics in the fifteenth century is largely derived from the town accounts which record payments for all sorts of activities and meetings undertaken by officials and other people from

---

57   Harvey 1991.

Lydd.[58] When the accounts open in 1428 we enter into a remarkable world of a politicised and militarised small community of mostly peasant based petty traders, artisans, mariners and fishermen. As we will see, the government and financial organisation of the town and parish was mature, and it was mobilised to good effect in these years. The security of the small town parish depended largely on its ability to secure friendship and favour with the local and county gentry, the royal officials of the Cinque Ports, and leading aristocrats such as the Archbishop of Canterbury. There is no sense from this record that the gentry and aristocracy were shadowy figures in the lives of ordinary people in this period. People from Lydd were involved in incessant negotiations, and the payments of bribes to gentry and aristocracy in order 'to secure friendship' in dealings with other aristocrats and gentry are recorded in the accounts on an unashamedly frequent basis. Expenditure derived from the taxation of the precious income of a largely subsistence-based population had to be justified by the government to the rest of the freemen, the commonalty.

The years between the 1440s and 1460s were especially critical for the defence of custom and traditional production in Lydd. Members of the gentry had to be appealed to at this time in a system which in practice was dominated by social power as much as the rule of law. The government of Lydd also aimed as much as possible to be excused from crippling demands for men and resources to guard the seas or make rescues from over the English Channel.

Regarding the militarised aspect of the town and region, the accounts reveal that Lydd men frequently mustered themselves and undertook military training with archery on 'the butts'. The immediacy of the crown's wars to Lydd's inhabitants is revealed in the record of soldiers from elsewhere passing through the area, and, as I have mentioned earlier, in their defence of the coast from invasion at Dungeness. A zone of 12 miles wide along the Kent coast stretching from Sandwich in the east of the county to Appledore in the north-west of Romney Marsh, which included Lydd, was marked out by the crown as an area of legal royal purveyance from which purveyors might take livestock or grain exclusively for the supply of Calais and Dover Castle.[59] Lydd paid expenses on numerous occasions to the harbingers of various aristocratic lords who were charged with supplying their soldiers bound for wars on the continent. In the 1420s and 1430s the government of Lydd attempted to stop soldiers being quartered in the town. In 1437, a year when south-east England was on high alert against probable invasion, the situation became serious as soldiers were apparently helping themselves to goods from the shops in Lydd without paying for

58   Finn 1911.
59   Harvey 1991, p. 14.

them and thereby causing what must have been serious disturbances. Men from Lydd presented themselves at Winchelsea before the earl of Warwick and sued for peace between themselves and the soldiers, and the latter were eventually discharged.[60] It was such outrages by soldiers in this region that Harvey cites as fuelling the grievances of the rebels from Kent in 1450, particularly as the wars with France were being lost through incompetence, and taxation squandered.[61]

The years leading up to Cade's rebellion in 1450 were particularly eventful. Numerous men from Lydd were indicted in Maidstone, Canterbury, London and elsewhere in Kent in the second half of the 1440s in the context of a break down in national government and a corrupt court affinity committing arbitrary acts against local producers. A number appear to have been accused by the Archbishop of Canterbury in the Easter of 1450.[62] By the later 1440s the royal leadership was in the hands of what was seen as an unscrupulous court party headed by the Duke of Suffolk, William de la Pole, the bishops of Salisbury and Chichester, and others, and war failures were blamed on these people, the Duke of Suffolk in particular. The lower echelon of the Duke of Suffolk's affinity was made up of a layer of hated men, particularly in Kent, who filled chief royal offices. These men, in a remarkably reckless manner, used these leading judicial offices, including the sheriff of Kent and warden of the Cinque Ports, to augment their incomes through extortion in legal process and oppression through arbitrary evictions of some tenants and the raising of fines on others. Historians have commented on the particularly rapacious and violent manner in which some went about buying up the estates of other gentry. Two of the most hated men were Robert Est, keeper of Maidstone jail and a chief officer of the archbishop of Canterbury's lordship, and Stephen Slegge, MP for Hythe and Dover and sheriff of Kent from 1448.[63] These men were in Lydd in these years. In 1446 both of them were in the town with the surveyor of the archbishop of Canterbury to enquire into the way in which a certain Thomas Shalwell of Lydd was arrested in the town and taken to Dover Castle. The following year Slegge returned regarding men from Lydd who had been indicted outside the town.[64]

Jack Cade, the leader or 'captain' of the rebellion in 1450, seems to have helped one of these indicted men of Lydd just before the rebellion started, as

---

60   Finn 1911, pp. 68–9. For threat of invasion in 1437 see Griffiths 1998, pp. 206–8.
61   Harvey 1991, p. 12.
62   Finn 1911, p. 140.
63   Harvey 1991, chapters 1–3.
64   Finn 1911, pp. 111–12, 123.

one entry in the account of 1450 records the payment of 2s 'to two men to bring a letter from the captain at the suit of Henry Lucas'. It is sometimes argued that these small communities hedged their bets when it came to siding with Cade in 1450, and that they opted on the side of caution for fear of bloody retribution from the crown and aristocracy. For example while the rebellion was underway in London the accounts record that the jurats and commoners of Lydd sent a porpoise to be presented to Cade – a gift usually reserved for sweetening aristocrats and the king – whom the clerk of Lydd who wrote the entry described as 'the captain of the host'. In a further entry, expenses were recorded for sending a letter to Cade in order 'to excuse the town', presumably from taking part in the rebellion and from sending a military retinue to London.[65] However, given the troubles that many men from Lydd found themselves in, that Cade had personally intervened on the town's behalf, that Lydd referred to him as 'captain' in their own records, and that at least one man from Lydd was on the pardon roll granted by the king after the rebellion, we must surely conclude that the town was deeply implicated in the rebellion. It is probable that communities on the coast were charged with defending the country from invasion while the aristocracy, the crown, and large numbers of men were taken out in the rebellion. The same precautions were taken during the rebellion of 1381 in which Kent had been one of the leading protagonists. What confirms Lydd's support for Cade is its allegiance to the Yorkist cause in the early throes of the Wars of the Roses which aimed to install the Lancastrian regime of Henry VI; Richard Duke of York was, for now, untainted in the popular mind. For example, 34 men (and 'two strangers') were sent by Lydd to the battle at St Albans, just north of London, in 1461.[66]

Accounts of the transition to capitalism, whether influenced by commercialisation or orthodox Marxist perspectives, assume that capitalist farmers appeared, developed and became dominant on the basis of their own self-activity. One need therefore only refer to their presence to account for their development through engrossment and enclosure. In reality they often came up against robust communities such as Lydd. But as the foregoing hopefully goes some way to demonstrate, this was not the kind of community that was simply going to allow a large part of its productive base and livelihood to be undermined by three or four farmers. Without alliances with powerful political interests from outside the enterprises of these farmers would have remained modest, within a more broadly subsistence-based culture. Further analysis of Lydd's political institutions below serves to confirm this conclusion.

---

65   Finn 1911, pp. 141–2.

66   Finn 1911, p. 196.

v   The Crown and the Cinque Ports

Although informally connected before the Norman Conquest, by virtue of its
charter of 1156 Lydd was a corporate member of the federated organisation of
the Cinque Ports. This federation gained its authority from the crown although
it assumed a good deal of self-government. In the fifteenth century these ports
were a string of small and medium-sized towns situated along the coast of
Sussex and Kent, with an increasing number of affiliated corporate and non-
corporate members of varying settlement status both on the coast and in-land.
The original five ports were Hastings, New Romney, Hythe, Dover and
Sandwich, and they had the status of 'head ports'; Winchelsea and Rye were
added to their number by 1400. Lydd was a member of the head port of New
Romney. The organisation was designed to protect the Kent and Sussex coast
which was particularly vulnerable to foreign invasion, and to provide 56 ships
for two weeks annually for the use of the crown. It formed the origin of the
British navy. New Romney's allocation was five ships to which Lydd was obliged
to contribute one, although this was commuted for money by the end of the
fifteenth century. This was a good deal for Lydd because, although New Romney
was still significantly larger than Lydd in the fifteenth century, it had been far
bigger in the twelfth and thirteenth centuries when the original allocations
were made. In return for this service to the crown the ports as a whole received
certain franchises applicable to all. The organisation was also significant
because it attempted to maintain and protect the common economic interests
of the ports, and dealt with internal disputes, usually of a trading nature,
between freemen from different ports.[67]

    The most important aspects of the Cinque Port franchise were as follows:
ports had freedom from county jurisdiction and law courts in Kent and Sussex;
freedom from all internal customs dues within the whole realm; freedom from
all royal taxation; the right to hold courts and have the profits from them; the
right to determine all pleas of the crown except treason; the right to punish
offenders of the law including implementation of the death penalty; freedom
from outside arrests and attachments for service; the right to have fines from
those infringing the rules of local markets; the right to the profits from wrecked
ships; the power for mayors or bailiffs and jurats, with the consent of the commons, to amend the customs and practices of the individual ports; the ability
for each head port to elect a member of parliament; and finally, where any
alleged injustice was done within a port and could not be settled locally, the

---

67   Murray 1935, p. 1; HMC 1896, p. 532.

Lord Warden of the Cinque Ports had the power to hear and determine the case through his chancery court at Dover.

However, and most importantly, many of the ports remained in the hands of private lordships. In practice there were variations in each town's franchise and liberties because the ancient rights of these lordships appear generally to have remained dominant within this struggle for jurisdictional co-existence. A number of ports did not even fulfil the powers given them by the Cinque Port franchise to elect their own head officer, the bailiff or mayor. Murray has argued that these franchises were not as exceptional as they may at first appear; most of them could be found in other incorporated boroughs throughout England. Theoretically, the freemen or 'barons' to whom the franchise applied could only be summoned to appear before the Lord Warden's courts at Dover, rather than the royal courts at Westminster, if disputes could not be settled in their own borough courts. However the Dover court was still a crown institution attended by royal justices and ministers, and so it is debatable as to how much was gained by this diversion. In fact, as Murray argues, even these were not unassailable in practice, and one can find examples of individuals or groups being summoned to Westminster and certain ports being subjected to the itinerant royal justices in Eyre.

Independent of these royal courts was the more informal Cinque Port institution of the Brotherhood of the Ports or, more typically, the 'Brodhull'. The Brodhull developed during the fourteenth century and its main aim was to ensure the legal and financial support of the whole confederation for ports experiencing encroachments on the franchise from powerful outsiders as well as from their own particular overlords. However the Brodhull from the late fifteenth century increasingly reflected the interests of the official class of the ports, involving itself in the constitutions of elections. It became inimical to popular government during the sixteenth century and is implicated in the political struggles which served to reinforce the economic transformation.[68]

On balance Murray is correct in her assertion that these Cinque Port franchises were not exceptional in practice, given the complexity of jurisdictions with which they had to contend. However, the franchise gave freemen in the ports greater room to manoeuvre against their local overlords than would have been the case without it; and what we see with the development of the Brodhull and the constant communications between the ports is the high level of politicisation and intimate knowledge of the law that was achieved by a broad range of peasants, petty traders and fishermen in the region in the fifteenth century.

---

68   Murray 1935.

vi   The Government of Lydd

The earliest surviving town custumal of Lydd was written by Thomas Caxton, town clerk, in 1476.[69] At the beginning it lays out the constitution regarding the election of government officials. At this stage elections appear relatively democratic. The 'commons' or 'commonalty' who were the freemen or Cinque Port 'barons' of the town, elected annually a bailiff, twelve 'jurats' or 'swornmen', and a deputy bailiff. Of these 12 jurats, eight represented the town of Lydd and four represented Dengemarsh. Additional information is provided in the chamberlain's accounts or town accounts which list the names of all the jurats elected each year at the head of each account. These show that during the fifteenth century exactly half of the jurats were changed each year.[70]

The ability of the commonalty to elect the bailiff had only been achieved in 1467. Prior to this date, the bailiff, also known as the constable in the early fifteenth century, would have been appointed by the Archbishop of Canterbury's officials because the town was part of the Archbishop's Aldington manor. But in 1467 the town became to a large extent an incorporated borough in its own right. It paid £7 8s 3d rent and 30s common fine to the lord and received controls of various extensive common lands.[71] Lydd's freemen could now name themselves 'bailiff, jurats and commons of Lydd'. The motivation for this concession by the Archbishop is not clear: there is, for example, no evidence of a struggle to achieve this status at Lydd, a status that was so bitterly fought for and denied in other ports.[72]

The 1460s and 1470s were a period of significant economic and political changes in Lydd. In terms of politics and constitutional matters, between the beginning of the record in 1428 and 1462 the customs surrounding the election of eight jurats representing Lydd and four representing Dengemarsh were strictly adhered to, with half being replaced every year. After 1462 references to Dengemarsh jurats begin to disappear on and off from the record. The last time

69   EKAC, Ly/LC 1: a later copy written in 1587 can be found at Canterbury Cathedral Library, Lit. MS. B2.
70   Finn 1911. Because of the ease with which these officials can be found at the beginning of each account, transcribed in Finn, I have throughout this study inferred that the dates of a particular individual's term of office are sufficient for reference. The only exception to this is if the term of office falls in the missing years of the chamberlains' accounts between 1485 and 1512. In this case the source of the information has been referenced.
71   HMC 1896, p. 531; Du Boulay 1966, pp. 141–2; Finn 1911, p. 220.
72   For example, New Romney's petition to elect its own mayor failed in 1484. See also the conflicts at Fordwich: Murray 1935, pp. 51–2. For the nature of conflicts over liberties and jurisdictions in the ports, see Croft 1997.

they are mentioned is 1477. This year coincides with the victory of the abbot of Battle Abbey over 'the town' in a centuries old franchise dispute that was revisited with a vengeance in 1466 over the right to shipwrecks on the Dengemarsh coast. It also coincided with disputes over the engrossment of Dengemarsh by the Abbey's farmer, and these conflicts will be addressed in more detail in the following chapter. Remember that Caxton's town custumal was also written in 1477, the year of the Abbey's legal victory against the town, and that he still kept Dengemarsh's representation in the written constitution. The town had lost legal battles over Dengemarsh before, notably in the early fourteenth century, but Caxton's custumal reveals that these losses would not be recognised.

The biggest changes in the constitution of Lydd were yet to come with the development of permanent oligarchic government in the early sixteenth century. What we see in Lydd in the fifteenth century with half of the jurats standing down each year was a broad representation of freemen and the commonalty within the central government. The custumal states that the prerequisite to become a freeman was that a man should be 'of good name and good condition' – that is, respectable and financially stable. It was up to the bailiff and jurats in any particular year to decide if a particular candidate was suitable. The admission to the freedom was secured by a fine which seems to have been assessed on income, and freemen as barons of the Cinque Ports were also taxed separately from the rest of the town in order to fulfil their obligations to the crown. However the large number of Lydd freemen in 1446 who probably accounted for well over a third of the households of the town and Dengemarsh, and the broad range of tax assessments, suggest that freemen status was hardly exclusive at this stage. Anyone with a reasonable stake in the town and Dengemarsh was probably a freeman.

In the fifteenth century it was the whole body of freemen that was described as 'the commons' or 'the commonalty'. There is little indication at this stage that these terms referred to a narrow 'common council', or an inner 24 or 48, which represented the general population of freemen as one finds in the larger English towns. Moreover, the accounts reveal that in the fifteenth century the commonalty was regarded as the most important institution in the government of the town. The commonalty were the Cinque Port barons of Lydd and were synonymous with the town. Errands were made and legal activities undertaken 'in the name of the commonalty', and debts were owed and fines were paid 'to the commonalty'. The chief officers of the town, the bailiff and jurats, were part of the commonalty, and answerable to them. The Town Hall was called The Common Hall.

The bailiff was the chief representative of the town in formal or informal assemblies and negotiations, either through the Brodhull or in meetings with aristocracy, gentry or representatives of the law for the purpose of securing favour or advice. He was chief judge in the borough court, and was also assigned the responsibilities of coroner and 'clerk of the market'. The latter ensured that trading customs were adhered to. In all of these activities he was advised and assisted by the jurats. Before the introduction of specialist chamberlains in the 1480s the jurats were responsible for the financial affairs of the town, including setting the rate of the common tax or 'scot', organising its collection and preparing the accounts of the town's income and expenditure. In the fifteenth century, because of the electoral fluidity between bailiffs, jurats and commonalty, these roles would have been regarded as a necessary but temporary division of labour, as well as authority, in order to best organise the town's affairs, and this obligation was spread among many inhabitants. Part of the basis of this fluidity is written in the custumal, and a clause within it states that the bailiff and jurats may not retail any form of merchandise during their period of office 'so that they are unable to increase their prices on the basis of the power of their office'. This was clearly recognition in this period of the potential for corruption in the system of permanent government. One can therefore see another reason for the rotation of half of the jurats each year: it was to enable retailers to continue their businesses. A political constitution such as this would encourage a communal consciousness appropriate to the central institution of the town, the commonalty, and be consistent with non-capitalist subsistence-orientated production and organisation, albeit partially commercialised. This attitude is well demonstrated by the unremitting defence of custom by members of the government in the fifteenth century.

vii   Romney Marsh Institutions and Infrastructure

Manorial lordships and Cinque Port liberties were not the only institutions that affected the lives of Lydd's inhabitants. This region of valuable fertile marshland was an artificial product generated by walling back the sea and draining salt marsh since centuries before the Norman Conquest, much like parts of the Netherlands. As with the other jurisdictions conflict was endemic, in this case over who paid for the maintenance and who controlled the administration. Formal organisation of the maintenance of the walls and drains in the Level of Romney Marsh above the Rhee Wall to the north of Lydd in the form of an early body of custom known as *Lex Marisci* (laws of the Marsh) was in place from at least the twelfth century, and these were developed and standardised in the thirteenth century. Before the thirteenth century, payments for Marsh maintenance owed by tenants were made according to

private agreements with landowners, but thereafter every landholder or occupier in the Marsh had to contribute whether their lands benefited directly or
indirectly from repairs. In 1308 new laws were brought into force for the district
south of the Rhee Wall which included Lydd. These required a constitution of
24 jurats, elected by a commonalty of representatives of ordinary landholders,
and a common bailiff who was elected by the manorial lords of the Marsh.
The role of this 'government' was to enforce the taxation of landholders for the
maintenance of sea walls and watercourses for the common benefit. When an
emergency arose the 24 jurats met and decided on whom the responsibility for
repair fell. The bailiff was told of the jurats' decision and if those responsible
neglected their duty he could arrange to have the damages repaired and charge
those responsible double the original amount required. The lords, however,
were apparently not satisfied with their controls through the election of the
bailiff, and various disputes resulted leading to a royal commission in 1361.
The report from the latter suggested that the lords and their bailiff could now
participate in the election of jurats, previously the sole right of the commonalty of ordinary landholders, and they could also now take part in the crucial
tax assessments.[73] There is no evidence to suggest however that the report was
followed up by an actual ordinance giving the landowners statutory powers to
intervene in this way.

So in the process of development of the social organisation of the maintenance of Romney Marsh, occupiers of the land rather than the owners of the
land became responsible for paying for its maintenance and, theoretically at
least, the owners of the land had an increasing say in the elections of officials
and the assessments of taxes. Lords' attempts to take control of the administration of the Marsh and tax assessments in 1361 is consistent with a much broader
'seigneurial reaction' against peasant tenants which tried to address lords'
declining influence and income in this period. Like other aspects of that 'reaction' such as attempts to pin back wages, and to maintain rents and serfdom
dues at pre-plague levels, this would most likely fail after 1381, at least temporarily. Indeed, before the second half of the fifteenth century little is heard
about changing political controls over the Marshes. However in 1474 the crown
was informed of decaying sea defences and marshland vulnerable to flooding
all the way along the Romney Marsh coast. This situation was blamed upon
landholders not paying their taxes. A 'commission' of 12 knights was sent to
force the defaulting holders to pay their dues, presumably at the points of their
swords. In addition 'faithful guardians' were appointed to take control of the

---

73   Teichman-Derville 1936, pp. 6–30.

maintenance of the Marshes and to hear accounts. The success of this commission is in doubt because a further royal commission four years later in 1478
reported that because of the default of repair of banks and drains, all of the
lands between the coast and a line running from near New Romney through
Lydd high street and along the coast from the west of Dengemarsh, and so
therefore including Dengemarsh, were in danger of 'inestimable losses' due to
violent tides and overflows of freshwater that were breaking defences. The two
commissioners appointed were Wealden gentry, Eldrington and Guildford,
who had both invested large amounts of money in large innings in the far west
of Romney Marsh near Rye. They clearly therefore had an agenda to protect
their own lands from the sea and get others to pay for the maintenance. Indeed,
they falsely stated that the affected lands 'were never settled under any certain
and fit statutes or ordinances, by any authority, for their secure defence and
preservation'. Plans were made to repair various walls in the south-west of
Lydd parish, and a new sewer was developed further west in the marshes
beyond Lydd parish.[74] What may have caused these defaults in the payment of
tax is that land holders no doubt felt it unfair that they should be forced to
improve or maintain land not their own. Also the depopulation of Dengemarsh
in the 1460s, and probably elsewhere in the Marsh, which we shall examine in
detail in the following chapter, would have seriously disrupted the earlier
Marsh organisation.

A new Marsh constitution was drawn up and this would form the basis of
practice during the next hundred years. The main officials were now two bailiffs, 24 jurats and two spenders. It is telling that two of the names of the jurats
provided in the report were Henry and Andrew Bate. The latter was the farmer
of Dengemarsh demesne and it was he who in the 1460s was responsible for
the depopulation. The manorial lords chose the bailiffs whose offices were
now permanent. The offices of the 24 jurats were also now permanent. These
were 'elected' following the deaths of other jurats by the manorial lords, bailiffs, and between eight to 10 of the jurats, the latter to be chosen 'out of the
most trusty, discreet and wealthy landholders within those lands and marshes'.[75] No longer was there a place in the election process for the majority of tax
payers, those who had not been forced from their lands. The jurats of this
administration were mostly from Lydd, and it is notable that the development
of oligarchy in the administration of the Marsh as a response to the recalcitrance of tenants subject to taxes on land not their own predated the develop-

74   Dugdale, 1662, pp. 47–51, 59.
75   Dugdale 1662, pp. 51–9.

ment of oligarchy in the town itself by 30 years or so. It seems probable therefore that, during the turmoil on Dengemarsh following violent depopulation in the 1460s, a number of the wealthier farmers in Lydd – including those holding the Dengemarsh demesne leases – would have lobbied for their permanent installation in the town government too.

In conclusion, the evidence for Lydd in the first half of the fifteenth century provides us with glimpses of what could have been the start of an alternative future to both feudalism and capitalism. This was a relatively well-populated area given the post-Black Death context, which no doubt reflected its attractiveness in what was a period of mobility for the peasantry in the context of declining feudal controls. The inhabitants were multi-skilled with deep roots in subsistent land holding, paying low rents without servile disabilities. They were substantially integrated into markets – domestic and overseas – although not market dependent. They had generated robust and relatively democratic institutions by the early fifteenth century at latest, and they were very well organised politically not only internally but in relation to outside political interests. As holders of a royal franchise they owed obligations to a feudal lord, the crown, and as tenants to other seigneurial lords, mainly ecclesiastical, they owed other customary obligations besides rents, although these dues were subject to perennial dispute. The social structure had a broad middle. A small handful of yeomen farmers were by the 1440s a distinct wealthy stratum within the parish, and they were wealthy on the basis of large leases granted by lords such as Battle Abbey and All Souls College, Oxford. They were, however, by no means a dominant force in economic and political terms at this stage, although because of their increasing association and mutuality with seigneurial lordship, and because these associations were being replicated across the region, cracks were beginning to appear in the newly emerging self-governing structure.

Engrossment, Enclosure and Resistance in the Fifteenth Century

Engrossment and enclosure developed to such an extent on Romney Marsh in Kent in the sixteenth century that by 1580 its landscape had modern agrarian capitalist attributes. It was a patchwork of large enclosed fields, traditional routes and rights of way were blocked off, and habitation had been greatly reduced with most people confined to the streets of the small towns and larger villages around its edges.[1] The extent of engrossment and enclosure was not a sixteenth-century phenomenon however, as is often assumed. Already in 1525, Sir Edward Guildford (1479–1534), who came from an established family of gentry in the Weald, could state that 'Romney Marsh where corn and cattle were plentiful, has fallen into decay. Many great farms and holdings are held by persons who neither reside on them, nor till or breed cattle, but use them for grazing'. This was not the opinion of one of the radical commonwealthmen whose impassioned complaints against such changes many historians attend to with raised eyebrows, but an absentee holder of one of the great farms in the Marsh which his father had developed in the middle third of the fifteenth century.[2]

In the discussion on demography in the previous chapter I concluded that Romney Marsh experienced unprecedented depopulation between the middle of the fifteenth century and the 1520s. This contrasted with the unprecedented increase in population of the nearby Weald in the same period. I also concluded that the primary cause of this demographic change was not plague or environmental factors such as flooding or the silting up of harbours, but rather the widespread change of agrarian production from mixed farming to sheep grazing on the Marsh in symbiosis with rural industrial development in the Weald. The question is, how was the transformation from subsistence-based mixed farming to large farms and sheep grazing and its associated depopulation possible before 1520? Historians cannot legitimately point to the stimulation of demand and assume that in response all the supply side levers

---

1   See below in Chapters Three and Four.
2   Cited in Gardiner 1998, p. 140. The lack of grain and dairy produce in the area would increasingly become a serious feature during the sixteenth century, as we shall see in Chapter Twelve.

naturally click into place. In other words, they cannot assume that peasants will choose to specialise and give up their subsistence holdings in response to market opportunities. This chapter will examine the immediate causes of the transformation in this part of Kent in the fifteenth and early sixteenth centuries. It will look in detail at what forms engrossment and enclosure took in the area, at who promoted and carried it out, and at who resisted it and the forms this resistance took.

Studies of engrossment and enclosure often treat the process in a political vacuum. We are presented with statistics on increases in plot size on any given rural manor and we are told, usually on the basis of evidence of land transactions in manorial court rolls, that these accumulations were generated through buying and selling of land without pressure. With the evidence available for Lydd in the fifteenth century we are able to attempt a detailed description of the political context of engrossment and enclosure both at the local level and at the national level. As we will see, one cannot dissociate engrossment and enclosure in Lydd in the 1440s from the conflicts over jurisdiction and custom in the parish, the wider break down in government in Kent and its attendant political disorder, the catastrophic loss of English territory in Normandy, and Cade's Rebellion in 1450, which was particularly significant for Kent.

It was in the middle third of the fifteenth century that the people of Lydd and Dengemarsh faced attacks on their customs and their landholdings both from outside and within. The most transparent case of forced engrossment of land in Lydd parish began in the 1460s. Attempts to force people out of their holdings on Dengemarsh began while the government of Lydd sought to maintain its jurisdictional interests in the manor against the claims of Battle Abbey. However, conflict over jurisdiction and custom was also associated with what on the face of it were less confrontational forms of engrossment and enclosure in the 1440s in the west of Lydd parish.

Before looking at engrossment, enclosure and the conflicts surrounding them in Lydd parish, it will be useful to locate them in the context of changes that were taking place in the Marsh as a whole at the same time. The period between the 1430s and 1470s was one of very substantial investment by ecclesiastical lords and Wealden-based gentry in repairs of sea walls, and reclamation and inning on Romney Marsh. John Elrington and Richard Guildford, esquires, undertook massive inning projects in the south-west of the Marsh near Rye in this period. These served to block up Rye harbour and the estuary linking the Weald to the coast by the middle of the sixteenth century. Among other projects Canterbury Cathedral Priory spent at least £1500 on the reclamation of 600 acres at Appledore on the western edge of the Marsh between 1449 and 1472, although substantial projects had begun there around 1400. The steady accumulation of plots witnessed in the manorial court rolls of Appledore in the same period, as mentioned in the previous chapter, should be seen in the context of this investment and its implications for capitalist leasing. A further 200 marks was provided to finish the work and to take in another 200 acres at Agney, a few miles to the west of Lydd parish. In 1477–8, William Brockhill, the new tenant of the Archbishop of Canterbury's manor of Cheyne Court, again not far to the south-west of Lydd parish, invested £43 in repairs and in enclosing the demesne and he was supplied with 800 sheep. By 1484 he was leasing 829 acres of the Archbishop's manors on the Marsh, and in 1496 a further 300 acres. The Knatchbulls, a yeoman family from Mersam in the Weald, replaced the Brokhills as the principal sheep farming lessees in the early sixteenth century and they would become significant gentry on this basis, sub-leasing the land to farmers from Lydd.[3]

i   Conflict in the 1440s: The Vicar, the Jurat and All Souls College

In the west of Lydd parish, it is the endowment and foundation of All Souls College, Oxford, between 1438 and 1443 by the Archbishop of Canterbury[4] with an area of land appropriately called Newland and the demesne of Scotney manor that more particularly concerns us. These farms were both developed in order to be leased. With regard to the inning, reclamation and enclosure to the west of Lydd parish we do not have information as to whether it involved depopulation, either forced or through land sales. Certainly in the more densely populated parish of Lydd the formation of enclosed leased blocks of land required not reclamation or inning, but the engrossment of small plots. In her work on the All Souls endowment and foundation, Gill Draper has found that the Archbishop worked with intermediaries who accumulated land and then passed it on to the lordship. We have seen in the previous chapter that Henry Aleyn of Lydd had a close association with All Souls College: he sold land to it, acted as a feoffee in its land transactions, and then became the first lessee of Scotney demesne and its large flock of sheep by 1446. The origin of

---

3   Smith 1943, p. 203; Mate 1991, pp. 131–2; Mate 1987, pp. 532–4; Draper 1998, pp. 111–13; Gardiner 1998, pp. 130–2; Hipkin 1995, pp. 138–9.
4   Henry Chichele's official motivation for the foundation was 'to train the "unarmed soldiery" of the Church militant and to build a chantry commemorating the generation who had fought under Henry V'. These were to be priests who could make 'the famous kingdom of England formidable to its enemies and renowned among foreign nations'. However, like New College, Oxford, another recent foundation, All Souls typically produced civil lawyers: Harris 2005, pp. 319, 348–50.

Newland has been traced back to the accumulation of small plots by one Thomas Godfrey, husbandman, between 1390 and 1423. Draper says that the sellers of these plots to Godfrey were mainly of peasant status and of limited means, and that they were selling off inherited land. It is not clear why they did this or whether indeed they were from the area. Godfrey then transferred these plots in a consolidated block to Andrew Ayllewyn and other men between 1427 and 1430. Ayllewyn was vicar of nearby Broomhill church, acting vicar in Lydd, and master of a hospital in New Romney. The land was then passed to Archbishop Chichele who endowed All Souls with the property in 1443.[5] Ayllewyn and Richard Clitherow, esquire and MP for New Romney, were the first lessees from that year.

It is just before the endowment in 1443 when we can locate the origin of disputes between Ayllewyn and the town of Lydd over taxation on Ayllewyn's livestock in Lydd parish, and on his suitability as Lydd's vicar. There are two sides to Ayllewyn's case which are both recorded in the account of 1446–7, although they stem from 1441–2.[6] At that earlier date Ayllewyn was implicated in the replacement of William Hebbinge who had been Lydd's resident vicar since 1435. For reasons unknown, Hebbinge was replaced by an absentee vicar who lived in Rome, and it was Ayllewyn who was chosen by the church authorities to act as vicar on his behalf. The town wanted a fully fledged resident vicar and reacted in 1446–7 by seeking legal counsel in London, and by petitioning the Archbishop of Canterbury for the purpose of either having Hebbinge back as vicar or someone other than Ayllewyn. Ayllewyn countered by procuring at great expense the impeachment of a number of men from Lydd to London and Maidstone, and the arrest and imprisonment in London of jurat William Bette who had been in London putting the case for Hebbinge.[7] The outcome of this case is unclear: it appears that Hebbinge was reinstalled as vicar temporarily but later arrested. On 3rd August 1450, during the bloody suppression of Cade's rebellion, Hebbinge was led up to the Archbishop of Canterbury by men of Lydd and by those of the king who came to fetch him; for what reason we do not know. It is at this point that William Gros, Lydd's common serjeant, was imprisoned in Canterbury Castle. Early the following year there appears to have been a meeting in New Romney between men from Lydd and Andrew Ayllewyn. Ayllewyn left for Rome soon after this meeting, and yet he appears to have been vicar of Lydd when he died in 1458.[8]

5   Draper 1998, pp. 115–16, p. 126 note 47.
6   Finn 1911, pp. 117–20.
7   Finn 1911, pp. 117–18; Robertson 1880, p. 445.
8   Finn 1911, pp. 141–8; Robertson 1880, p. 445.

What is of great significance about this case is the social power – in addition to his deep pockets – that Andrew Ayllewyn wielded against Lydd's government. Certain 'maintainers' of Ayllewyn told the body of commoners in Lydd, who were, as I have stressed, the dominant institution in the town in the fifteenth century, that the jurats had 'made a false quarrel' against Ayllewyn and wasted a large amount of the town's money in trying to get Hebbinge installed as vicar. The jurats, however, justified the magnitude of the expenditure by assuring the commoners that were it not for this 'great maintenance' of Andrew 'being within us', something which was 'openly known', then no expenditure would have been required.

The town's reservations over having Ayllewyn as their vicar become clearer when we turn to the other side of Ayllewyn's case. Making their case against him in 1446–7 the jurats alleged that for the previous five years Ayllewyn had refused to pay his required scot or tax on the cattle he owned in the 'diverse farms' he held in the parish. They again argued that 'we have not been able to compel him to pay the scots which are due because of the great maintenance of diverse persons being within us and against due correction of the town'. That phrase, 'great maintainers', reverberates from the memoranda in this case: what this appears to reflect is the vulnerability of the major part of the jurats to some of the wealthier yeomen with the ear of powerful external patrons. This point is given added weight if we remember the context of political disorder that emerges at exactly this time.[9]

In summary, Ayllewyn became lessee of All Souls in Lydd parish soon after he had taken over the vicarage as local representative of an absentee vicar in Rome, replacing Lydd's preferred resident vicar. He also held other farms in Lydd parish and aimed to use his authority to side step the customs and usages of the town with regard to taxation on livestock. With his rapidly expanding economic base and backing, it is likely that Ayllewyn's designs on a power base in Lydd was regarded as a threat to the economic and political stability of the town by the major part of what appears to have become a government that was starting to split into factions between the most powerful few and the rest.

Less than a year earlier there was another serious attack on the customs and usages of the town by James Ayllewyn who was possibly a close relation to Andrew.[10] On 14 March 1446 the lieutenant of the Cinque Ports came to Lydd 'to make an end of one matter in dispute between the town and James Ayllewyn'. Although a long-standing jurat, James was not among the leading handful of men of Lydd in terms of wealth. In this year he was assessed at 2s, similar to John Sarlis, and like Sarlis was prominent in the town's affairs. Up until this point there is no indication of any animosity between James Ayllewyn and the town government. However this year he held a 'grievance' against the town constable or bailiff, William Melale, and 'a commoner', probably William Gros who was very active in the government as common serjeant at this time.[11] But instead of taking his complaint first to the jurats of Lydd, he 'wilfully' sued them at Dover Castle to the chief court of the Cinque Ports, and in doing so he had disregarded the town's customs and usages and put the town to great expense. James had also disregarded the town's Cinque Port franchises with regard to due process over arrests of both people and commodities. It was said that he:

> reviled, mis-said, and strangely rebuked diverse sworn men [jurats] with tedious and odious language, and drew his dagger against the king's peace and struck some of them with it. Furthermore the said James, recognising no officer here, and following no process ever by us ordained or awarded, took it upon himself to arrest one Joan Ivysshe, put her in the town jail, and hold her in prison for a day and a night without reasonable cause.
>
> And also the said James took it upon himself to arrest diverse goods at the coast here and kept them in his own hands. By our lord's commandment [the Cinque Port franchise granted by the king] these goods belong to the bailiff and jurats and to no other man, unless they default in their duty and so by due process the goods are awarded to another man.

The entries written on behalf of the town finish with '[t]hese injuries and wrongs we could not hastily put into execution by the law on our lord's behalf because of his [James's] great menace'. After the inquisition on March 14, 1446 James Ayllewyn was bound by a sum of money to keep the town customs. He did so and continued to be prominent in the town's affairs.

It is clear that collective attempts were being made at this time to undermine the traditional authority of the government of Lydd with implications for controls over the developments of new farms and landholding within its jurisdiction. This seems to me to be of great importance in a consideration of a

---

11   Finn has transcribed this name as 'Growte' but there is no evidence for a commoner of
      this name, and it is probable that he has mistaken the 't' for an 's', letters that are difficult
      to distinguish in the fifteenth century. The name would then be 'Growse' an alternative
      spelling for Gros.

transition to a new social-property structure. The problem with external main-tainers led the government to make a new constitutional arrangement in October 1448, a year or so after Andrew Ayllewyn's case and during the political disorder in the lead up to Cade's rebellion. Some jurats were allegedly refusing to provide knowledge of counsel they had received and this was 'hindering' the town in its legal affairs: these affairs had stretched the government to the limit at this time because men from Lydd were indicted all over Kent and they required legal representation and support. The ordinance which was agreed among the jurats and commoners stated that the jurats, bailiff and 24 com-moners could examine a jurat who was keeping counsel to himself in order to determine whether he had a legal right or excuse to do so, and if he had no such excuse he was to be discharged from the government.[12]

The town was involved in other serious disputes, again in the summer of rebellion in 1450, a few weeks before Hebbinge was taken to London. This time the enemy was John Cobbes, a gentleman of Newchurch in Romney Marsh proper, and six others from the same place acting in his name. They were bound in £40 'not to legally charge, vex, or procure to legally charge' anyone of Lydd. As receiver, steward and bedell of All Souls College, Cobbes was its chief official, and therefore someone with strong connections with people like Andrew Ayllewyn and Henry Aleyn. At least one of those acting in Cobbe's name, Henry Goddard of Newchurch was, like Ayllewyn and Cobbe himself, a lessee of the College.[13] So conflict between the new leasehold farmers of All Souls College and upholders of the ancient custom and usages in Lydd seems to have been endemic from the beginning of the College's foundation. At this point the body of commoners in the town and parish were holding their own.

ii   Conflict in the 1460s and beyond: Battle Abbey and Its Farmers

The conflicts in the 1460s were the result of the engrossment of holdings and disputes over customs and jurisdiction on the manor of Dengemarsh in the east of the parish of Lydd. We are fortunate in the survival of detailed sources for this manor, and I will begin by examining in detail the nature of landhold-ing and agrarian production prior to the conflicts and the momentous changes that took place there.

---

12   Finn 1911, p. 136.
13   Finn 1911, p. 143; Draper 1988, p. 115.

In the second half of the fourteenth century and early fifteenth century lords in England withdrew from the direct management of their large manorial demesnes because prices had dropped and wages had risen dramatically following the feudal crisis and subsequent reduction in population. The demesnes were leased to the more well-heeled peasant farmers in order for lords to maintain a reasonable and steady income. In the thirteenth century and first half of the fourteenth century Dengemarsh was one of a number of manors provisioning Battle Abbey which lay some 30 miles west along the coast in Sussex. As a 'provision manor' the produce of Dengemarsh's demesne was allocated for the abbey's direct consumption. The produce of the demesnes of the abbey's manors that were at a greater distance was sold for a money income. All of the provision manors sent a range of products such as fish, livestock and dairy products, and over half of the value of the produce was in corn. Between the 1340s and the 1380s the abbey's manors experienced a decline in income of 27 percent. Hence from as early as 1346 Dengemarsh began to be leased, although at this stage it was frequently back in the abbey's hands. The abbey did not have a good relationship with its tenants on Dengemarsh and with the town of Lydd in the fourteenth century because of the endemic conflict over custom, particularly right of wreck. As I mentioned in the previous chapter, in the 1350s the abbey was forced to complain to the king that its officials were harassed by men from Lydd when they went there. So finding suitable candidates to farm its manor there would be a challenge. There was no wealthy stratum of proto-capitalists straining to become market-dependent and break into capitalist development as orthodox Marxists suppose. This endemic conflict over custom would come to influence the abbey's policy on engrossment and enclosure in the manor in the 1460s and I examine the abbey's thinking on this below. For now we should recognise that Dengemarsh was still supplying large amounts of corn to the abbey in the late fourteenth century, and at this time Lydd itself was one of the main markets which the abbey used to buy its corn. The marshes around Lydd, Dengemarsh in particular, were traditionally engaged in significant arable cultivation and were not as yet used primarily for livestock.[14]

Probably the last time the demesne was taken back into the hands of the abbey was between 1429 and 1431. A balanced, mixed farming was *still* evident on the manorial demesne in 1430.[15] Income was clearly erratic at this point

---

14   Searle 1974, pp. 251–9; TNA, SC 6, 889/13–27; SC 6, 890/1–6.

15   The lordship accounts are damaged in these years making overall calculations for each year impossible. However with regard to arable cultivation they reveal the employment of three sets of plough teams on the manorial demesne and the employment of labourers

and this doubtless reflects the temporary nature of the abbey's involvement. It appears that the demesne had been recently leased to a John Pevensey because the 1429–30 account details much of the stock and produce as being seized from him back into the hands of the abbey. The 1430–1 account reveals that a substantial £14 12s was spent that year on a new embankment, and this suggests that the abbey was preparing a more attractive lease for another farmer. Searle points out that unlike Westminster and Ramsay Abbeys in the fourteenth century which were only interested in renting their home farm or demesne, Battle Abbey was interested in farmers who could take over the whole manor, including 'rent roll, demesne, stock, equipment and buildings for terms that varied from five years to lifetime leases, most being 10 year terms'.[16] We know that John Bate of Lydd was leasing Dengemarsh manor by 1441, and may well have been as early as 1432.[17]

A clear picture of the nature of landholdings, customary rents and demesne on Dengemarsh can be gained from rentals and a taxation list that survive for approximately 60 years before 1432. For the year 1432 two related rentals of particular detail survive.[18] In addition there is a rental for 1402, and a marshland drainage taxation list dated within the reign of Edward III (1327–77).[19] The latter lists the occupiers of land within 'the 'Watering' of Dengemarsh who were subject to taxation for the maintenance of the drains and sea walls. Half of the people recorded on this taxation list survived to be recorded on the 1402 list, and a quarter of them were still alive in 1432. So the date of the earlier list

---

for threshing corn and mowing hay. In 1429–30 arable produce amounted to 14 quarters of wheat, 24 quarters of oats and 14 quarters of barley malt. The accounts are damaged where the details of acreage sown are given, but indications that a quarter measure of corn was produced on each acre suggest that the acreage sown that year was in the range of 100 acres, which accounted for a third of the demesne acreage. In 1430–1 the total livestock in the manor consisted of 11 horses, 72 cattle and some pigs. This does not represent a large amount of livestock for this year. However the abbey allowed sheep from other owners to pasture on the demesne for a sum of money: in 1429–30 this amounted to £4 for 282 sheep belonging to three men, dropping to only 3s 4d for 30 sheep owned by one man in 1430–1. More significant income was derived from 'agistment in broco' – that is, renting scrub land temporarily: £8 10s in 1429–30, and £6 12s in 1430–1.

16   Searle 1974, pp. 258–9.
17   The reference has been lost.
18   TNA, E 315/56, pp. 226–41; TNA, E 315/386. The former is enshrined within a large book containing all the Battle Abbey rentals within the overall manor of Wye to which Dengemarsh, a coastal attachment, belonged. The latter forms a compact book by itself making it practical for mobile use.
19   TNA, SC 11/347; TNA, E 315/57, pp. 30, 108.

can be placed at the end of Edward III's reign, circa 1370s. The total acreage of the manor recorded in the 1370s was 967 acres including the demesne. The demesne acreage was 307 acres leaving 660 acres of customary tenant land. 120 acres of the demesne was farmed out in 19 separate plots at this stage. So the demesne represented a third of the total manorial acreage, a typically large English demesne, similar to the proportionate size found for the English midlands in the thirteenth century.[20] Whoever leased this demesne as a farm was therefore undertaking a very large enterprise. The most detailed rental of 1432 records 658 acres of customary tenant land outside of the demesne making its acreage identical to that of the 1370s. This evidence clearly demonstrates that there was no change at all between the size of the demesne and the rest of the manor, and indeed in the size of the manor as a whole, between the 1370s and 1432.

We can now turn in detail to the customary holdings. There were, as I have said, at least 49 inhabited messuages recorded in the Dengemarsh rental of 1432. These were well-spread throughout the structure of occupiers, and included seven people or families who lived in messuages with only half an acre attached. These were most probably labourer's cottages. There was therefore a high density of habitation in the manor and outside of the town at this stage. The overwhelming majority of the 658 acres in 1432 were very small; mostly less than a few acres, many containing just fractions of acres of land. Three knights and gentry held approximately 50 to 60 acres each. These families did not participate in the government of the town, and it is not clear if they were resident. Aside from these the plot size ranged from a quarter of an acre to 17 acres. There was only one example of the latter and only two cases of 10 acres, the next largest size. There were 85 occupiers in the 1370s and 81 occupiers plus the abbey and the churchwardens of Lydd in 1432. Those 85 occupiers in the 1370s were divided between 51 different family names. However the 81 in 1432 were divided between as many as 64 different family names. Regarding the structure of holdings, including the holdings of the gentry, in the 1370s the highest amount of acreage held by an individual or by the heirs of an individual was 50 and the lowest was a quarter of an acre. In 1432 the highest was 59.5 acres and the lowest was half an acre. Within these similar outer limits the structure of holdings appears at first very similar. The traditional subsistence holding of half a virgate is generally regarded – given certain regional variations – as being no more than 15 acres in lowland England. Only 11 of the 85 people in the 1370s held 16 acres or more, and 12 of the 81 in 1432 did so. A traditional smallholding is regarded as being no more than five acres. The number

---

20   Kosminsky 1956, p. 92.

holding five acres and below in the 1370s was 51, and in 1432 it was 50. However when we examine the smaller holdings, significant differences appear between the two dates. The number holding less than three acres in the 1370s was 30, and yet in 1432 it was up to 37. And the number holding less than two acres in the 1370s was 25, and up to 29 in 1432. Finally, the number holding less than one acre in the 1370s was eight, and up to 16 in 1432. This evidence of a significant increase in family names occupying land in the manor, and of a significant increase in the number of people occupying less than three acres of land between the 1370s and 1432, suggests that there was an increase in demand for land between these dates and the result was a fragmentation of holdings at the bottom of the holding scale.

In 1432, 85 percent of occupiers held a bare subsistence holding of 16 acres or fewer, and 46 percent held less than three acres. Without other holdings in adjacent manors or the support of another trade, especially fishing, the vast majority of these occupiers would not have survived. Why this fragmentation of holdings occurred on Dengemarsh during a period of general population downturn is not clear. The period between the 1370s and 1430s marks the decline of serfdom in England. So can the fragmentation of holdings in Dengemarsh and Lydd be attributed to the migration of peasants from harsher servile tenures, perhaps attracted by the Cinque Port liberties and occupational opportunities? Or was it because people were being forced from their holdings elsewhere in the parish or from elsewhere in the Marsh?

Virtually all occupiers who held more than one plot held them in different locations (within the manor) where they were used for different purposes, that is, for arable or pasture. Many held land in an area called 'Southmede', a name that suggests meadow or pasture. This was a large district and yet plot size here was the smallest, the largest being two acres. So like all of the other plots in the manor this pasture was held in very small severalty or in small enclosed fields. Small numbers of animals would have been kept in these fields. They would have provided a balanced diet, a crucial source of manure-based fertilizer to support arable production in the other fields, and also a means of transportation if they could accommodate a horse. There were notably therefore no common lands in this manor laid aside for pasture for all of the animals in the manor.

The absence of open fields and common lands in Dengemarsh manor points, on the face of it, to a lack of communal organisation and of communal responsibility. Manors such as this were typical in Kent from the thirteenth century, and coupled with relatively free tenure some historians have assumed they represent a spirit of individualism and private enterprise. This form of 'old enclosure' is seen as already one step towards capitalism.[21] However, these enclosures on Dengemarsh were fragmented and non-consolidated, a deliberate strategy which enabled individual cultivators to have access to diverse land use. There had been no attempt to build up larger consolidated farms in the years before 1432; indeed the opposite had happened. The Dengemarsh court rolls that survive in a mostly complete form between 1430 and 1450 reveal a busy land market in the two decades after 1432. These transactions generally took the form of a balance of buying and selling by those most involved. There is only one example of a tenant accumulating land in any significant way, that of Laurence Elys. Laurence was one of three Elys's who spent time in the juratcy from 1428, the year that the record of government representation begins. Laurence and Stephen represented Dengemarsh. William and Stephen Elys were both mariners, while Laurence focused on farming. In 1432 Laurence held approximately 12 acres on Dengemarsh plus the messuage that he lived in there, and Stephen held approximately six acres and his messuage. Between 1432 and 1450 (the year he died), he was involved in another 15 transactions involving very small amounts of acreage: for example, 13 of these were acquisitions from 12 different individuals. These amounted to approximately 60 acres, and he bequeathed them to his heirs collectively, placing these heirs amongst the highest holders in the manor.[22] However this acreage did not form a consolidated farm and it was shared or dispersed between these heirs in any case. This type of accumulation and dispersal upon the death of the accumulator is typical of those accumulations that are found around 1300, in contrast to the second half of the fifteenth and sixteenth centuries when accumulations were consolidated and passed on to an individual as a single unit.

Even if one accepts that such Kentish manors containing fragmented enclosed plots, no common lands, and a free land market in the late medieval period produced 'an atmosphere of individualism and private enterprise' as Du Boulay has suggested, this atmosphere had not stimulated any movement towards agrarian capitalism before the middle of the fifteenth century. This was because, even with such an arrangement, important communal responsibilities existed. These responsibilities could be found in the maintenance of rights of way, in the important values of 'neighbourliness', and in the occupations that supported these fragmented plots such as fishing. Those who occupied land on the manor also had other common foci, namely the important franchises they claimed such as right of wreck, and their political

---

21 Du Boulay 1966, p. 134. See the discussion in Part I, Chapter Seven.

22 TNA, SC 2, 180/60–5.

representation amongst the commoners in the Cinque Port of Lydd. There was no common land on Dengemarsh but there were four large areas of common land attached to the borough of Lydd; and those on Dengemarsh who also held small plots in the manor of Aldington would have had access to these commons. As we have seen in the previous chapter it was normal for inhabitants in the parish to hold lands in both manors, including petty traders and artisans who lived in the town. Structures of holdings in manors cannot be treated in isolation as every rural historian knows, and relationships between these manors, towns, commons and customs were highly complex.

The geographical relationship between the demesne and the customary holdings can be identified in the rental of 1432. The presence of the demesne lands of the 'Abbot and Convent of Battle' in close proximity to the customary holdings is clear. The tenants' holdings are in many cases described as being between these demesne lands and another tenant, leading up to these lands, and lying next to them. There are also references which are less frequent which describe tenants' lands being within those of the demesne, surrounded by them, enclosed on all sides by them, and interestingly 'within Le Batayllondgate'. This evidence reveals that the demesne must have been dispersed to some extent among the customary holdings. This has implications for the processes of engrossment which are examined below.

Regarding the important subject of tenurial status, in 1432 the vast majority of holdings were non-servile customary holdings. Eleven small plots are described as being held 'in servicio' and this may represent a residual aspect of the 'great gavelmead' tenure that was discussed in the previous chapter. Tenants holding this tenure in the fourteenth century, which only related to 36 acres in the manor, had to provide 16 horses and riders between them for certain carrying services for the abbey. The rent per acre was very high at 3s 4d. In return they were allowed 16 sheep per acre held to graze upon the rough coastal shingle. In 1432 there were no longer rents of a higher magnitude, distinguishable from the rest. However a reciprocal relationship in which carrying services were owed in exchange for the grazing of sheep may have remained. There were also eight plots held 'in feod firma' – leased. These were probably small plots that fell into the lord's hands, either because tenants did not want them at some point because they carried high rents and servile customs, or because a tenant died without heirs and the lord took over them by default.

The vast majority of holdings, as I have said, were not freeholds but rather non-servile customary holdings. However, like freeholds, restrictions on the heritability, alienation or sale of these holdings did not apply to them as the busy courts rolls bear witness. Entry fines were low at the equivalent of a year's rent. There were frequently significant differences in entry fines even though they related to plots of similar size, but this can be put down to the diverse range in the quality of the land in question, some of it including stony and salty areas. The size of the attached messuage would also be an important factor in the magnitude of the fine. For example the lowest rent paid was 0.38d per acre and the highest was 12d per acre including messuages. However most rents were between 4d and 6d per acre and the main base was 4d. Rent at 4d per acre was relatively low in comparison with rents elsewhere in England: it was indeed the value deemed acceptable by the rebels of 1381 in their list of radical demands. This value remained the same at Dengemarsh throughout the period between 1430 and 1535 for which we have manorial records. Rents were also 4d per acre in Old Langport manor in 1551. By then, however, parts of the latter manor had been developed into competitive leasehold rents and these were very high. The Aldington rental of 1556 which included the urban streets of Lydd reveals that rents were and remained even lower in this manor, working out at only 1d per acre and 2d for a basic tenement.

The customary holdings on Dengemarsh in 1432 were therefore among the most secure with regard to tenurial status. They were not copyholds for lives or for terms of years which would have left them subject to the highest bidder when these terms elapsed; they were heritable and held 'in perpetuum'. The lord could not increase the rents legally, or without violence, except when holdings fell back into his hands through default of heirs. The peasants therefore paid what would increasingly be below the market value of their land. If such a situation would have continued throughout the country land would – as in France – have become increasingly worthless to the lords and, theoretically, the broader demands of the rebels of 1381 (such as the removal of lordship) would have become a reality. One can perhaps see why ecclesiastical lords and gentry in this region were so keen to improve land and develop new leases across the Marsh that carried the market value of land. It is important to state here that those occupying small plots on Dengemarsh were not subletters and paying a market rate to a larger holder. The rental clearly shows that the occupiers holding the increasingly fragmented plots were all paying the basic ground rent directly to the lord.

As it turned out, Battle Abbey and its associates were not prepared to accept an increasingly low income from its Dengemarsh rents, and a rental of 1538 associated with the dissolution of the monasteries reveals a very different situation from that in the first half of the fifteenth century.[23] Indeed a transformation just short of a revolution in land holding had taken place. The demesne was no longer 307 acres in size, which was already large, but 408 acres. It was

---

23   TNA, SC 6, Hen 8/3675.

split into two farms worth £22 and £21 per annum. The second one was called Northlade, 'a parcel of marsh newly enclosed'. Northlade was developed in the second half of the fifteenth century. It was worth £10 in 1470 and £13 in 1480.[24] As mentioned earlier, part of the demesne, 120 acres of the total 307 acres, had much earlier been leased out in small separate plots until at least the 1370s, and many demesne plots were dispersed among the customary assize holdings. The manorial accounts for Dengemarsh reveal that a total lease of 100s or £5 was paid annually for 'diverse land and pasture' at Northlade in 1358–9, and this was not consolidated land at this stage.[25] It is certain therefore that this leasehold farm at Northlade which was growing in value and probably in size in the 1470s and 1480s was only a very recent development.

The number of tenants recorded in 1538 was 31 and the number of holdings had been reduced to 35. Of the 31 remaining tenants, six were gentry, and at least 15 were Lydd jurats and their families. This reveals a striking increase in the exclusivity of landholding amongst the enlarged and increasingly wealthy political elite. At least three consolidated farms of 75 acres, 80 acres and 100 acres with their own messuages had been developed in the 1470s and 1480s amongst the customary holdings: the latter two were situated together, divided by the road leading from the town to Dungeness. The remaining rents were no longer of customary tenure but had been converted to freeholds.

So what exactly happened on Dengemarsh in the years between 1432 and 1538 which resulted in large consolidations among the customary assize rents, the substantial enlargement of the demesne and consequentially the severe depopulation?

The expansion of the demesne occurred as early as the 1460s at the same time as a serious jurisdictional dispute between the people of Lydd and Dengemarsh and Battle Abbey reached a climax. The origin of the dispute was Battle Abbey's claim to right of wreck and other franchises from its Dengemarsh manor. The people of Dengemarsh and Lydd claimed the same rights by virtue of their royal jurisdiction as Cinque Port associates. As with many such disputes in medieval England they stemmed from precedents in the late thirteenth and early fourteenth centuries, a period when lords in England were at the height of their powers against their peasant tenants, although also on the verge of crisis. The disputes generated from this period were typically played out in the rebellion of 1381. The dispute on Dengemarsh over these liberties in the early fourteenth century lasted for five years, between 1310 and 1315. Certain men who are described 'of Lydd' lost the dispute by default in the end because

---

24   TNA, SC 6, 1107/9–10.
25   TNA, SC 6, 889/17.

they consistently asserted their jurisdictional right as Cinque Port freemen or 'barons' to be tried at Shepway, the royal court for the Cinque Ports at that time; and they refused to attend external courts at Westminster in London and at Canterbury when summoned.[26] This recalcitrance on the part of the people of Lydd and Dengemarsh was not diminished by the official defeat. In the 1320s there was an inquisition in Dengemarsh court by Battle Abbey because ships from France, Portugal and Newcastle that had been wrecked at Dungeness had their cargo distributed and sold by people of Dengemarsh.[27] And in the 1350s, as I have mentioned above, the abbey was forced to seek intervention from the crown because people of Dengemarsh would not allow its officials to have physical access to the manor in order to collect rents and do business. As soon as Lydd's accounts open in the fifteenth century issues with the abbey are apparent. In 1431–2 Lydd's jurats paid a lawyer at New Romney for 'a certain matter pending between the Abbot of Battle and certain men of Lydd'. Three years later, while continuous meetings were held between Lydd jurats and officials of the ports at Dover, money was paid to a John Scoleg to ride to London with fish for the Abbot: the aim was doubtless to appease him in the courts there.[28]

The climax of the franchise dispute was in the years between 1466 and 1469, although in this latest manifestation it began earlier in 1462 and did not end until 1477. In 1462 Lydd was buffeted by debts, a result of funding 34 men and some 'strangers' to march to St Albans on the other side of London during the Wars of the Roses the year before, and of funding the more immediate challenge of defending the coast against foreign navies and providing soldiers for Calais. Lydd sought new sources of income and in the same year the jurats decided to tax fishermen from outside of the liberty.[29] These fishermen came from Devon and Cornwall to benefit from the seasonal fishing on the Kent coast and the market and cabins at Dungeness. In the following few years the accounts reveal that these 'Westernmen' were prepared to pay the tax, although in the summer of 1465 they appear to have demonstrated some reluctance to do so. Hence an ordinance was written on June 9 that year threatening them with prison if they failed to pay. As we shall see the reluctance to pay the tax to the town appears to have resulted from the involvement of Battle lordship in the issue. On 1 May the following year (1466), 12 Lydd jurats rode to the abbey in Battle in East Sussex to speak with the Abbot about Dengemarsh 'for

26 Daniel-Tyssen and Lower 1886, pp. 155–63.
27 TNA, SC 2/180/57.
28 Finn 1911, pp. 39, 61.
29 Finn 1911, p. 205.

keeping the franchise'. In the same year three lawyers and a number of Lydd jurats came together 'to make the town's customs'. On another occasion that year a man was paid to fetch the abbot's charter that was with the surveyor of the Archbishop of Canterbury, and William Bette and Thomas Caxton of Lydd rode to London to arrange a meeting with the Abbot for 'a treaty' between Battle Abbey and the town.[30]

During the following two years a number of Lydd men, particularly Thomas Caxton, frequently attended the courts at Westminster in London, often for months at a time, fighting against a suit made by the Abbot against the town. Fish, mainly barrels of sprats, from Dungeness, and tavern lunches and drinks in London were lavished on leading Kentish aristocrats such as Sir John Fogg, Sir John Scott and Sir John Guildford, and on local and London attorneys in these years for the purpose of maintaining Dengemarsh's Cinque Port franchise. Patronage from such men was deemed crucial.

Returning to the details of the case, what seems to have deterred these fishermen of Devon and Cornwall from paying tax to the coffers of Lydd was that the Abbot's officials, namely the farmer of Dengemarsh manor and the beadle, both Lydd men, were *also* attempting to tax them. The farmer of the manor, Andrew Bate, who was instrumental in the demesne expansion at the same time, was challenged on this issue of taxing fishermen in Lydd's borough court on 21 September 1467. Bate rejected the charge, and responded by asserting that any fish or money he may have received was freely given as a gift. That Bate denied the charge suggests that he recognised that had no legal right under the asserted franchise of Battle Abbey to tax fishermen. The beadle, Laurence Holderness, who received his orders from the manor's farmer, was in the same court a few weeks later, and he entirely contradicted Bate's version of events. He stated that by the assignment of Andrew Bate he did tax them, and he revealed that Bate had told him to say that any fish given to him was given as a gift without being taxed, and yet some years he took a 1,000 fish from them, and in one year 1400; in addition he took 50 fish from every boat.[31]

It was clear that the conflict between the abbey and the town in the years between 1466 and 1469 was not simply about the ability to tax fishermen, however important the implications were for the town's customs and income in difficult times. The borough court record only survives in these years because the entries of this serious case were copied into the chamberlains' accounts along with other important memoranda and ordinances. Directly underneath the record of the above dispute in the accounts is a list of memoranda

---

30   Finn 1911, pp. 216–18, 280.

31   Finn 1911, p. 323.

concerning numerous elements of the conflict and possible solutions. These memoranda were written in a very different, neat, monkish hand in gold ink, probably by a scribe from the abbey. The entries in full are as follows:

> It is said that the farmer of Dengemarsh compelled Westernmen to pay him 300 dried whiting [fish] against their will.
>
> The same farmer took a cabin or two by the assignment of the abbot [of Battle], in prejudice of common rights.
>
> There have been wasted and put away from Dengemarsh 70 households. As a result there are now fewer than eight men of Dengemarsh capable of going to the beach to defend the coast from the king's enemies.
>
> Caxton [Thomas] says that William Rolf [of Lydd] offers more money for the manor of Dengemarsh than Andrew [Bate] has paid up to now. He [Caxton] also offers all manner of franchises and liberties to be reserved to the lord, such as wrecks, fishings, waifs and strays, and the profits from the cabins etc.[32]

This remarkable series of entries reveals that the franchise dispute was tied up with the forced and momentous depopulation of Dengemarsh by the abbey's farmer. The most striking clause is that which refers to 70 households being 'wasted and put away' from the manor, and we will return to this below. As for the remaining clauses, Thomas Caxton, the town clerk who had been working on the case for the town and Dengemarsh for the previous two years, reiterated the issue of the farmer of Dengemarsh manor's illegal taxation of fishermen from the West Country, and of his apparent confiscation of some of the fishing cabins on the coast in the name of the abbey and in disregard of common rights. As a means of resolving the dispute, and at the same time preserving Dengemarsh for its tenants, William Rolf (a Lydd jurat and Dengemarsh land holder), either at the instigation or with the help of Caxton, offered the abbey more for the lease of the manor than the current farmer, Andrew Bate, was paying; and, in the name of Lydd and the Dengemarsh tenants, Caxton offered to give up the long-term claim of the town on the various franchises and liberties of the manor.

The abbey refused the compromise and continued to work with Bate to achieve its ends. A few months later on 16 January 1468, John Andrew, 'bailiff of the liberty of the abbot of Battle', at the instigation of Andrew Bate, and it seems by the authority of the sheriff of Kent, brought a summons against John

---

32   Finn 1911, p. 323.

Sarlis and Thomas Caxton of Lydd to answer the Abbot of Battle in the courts of Westminster in a plea of trespass.[33] Caxton and Sarlis were charged with 'taking away 10,000 whiting at Dungeness'. The 'trespass' was clearly done in the name of 'the commons' of Lydd because Caxton rode to Lydd from London a few weeks later on February 2nd to inform them of the progress of 'the abbot's wrongful suit', and returned to London with their response.[34]

It was the farmer, Andrew Bate of Lydd, who instigated this plea of trespass and to do so he involved the bailiff of Battle. Regarding the latter, Searle has shown that by the middle third of the fifteenth century the burgesses of Battle were, like those in other larger towns in England, a self-perpetuating ruling clique of merchants and lawyers, and they were benefiting from large accumulations of land in the Sussex countryside. As sub-stewards of the abbey, by the time of the Dengemarsh conflict in the late 1460s they also dominated the administration of the abbey itself. In the fourteenth century, when the abbey experienced a steep decline in income, it farmed out its manors wholesale and, in a further cost-cutting drive, its aristocratic retainers who helped it collect rents and maintain its social power were cut from the budget. However, by the time of the conflict on Dengemarsh the aristocratic retainers were re-employed and the sub-stewards were riding out collecting the rents again, as well as involving themselves in land speculation. Andrew Bate and his partner Henry Bate were in fact co-holders of eight acres of land in Lydd parish with John Bokeland of Battle: the latter was an attorney and held the two offices of abbot's chamberlain and sub-steward from the 1470s, and he engrossed land around the town of Battle as well.[35]

It is this resurgence of Battle Abbey and the connections and the social power of its farmer in the 1460s that enabled him to have such an impact on the customs and tenants in the parish of Lydd. One cannot otherwise see how it would have been possible for him and people like him across England in this period to create such catastrophic changes in such populated areas. One can only point to a mutual relationship between these farmers and the lordship administrations from which they leased their lands. Given this mutual relationship it comes as no surprise that, in 1477, Andrew and Henry Bate were chosen as chief officers by the aristocratic royal sewer commissioners to

33   Finn 1911, p. 322.
34   Finn 1911, p. 245.
35   Searle 1974, pp. 365–80, 418–37; Finn 1911, p. 240.

develop a new Marsh administration in the face of tenants allegedly defaulting in their land tax payments.[36]

In the formal charge of trespass against Thomas Caxton and John Sarlis, both of them were described as 'yeomen'. It is important to distinguish them, however, from others with the same title who farmed hundreds of acres and were on some occasions, particularly in the sixteenth century, also described as gentlemen on the basis of their wealth. It is a mistake to assume that those described as yeomen in the late fifteenth and sixteenth centuries were subsistent peasants of a traditional type. If Robert Allen has found examples of this in the seventeenth century, then the term had by then changed its meaning. It was very rare for anyone in Lydd without substantial leases to be described as a yeoman from the early sixteenth century. In the middle third of the fifteenth century this was still not unusual. Caxton and Sarlis were not among the big lease-holders in the parish and town government. They were nevertheless leading representatives of the commons of a well-organised small-town community that had a different raison d'être; one that, out of necessity combined certain communal values with modest success in trade and in landholding without serfdom. Caxton and Sarlis were small farmers and tradesmen of relatively middling wealth. Sarlis was a baker, brewer, and fisherman; Caxton a small-town trader and litigious clerk. It was this raison d'être, the basis for an alternative future to feudalism and capitalism, which was being challenged by emerging capitalist farmers and their patrons. People like Caxton, Sarlis and others led the resistance.

This brings us to the expansion of the demesne on Dengemarsh. To begin with we must take account of the charge put to Battle Abbey in September 1467 that 70 households had been removed from Dengemarsh, and that there was as a consequence by then only eight men able to defend the coast there against England's enemies. This development was presented as an act of violence as the charge included terms such as 'wasted' and 'put away'.

On 23 November 1466, a year before this serious and momentous charge, and during the initial throes of the dispute over the franchises, the demesne farmer Andrew Bate, whose role had also been central in the franchise dispute, appeared as a plaintiff in Lydd's borough court against John Sedley of Lydd in what appears to be a case of defamation or libel. As important memoranda derived from the borough court this record was copied in the town accounts. Bate stated that Sedley said he was 'an extortioner' and that 'he had driven away half of Dengemarsh'. Sedley denied that he had said these words, but

---

36   Dugdale 1662, pp. 47–55.

rather that 'Andrew should [as in, 'would' or 'will'] drive men out of Dengemarsh, as men had been saying'. Four witnesses confirmed that Sedley said that 'Andrew Bate will force ['a wroke'] men out of the north end of Dengemarsh as men had been saying'.[37]

Like Caxton and Sarlis, John Sedley was a Lydd jurat who appears to have been voicing a general concern to Bate about what was going on. Why it took Bate to initiate legal proceedings against him rather than the other way around is not clear and I will explore this point below. But whether Bate had *already* driven half of the people from Dengemarsh he certainly appears to have been in the process of doing so. On the same day a number of further witnesses came to court and recounted their experiences. Here are the court depositions that were copied into the accounts:

> William Smyth informed the bailiff and jurats that the Abbot has a herd of cattle in the north end of Dengemarsh which was hurting the people dwelling there. And that, by his faith, he no longer occupied his lands because of the hurt that Andrew Bate's cattle did to him. He was forced to sublet his lands.
>
> Roger Cokered also said that because of the overpressing of Andrew Bate's cattle, he had lost 21 cows and six horses. He might have saved them if his pasture had not been destroyed by Andrew Bate. He no longer dared to occupy his lands because of the destruction of Andrew Bate's cattle.
>
> Nicholas Howlyn said that if he might have held his house and land in peace, without the hurt caused by Andrew Bate's cattle, he would not have sold it. The destruction in one part by Andrew's cattle caused him to sell his place for 13s 4d, better cheap rather than what the said Andrew had offered him.
>
> Laurence Garard and Agnes, the wife of Thomas Cliprank, said that the said Thomas departed from Dengemarsh because of the hurt of Andrew Bate. The said Thomas swore to Stephen Hoigge and the said Laurence that he would never have departed from Dengemarsh if it was not for the overpressing of the said Andrew who often threatened and forced him.
>
> Thomas Smyth said he would not have sold his lands at Dengemarsh for double the silver if he could have occupied them in peace as neighbourhood required, and that because of the cattle of Andrew Bate he was grievously hurt and yearly lost his corn causing him to sell his lands.

37   Finn 1911, p. 278.

The said Andrew drove his mare into the mire which was the cause of her death. Also the said Andrew asked the said Thomas if he would sue him, and he threatened him saying that if he did sue him he would pay him back at some or other place.

Thomas Shalwell also said that the said Andrew had hurt him often to the value of 20 nobles [20 × 6s 8d]. And because this occurred yearly he stopped sowing and occupying his land. He will depart from Dengemarsh if he cannot live in peace – better than before.[38]

So there was no formal eviction of tenants by the lord. The lord's farmer, a butcher-grazier, simply drove his herd of cattle on to the surrounding small plots of arable and pasture and 'destroyed' them. This strategy had the same effect as direct eviction. He then issued threats to those who dared try to sue or remonstrate with him. At the same time he offered to buy them out. He did this 'often' and 'yearly' and this suggests that he had done it for at least two years. Those deposing against Bate were among the commons of Lydd, some with experience in the juratcy. These would have carried weight in the borough court and most probably would been regarded as representatives of the commoners who were losing their lands. The one example where this was not the case was that of Thomas Cliprank of whom we have no other record than this entry. His fear of Bate apparently led his wife to seek help from Stephen Hogge, one of the more experienced commoners and jurats in Lydd, and a landholder on Dengemarsh.[39] Cliprank and his wife were probably among the poorer households that were removed from Dengemarsh, a significant number of which had small cottages tied to small plots.

No-one did in fact sue Bate it seems. The reason for this is not easy to explain. The strategy of resistance that seems to have been adopted from November 1466 began with the affected landholders to come to the borough court in order to support Sedley's statement, after Bate had instigated a plea of defamation against him. Was the social power that Bate wielded so effective that people dared not seek redress in court even given the magnitude of the offence? The answer may lie in the different jurisdictions in the parish. Legal redress against Bate for offences done on Dengemarsh would have been obliged to have taken place in the manorial court of Dengemarsh. The court rolls do not survive for this period and so we do not know if the tenants did try to stop him there to begin with. As farmer of all aspects of the manor besides the demesne Bate would have been as its own lord and it is likely that bringing him to

---

38   Finn 1911, pp. 278–9.

39   In his will of 1489 he is called Stephen Cheseman alias Hogge senior.

his own court may have presented difficulties. But by instigating a plea of defamation against a Lydd jurat Bate may well have inadvertently fallen in to a trap set for him by the aggrieved Dengemarsh tenants, as this was the type of case that could be tried in the borough.⁴⁰

Another reason for the vulnerability of these tenants may have been the more individualised nature of production on the manor. All of the plots were held in severalty and without common pasture. There was therefore no local war over the absorption of the commons and the consequent extinguishing of common rights which affected all of the tenants simultaneously. Violent illegal engrossment was undoubtedly easier in these circumstances. Nevertheless, the tenants still demonstrated an attachment to certain communal values. Thomas Smyth stated that Bate disregarded the requirement or custom of 'neighbourhood', and by stating this in a court of law he was therefore expecting this custom to carry a good deal of weight. Nicholas Howlyn said he preferred to sell his land to someone other than Bate, and at a cheaper price than Bate had offered him after destroying his place. This was an act of solidarity against Bate's expansionist project. Two days after these depositions three Lydd butchers and a servant of Henry Bate came to the court and deposed against both Henry and Andrew Bate who were also butchers. They said that Henry Bate sold a pig and a sheep that were unwholesome and that 'Andrew Bate uses the art of a butcher to the hurt and undoing of the artificers there'.⁴¹ Opposition to Andrew Bate and his relation and colleague Henry Bate had mounted in more than one quarter into an organised and concerted attack. The most important communal focus for these tenants of Dengemarsh, in the absence of common lands, was doubtless their customs in common that they had observed and defended for centuries, particularly right of wreck. These were being undermined at the same time as tenants were being driven from their holdings by Bate and the abbey. One strategy for the tenants, as we have seen in the depositions above, was to formally relinquish these rights in return for the removal of Bate from the manor in return for peaceful tenancy. This was stated in stark terms the following year when William Rolf also offered to pay more for the lease of the manor than Bate was paying.

The resistance clearly failed. The struggle over the franchises continued into the 1470s, and by 1477 it seems that Dengemarsh had lost its Cinque Port status and therefore its formal franchise. Although Caxton maintained this status in the custumal that he produced in 1477, the jurats representing Dengemarsh

40   This is a useful example of the way in which fragmented jurisdictions in England provided the peasantry with room to manoeuvre in their resistance against lords and their agents. See Rigby's arguments on this point and my critique in Part I, Chapter Two above.
41   Finn 1911, p. 277. This is Finn's translation of a latin text.

were no longer recorded at the head of the town accounts. In the latter record all jurats were now stated as from the borough of Lydd. The absence of representation in Lydd's government for Dengemarsh tenants also reflected the depopulation of the manor. The area where the main destruction of the tenants' lands took place was almost certainly 'Northlade', referred to as the 'north end' of the manor in the depositions. Only two or three years later in 1470, after the charge was made that '70 households had been wasted and put away' from Dengemarsh, it seems that the area of formerly scattered demesne plots called Northlade had been engrossed with the surrounding customary tenants' land and leased to Andrew Bate for £10 per annum. That year a young Thomas Robyn replaced Bate as the farmer of the central demesne which was worth £22. A decade later in 1480 Robyn, having begun his career as a Lydd jurat two years earlier, had taken over both leases with the value of the Northlade lease having increased to £13.[42]

Thus violent inroads were made into tenants' holdings in the north end of Dengemarsh manor during the 1460s. The origin of the attack came from the demesne farm. We know that Northlade had been further enlarged and enclosed by 1538. It was valued at £20 in that year, and the demesne acreage as a whole had grown to 408 acres, 100 acres more than it had been in 1432. We also know that tenants' holdings in the rest of the manor had been consolidated and transformed by 1538, and that Thomas Robyn himself had engrossed and consolidated two substantial farms of 100 acres and 75 acres amongst them by 1520. The rest of the chapter will examine how this was done and the impact it had.

The survival of the Dengemarsh court rolls after 1450 is limited when compared with the almost full record for the two previous decades. There is one fragment relating to 1482 and they survive only intermittently from 1487.[43] Nevertheless these limited records reveal that Thomas Robyn acquired 13 acres from four transactions in 1482, and in 1489 alone he acquired well over 130 acres in 18 transactions from 18 different holders.[44] To be more accurate the accumulations in 1489 amounted to 129 acres plus the acreage from four more transactions the record of which is unreadable. Only one of these transactions concerned his inheritance from his father which amounted to three acres. It is significant that 1489 was the year in which most of Robyn's accumulations were recorded because this was of course the year of the first antidepopulation legislation produced by the English state. The introduction of this legislation in this year is a clear indication that the actions of Thomas

---

42   TNA, SC 6, 1107/9–10.

43   TNA, SC 2, 180/61–5.

44   TNA, SC 2, 180/61, p. 3.

Robyn, and of Bate before him, was being matched by others like him across England in the years leading up to it. Robyn was the manorial farmer of two large demesne leases by 1480, and of the largest one since 1470, and so he was already undertaking a very large enterprise before these further accumulations. His attempt to recover 25 quarters of wool 'of merchant ware' from William Essex of New Romney in 1487 indicates his involvement in substantial wool production before 1489.[45] The cattle herd of Bate, the butcher-grazier, had been replaced by sheep for the production of wool; and most of this was undoubtedly headed for the expanding cloth industry in the Weald.

Did Robyn achieve this accumulation through violence and intimidation *a la* Andrew Bate? Did he destroy the remaining tenants' crops and pasture grounds and then offer to buy them out? Or did he accumulate through a more innocuous process of buying and selling, offending no-one, as historians often assume as they read the record of land transactions at face value? The land transactions recorded in the court rolls are very matter of fact, confining the record to the transaction being undertaken and the fine due to the lord or farmer of the manor. There are no memoranda accompanying the business in hand which might provide detail on any issues relating to the manor. We can only gain a picture of relations on the manor by examining the nature of the other business recorded in the same source which produced fines for the lord.

A comparison of the court record between 1430 and 1450 with the post-1487 period is revealing. In the earlier period 42 cases of trespass and 80 cases of debt are recorded and these two forms of plea were sometimes linked. There was in addition one case of assault with a stick which drew blood in 1448. As we have seen there was limited accumulation by Laurence Elys in this period and this does not appear to have translated into aggressive trespass elsewhere in the court rolls. From 1487 cases of debt were not recorded, but there were 68 cases of trespass, mostly before 1520 after which the record dwindles. In striking contrast to earlier, all of the cases between 1487 and the 1520s were violent. They took the form of simple assaults with sticks and knives, or of armed individuals or groups of people breaking and entering property and driving out or carrying off other people's animals, cloth or canvas. Also, in time-honoured fashion, goods were taken from wrecks on the coast. Significantly, 20 of the 68 cases involved Thomas Robyn and his family, although mainly Thomas. Some of these conflicts with the Robyns involved members of the government of Lydd and jurors of Dengemarsh court. Particularly interesting is a series of conflicts between the Robyns' and the Holdernesses between 1505 and 1507. Cows and lambs were driven from the property of both sides, and both sides assaulted

---

45   CKS, NR/JW 3.

each other on other occasions. Thomas Holderness, an earlier jurat of Lydd, was Thomas Robyn's servant at one point in this struggle. Laurence Holderness, who had been manorial beadle in 1467 when he deposed in court against Bate regarding the conflict over the franchises, was attacked by the Robyns on a number of occasions between 1505 and 1507. Many trespasses involved people who were not Lydd jurats and do not appear in any other record. This suggests that they were, like Thomas Cliprank, amongst those of least means in the parish.[46] These attacks on Robyn by representatives of the poorest parishioners occurred in the two decades after Robyn's main accumulations of holdings. They reflect his unpopularity, a break down in law and order, and the emergence of new lines of class conflict.

It is true that the majority of trespasses in the surviving court rolls did not involve the Robyns. Nine additional cases, however, involved the lordship of Battle Abbey more generally thereby challenging Thomas Robyn as the manorial farmer indirectly. Individuals or groups of men either broke into the Abbot's property, possibly buildings for goods' storage, or took goods from wrecks on the coast.[47] For example in 1487, six men armed themselves and stole cloth at Dungeness. Added to these cases was one occasion when Thomas Robyn himself committed trespass against Battle property when he was no longer the farmer. Most of these cases involved jurats of Lydd, and those such as Thomas Holderness who had been a jurat at one time. These trespasses bear witness to the continuing tensions over the recent victory of the Abbot of Battle over the franchises, something that had clearly not been accepted. To be fair to the abbot, even if he had agreed to compromise with the commons of Lydd and agreed to remove Bate as the farmer of Dengemarsh in exchange for the franchise, it is unlikely that – given the history between the two parties – tenants of Dengemarsh would have refrained from what they viewed as rightful plunder on the coast.

The Robyns and the lordship together accounted for 29 of the 68 cases of trespass. The other 39 cases reveal no clear patterns among those of different

---

46   For example in 1491 Robert Brokman was armed against Thomas Robyn and he 'broke entry' and drove off six cows. In 1492 Richard Tuppe and Henry Tuke was armed against Thomas Robyn and his wife Isabelle and he broke entry and stole some of their goods. In 1510 John Crowde was armed against Thomas Robyn and he rescued 30 sheep and drove them away. In 1517 Margaret Pelland was armed against Thomas Robyn and she carried off his canvas. In 1508 there was a case of trespass involving a 'Thomas' but his surname is indecipherable from the manuscript. He was armed and broke entry against 'diverse tenants of Dengemarsh': TNA, SC 2, 180/61, p. 6; 180/63, p. 3; 180/64, pp. 2–6.

47   TNA, SC 2, 180/61, pp. 2–7; 180/63, p. 1; 180/65, p. 5.

wealth and status, and very few of those involved were jurats. It is notable that
of the 20 cases involving the Robyns, only four were separate incidents of
assault as opposed to breaking and entering property, while by contrast 23 of
the other 39 cases were incidents of assault without reference to theft. These
acts of violence among the general population are indicative of significant
changes in social relationships in Lydd parish in the late fifteenth and early
sixteenth centuries. The conflicts and tensions followed the severe engrossment and depopulation of Dengemarsh and the break up of its community
and common customs. One must necessarily attribute their cause to the revolutionary changes that occurred in the previous two decades which, besides
removing people unwillingly from their holdings, seems to have caused widespread resentment and encouraged criminality. However, within this recorded
criminality and violent behaviour among the remaining tenants and servants
on Dengemarsh, class lines were being defined, as an overwhelming disproportion of this activity was directed towards or initiated by the manorial farmer
and the abbey who forced through the changes. In fact the trespass cases
involving the farmer and the abbey which were directly related to property
theft, and which contain clearer elements of class conflict, account for 25 of 41
such cases, an even greater disproportion.

Lydd and Dengemarsh failed to resist this first and most significant wave of
enclosure which broke through both local custom and traditional subsistent
land holding. This crushing defeat was largely due to the fact that at least one
leading family in these communities saw their interests in accord with outsiders of higher status and wealth: first the Ayllewyns, then the Bates and the
Robyns. Faced with 'great maintainers' that aimed to undermine its political
and economic structures, Lydd was forced to invest in patronage of their own;
in men like Sir John Scott, Sir John Fogg and Sir John Guildford. These leading
Kentish aristocrats, who also acted as officers of the crown in various capaci-
ties, may have had sympathy with Dengemarsh's struggle to keep its asserted
Cinque Port franchise, and – for a price – may have helped the town when the
case came to the law courts in London. However, they would have probably
shown less interest in the demesne expansion and engrossment of holdings.
The latter, although it had momentous, epoch-making significance, was a matter for local courts at this stage. There was no royal statute against it until 1489,
and as we have discussed in Part I, this statute relied on lords to prosecute their
own farmers. In the evidence presented above one can see how indifferent the
Abbot of Battle would have been to this expectation. As Beresford concluded,
'dumb defiance' was the general response.

As for the aristocratic patrons from whom the commons of Lydd sought
influence, Sir John Guildford was himself spearheading changes in the west of

Romney Marsh, and in the 1470s he would be one of the royal commissioners of sewers aiming to institute greater controls over the remaining occupiers of the land. His family invested in the reclamation of salt marshes and the creation of new innings from the middle of the fifteenth century as has already been mentioned, the same time as the conflict over engrossment on Dengemarsh. Like Elrington's innings nearby, Guildford's inning was leased in large parcels to substantial farmers, and these farmers would have supplied wool to the Weald where Guildford himself was based and where he had substantial industrial interests. His is just one example of the recognition of the way forward by landlords and farmers alike. Guildford was as ruthless in these processes as any. His inning had by the middle of the sixteenth century led to the silting up of Rye's harbour and the Rother estuary in the west of the Marsh. An inquiry in 1561 concluded that it was 'the insatiable covetous inning' such as Guildford's that was responsible for the 'wonderfully decayed' state of the harbour.[48] Sea-going trade and shipping could not compete with the new grazier capitalists of Marsh and Weald.

Scott and Fogg as leading Wealden gentry had, with Robert Horn, invested £333 towards the crushing of Cade's rebellion 16 years earlier, a rebellion that if successful would have placed such communities as Lydd and Dengemarsh on a much surer footing politically.[49] However, gentry such as these may well have been concerned about the depopulation of coastal communities given their role in defending the realm. This role was specifically mentioned in the charges against Bate that were put to the abbey, and probably others, by Caxton in 1467. It was therefore clearly regarded by the people of Lydd and Dengemarsh as an important issue and one of the pillars of their case. Depopulation and its implications for the defence of the realm was a theme that influenced the reasoning behind the royal statute of 1489, and it is possible that it was the particular conflicts over enclosure in communities on the Kent coast that those who drew up the statute had in mind. Whatever reservations gentry may have had over the depopulation of Dengemarsh, in the end the balance of interests and influence had turned against the commons of Lydd and Dengemarsh.

In conclusion, the evidence for Romney Marsh provides an important example of the serious transforming engrossment and enclosure that was taking place in England well before the first anti-depopulation act of 1489, and it can be cited as strong support for the evidence and arguments of contemporaries Rous and later Hales, and for modern historians such as Beresford and Fryde. Further research might elicit greater connections with the political

---

48   Hipkin 1998, p. 138.
49   Fleming 2004.

conflicts of the day as Fryde says, and locate enclosure in the fifteenth century into the wider feudal social-property structure – that is, into the relationship between the court party of the monarchy and provincial offices, and inter-lord-ship and inter-state conflict. It also underscores my argument that one cannot judge certain counties such as Kent as already enclosed in the medieval period on the basis of 'old enclosure' and thereby exempt them from calculations of new enclosure from the fifteenth century. As we have seen with the evidence for Dengemarsh, such 'old enclosure' was compatible with subsistent farming communities and feudal landlordship. It had to be subsequently transformed by large-scale engrossment and new enclosure from the 1460s. The relatively free customary tenures in this region cannot be cited as a cause for these developments. On the contrary they could have determined the opposite effect, as happened in the period between 1370 and 1430 when the land holdings became increasingly fragmented.

CHAPTER 11

An Emerging Capitalist Social-Property Structure

It has been my contention that a capitalist social-property structure in agrarian society and rural industry was becoming clearly visible and taking large strides in England by the middle of the sixteenth century; earlier in some areas and later in others. This view receives support from historians such as Jane Whittle and Andy Wood with their recent acknowledgement that the widespread anti-enclosure rebellions of the 1530s and 1540s were a symptom of emerging agrarian capitalism, and by Keith Wrightson who has recognised that changes in the fifteenth and early sixteenth century were profound and set the context for subsequent change. While one might have some sympathy with Wrightson's argument that the decisive periods of transformation were still in the future – where a point of no return was reached – his conclusion that farming in England was still predominantly subsistent in the 1520s and that there was no burgeoning capitalist mentality by that time appears as a contradiction to his other conclusion that changes had been profound.

The classic agrarian capitalist class structure in England took the form of the triad of commercial landlord, leaseholding tenant and landless wage labourer. It was never so neat and tidy however and would only become sharply defined and generalised across the whole of England during the seventeenth century. Nevertheless, a less sharply defined but functioning agrarian capitalist social-property structure operating, in Ellen Meiksins Wood's words, 'according to principles and "laws of motion" different from those prevailing in any other society since the dawn of history', and based in particular on the first two elements of the triad, was in place much earlier. In this chapter I will examine developments in Lydd and its region over the course of the sixteenth century, and assess the extent to which an agrarian capitalist social-property structure and capitalist mentalities had developed by the 1530s as a result of fifteenth and early sixteenth-century enclosure.[1]

i   Commercial Landlords and Capitalist Tenant Farmers

The decline of serfdom and transformations in the organisation of the lords' estates between the late fourteenth and early sixteenth centuries fundamentally changed the character of English feudal lordship. After the Tudor state

---

1   Wood 2002, p. 131.

dissolved the monasteries in England and Wales in the 1530s, that character took another decisive turn. During the late medieval period it was ecclesiastical lords who dominated ownership of landholding in Lydd and its region. Large leaseholding capitalist farmers emerged in this region as a result of *their* policies. As we have seen in the previous chapter, in this region at least these lords were often as aggressive as the farmers in expropriating the peasantry. The Archbishop's Aldington manor which contained the borough of Lydd, and All Souls College which held lands in the west of Lydd parish and beyond, survived the cull of ecclesiastical institutions in the 1530s. However, the lands of Canterbury Cathedral Priory and Battle Abbey were dissolved and the ownership of the farmer's leases passed into the hands of lay aristocracy and a highly acquisitive gentry. Large capitalist farmers known as yeomen and small gentlemen sometimes acted as landlords and leased their own freehold lands to other farmers and family as it suited them, and they also sub-leased from larger gentry. However, land *ownership* continued to be dominated by the larger gentry and aristocracy, and their ownership of freehold land in England would increase at the expense of smaller freeholders and be subsequently transferred to the capitalist leasehold sector.

Regarding developments by the seventeenth century, Stephen Hipkin has shown that medium-sized and large farmers on Romney Marsh Level in the 1650s received their leases from a number of owners, including from smallholders. He frames this evidence as contradicting Brenner's picture of a classic triad of large landlord, capitalist farmer and labourer by the seventeenth century. And yet (in support of Brenner) he finds that *the majority* of large leaseholders' lands were typically leased from *one* owner, and that during the seventeenth century the sometimes blurred line between owner and lessee became increasingly clear and defined. He also shows that sub-leasing was not a significant feature, accounting for only about ten percent of holder's lands.[2] Limited sub-leasing by capitalist farmers did not therefore blur the picture of these large capitalist farmers holding and farming huge acreages from the greater gentry. The first two elements of the agrarian capitalist triad were firmly installed in the seventeenth century.

The decline of relatively modest occupying freeholders began much earlier however. The gentry capitalised on the earlier achievements of Lydd's yeoman farmers and at the same time they benefited from grants of monastic property from the crown. We have seen how farmers in Lydd parish in the fifteenth century developed demesne leases on behalf of their ecclesiastical lordship lessors by drawing in neighbouring tenements, and how significant farms were developed by yeomen such as the Robyns through the large-scale engrossment

---

2   Hipkin 2000, p. 655.

and consolidation of tenements in the wider sea of holdings. However, in the 1530s gentry began to buy up these consolidations and lease them out. For example, the consolidations of the Robyns were sold to John Mayne, esquire, who then leased the property back to them at a competitive rent. Mayne also bought 300 acres from Thomas Swan of Lydd in 1533, presumably for the same purpose.[3] Two phases in the leasing of land on Romney Marsh from All Souls College and Canterbury Cathedral Priory between 1450 and 1545 have also been identified. Between 1450 and the 1520s Marsh leases were taken up for short terms and relatively low rents by 'peasant' farmers. In the second phase from the 1520s the farmers were increasingly members of the gentry who did not live on the Marsh. They held longer leases, but the farms had increased in value.[4]

In the 1530s the leading gentry of Kent, who also formed part of the county oligarchy of the centralising Tudor state, took control of the dissolved monastic estates and those of other lords in Lydd parish.[5] It is the increasingly influential and wealthy lay gentry of Kent who were the landlords in this new agrarian capitalist social-property structure. From the 1530s they augmented their estates and thereby increased their controls over the land. They drew in the earlier accumulations of freehold and customary tenements and leased them out; and, through their influence in the county oligarchy, they added the property of the monasteries to their increasing estates. This newly available property was more likely to be seen as a commodity than a rent roll, given the feeding frenzy during the dissolution of the monasteries, and inevitably

---

3 For example, James Robyn senior sold his 80 acres to Mayne in 1533, which he had inherited from his father in 1526. James Robyn junior relinquished his inheritance of a messuage and 100 acres in the same place to the third brother Robert Robyn. Robert also appears to have sold this to Mayne, and subsequently bought the lease back in 1537 at 20 marks per annum for 20 years, giving it to his son John: TNA, SC 2, 180/64, p. 11; TNA, SC 6, Hen 8/3675; EKAC, Ly/JB 4, p. 3; EKAC, Ly/JB 3, p. 76.

4 Draper 1998, pp. 119–20.

5 In 1537 an indenture was made between Sir John Dudley, knight, of Halden in the Weald, and Thomas Wriothesley of London, esquire, 'for all those fresh and salt marshes now being in the tenure and occupation of one Thomas Strogull of Lydd lying in the parishes of Lydd and Broomhill'. Strogull also saw the ownership of his farm of Northlade on Dengemarsh pass from Battle Abbey to Sir Walter Hendley in 1547. Hendley was a senior official in the Court of Augmentations which oversaw the grants of monastic lands. He was executor of the recently deceased Sir Thomas Hawte, knight (also from the Weald), and in 1539 he made an indenture with Thomas Colpeper, esquire, of Goudhurst in the Weald for the farm of Scotney and its sheep to the value of £506 (reserving 400 sheep to Hawte's widow); British Library (BL), Harleian 77, G 17; BL, Harleian 78, G 29; BL, Harleian Roll, S 34; Calendar of Patent Rolls, Volume 1, Edward VI, Part V, p. 157. See Clark, 1974, pp. 52–4, 70 for information on these gentry, including their county offices.

even less regard would be shown to existing small customary tenants as a consequence.

Turning to the farmers, in the previous two chapters it has been demonstrated that in the 1440s there were only three substantial farmers in Lydd. Two held large demesne leases containing hundreds of acres and were compelled to produce on a large scale for the market in the mould of Brenner's first capitalist farmers and Dyer's new men. While clearly novel, they were as yet by no means a dominant force in densely populated parishes such as Lydd. They formed a small minority in Lydd's government which was socially diverse and dominated by mariners, fishermen, petty traders with subsistent customary holdings, and husbandmen. However, from the 1440s onwards, conflict over custom and the engrossment of holdings, the forced depopulation of Dengemarsh, and the stepping up of investment in the Marsh by ecclesiastical lords and Wealden gentry began to transform the social-property structure. The dominant strategy of the broad-based and annually rotated fifteenth-century government of Lydd was to resist these changes. This was because the latter militated against custom and traditional landholding as the basic subsistent element of the existing multi-occupational household economies. Thomas Caxton and others in the government spent years in London and elsewhere trying to resist Battle Abbey and its farmer Andrew Bate from making catastrophic inroads into the customary holdings and Cinque Port liberties on Dengemarsh. They even appealed to the Abbey's pockets by outbidding Bate for the lease. This concerted resistance failed and as we have seen Thomas Robyn, as farmer of two large demesne leases, carved two other yeoman farms from the customary holdings on Dengemarsh after the back of the resistance had been broken.

Consistent with the polarisation of wealth was the polarisation of political power. At some point between 1509 and 1512 the jurats in the government of Lydd became permanently installed, only standing down through death or if they became embroiled in serious disputes. The bailiff stood down each year and a new one was chosen from among the permanent jurats: he was elected by the commonalty, and this was their only remaining role in elections. The effect upon the numerical representation in the central government can be shown from a simple comparison of the number of jurats elected in the thirty years between 1454–5 and 1484–5 and the thirty years between 1512–13 and 1542–3. In the former there were 78, and in the latter only 37. In the early sixteenth century it is clear that the commonalty was no longer the central institution: that role had now been taken by the bailiff and jurats. The commonalty were still required to assent to important decrees, and they even made decrees themselves with the assent of the bailiff and jurats. However, a further narrowing of representation of the commonalty occurred in 1526, and this affected the ports as a whole. The Brodhull, represented by the jurats and bailiffs or mayors of the ports, decreed that due to a continuity of serious tensions that had arisen in recent years at elections, only 37 freemen would be eligible to vote from then onwards. These were to be chosen by the jurats from the larger body of the commonalty. This narrow section of the commonalty would then elect the bailiff from one of the jurats, and the bailiff would then elect the jurats.[6] The latter clause did not apply to Lydd at least because the jurats remained permanent.

By the second half of the sixteenth century the numbers of commonalty involved in the election of bailiff was reduced to as few as 21, and these were called the 'combarons': by the turn of the seventeenth century they had no involvement in the elections at all. A charter of James I's reign (1603–25) states that the permanent jurats elected the bailiff, and asserts that it was confirming existing practice.[7] Peter Clark has argued that this process of narrowing oligarchy in the Cinque Ports in the sixteenth century was the direct policy of Tudor government as part of its centralisation programme. It began in the 1480s with Henry VII and was given added impetus by Wolsey's regime from 1513. The main strategy was to reduce the number, power and independence of the commonalty in order to make these strongly enfranchised towns more pliable to the crown. As early as 1504, 'in the Cinque Ports the first steps towards municipal government by clique had been approved'.[8]

So around 1512, in the context of tensions and violence on Dengemarsh, Lydd's government became a permanent oligarchy. Its membership was for life and, apart from a few rare exceptions in the first half of the sixteenth century, jurats were only replaced after their deaths. In the first half of the sixteenth century the government became dominated by large capitalist farmers. In 1528, of the 11 jurats and one bailiff six were large or very large farmers who both farmed and sub-leased accumulated property. A seventh significant farmer was described as a yeoman but appears to have been of comparatively more middling wealth. Four were high-street traders with land – two of these substantial, and one was a husbandman or relatively small farmer. The latter, John Colyn senior, found his way into the government between 1528 and 1535, but he would be the last of his kind to do so. In all, eight of the 12 were significant farmers and this is a measure of the wider transformation that had taken

---

6 Centre for Kentish Studies (CKS), CP/B1, pp. 206–7.

7 EKAC, Ly/I 7.

8 Clark 1977, p. 20.

place by the 1520s. This level of domination would continue in the following decades and increase in the second half of the sixteenth century.

Already by the 1520s, in stark contrast to the 1460s, the interest and approach of the membership of the government was not to resist but to facilitate the expansion of agrarian capitalism. By 1580 the whole government was made up of large capitalist farmers and rentiers whether these were described as yeomen or gentry. From the middle of the fifteenth century agrarian customs and neighbourliness became values increasingly in opposition to the interests of the farmers in government. By the early sixteenth century the strategy for these farmers was to expand their enterprises by the following means: first, by speculation, accumulation, and the automatic reinvestment of profits; second, through inheritance practices designed to maintain and expand consolidated accumulations of property; third, by maintaining the representation of the family line in government. Perhaps because of the attractiveness of this new regime during the course of the sixteenth century, the membership of Lydd's government became increasingly filled by wealthy immigrants.

It is with the evidence of the extent of property held by those farmers who became jurats of Lydd in the 1520s and 1530s that we become aware of the expansion of capitalist farming enterprises in this region. Those Lydd families that built upon the achievements of their ancestors – the new men of the fifteenth century – were the Godfreys, the Bates and the Robyns, although their success would be consolidated and enclosed within one or two family lines only.

Thomas Godfrey senior stands out from the rest in the 1520s because as early as 1528 he is described in one source as an 'esquire'. This was the year that he acquired two thirds of the manor of Old Langport, including a residence suitable for minor gentry. This manor took in the nearby parish of Old Romney and part of the north end of Lydd town. Thomas had also benefited from three lucrative marriages gaining title to lands in various parts Kent, including More Court at Ivychurch in the Marsh.[9] Both before and after his death in 1543 he devolved to his two sons about 350 acres of both freehold and secure customary property, although he also held an unstated amount of land elsewhere in Kent.

The brief glimpse we have of the type of enterprise Thomas Godfrey senior was operating points to sheep farming, and in continuity from the mid-to-late fifteenth century it was wool that was the main commercial product of these farmers. Andrew Bate, a jurat between 1523 and 1532 and descendant of the fifteenth-century farmer of Dengemarsh of the same name, devolved

---

9   Hasted 1972, pp. 426–7.

600 sheep plus a range of other livestock and horses to his four sons in his will of 1532. His eldest son Thomas Bate who became a jurat in 1538 also benefited in terms of property from his marriage, and he received the lion's share of his father's will described above besides unstated lands which he was already farming. In his will of 1577 he reveals holdings that were widespread across Romney Marsh including 90 acres sub-leased to a Robert Tookey. The amount of potential profit in this property is indicated in a clause demanding that if his wife was pregnant when he died the newly-born child was to receive £300 out of his other sons' lands.

Thomas Robyn, the engrosser and encloser of Dengemarsh, was described as a yeoman and he had been a jurat since 1478. He devolved three freehold farms on Dengemarsh amounting to 255 acres to three sons in his will in 1526. As pointed out above these freeholds, which were themselves only a few years earlier converted from customary tenure, would within 10 years be bought by gentry and granted back to the Robyns as leases. As we have seen in the previous chapter, Thomas Robyn was already a sheep farmer of some note in the 1480s and given his age by 1526 it is more than probable that at least two of his sons were already farming his lands independently and on some scale. The eldest, Robert Robyn, was already a jurat in 1523 and we must assume he had a solid property base to accomplish this political base before the inheritance of another farm of 75 acres in 1526. James senior, who became a jurat in 1528, was already farming an 80 acre farm on Dengemarsh which was not mentioned in his father's will.[10] Robert then proceeded to accumulate both of his brothers' inheritances and became the chief beneficiary and propagator of the Robyn's family line in property and government as we shall see. His inventory was worth a striking £440 in 1551.

The trend of wealthy immigrants to Lydd was set by Thomas Strogull who probably originated from the far west of the Marsh or the southern Weald.[11] He entered the juratcy in 1522, the year before Thomas Godfrey senior. He seems to have moved to Lydd in 1515 after his marriage to a jurat's daughter.[12] Before he entered the government Strogull was already a big sheep farmer. In 1520 he was granted the partnership of the lease of Scotney from All Souls College in the south-west of the parish. As we have seen in Chapter Nine, in 1508 this lease was valued at a very high £64 per annum because it included a stock of 800 sheep and 200 lambs, a very big enterprise in wool. By 1524 Strogull had

10   For evidence of him selling it in 1533, see, TNA, SC 2, 180/64, p. 11.
11   A John Strogull from Warehorne in the Weald appeared in Lydd's court in 1519: EKAC, Ly/JB 2, pp. 15–16.
12   See Typpe's will of 1515. For the entry fine see EKAC, Ly/fac 2, p. 22.

taken over the whole lease, and by 1533 he held another large lease from All Souls College called Priors Marsh worth just over £20 per annum.[13] The demesne of Dengemarsh was split into two leases in the 1530s amounting to 408 acres, and by 1536 Strogull held both of them. Northlade, which originated from Andrew Bate's cattle 'overpressing' onto the customary holdings in the 1460s, was now worth approximately £20 annually, and the other original demesne lease was worth £22.[14] In addition to this extensive array of leases he held over 80 acres of customary land in Old Langport manor by 1551. These acres were mostly made up of accumulated adjacent small plots which abutted onto other lands of his in adjacent manors, and he sublet them to people in other Strogull family lines. He also must have held at one point approximately 140 acres in and close by the town (Aldington manor) which were in the possession of his son John in 1556.[15] In his will of 1551 there was substantially more besides including lands in Snargate on the other side of the Marsh.

Richard Stuppeny moved from the New Romney juratcy to Lydd's in 1528 and then back to New Romney again in 1537 where he died in 1540.[16] Stuppeny became increasingly involved in leaseholding in the early sixteenth century, taking ever larger farms during his lifetime. He did not work alone however and was involved with other men with 'extensive concerns in reclamation and property-holding'. He held the 227 acre farm of Newland in the 1520s for £27 per annum and also Ketepen or 'Stopene Marsh' – named after himself – which lay further west worth £8–9. Newland was of course the farm that laid the foundation of All Souls College in the 1440s and was associated with Ayllewyn's controversy in Lydd at that time. Stuppeny's collaboration with others is indicated by his involvement in 1516 in the enclosure of a salt marsh adjacent to Newland with another big farmer on the Marsh, William Brokhill, and John at Hale of Tenterden in the Weald who was a servant of Wealden knight Richard Guildford.[17] He was therefore at his economic peak when he entered the Lydd juratcy in 1528. In his will of 1540 we find that while he farmed many of the leases he had accumulated, he sub-leased others. These went to his son Laurence along with all the sheep and lambs.

13   For All Souls College farmers see Draper 1998; for the other leases see BL, Harl. 77, G 17; BL, Harl. 78, G 29; BL, Harl. Roll, S 34.
14   TNA, SC 6, Hen 8/3675; Caley and Hunter 1810–1833, p. 347.
15   For Old Langport see CKS, U1043/M4; for Aldington see EKAC, Ly/ZM 1. For the town scot of 1556 see EKAC, Ly/FR 1. For further references to these documents refer here.
16   CKS, CP/B 1, pp. 137–227.
17   Draper 1998, pp. 119–20.

All of these men were jurats of Lydd in the 1520s. The record is not always explicit about the amount of acreage held at this time but, apart from Godfrey whose lands were mostly made up of freehold and customary lands, we can characterise them as holders of multiple leases containing hundreds of acres, with significant customary and freehold land as well. It would be inaccurate to say that they had to compete or starve at this stage because they still held their own freehold or secure customary lands, even if these formed a minority of their accumulations. Nevertheless, the imperative to maintain or improve the wealth and political position they inherited ensured that their approach to production was competitive and geared to investment in further accumulation. They were described by contemporaries as both yeomen and gentlemen; these terms were used loosely and were often interchangeable. The vast amount of focus was on sheep in line with the developments in the cloth industry in the Weald. Leases such as Scotney contained at least 1,000 sheep by 1508, and Dengemarsh was being farmed commercially on a large scale for sheep production by Thomas Robyn from the 1480s at the latest. One cannot therefore speak of a predominantly subsistence-based farming in the 1520s and 1530s in this region given the enterprises of its ruling elite, enterprises that were constantly expanding. It seems that when accumulations became too large or inconveniently situated, they were sub-leased. As we shall see a good deal of subsistence production was still undertaken by the rest of the population, but already this was no longer the dominant culture and it was under further threat.

Clearer taxation evidence relating to the maintenance of the Marsh in the 1580s reveals the extent of this expansion during the following 50 years. Thomas Godfrey junior held 341 acres of his own freehold land in South Walland Marsh which was situated to the west of Lydd parish, and another 40 acres in the same area which he leased from two larger gentry. In addition he leased 490 acres in White Kempe to the north and west from local minor gentry. The extent of his freehold acreage ensured that he was styled 'gentleman' during a legal case against him in 1583 which we will look at in detail in the next chapter. But his overall holdings were modest compared to John Berry. Berry was styled 'yeoman', doubtless because the vast majority of his holdings were leases. He held 353 acres in Lydd parish but most of his farms were held of significant Kent gentry in White Kempe, an area of marsh to the west of Lydd which stretched over towards Rye. Including 207 acres of his own lands, his holdings amounted to 1,978 acres in 1586, and these were held of various minor and larger county gentry.[18] This taxation evidence refers to the marshes in Lydd

---

18   EKAC, Ly/ZR 2, pp. 1, 7–8, 11, 13, 21–2.

parish, Walland and White Kempe, which were situated below the Rhee Wall. Berry's will of 1592 reveals he had other holdings above the Rhee wall including in Ivychurch from where he originated. Berry's will reveals his strong links with London and wool drapers, and his wife Katherine's will of 1612 reveals links with a clothier from Cranbrook in the industrial Weald. This evidence is a useful insight into lucrative trading links as well as the nature of the product. Godfrey's will of 1624 provides details of his property which was spread across the Marsh and Weald. The inclusion of 'manors' in the description of his property is clearly significant and a feature of the growing wealth of this class in Lydd in this period.

John Berry and Thomas Godfrey were by no means the only Lydd jurats with big estates by the 1580s. Most of the jurats leased over 200 acres.[19] However in 1586 Peter Godfrey held at least 653 acres, Matthew Knight held at least 698 acres, Willam Dallett 720 acres, and Thomas Harneden 908 acres.[20] Clearly most of the land in Lydd's parish as well as much of the rest of Romney Marsh was by the 1580s in the possession of the farmers who governed Lydd. While it is clear that progress had been made in the accumulation of leases between 1530 and 1580, there was no qualitative difference between the farmers in 1580 and some of those in 1530. Indeed some of the farmers of the 1520s and 1530s in Lydd would not have been out of place in the mid-seventeenth century. The main change was that by 1580 there were more of them reaching the level of the wealthiest in 1530, and that they had by then entirely taken over the government of the town.

As the farmers continued to accumulate leases, the landlords reaped the benefits of increasing rents. Perhaps the most useful example is that of Northlade on Dengemarsh. From a cluster of scattered ecclesiastic demesne holdings in the fourteenth century worth £5 per annum, it developed into two substantial enclosed leases during the fifteenth century and they were worth over £40 in 1538 at the dissolution of Battle Abbey. By 1596 the Northlade lease contained approximately 350 enclosed acres worth £160 per annum to Mr Edward Bacon, the absentee owner, and ensured that the lessee Matthew Knight would be presented in Lydd court for having over 2,000 sheep, a figure that infringed the anti-enclosure statutes.[21]

19 The various taxation lists between 1583 and 1586 recorded in EKAC, Ly/ZR 2 reveal that John Bateman, Thomas Knight, Alexander Weston, Robert Tookey and John Wells held 262, 260, 221, 240 and 248 acres respectively in Dengemarsh and South Walland.
20 EKAC, Ly/ZR 2.
21 EKAC, Ly/Qs 1, pp. 171–4. For more detail on Knight see Chapter Twelve.

ii   Contrasting Mentalities in the 1520s: Capitalist and Non-Capitalist

What is meant by 'capitalist mentality' and is there is any evidence for it by the 1520s? Christopher Dyer defined the accumulating farmers of the late fifteenth century as ruthless economic men. In itself being ruthless is not an attribute reserved solely for capitalists of course. The aristocracy and gentry throughout the epoch of feudal society displayed an unparalleled ruthlessness. It is the phrase 'economic men' that represents what is ruthless about capitalists in particular. For example what was driving people such as Andrew Bate and Thomas Robyn of Lydd in the second half of the fifteenth century? What would make members of a peasant elite such as these disregard custom and their community in such a way as to become separated from their traditional roots? Was this not a different form of ruthlessness born out of experience in running a large competitive leaseholding enterprise? Was it not this that produced a cultural change, made them 'economic men', and led them to adopt capitalist rules for reproduction?

Dyer contrasted these ruthless economic men – and it was men such as Bate and Robyn that he had in mind – with those peasants who accumulated land in the late thirteenth and early fourteenth century. The latter did not develop wealthy dynasties out of these accumulations by providing one son with the lion's share, but instead divided their property among their offspring. In any case their accumulations were never consolidated farms and never on the scale of the leaseholds of the fifteenth century. The economic men – capitalist yeomen – that were widespread by the late fifteenth century had developed a new culture of competitive leasehold farming that made them interested in maintaining a large enterprise and expanding it through the next generation. In order for an enterprise to expand, it meant that a viable central enterprise able to compete had to be passed on from one generation to the next, and this meant that decisions had to be made regarding which son was to receive the largest enterprise. Capitalist businessmen do not build large enterprises in their lifetimes, hopefully with a monopoly, extensive business networks and political influence, and then divide them up into small concerns without political influence upon their deaths.

Vincent Daniel was a large leaseholding farmer of Scotney in the first two decades of the sixteenth century, and in his will of 1520 he spoke of his own 'wool man' or wool factor to whom he sold his produce and his own shepherd. He was one of three sons of John Danyell, a Lydd jurat who died in 1487. In contrast to his wealth, Vincent's brothers Richard and William Danyell were smallholding fishermen having been provided for as such by their mother Joanna's will in 1490. Vincent was not mentioned in her will and he had undoubtedly already been provided for with his father's main property. This placed him in a position to take over the large Scotney lease in 1508 and then become a jurat of Lydd. Besides the Scotney lease he held his own lands and farmed approximately 700 sheep and a range of livestock and horses in 1520. He died without surviving children, but instead of dividing his inheritance equally among his family he chose only one of his three nephews to continue his enterprise. He provided his nephew Thomas Danyell with his tenement and attached lands on Dengemarsh, 200 sheep and a range of other livestock. This was the preferred strategy rather than making all of the nephews comfortable. In 1510 Vincent had bought an acre from another nephew, John Danyell, and returned it in his will along with a cow and £2 plus another £2 on condition that John made a new boat. The other nephew, Richard Danyell, received £2 plus another £10 towards the making of a new boat on condition that Richard sold an acre of land to Thomas, Vincent's preferred beneficiary. That acre lay amongst the lands on Dengemarsh that Vincent passed on to Thomas and was presumably a hindrance to engrossment. Vincent passed nominal amounts of 3s 4d to 'poor maidens' in his lineage. Compare this to the £10 each he gave to his executors to administer the will.

In his will of 1532, Andrew Bate was faced with devolving his property to four sons, all of age. The acreage passed on is unstated, although three of the sons received two cows and 100 sheep each. The other son, Thomas Bate, who was already farming some of his father lands, received his father's main residence plus 300 sheep – three times as many as his brothers, eight horses, a range of other livestock, two couples of oxen, a wagon, a plough, cart and harrow, and land enough to provide six seams of wheat, ten seams of barley, four seams of oats and one seam of beans. Five years later it was Thomas who would become a jurat on the basis of this unequal allocation.

Thomas Robyn devolved his property to five sons. But Robert Robyn was the chief beneficiary of the Robyn's family line in Lydd. The fact that he was already a jurat in 1523, three years before his father Thomas's will in 1526, more than suggests that for a number of years he had been provided with a large share of his father's property. He received in 1526 a further messuage and 75 acres on Dengemarsh. In subsequent years he appears to have bought up the Dengemarsh farms of his two brothers, John junior and John senior who held a messuage and 100 acres and a messuage and 80 acres respectively. The farms of 75 and 80 acres would be passed on to two of his sons in 1551: his other son, John Robyn, was already working the larger farm on Dengemarsh of 100 acres, plus 42 acres of recently accumulated lands and more elsewhere. It was Robert's son John who was therefore provided with the much larger capitalist enterprise and as a consequence he would continue the family tradition in the juratcy two years later from 1553. We do not have a will for Robert's brother James Robyn junior, but James senior who did make it into the juratcy in 1528 and so must have still held his farm at that time died intestate in 1545 and with a notably modest inventory total of £12 10s and debts and legacies of £20. Compare this to Robert's valuation of £440 in 1551.[22]

The inheritance strategy among this new class in the 1520s and much earlier was clear. The partible inheritance custom had to be compromised and one son was to be provided with the lion's share of the inheritance. This compromise ensured the perpetuation of at least one line of the family within this class through a larger economic base, the expansion of the latter and, equally important, increasingly powerful representation in the central government of the town. This perpetuation of the status of one line was achieved to the detriment of other siblings, and the wider family. Concentration of property opened doors to economic expansion and legal and political patronage.

Stephen Hipkin, who demonstrates no knowledge of this process, speculates that even in the late sixteenth and seventeenth century large capitalist farmers in Kent were adhering to the medieval inheritance custom of gavelkind that required the inheritance to be divided equally. He calculates that there were 448 private owners on the Level of Romney Marsh in 1654 (above the Rhee Wall) and he asserts that the fragmentation of holdings 'fostered by partible inheritance is reflected in the existence of 188 owners of less than 20 acres'. He chooses Thomas Godfrey of Lydd – who we have discussed above – as an example of a big farmer dividing up his inheritance along these lines. He is described as 'the Elizabethan bailiff of the Marsh'. In the next chapter we will come across him defending charges against him of owning over 2,000 sheep and engrossing most of the marsh in that area into his own hands. That Thomas was bailiff of the Level administration reveals that Lydd men had strong controls over the administration of the Marsh above as well as below the Rhee Wall. Hipkin identifies six men among the descendants of Thomas in 1654 who owned between them 339 acres in the Level, and from this finding he concludes that this is evidence of the impact of gavelkind on the distribution of land ownership.[23] But there was more than one Godfrey farmer in Lydd in the late sixteenth century, and those 339 acres were only a limited part of his overall enterprise, as we have seen. Lydd peasants with limited means still divided their inheritance as we shall see below, and that accounts for the large number

---

22   Zell calculates that yeomen in Kent in the early seventeenth century left goods on average worth £100 to £150: Zell 2000, p. 71.

23   Hipkin 2000, pp. 665–60.

of owners with less than 20 acres in 1654, although these numbers were always dwindling.[24]

Another aspect of a capitalist mentality and capitalist rules for reproduction is a meticulous approach to accountancy and a focus on accumulation and productive expenditure. The greater gentry, or aristocracy, had during the late medieval period typically used political networks and warfare to expand their property, and they devolved their property in order to accumulate political alliances. They often kept detailed accounts but typically used the profits for non-productive expenditure – that is, for warfare and display for the purpose of further political accumulation. By contrast the profits of capitalist farmers were reinvested systematically into a productive enterprise in order to expand it and this can be demonstrated in Lydd.

For example Peter Godfrey, in his will of 1567, details his position as executor and custodian of the bequests of inherited property in a list of other people's wills, and of the profits arising from these. He had been charged by testators to manage their property while their children were still minors, and under his administration he had turned these bequests into interest-bearing loans. His will reveals that within this class money bequests to minors were treated as investments to ensure a surplus when they fell due – that is, when the minors reached 21 years of age. Indeed, Godfrey expected executors to draw up an account of the profits accrued from his *own* lands that he had bequeathed to his younger son when the latter became of age. So no inherited property was left dormant while heirs took years to come of age and receive it. Testators employed executors to extract whatever could be squeezed from the property in the mean time. Godfrey's was a highly business-like will, one of a highly accomplished speculator in property. A similar clause can be found in Richard Stuppeny's will of 1540. One of Richard's sons Laurence was to receive all of his father's sheep and lambs and all of the profits of his farms which Richard held by leasehold. Some of these leases Richard had occupied himself and some were occupied by William Walter and John Heyward of New Romney. These men were to act as his executors. They were charged with drawing up an account of his yearly profits from his leases and when the profits reached £30 or £40 they were to immediately invest in more lands for Laurence.

Large amounts of money were invested by large capitalist farmers in men trusted to organise their affairs. We have seen Vincent Daniel spending £10 to organise his will in 1520. Peter Godfrey was paying £30 annuity to Robert Riestone, esquire, and a £16 annuity to John Cheeseman – presumably for this

---

24   For an analysis of developments in the seventeenth century see the postscript in Chapter Twelve.

purpose – and he also patronised Sir Thomas Wootton esquire, a lawyer. Ralph Wilcockes, a jurat of Lydd for only one year in 1554–5, left £60 for the execution and oversight of his will alone. This was carried out by four men. The most significant was his overseer, Sir John Baker of Cranbrook and Sissinghurst in the Weald, a member of the county gentry and very active in the Tudor state oligarchy. His executors were Richard Knatchbull of Mersam, yeoman, John Berry of Ivychurch, yeoman – who immediately replaced Wilcockes in the Lydd juratcy the following year – and our Peter Godfrey of Lydd, yeoman. These three were probably the largest sheep farmers in the area.

In contrast to developments in the nineteenth century, technological innovation in agriculture was limited in the early modern period in England, beyond the widespread extension and systematic implementation of already available techniques: apart from the development of convertible husbandry, much of the increasing labour productivity of English agriculture was the result of lords rationalising their estates, the approach of capitalist farmers to competition in production and accumulation, and the removal of peasant customary controls on production. I have argued that a capitalist mentality can be identified by its disregard for non-capitalist mentalities such those recognising traditional customs in common, and values of 'neighbourliness'. This was not of course merely a culture clash: as an emerging capitalist rule for reproduction the removal of peasant customs and common rights was essential for improvements in efficiency and productivity as capitalist farmers sought to maximise profits and increase the available land for capitalisation. In the medieval period these traditional customs and values had significant traction and could be cited in court by communities in defensive actions against enclosers. A capitalist mentality can also be identified by its disregard of those (non-capitalist) statutes introduced by the Tudor state from 1489 to prevent depopulating enclosure and overspecialisation. Concerns for neighbours' supply of dairy products and bread do not arise when one is – in a capitalist manner – orientating the business towards optimum rewards in a particular context of demand. The enterprises of the offspring of those jurats in Lydd in the 1520s that developed in the second half of the sixteenth century disregarded statutes against overspecialisation and depopulation as a hindrance against optimising their return and ongoing competitiveness, and this will be examined in detail in the next chapter. There is a common link between the mentality of the new men of the fifteenth century to those of the 1520s and those in the subsequent generations, and that is the expansion of capital. On the basis of the foregoing I would argue – against Wrightson – that there *was* a burgeoning capitalist mentality by the 1520s and much earlier in Lydd and its region. As I have said, those farmers in the 1520s would not have looked out of place in the mid-seventeenth century, a period in which Wrightson would not deny that such a mentality was dominant.

It has been my contention that we cannot speak of capitalist development as a revolutionary aim from below. This contention can be demonstrated in part by showing aspects of the mentalities of the majority of peasant society which strikingly contrast with those of the large farmers. John Caxton was a jurat between 1525 and 1540 and a contemporary of the farmers analysed earlier. He was referred to as 'mercer' in the court books of 1519, and he supplied a broad range of articles such as armoury and hardware as well as finished cloth in his high-street shop. He was also involved in fishing, and he owned a range of nets. His father was Thomas Caxton, the town clerk, who as we have seen in the previous chapter tirelessly fought to prevent the engrossment and enclosure of Dengemarsh by Battle Abbey's Lydd farmers, and to protect Cinque Port customs against Battle Abbey in the 1460s. Thomas Caxton came to Lydd from Tenterden in 1458 and became jurat between the years 1468 and 1471. Thomas was described as both 'yeoman' and 'chapman' in 1468 and 1472 respectively, the former during the conflict on Dengemarsh when he was sued to Westminster by the bailiff of Battle at the instigation of Andrew Bate having sided with those whose livelihoods Bate had damaged.[25] His political assertiveness led to him receiving a royal pardon for his role in Fauconburg's rebellion three years later, being the named representative of others from Lydd who were also involved.[26] We know he was lessee of Bletching for at least the years 1468–70, although this was a very small property at 16 acres, and he held various tenements in the town in or near the High Street which suggests that they were shops. These tenements laid the foundation in his will for the livelihoods of the above-mentioned John Caxton and his two younger sons, William and Thomas. These sons were all set up individually and equally in 1495. However, William died in 1513 without mentioning property in his will, and we do not know what happened to Thomas although he was presented as a brewer and innkeeper in 1489. In his will of 1540 John Caxton bequeathed all of his lands and tenements in Lydd town to his wife for her lifetime, and they were then to be passed to his sons Augustine and Sebastian. The property was to be shared equally and so John's approach to inheritance proceeded in the same manner as his father. Augustine was also given a range of fishing nets at this point. Neither son entered the government; they probably continued as multioccupational traders with fishing links.[27]

---

25   EKAC, Ly/fac 1, fol. 122v, 179v.

26   TNA, Ancient Correspondence, Chancery and Exchequer, vol. 57, no. 108.

27   EKAC, Ly/AL 4.

It is interesting to note that William Rolf, one of Thomas Caxton's fellow jurats and collaborators in the battle against Andrew Bate on Dengemarsh in the 1460s, adopted the same inheritance customs and values as his colleague. In his will of 1473 Rolf instructed his three sons to share his inheritance when they were of age. This may have been the tenement and 38 acres called 'Rolvys' in Lydd parish which turned up in the will of John Holme, jurat, in 1496, and still bore William's name who therefore must have earlier been its long-term holder. William was a peasant farmer therefore of some note by medieval standards, and as such was in a position to apply for the Dengemarsh lease at a higher rate than Andrew Bate paid. This offer was of course refused by Battle Abbey as we have seen, perhaps because the abbey suspected that Rolf was not about to go enlarging it at his neighbours' expense or act as the Abbey's fifth column in the town. Simon Rolf was probably one of William's sons and in his will of 1526 he passed on two tenements. After his wife died one tenement was to go to his son Clement and the other in which he and his wife dwelt was to go to his daughter Agnes. So again the inheritance was shared and Simon, like John Caxton, followed the tradition of his father. On the basis of this inheritance Clement Rolf became a labourer and servant of jurat Simon Typpe. In his will of 1544 in which he was unusually styled 'labourer,' Clement bequeathed to his son John 22 sheep, a lamb and a cow, and to his daughters, a cow and a lamb each. His two overseers, one of whom was his master were to have half an acre of wheat if they helped his son John to save the rest. He bequeathed his only tenement in which he dwelt to his son John.[28]

So the heirs of the key players who tried to uphold custom and prevent engrossment in the momentous struggle on Dengemarsh in the second half of the fifteenth century became small-holding labourers, fishermen, and at best petty shopkeepers with limited property in the first half of the sixteenth century. They also no longer had representation in government. At the same time the property of the heirs of the engrossers expanded, and their representation in the government became increasingly secure. More will be said of this marked and momentous polarising process below.

A similar mentality towards inheritance can be identified for Thomas Smyth who was a jurat between 1523 and 1534. He was described as yeoman in his will of 1534, but he was not a large leaseholder like the other farmers. Thomas and his brother Laurence were sons of John Smyth and beneficiaries of his will in 1513. The will lacks a description of holdings but on the whole appears modest. Thomas also distributed his property evenly in his will of 1534, and his sons

---

28   This was worth 13d rent in the Aldington rental of 1556, and this value meant it had a few acres attached to it.

became co-holders of the principal tenement and the residue of the freehold lands.[29] So even among the more well-to-do jurats we can identify clear demarcations in mentalities with regard to property and wealth and its distribution, and this demarcation separates the larger mostly leaseholding farmers from the rest of the town. Leading representatives of the town such as Thomas Caxton and those peasant farmers of more solid middling wealth such as Thomas Smyth maintained traditional mentalities which did not favour particular heirs in a bid to consolidate property and expand capital.

Sharing the inheritance most particularly characterised the less well-to-do commoners and was typified by the smallholding fishermen. A clear example is provided by the Dyne family. Adrian Dyne set up all of his four sons as viable fishermen in his will of 1519, including his partnerships in boats. The three youngest were also to *share* their father's tenement in which he dwelt after his wife's life, which was almost immediately, Adrian senior presumably having already been taken care of. Adrian's wife divided her substantial fishing equipment among them *equally* the following year. John Dyne senior had three sons, and his strategy in his will of 1548 was virtually the same as his father Adrian's, although John also included his brother Robert in the share. He gave his brother Robert the moiety of his boat called 'The Michael' – which his father had given him (John) 29 years earlier – and the other moiety to his first son. Robert also received John's 'middle' cabin at the Ness. John's second son received the moiety of his boat called 'The John' together with various hooks and nets and the fourth cabin at the Ness. So presumably he would have been in partnership with someone else who held the other moieties. The three sons were to share the rest of his cabins. The third son received six fishing nets and a cow. Regarding his landholdings, he bequeathed his 16 acres, two tenements and a close in Lydd and Brookland to his wife for her life, and then to be shared among his three sons.[30] The continuity of inheritance strategies in this family in terms of the integration of siblings in all wills and the sharing, as far as was possible, of *all* trade equipment and landholdings among male heirs is striking here. Attempts to improve one line were eschewed in favour of a combination of equal division and pooling of family resources beyond individual households. The contrast with the capitalist farmers could not be starker.

---

29   21 acres of land and other features in the Old Langport rental of 1551 appear under the title of 'heirs of Thomas Smyth'.

30   These properties in Lydd survive in the 1556 Aldington rental under the title the 'heirs of John Dyne'.

iii   Proletarianisation and Dependence in the Sixteenth Century

The first two elements in the class structure of agrarian capitalism, namely commercial landlords and tenant farmers, had become a dominant feature of Lydd and its region by the 1530s. The third element is of course the wage labourer. In Chapter Eight I argued (in agreement with Ellen Meiksins Wood) that the origin and development of agrarian capitalism was a process of expropriation that resulted in the increasing proletarianisation and dependence of the population. That origin and development was not the result of an already existing proletariat. With regard to Lydd and its region we know there had been a massive reduction in subsistent landholding possibilities in Lydd parish and beyond by the 1520s given the amount of engrossment and enclosure that had taken place. Certainly in the 1550s the structure of wealth in Lydd appears polarised with two-thirds or 166 of the 235 names rated in a common scot of 1556 at 1s and below, the highest being 26s 8d.[31] This situation is comparable to the levels of proletarianisation in the industrial Weald. Michael Zell has demonstrated from the taxation returns of 1524–5 that the small cloth town and district of Cranbrook in the Weald of Kent was one of the wealthiest districts there, and yet the polarisation of wealth was particularly acute, with over sixty percent of the population in the two poorest wealth bands.[32]

In the absence of detailed periodical taxation evidence, in the rest of this chapter I explore proletarianisation and dependency in Lydd through other evidence of social polarisation: increasing poverty and vagrancy, susceptibility to bad harvests, and the criminalisation of the poor.

Traditional official provision of poor relief is recorded in the Lydd's town accounts as a bi-annual doling of corn, and in the churchwardens' accounts as an annual money dole of 3s 4d on All Saints Day. The recording of this provision was erratic for most of the fifteenth century and this may reflect a relative lack of need in this period. However the reference in 1475 to the 'writing of a new bill of the alms people' points towards the development of more systematic provision in Lydd. Already in 1486 a mandate was sent from Dover Castle to New Romney, enquiring into vagabonds and beggars, and this mandate would have been recorded at Lydd if the accounts would have survived between 1485 and 1512. The unusual sparcity of the wills of Lydd in terms of their content in the decades straddling 1500 is evidence of a high incidence of inter-vivos devolution of property: in other words property was typically transferred by parents to offspring within the lifetime of the parent instead of at the time

---

31   EKAC, Ly/FR 1.
32   Zell 1994, p. 145.

of their death. This strategy suggests an increase in insecurity and uncertainty in this period.[33]

The first indicators of serious imbalances in production and distribution in the region due to increased market dependency on food are in the 1520s during a series of bad harvests. Food shortages first become apparent in the local record in 1519 in the form of letters of proclamation from the Admiralty of the Cinque Ports at Dover, and from New Romney which called for restraints upon the sending of corn, butter and cheese overseas – the English garrison at Calais excepted.[34] In 1520–1 expenses were paid 'for six people assigned by the bailiff and jurats to go and search for what stores of wheat, barley and oats were in men's barns and houses, because some people made a complaint that the town will lack corn because of carrying over the water'.[35] This indicates that farmers may have been withholding grain until they could get a higher price, or selling it in French markets where they could get a better return. The widespread transference of arable to pastoral farming also massively increased imbalances between local grain and wool production in what used to be a grain-growing area. As we shall see in the next chapter, further into the sixteenth century Tudor statutes against overspecialisation and attempts to enforce farmers on Romney Marsh to grow much more grain fell on deaf ears.

Evidence of increasing poverty in the early sixteenth century comes in the form of a number of lists of people in the town accounts who were unable to pay the local tax or 'common scot' which was levied upon all moveables including livestock and grain. Abatements of this tax are recorded for people of a wide range of means, and 'stresses' (perhaps short for *dis*tresses) were also recorded revealing that those of the least means were selling or pawning their belongings in order to survive. In 1519–20 there were ominous signs for the future as a 'complaint' was made to the bailiff and jurats 'by diverse of the commoners that the common scot was too much'. A significant weight of responsibility for the provision of the navy for Henry VIII's wars fell upon the town and the other ports and in these years the accounts describe the town continuously preparing for war, stocking ships and defending the coast against armies attempting to invade. Men of Lydd were injured and killed on the coast and fishing cabins burned in the early 1520s taking away breadwinners and tools from households. The tax had been set at a relatively high level at this time, but such levels were not uncommon during the various extended crises of warfare

---

33   EKAC, Ly/fac 1, p. 149; HMC 1896, p. 547. For the implications of inter-vivos transfers see R. M. Smith 1984, p. 159.

34   EKAC, Ly/fac 2, pp. 42–56, 165.

35   EKAC, Ly/fac 2, p. 53.

and building projects in the fifteenth century, and without causing distress in such numbers and for such extended periods. The lists of those unable to pay began seriously in 1520–1 reflecting the bad harvest of that year, but the situation became worse between 1525–6 and 1531–2. The lists of stresses and abatements appear more serious from the 1527–8 account following the bad harvest of that year, and frequent proclamations and precepts are recorded that had been sent to Lydd for the punishment of vagabonds, beggars and heretics. For the first time there is an air of the criminalisation of the poor. 'Privy searches' for beggars took place until 1536–7, the number peaking between 1527–8 and 1530–1. After 1531–2 only scot abatement lists are recorded because punitive legislation was introduced which ordered that there were to be no more stresses taken for the common scot. Those people who did not pay on the day legally assigned by the bailiff and jurats were to be imprisoned until they could pay. In the same year a letter was sent from Lydd to Dover Castle regarding 'certain beggars imprisoned at Lydd', indicating that this was no idle threat, or otherwise revealing the results of privy searches. Some people opted to leave the parish: in 1530–1 the chamberlains were forced to make allowances in their calculations for 'diverse persons who had departed out of the town', as well as for the rest of the scot abatements.[36] Also in 1530 and 1531, key years of punitive legislation against the poor, people are found in Lydd's borough court calling in debts owed to them by their tenants to whom they had sublet various plots.[37] At the same time unrest became widespread at elections across the ports, and certain jurats of Lydd had their houses burned down.[38]

Charitable bequests in the wills reinforce the evidence in the accounts of increasing poverty. The form of these bequests took a decisive turn in and from the 1520s. Earlier bequests to the poor were contingent upon the survival of a testator's heirs, or wrapped up in general clauses which bequeathed the residue of a testator's moveables towards charitable works. Direct non-contingent bequests to the poor – often to named individuals – continued to rise sharply from the 1520s.

We are fortunate in that two lists of names survive for the accounting year beginning in September 1528. These can be added to the list of jurats in the 1520s that we have analysed above, and we can base our analysis on these. The first is a list of 38 freemen or 'combarons' who were chosen by the bailiff and jurats to elect one of the permanently installed jurats as bailiff for the year. This list represented a narrowing of those representing the commonality in the

36   EKAC, Ly/fac 2, pp. 53, 82, 96, 123–67.
37   EKAC, Ly/JB, pp. 14–16, 19, 30.
38   See below and Chapter Thirteen.

town as previously all freemen were eligible to vote. The decree for this change
came from the Brodhull (Brotherhood of the Cinque Ports) which as we have
seen was a regular meeting of the mayors, bailiffs and jurats of all the Ports. It
followed serious dissensions across the ports at elections in 1526, the legacy of
recent widespread developments in oligarchic government. More will be said
of this in context of resistance to changes in following chapter.[39] The other
list of 1528–9 records 35 'Poor People' who were deemed worthy of receiving a
dole of corn that year.[40]

With their families included, the 38 freemen on this list in 1528 represented
about a fifth of the population of Lydd. They also represented – on the face of
it – the wealthiest fifth of the population and we can gain a perspective on the
status of the rest of the population from them. Having said that, the choice of
the 38 was a political choice, and so it is likely that troublemakers, such as
those causing problems at elections, were excluded. The 38 were not a homo-
geneous group. They contained wealthy farmers who would become jurats
when the present incumbents in the government died, a mercer of modest
means, middling farmers and small peasants, fishermen and fishermen-farmers, and agricultural labourers. A number of these were also probably traders
with shops in the town. At least one of the labourers was poor enough to also
find himself on the poor list of that year, and at least five were adult servants of
jurats. Because the wealth and status of these freemen overlapped with that of
the poor list we may conclude, with the caveat that the 38 were a political
choice, that a large majority of the population were barely scratching a living
with a combination of wage labour, smallholding and fishing, and this conclusion for the 1520s corresponds with the assessments of wealth in the scot list of
1556 mentioned above.

It is the continuity of the fishing industry in Lydd in the sixteenth century,
and for centuries later for that matter, that provided for the means of subsistence and culture for large section of Lydd's population. The communal
pooling of resources provided an alternative culture to the capitalist farmers,

---

39   EKAC, Ly/fac 2, pp. 115, 129, 139–40; EKAC, CP/B 1, pp. 206–7, 211.

40   The dating of this list is slightly more complex, as it is found at the back of the accounts
     book along with the lists of stresses (that is, items pawned to the government by those
     who couldn't afford to pay their scots). Reference is made to these appendices in the body
     of the accounts for the late 1520s (particularly for 1528 and 1529), recognising their
     placement in the back, and the hands in both sections are identical. The list can also be
     dated between account 1526–7 when Thomas Butcher – the first poor person on the list
     – abated his scot, and the account of 1528–9 when his widow first appears abating a scot
     which would have been the scot he *recently* left through his decease. The latter date seems
     therefore the most likely: EKAC, Ly/fac 2, p. 124, 132, 142, 256.

and this culture included networks which provided for the poor. It is telling in this respect that Lydd's hermit who was responsible for the poor list was a fisherman. Engrossment and enclosure were particularly apparent on Dengemarsh – the base of the fishermen in the fifteenth century – and we can now examine examples of the economic decline of a section of fishermen in relation to these changes. What follows are the mini-biographies of four people who found themselves on the poor list in 1528–9.

William Kempe was styled 'fisherman' in the courts in 1520 and was on the poor list of 1528–9. He was probably the son of John Kempe who had been a jurat between 1465 and 1494.[41] He appears to have fallen into difficulties with his debts in the first decade of the sixteenth century. He was involved in an obligation worth £10 with Andrew Bate junior in 1508, and the following year he was defending a charge against him of a £3 debt to James Swan, one of the wealthier jurats. In 1510 and 1511 he was involved in a number of trespass disputes on Dengemarsh, at least one of these being a violent confrontation. He was mostly the plaintiff in these trespass cases. He was stabbed in the only case we have details for and he may well have been severely damaged in the other cases. By 1520 he was defendant in the borough court against a small debt, a plea of account and a plea of broken contract. The latter two cases involved other fishermen. His wife was given clothes by a widow in 1527, as were other poor, and as his widow in 1531 she was discharged of his first scot.[42]

Stephen Strete was also the son of a jurat in the early years of the sixteenth century before the juratcy became permanent. His father was William Strete, a fisherman. William bequeathed to Stephen only 40s and household goods in his will of 1512, and 20s was bequeathed to each of Stephen's children. As Stephen was already established by that time, his father had no doubt set him up in his trade long before this. We first come across Stephen Strete in 1508 assaulting and being assaulted by Robert Typpe on Dengemarsh. The Typpes were prosperous farmers in the juratcy by the 1530s. Strete was brought before the borough court between 1518 and 1520 because of a series of debts he allegedly owed, including 13s 4d to William Greneway, and 40s to wealthy butcher John Adam. He also had a plea of account brought against him by Peter Typpe.[43] In the 1520s Strete lived in a small tenement with a few acres attached in or near the town. By 1527–8 his debts had probably caused him to sink further into poverty. He was in this year stressed a 'mawnd' and a sheet for 12d. He was on the poor list of 1528–9, discharged of 4d from the first scot of 1531–2,

41   EKAC, Ly/JB 2, p. 23.
42   EKAC, Ly/JB 1, pp. 14–31; TNA, SC 2, 180/65, p. 3; EKAC, Ly/fac 2, p. 167.
43   EKAC, Ly/JB , pp. 24–30; EKAC, Ly/JB 3, pp. 2, 31; TNA SC 2, 180/65, p. 1.

and had died by 1535–6, his widow having abated her scot that year.[44] It is possible that the networks of fishermen revived the family's fortunes. Thomas and Edward Strete may have been Stephen's sons. Thomas abated his scot in 1530 and we hear no more of him in the Lydd record. However in 1533 Edward Strete was involved in a surety with John Butcher, a fisherman-ripier. The latter was a supervisor of the alms house and because Edward was a witness of the hermit Robert Sperpoynt's will in 1541 we can infer that Butcher and Sperpoynt found work for him, he being a youth with his father on the poor list. Indeed, Edward became a fisherman and like the other Lydd fishermen went to the king's works to build defences or to transport materials for the defences further east along the Kent coast at Deal in 1538.[45] However an Elizabeth Strete and a 'Mother Strete' were bequeathed clothes by a jurat's widow in 1550. A family having someone described officially as 'Mother' in it and being bequeathed clothes by wealthy widows was, almost without exception, a sign of poverty. There were three 'Mothers' on the poor list of 1528–9.

Harry or Henry Notie suffered from a combination of his father Richard Notie's debts and the division of the patrimony. Richard Notie had been a fisherman of some note until his death in 1510. His will displayed as much fishing property as any fisherman in this period. However he had accumulated debts and to pay for these he had to sell two boats (batellas), four cabins, and five nets. The rest of his 'fishing craft' was divided in four equal parts between his wife and his three sons. Each of them – including Henry – received four nets, but this paled into insignificance without the boats and cabins meaning that Henry and his brothers were to struggle as very basic fishermen. The Noties, like the others who found themselves struggling in the first decades of the sixteenth century, had their fair share of battles on Dengemarsh. Henry's father Richard stabbed Stephen Mekyn in 1504, and Henry's wife armed herself and broke into a widow's house and stole goods.[46] As with much of the violence on Dengemarsh and subsequently these incidents were linked to debts owed in the borough court, in this case by Henry Notie. Like Stephen Strete's, Henry's recorded debts in court begin in 1518 with a 6s debt, three in the following year totalling 27s plus a plea of account. The following year he was in court owing three more debts totalling 19s 9d and he was subject to another plea of account, mostly against jurats and those on the privileged commoners' list of 1528–9. Henry abated his 8d scot in 1528–9 twice but was forgiven the second time

---

44   EKAC, Ly/fac 2, pp. 132, 142, 167, 197–8.
45   EKAC, Ly/fac 2, pp. 57, 178, 221.
46   TNA, SC 2, 180/63, p. 4; SC 2, 180/65, p. 4.

presumably because he was on the poor list.[47] The only other record of the Notie family after this was in 1541 when Elizabeth was bequeathed bedding by Sperpoynt the hermit, and in 1549 when Margaret was bequeathed a ship's chest by Phillip Martin.

Stephen Wyberd or Wybarne was also a fisherman. It is probable that his father was John Wyberd, a jurat in 1508 before the beginning of oligarchy.[48] The first we hear of Stephen is also in 1508 when he was in court in a plea against John Godfrey who owed him 4s.[49] However by the 1520s there are ominous signs of poverty. In 1521 John Boldyng, a Dengemarsh husbandman, bequeathed to him a blue coat, a ewe and a lamb, and two years later a John Watte bequeathed to him a russet coat. These are examples in these years of direct bequests to the poor. In 1527–8 he was stressed a fishing net which may have left him without the means to find work, and consequently was on the poor list the following year.[50] The next we hear of him after this is in 1531 when he set fire to jurat Robert Ferrour's house and was clearly expressing some anger about his situation.[51] He was granted a small cottage and garden in the town by a Lydd woman who married and moved to New Romney in 1535, and this still remained with his heirs in 1556.[52] One of those heirs was possibly another Stephen Wyberd who in 1549 was bequeathed his servants wages and 6s towards a new coat by wealthy jurat and trader Thomas Tye.

Another Wyberd, possibly Stephen's brother, also struggled. From 1508 Peter Wyberd was frequently in Lydd's borough court and Dengemarsh's manor court. In 1508, 1510 and 1511 he was charged with assaulting different men on Dengemarsh with sticks and knives and at the same time between 1507 and 1513 he was frequently in the borough court as plaintiff and defendant in cases mostly involving debt. One of these in 1508 was a large plea of account for £3 10s, in which he was charged by Simon Rolf. In another case in 1510, jurat Thomas Rey took three sheep and three lambs from him valuing them at 6s presumably to cover a debt. Wyberd made a counter plea that his property had been unjustly detained. Most of the other cases concern people indebted to him although for relatively small amounts. He too was in trouble in 1527–8

47   EKAC, Ly/JB 2, pp. 8, 20–31, 142–5.
48   EKAC, Ly/JB 1, p. 12.
49   EKAC, Ly/JB 1, p. 8.
50   EKAC, Ly/fac 2, pp. 132, 137.
51   EKAC, Ly/JB 3, p. 38.
52   EKAC, Ly/JB 4, p. 14.

having to sell a pan made of laten. He had to abate his scot that year, the follow-ing year and in 1534–5.[53]

These examples indicate that an important section of Lydd's population experienced decline in the early decades of the sixteenth century. These were skilled tradesmen with family that had recently had the means and desire to join the government. The relationship between debts and violence on Dengemarsh in the context of continuing accumulation there is clear. Also a significant development was the criminalisation of the poor who could not pay their debts to the town at specific times, and the creation of a debtor's prison. The dispossessed were now categorised as 'beggars and vagabonds' and even heretics.

During the following decades engrossment and enclosure continued and we shall examine this in more detail in the next chapter. This intolerant attitude by the government towards the poor became increasingly intense during the rest of the sixteenth century as dependency increased. Presentments in the assembly book of 1566–1604 provide evidence of increasing controls on the workforce and heightened suspicion on the part of the government of the activities of that increasingly broad section of the social structure referred to as 'The Poor'.[54] Among the most common presentments were of men and women without masters. These were categorised as 'idle' or if working they did so illegally, 'out of covenant', or unlicensed and 'going at their own hands'. Up to 10 people at a time were presented for these offences, and the numbers of presentments increased towards the end of the century. Servants were a par-ticular focus of notoriety, and a combination of servants, apprentices, 'idle per-sons', vagabonds and 'other poor' continuously found themselves in large numbers before the court charged with illegal lewd behaviour – that is, late-night drinking, tavern haunting, night walking, affrays, unlawful games, pass-ing on stolen goods, and for not following their living, or for not having the means to live.

The inference that not having the means to live had become a crime was etched deeper into contemporary consciousness with a new entry written in the town custumal in the 1550s at the request of the government of farmers. It stated that 'every poor man within this town should have ready for inspection in his house at Michaelmas every year at least three loads of fuel wood on pain of imprisonment and to be found suspicious of hedge picking and wood

---

53   EKAC, Ly/fac 2, pp. 132–42, 191, 250–1; TNA, SC 2, 180/65 pp. 1–3, 10; EKAC, Ly/JB 1, pp. 4–40; EKAC, Ly/JB 4, p. 14.
54   EKAC, Ly/JQs 1.

stealing'.[55] The hedges and wood being referred to were usually those forming the hedges and fences of the extensive enclosures of the farmers. It was also made an offence to collect wood from the previously common land and scrub-wooded area called the 'Holmstone' to the south of the town, and this was a new law which criminalised numerous people who were now presented for offending it. Use of the commons was probably made an offence in spite of the implications for fuel poverty because, as the drainage and sea defence accounts clearly show, materials for maintaining sea defences were running out in the 1560s and broom from the Holmstone was increasingly used.[56] Inundations from the sea would have been perceived as potentially disastrous for farmers investing in commercial land.

With their increasing ownership and controls of all means of production and survival, the government appear to have placed people in an impossible position. It comes as no surprise therefore that the property of the jurats and other yeomen, mostly sheep and enclosure materials, was the main target for theft. Here is a flavour of the presentments. In 1570 'Watt's widow' was charged 'for plucking wool from a sheep of John Heblethwaite'. On 8 April 1570 'the son and the daughter of John Bigges, carpenter' were presented for 'picking hedges'. Bigges himself was presented the following year 'because he had not provided wood for his winter store'. On 1 July 1570 William Golding was charged for being 'a privy picker and a suspicious liver', and later for being a vagabond. In 1571 Bead Bargro, Henry Vyam, Thomas Knox, Thomas Meere and Nicholas Asinden were charged 'for keeping dogs suspicious for killing sheep'. In 1572 Mrs Rycraft ('Rycraftes wyf') was charged for 'stealing railings from Mr [John] Berry's land' and her daughter was charged for 'stealing barley out of Mr Bateman's barn'. 'Rycraft' had earlier been presented for being masterless and out of covenant. The same year Christopher Lambert was presented for 'stealing wood out of Mr Bateman's close', and Robert Masley was presented 'for flaying [skinning] Mr Strogull's sheep and Mr Barnes's sheep'. In October 1576 it was William Lucas 'Palmer's wife's son' presented for 'picking from hedges' at service time ('divine service') in church, and in the same year Stephen Mellowe, a husband-man, was indicted for driving away three ewes of jurat William Dallet. In 1586 Robert Kempe, labourer, was indicted for driving away a ewe of Vincent Puckell, butcher, and the following year for stealing one 'yextrenger' and one 'staple' from John Strogull's court. The same year Clement Downe was charged with selling to William White 'two cheeks of a plough suspected to be stolen by him

---

55   EKAC, Ly/LC 1, pp. 31–2. Michaelmas was a feast day at the end of September. By this date Lydd's inhabitants were expected to be stocked up on fuel ready for the winter.

56   EKAC, Ly/ZS.

from Matthew Knight', and James Wood of Ivychurch, husbandman, was indicted for stealing six sheep and two lambs from Thomas Godfrey junior. On 12 May 1593 John Carpenter, 'William Hooke's boy' and 'John Skiptoone' were presented for 'picking other men's hedges in the night time'.[57] These are the examples in the presentments that enter the names of the victims as well as those of the alleged thieves. The thieves were of husbandman status and below, and the former were mostly the wealthiest farmers in the juratcy such as Berry, Godfrey, Strogull, Bateman and Knight. The class divisions between these two groups were sharper than those exhibited in the conflict on Dengemarsh in the decades around 1500. In addition to these examples numerous memoranda are recorded in these years of serious felonies by 'malefactors' – which included some of the alleged thieves mentioned above, who were imprisoned – but without describing the actual offences and their victims. The jurats also bore the brunt of the recorded verbalised ill-feeling in the town. For example on 24 January 1574, William Bennes was 'imprisoned, fined and punished according to our custom for evil reporting and miscalling of John Berry, jurat' and in 1588 William Griggesby, a serial tavern brawler, was presented 'for abusing Mr Bailiff of Lydd with irreverent and unseemly words behind his back'.[58]

As we enter the 1590s we enter a crisis of epidemics and rapidly increasing poverty on a much larger scale than in the 1520s. There was a steady increase in expenditure on poor relief between 1590 and 1612. In 1590 the amount received by the overseers of the poor was £46 18s 5d, and in 1612 it had risen to £74 15s 8d. By the 1630s it was said to be '£140 yearly and it increases daily'.[59]

This evidence of proletarianisation and dependence in Lydd appears typical of other developing pastoral farming regions by the early seventeenth century, as the last remnants of subsistence possibilities were enclosed. Joan Thirsk found that:

> When some pastoral regions in the seventeenth century ceased to grow even a modest quota of cereals for their own support, and depended increasingly on grain supplied from the arable zones, they aggravated their own latent problem of underemployment or unemployment. An account of the pastoral vale of Tewkesbury at the beginning of the seventeenth century crisply described a condition typical of many other pastoral areas: 'there being no kind of trade to employ men, and very small tillage, necessity compelled poor men to ... stealing of sheep and other

---

57   EKAC, Ly/JQs 1, pp. 52–80, 123–5, 132, 147, 158–62.

58   EKAC, Ly/JQs 1, pp. 72, 91, 131.

59   Elks 1989, pp. 74–5.

cattle, breaking of hedges, robbing of orchards, and what not; insomuch that the place became famous for rogues ... and Bridewell was erected there to be a terror to idle persons'.[60]

In conclusion, in two or three generations between the 1460s and the 1520s the social structure of Lydd underwent a marked polarisation that amounted to a social transformation. By the 1520s a class of capitalist farmers dominated property holding and the government of Lydd. Following the development of new leases in the parish in the fifteenth century as a result of reclamation, engrossment and enclosure, their enterprises had expanded by the 1520s so that they typically held multiple leases of hundreds of acres. Their rise accompanied the imposition of government oligarchy in the town from around 1512 and this gave their economic interests direct political representation. Like feudal lords capitalist farmers also aimed to reproduce themselves through a form of political accumulation, but this time it was very different. Rather than a means to squeeze the peasantry extra-economically, political accumulation for these farmers was a means to further expand their capital through economic accumulation via the expropriation of the peasantry and the maintenance of a cheap workforce. At the same time, and as the inverse of the same process, peasants, fishermen and petty traders who formed the dominant culture in the fifteenth century, and whose interests were reflected in the outlook of the government at that time, experienced decline, proletarianisation and dependency through indebtedness as their land base became eroded due to the engrossment and enclosure by the farmers. The polarisation in economic interests was also reflected in the development of clearly contrasting mentalities between the capitalist farmers and the rest of the population towards property and family.

An agrarian capitalist social-property structure still had a long way to go before it was sharply defined into commercial landlord, capitalist tenant farmer and landless wage labourer. However, this structure had emerged in its fundamental outline in the first half of the sixteenth century. It was only with this profound change in the generations before the 1520s that the expansion of capitalist enterprises in subsequent periods was made possible. Gentry increasingly accumulated engrossed customary and freeholdings and leased

---

60 Thirsk 1978, pp. 163–4. Tewkesbury is in Gloucestershire in the south-west of the country. The Bridewell prison was developed in London for the disorderly poor and homeless children in the 1550s. The name became synonymous with prisons elsewhere. More detail on the further extension of enclosure for pastoral farming during the mid- and late sixteenth century is provided in the following chapter.

them back to their engrossers so that the class lines between land owners and land leasers became increasingly sharply defined. Accumulation of multiple leases and further engrossment by capitalist farmers also ensured a sharper definition between themselves and their increasingly dependent neighbours. This definition became increasingly marked as the population began to rise after 1540. This led to the real-terms reduction in the value of wages of an increasing majority of the population, and therefore to increased profits and increased rents for the farmers and lords. Having said this, for farmers to benefit from the increasing dependency and domestic demand for their products that their accumulations generated, wage labourers had to be able to afford them, and so blind destructive accumulation could not go on indefinitely. Supplying that demand in the long run would stimulate further the need to introduce labour-saving methods and produce more cheaply. The imperative to use as little labour as possible and yet at the same time have a mass demand for commodities is one of the deep contradictions of capitalism.

CHAPTER 12

Engrossment, Enclosure and Resistance in the Sixteenth Century

Historians have argued that the period between 1530 and 1580 witnessed a hiatus in the enclosure movement in England. One element contributing towards this conclusion is the statistic based on Wordie's chronological process of elimination that only two to three percent of England's surface was 'enclosed' during the whole of the sixteenth century. As I have argued this figure fails to take account of the engrossment of 'old enclosed' holdings in the south-east and elsewhere which may have made up 45 percent of England's surface by 1500.[1] Whether one chooses to adhere to the statistics or not, the reasons given for the so-called hiatus in enclosure present a pressing argument. The key causes cited are the crown's anti-enclosure statutes from the 1530s and resistance to enclosure by peasant armies in the 1530s and 1540s. The crown's sympathy with arguments against enclosure in this period was an expression of its fear of public disorder due to starvation, dislocation and fear of invasion due to depopulation of coastal areas. Hence it attempted to limit the accumulation of farms and curb over specialisation in sheep grazing to ensure enough tillage for the production of food grains, and the rearing of cattle for meat and dairy products.[2] The threat of widespread peasant rebellion may also have tamed the enthusiasm of enclosing yeomen and gentry for undermining the livelihoods of peasants. Rising grain prices due to demand from a rapidly rising population from the 1540s, an increasing proportion of which was landless and had to buy food to survive, also meant that the compulsion to engross and consolidate peasant holdings in order to clear the way for sheep walks was lessened. Big profits were now also to be made from growing grain for staples like bread, although pastoral farming remained more lucrative.[3]

This chapter examines these arguments in the light of evidence for Lydd. As we have seen in Chapters Ten and Eleven, large scale depopulating enclosure had already occurred in Lydd parish before 1530, and as a result large sheep graziers already dominated the government of Lydd. Most importantly for the present discussion, further massive accumulations of land in the form of

---

1 See Chapter Seven above.
2 Thirsk 1967, pp. 213–38.
3 Thirsk 1978, pp. 165–6.

multiple leases by 1580 were achieved by the same families of yeomen and small gentry in Lydd's government and by wealthy immigrants. So if engrossment and enclosure was clearly augmented and consolidated at Lydd and its region between 1530 and 1580, how was this achieved given the new statutory restrictions? Also, what form did any resistance take, and how successful was it?

i   Legal Resistance to Engrossment and Enclosure

A chance survival of a fragment of a case held before the royal court of the exchequer at Westminster (London) in 1576 reveals that John Berry of Lydd was charged that year with 'offences done against the statute for the maintenance of dairy cows'.[4] The record of only one witness survives, that of husbandman Clement Gallyen of Lydd, and he deposed in Berry's favour. He stated that Berry held the following properties: a mansion house at Cheyne Court and its 500 attached acres on Romney Marsh a few miles to the west of Lydd, a farm in Lydd parish where Berry lived, a farm at Broomhill, land at Newland, two farms called Abbots Marsh and Abbots Land – again to the west of Lydd parish – and other farms in Ivychurch and Brookland over on the west side of Romney Marsh. As we have seen in the previous chapter, in 1586 he held a farm of 353 acres in Lydd parish, and his other holdings to the south of the Rhee Wall alone contained approximately 1,978 acres. Of this accumulation, 207 acres were his freehold lands, and the rest were leases held from six Kent gentry. Gallyen stated that in 1576 Berry kept between 1,500 and 1,600 sheep, maintained 43 dairy cows and reared 40 calves. The law stated that if farmers kept more than 120 sheep, they had to keep one cow for every 60 sheep and rear one calf for every 120 sheep. If Gallyen was telling the truth, Berry was well within the law. The extent of Berry's landholdings at this time suggests that he was farming on much larger scale than even these large numbers of animals suggest. Berry was one of the wealthiest men in Lydd at this time. He migrated to Lydd from Ivychurch in the north of the Marsh in 1555. He arrived to immediately take up the space in Lydd's juratcy that had been left after the death of the Ralph Wilcockes that year. One might even say that it was reserved for him. He already had close ties with Lydd and was executor of Wilcockes's will. Not only that but he probably took over Cheyne Court and other farms from Wilcockes upon the latter's death. To further cement his future he married Peter Godfrey's daughter Katherine, and therefore nestled into the wealthiest Godfrey line.

---

4   TNA, E 133/2/351.

The case of 1576 indicates that Berry was stirring opposition in Lydd in the years leading up to it and I will examine this opposition in the 1560s and 1570s in more detail below. First we must address another related case at Westminster which was brought seven years later in 1583.

In that year a certain James Browne of Burnynges wrote a letter to Sir Thomas Bromley, knight, chancellor of England.[5] He informed the chancellor that he had recently presented at the court of common pleas at Westminster certain information against John Berry (again), and his relation Thomas Godfrey junior, both of Lydd, and charged them with infringing the royal statutes which had been instituted between 1535 and 1572. The infringements included the keeping of over 2,000 sheep, and the rearing of an insufficient proportion of dairy cows and calves. The defendants had pleaded not guilty and the trial was due at the same court. Browne's letter to the chancellor was a plea to allow him to immediately examine some of his witnesses to the case in the higher court of chancery. His reason for this request was to ensure that some of his witnesses did not die of old age before they could present their evidence and to ensure that others were not moved from the area through foul play:

> the chief witnesses that will prove my case are very aged men and shepherds and keepers of marsh grounds, not able to travel in winter when the case is to be tried, and likely to die before the trial from extreme age and weakness. Some of them are also bailiffs and domestic servants of the defendants who by that time will be sent either beyond the seas or so far from being found that I shall be prevented miraculously in my case.

Browne also enhanced his charge against Berry and Godfrey by stating that the defendants were,

> [m]en of wonderful [as in, 'unbelievable'] wealth, and tenants of marshlands in Romney Marsh and nearby to some of the most worshipful gentlemen of the county of Kent, whose aid and friendship the said defendants so greatly expect that they think to colour up their great faults which are in truth the engrossing up of the greatest part of the marsh lands in those parts into their own hands and turning it all to grazing. So that tillage for bread, the keeping of dairy cows for butter and cheese is not there used, and as a consequence the people of the area are destitute

5 TNA, C2/Eliz/B20/17. I cannot identify the place name 'Burnynges': however, a James Browne was rated at a fairly high 8s in a Lydd taxation document in 1556.

of both bread, butter and cheese, a general hindrance to the poor people
there about dwelling, and also as a consequence many of the villages in
the Marsh there are destroyed and laid waste.

Browne finished the letter by requesting that the chancellor command Berry
and Godfrey to come to the court of chancery at Westminster to explain why
he ought not to examine the witnesses in the way he had stated.

The joint response of Godfrey and Berry stated that Browne's 'bill of complaint ... is altogether uncertain, untrue and insufficient in the law as such to
require an answer ... altogether devised, framed and imagined, rather upon
malice than upon any just suit'. They argued that any delay in proceedings
which might have prejudiced the ability of the witnesses to attend trial was
caused by Browne himself in bringing this extra complaint. They suggested
that it was possible for the case to be tried at the next quarter sessions court in
the county where the witnesses would not have so far to travel and would not
have to wait so long. Finally they submitted to whatever course of action the
chancellor deemed appropriate.

This is unusually clear evidence of social power and its potential role in the
processes of engrossment and enclosure which created a new agrarian capitalist social-property structure. The allegation that as tenants to the county gentry they expected 'aid and friendship' in their business transactions and in
their protection from the law concurs with my assertion that there was an
effective mutual relationship between lessees and landlords, and with the evidence presented earlier of the relationship between lords and their farmers in
Lydd in the fifteenth century. Indeed, specifically with regard to Kent, Du
Boulay's study of the lessees of the Archbishop of Canterbury's estates concluded that in the early sixteenth century 'the interests of the rentier archbishop and the lessees of his demesne were fairly evenly balanced, and it is
hard to say that one side was operating at the expense of the other'.[6] The allegation that the defendants wielded overwhelming domination over their servants and labourers is not so easy to verify. However, evidence in the previous
chapter of the increasing controls by the Lydd juratcy over the poor in Lydd
parish in the 1570s and 1580s is suggestive for Browne's version of events.

This is the only evidence of the case that survives, but it is possible to judge
quite clearly the merits of both sides of the argument from evidence in the
court book of Lydd itself, and from Romney Marsh rentals and taxation evidence. Browne described Godfrey and Berry as men of 'wonderful wealth' and
he said that they were 'engrossing up ... the greatest part of the marsh lands in

6   Du Boulay 1966, p. 230.

those parts into their own hands and turning it all to grazing'. We know that this was by no means an exaggeration. The thousands of acres that make up part of Berry's land holdings at the time of the trial have been presented above, and in more detail in the previous chapter. I also showed in the previous chapter that Godfrey held, besides 341 acres of his own freeholdings, leases amounting to another 530 acres in Lydd and White Kempe Watering alone to the west of Lydd, and considerably more farms in other parts of the Marsh and Weald.

What of the accusation that as a consequence of this engrossment and social power there was a lack of tillage and dairy cows and more importantly an increase in poverty and depopulation? Lydd's assembly book begins in 1566 and in it we find continuous presentments against Godfrey, Berry, and many other men for all of the things that they had been accused of. Amongst the array of presentments for nuisance, affrays, illicit activities such as hedge and sheep picking, masterless labourers, unlicensed trade and felonies that have been described in the previous chapter, there are presentments concerned with decaying houses – particularly manor houses of minor gentry whose estates had been engrossed and the buildings left empty; the cutting adrift of a minimum of 20 acres allowed around these houses by statute; the bridges that were left to decay and the enclosure of land across common byways so that common ways were blocked; the continuous encroachment of rails and posts of enclosures onto highways and common lands; the grazing of an illegal number of sheep, and a related imbalance in the production of arable and dairy products in favour of wool.

The numerous manors and sub-manors in Lydd parish meant that there were a number of manor houses in the locality in the fifteenth century: at Scotney, Old Langport, Belgar, Jacques Court, and there was also at least one on Dengemarsh. The minor nature of the traditional gentry estates in Lydd parish was typical for Kent before the fifteenth century, and the cause is put down to the Kentish custom of gavelkind which advocated the fragmentation of estates among heirs. Apart from the strong ecclesiastical presence in Kent there was no overarching lay power in the county as a result.[7] Engrossment and enclosure on the scale mentioned earlier would not only remove peasant dwellings but also these numerous small gentry houses whose estates were also too small for the new men in Kent. We already know that by 1551 the manor place of Old Langport manor had been removed along with a number of peasant dwellings to make way for an expensive marshland lease. The lease was in possession of Peter Godfrey of Lydd at this time, possibly our defendant's father.[8] Evidence

7   Du Boulay 1966, pp. 65–8, 111; Fleming 2010.

8   CKS, U1043/M4

in the assembly book which begins in 1566 reveals that the other manor places were protected by statute at this time and the commonality of the town attempted to enforce it. The court held in Lydd, the proceedings of which were recorded in the assembly book, was described as the 'hundred and sessions' court, and so in contrast with the earlier borough (hundred) court it appears to have been provided with the jurisdiction of royal quarter sessions, with the bailiff and jurats given the authority of justices of the peace. The quarter sessions and these royal justices increasingly took over the legal business of the county in the second half of the sixteenth century, and the continuing independence of the Cinque Ports may have ensured at this stage that the government of Lydd were provided with this status. It was these royal justices who were of course charged with upholding the royal statutes. I present the evidence put by the jury of commoners to the bailiff and jurats in chronological order in order to provide the clearest impression possible of the continuous and cumulative process of change in the so-called years of hiatus. The court of 15 September 1566 heard:

> that the manor [house] of Belgar is greatly run to ruin and decay and the lands are severed from it contrary to statute. It is thought that a gentle letter should be sent to Edward Middleton and Arthur Middleton, owners of the same, to give them advertisement of the same presentment and to admonish them to re-edify and repair the same before the feast of St Bartholomew the Apostle next coming [24 August 1567], so that for default of amendment and reparation of the same the township has no cause to enter the same and to take its profits until it is re-edified according to the statute.[9]

These owners of Belgar manor, which lay to the east of the town and to the north of Dengemarsh and Northlade, were not resident and had left the manor and its land in the hands of farmers who were more interested in the profitability of the land than in maintaining the buildings that came with it. The 'gentle letter' that was sent to the owners was bolstered with the serious threat of an ongoing financial penalty; but this had no effect because the following September the jury again presented 'the manor house of Belgar because it is ruinous and in decay'. At the same time they presented that, in the same area, 'the lane leading from Costelore to Belgar and so forth to the sea is being encroached upon by the farmers of Belgar'. The same year the manor house of Jacques Court on the right hand edge of the town, and Sir Walter Hendley's

---

9   EKAC, Ly/JQs 1, p. 27.

tenement, probably on Dengemarsh, were presented because they did not have 20 acres employed to them. Belgar was again presented in October 1568 and April 1570 because the manor's mansion was ruinous and did not have 20 acres employed to it.[10]

On 26 January 1572 the presentments reveal that the problem had spread – but the focus was changing to the more immediate problem of lack of tillage and the shortage of arable produce in the area for the consumption of the poor. This was over 10 years before the case against Godfrey and Berry at Westminster. The jury presented that 'the manors of Jacques Court, Scotney, Belgar and also Mr Swan's farm that Mr Berry dwells in have been more used to tillage than they are at present, contrary to the statute'. This statute had stated that after an earlier date there was to be no more transference from tillage to pasture, and the land that had been transferred to pasture was to be returned to its former state.[11] In October of the same year, 15 men (including all of the permanent jurats and a few other farmers) were told that they had 'arable lands within the liberty according to the nature of the soil and ought to sow them yearly at least according to the statute, in addition to the lands which they already sow'; and each man was appointed to sow a specific number of extra acres. These appointments amounted to an extra 299 acres that were required to be sown in Lydd parish alone. John Berry had to sow 40 more acres and Thomas Godfrey junior 20 more, and these were among the more serious offenders, particularly Berry. At the same time (October 1572) Godfrey was presented 'for that he has 400 sheep and should keep 4 cows and breed 3 calves every year according to statute and he does not'. Godfrey, Berry and various other Lydd jurats had taken no notice of the law in this respect because they were presented again in 1573 and 1574 for lack of tillage, and Godfrey and his nephew were presented again in 1575 'for want of tillage, and that they keep neither cows nor breed calves'. In the meantime Belgar was presented again as still ruinous and was now joined by Anthony Mayne, esquire's, mansion on Dengemarsh, and John Bateman, jurat's, two places, one at Westbrook and one at New Langport (Scotney).[12]

Between 1566 and 1574 there was a catalogue of cases which firmly support most of Browne's later allegations in 1583 against Godfrey and Berry, although similar cases could have been brought against a number of others at this stage. Godfrey and Berry must have been singled out as the chief threats to the livelihoods of the smaller men on Romney Marsh. The offences against the

---

10   EKAC, Ly/JQs 1, pp. 29–32, 40, 53.

11   Thirsk 1967.

12   EKAC, Ly/JQs 1, pp. 72, 79, 81, 83, 87, 92.

statutes must have been going on for some years before 1566, and it seems as though the jury of commoners in Lydd had little power by this time in the face of the jurats of Lydd who were all big farmers and serial offenders against the statutes. It must have been difficult for these commoners of relatively meagre resources to continuously present these justices of the crown to themselves for infringing the statutes of the crown. Hence the need for matters to be taken out of the town to a higher court, and this was no mean feat considering the theoretical immunity of Lydd from such courts by virtue of the Cinque Port franchise.

Between 1575 and 1582, the years leading up to the trial of 1583, the presentments for offences against the statutes cease altogether and we will return to possible reasons for this below. After 1582 the presentments for decaying manor houses continued. Thomas Harneden, jurat, was presented for the decay of the Dering's gentry mansion called Nodde, previously in the possession of Peter Godfrey, and Belgar yet again.[13] But after 1587 there were no more presentments for decay, presumably because after at least 20 years of neglect and decay these mansions were now rubble in any case. The capitalist farmers of Lydd lived in newly-built substantial houses in the town which still survive today, and the marshes were mostly left to the limited number of shepherds and marsh keepers to dwell.[14] Between 1587 and 1589 the focus in the presentments continued to concern the need for tillage and the jurats and farmers were presented for having acreage which was 'apt for tillage', now in multiples of 60 acres each. In 1590 we enter a crisis of epidemics and rapidly increasing poverty on a much larger scale than that of 1528 when the first poor list appeared. It is from here that serious widespread poverty in England becomes a permanent structural feature rather than one that reared its head in any particular conjuncture. At the beginning of the crisis, in 1591, Godfrey was again presented for keeping above 2,000 sheep, as he had been by Browne at Westminster in 1583; and he was joined by Matthew Knight 'for the like'. Knight had taken over the leases of Belgar and Northlade by this time.[15]

Scarcity of corn in the area can be read into the more active measures taken towards provision of the poor from the 1570s. On 6 October 1574 provision was made for 'a market of corn to be kept every Saturday for the relief of the poor within the town who were not able to travel to foreign markets for their corn'. All of the jurats and 13 of the wealthier commoners and jurats-to-be were listed

13   EKAC, Ly/Qs 1, pp. 110, 125.

14   Private communication from Mrs Beryl Coattes, local historian for Lydd, based upon her unpublished work.

15   EKAC, Ly/JQs 1, pp. 126–34, 145, 171–4.

and allocated a particular amount of corn to supply the market each year. On 20 November 1595 during the crisis years another revealing decree was made by the bailiff, jurats and six of the wealthiest commoners. It stated that:

> Provision of corn should be made to the intent that the poor inhabitants of Lydd might, on any day of the week henceforth until [gap in text], have all manner of corn and grain for their money at the same prices as in other markets. The charges and expenses, including the carrying of the corn to the town, and the losses made by retailing in small measures such as tolvets, pecks etc, to be borne by the common charge of the town.[16]

These two decrees span the decades around the case of 1583 and the serious crisis of the 1590s. Some historians may interpret this evidence as marking the beginning of an enlightened modern attitude towards poverty. In fact it provides a good indication that these big farmers of Lydd who dominated the area politically and economically refused to adhere to the statutes and grow corn on the own lands to the extent required to supply an increasingly landless, dependent and impoverished population with basic food. The price of corn was rising in the country as a whole in this period due to increasing demand from a rapidly rising population and an ever-increasing proportion of people and families without landed subsistence who now had to pay for it. The problems for wage earners who formed the new structural poor would have been more acute on Romney Marsh where it is clear that demand for wool for rural industry still provided the best profits and where farmers were as a result reluctant to transfer their production. These decrees reveal that because of the scarcity of corn there had been pressure on Lydd's inhabitants to buy it from outside of the parish in other markets, and travel was expensive. They also suggest that these farmers had been reluctant to sell what corn they did grow in small measures to their own inhabitants because it was more convenient and lucrative for the farmers to sell in bulk elsewhere. The agreement to provide for the poor in the way laid out by the decrees seems to have come about, not as a result of pressure from the royal statutes, but because the cost of the provision was borne by the town as a whole and not only by the farmers. The impact of the tax on the farmers would therefore have been substantially reduced.

We can now turn to other indicators of the continuity of engrossment and enclosure between 1530 and 1580. The maintenance of bridges was the responsibility of land holders. The decay of bridges or their complete illegal removal blocked customary byways and this was a deliberate process in the privatisation

---

16   EKAC, Ly/JQs 1, pp. 90, 168.

of large areas of land that previously had public access. Between 1566 and 1604 there were 140 presentments of 58 people for this offence. A number of these were repeat presentments for the same bridges, the previous warnings having gone unheeded. Not surprisingly given the extent of their landholdings, 24 of these 58 people were Lydd jurats, four were gentry from outside the parish, and the rest were mainly other farmers of means from the combarons and families of the jurats. The jurats bore the brunt of the presentments. Thomas Godfrey junior in particular was presented 16 times in his lands which were all over the west of Lydd parish. Peter Godfrey was presented seven times, Thomas Harneden seven times and John Bateman nine times. Berry was only involved on a few occasions as most of his lands were outside of the liberty. Unlike the presentments for the decay of manor houses, those for the bridges continued throughout the period.

One way to increase the size of one's enclosures in this period was to simply extend the rails and posts of the fences around the enclosure outwards onto common highways and common land. There were 64 presentments involving 36 people in these years for this offence. This strategy eventually worked for Harneden and Berry. Following their continuous refusal to remove their posts from the common areas they were eventually allowed keep the enlargement and pay for their encroachment as an additional rent. Thomas Ederyk of New Romney actually threatened the jury of Lydd with physical harm for presenting him for a similar offence.[17]

The evidence from the assembly book alone provides a strong reinforcement of Brown's case in 1583 to be one of fact and not born out of something 'uncertain, untrue and insufficient in the law', or 'devised, framed and imagined' as the defendants Godfrey and Berry maintained from their positions as justices of the peace of the liberty. The very detail that Browne goes into regarding massive accumulation, food scarcity, exemption from the law, resulting decay and poverty and the culpability of the defendants in these respects reads as a summary of the presentments in the Assembly Book in the preceding decades.

ii   Illegal Resistance to Engrossment and Enclosure

Between 1548 and 1551 there was widespread anti-enclosure rebellion in Kent, as there was throughout England. Similar to the peasant camps that were set up around Norwich in Norfolk, a camp was set up around Canterbury in Kent.

---

17   EKAC, Ly/JQs 1, pp. 116, 212.

In view of the mass unrest and disorder that engrossment and enclosure had caused by this time Protector Somerset authorised commissions into illegal enclosure in 1548. The peasants, artisans and poor viewed these commissions as a green light of support for their anti-enclosure cause and they proceeded to take up the fences of enclosures. Demands in Kent were also made for a rise in wages. Much of the evidence and focus of antiquaries studying the rebellion which centred on 1549 was on East Anglia and Norfolk in particular – hence the rebellion has been known to posterity as 'Kett's Rebellion' after one of the leaders in that county. Now a more general 'English Rising' is increasingly coming to light, and Kent played its part in this one as it had done in the major risings of 1381 and 1450. On June 13, 1549 Hugh Paulet wrote from Kent that there had been 'a lewd uproar of the people in sundry places' although it had by then quietened down. A sign of the Duke of Somerset's popular support in Kent came on 6 October 1549 when in response to the Earl of Warwick's mustering of the bulk of the aristocracy's forces against him he was allegedly able to mobilise 'over 4,000 peasants' from Kent to protect him around Hampton Court where he was lodged with the king. He later went to Windsor Castle 'where a great number of peasants were daily assembling'. He was accused of sending the peasantry to oppress the nobility. Andy Wood has made the interesting comparison with Cade's rebellion and the support of the Kentish peasantry for the Duke of York in the decade that followed.[18] Two insurrections in the county were planned in early 1550 although they were not successful. According to a foreign witness, 10,000 peasants are alleged to have assembled near Sittingbourne in east Kent but were dispersed by a force of cavalry. He claimed that the gentry had seized the peasants' lands and doubled their rents.[19] In the following year another witness, Nicholas Ridley, complained that Robert Deane, the steward of Rochester Cathedral in Kent, had attacked tenant's rights and 'raised so excessively the rent, enhancing that what went for £14 unto £44 or more ... unto the great slander of all bishops ... that should consent and suffer their poor tenants so to be pilled and polled and their lands so excessively to be improved by such lease-mongers which are the utter undoing and very destruction of the commonwealth'.[20]

There is no evidence of overt rebellion in Lydd itself at this time although a dispute over marshland taxation in North Walland to the west of Lydd in 1549 and early 1550 would most likely have been connected to the wider rebellion. The jurats of North Walland Watering would have included a number of Lydd

---

18   Wood 2005, pp. 83–5.
19   Clark 1977, p. 79.
20   Clark 1977, p. 82.

farmers who had farms all over that area, and they complained to three leading Kent gentry, Sir John Baker, Sir Richard Sackville, and Sir Thomas Moyle, that the maintenance of the Marsh there was left in a bad state because of disagreements between the jurats and those that are described as 'tenants' and 'commons'. These gentry who clearly had more pressing military matters left the matter in the hands of Ralph Wilcockes who was described as lord of Cheyne Court, a manor just to the west of Lydd parish. The subsequent letter written by the dwindling number of jurats on 8 February 1550 to Wilcockes singled out a certain Richard Friend as the ringleader who was 'friendly' to the commons and 'reproachful' to them. They said that he speaks his mind in 'every audience' and that he intends to do so again when he comes before the lords. They finish with the expectation of support from Wilcockes and the other lords in the dispute.[21] We do not know the result of the dispute but interestingly, soon after this episode, Wilcockes chose to move to Lydd where he became a chamberlain in 1551 and a jurat in 1555. This was the first time that a man described as lord of a manor had joined the government of Lydd, and one wonders whether this was a defensive measure on his part in the face of opposition among the commoners in the Marsh.[22]

In the previous chapter I presented evidence of continuous hedge picking and sheep stealing by peasants and poor in Lydd from the 1560s. This in itself can be seen as a form of resistance to enclosure, and the criminalising of the poor for not having enough fuel was certainly an example of class conflict in this period. There are indications of potentially more serious disorders pertaining to anti-enclosure riot and electoral discontent in the first half of the 1570s in the parish. On 12 March 1572 Arnold Barrowe, John Eppes, Robert Huglen, William Bresinden and Saloman Adams were fined 10s each for the impressively alliterative charge of 'diverse disorders done at diverse men's doors at 12 o'clock in the night'. Five weeks later we find that these men had 'pulled up Mr Bailiff's and Mr Harneden's posts and rails' on their enclosures. This was of course exactly the time when the same jury were presenting people like Harneden for illegal encroachment of their posts and rails on the commons.[23]

---

21 CKS, S/W, AZ 2, pp. 11–16.
22 See his will of 1555. Besides his holdings in the Marsh he held a Park at Wrotham and a manor at Warhorne, both in the Weald. He spent £60 alone on the execution and oversight of his will. £800 worth of his moveables was to be spent on lands for his younger son Edward who became a Lydd jurat.
23 EKAC, Ly/JQs 1, p. 73.

Regarding the rioters, William Bresinden was described as an innholder and Saloman Adams, a tailor. Arnold Barrowe had a more illustrious background as the son of William Barrowe who was of small gentry status and for many years had been clerk of Lydd and then jurat before his death in 1555. Arnold's older brothers, William junior and Thomas, had both been in the combarons, and William in the juratcy for one year in 1567, after which he either died or migrated. The vast majority of William senior's estate was bequeathed to Arnold's brothers in 1555 when Arnold was still a minor: indeed he was still not 18 when his brother Thomas made his will in 1562. Arnold was bequeathed some of the residue of his father's lands in Lydd town and parish which his brothers had sublet in the meantime, and he was to receive the profits accrued from these lands when 21 years of age. In 1562 his brother gave him the option of receiving £30 for his schooling or £15 and the release to him of his inherited lands. So by 1572, when his rebellion first comes to light, while certainly not achieving the wealth and status of his brothers because of the nature of the inheritance strategies of his father, he may well have been educated and had a small amount of land. John Eppes and Robert Huglen who were also fined for their part in the anti-enclosure activity also carried the surnames of recent jurats although their representation in the government had ceased now that it had been entirely taken over by big farmers. The picture that emerges is a very vague one, but it is clear that these men were not represented in the government, and given the artisanal element of some, and lack of evidence of significant land holding of the others, they were probably among the more relatively middling commoners and trades people in the town. These were the type of people that were probably now in the front line of defence against continuing enclosure that threatened the common lands and the integrity of the remaining unconsolidated plots in the parish. They may also have nurtured a sense of disenfranchisement given the family backgrounds of some of them, especially Barrowe. There was agitation against oligarchic control by magisterial cliques across the ports in the 1560s and 1570s and this would continue to be a feature of politics into the seventeenth century.[24]

Significantly, the same Arnold Barrowe was presented in court a few years later on 22 October 1575 'for making a rescue against the Queen's officers of this town'. We do not know what this 'rescue' entailed but it sounds like the recovery of animals or some commodity that had been taken from him or others by the jurats. However it may relate to other serious disturbances the same year. A case involving Barrowe was reported to the Brodhull of the Cinque Ports by John Heblethwaite, a jurat and recent bailiff of Lydd, because he had had his

---

24   Clark 1977, p. 141.

authority undermined during actions he took against Barrowe. Heblethwaite had imprisoned Barrowe 'by reason of his former abuse' and bound him in the sum of £5 for his good behaviour. However, other jurats had released him from prison without such a bond even though he 'had in their sight and hearing menaced [Heblethwaite] and some other of the jurats or other officers saying these words: "some of you shall repent it"'.[25]

The decision of the Brodhull was that Barrowe was to make a bond in a certain sum of money or be imprisoned. What is intriguing is what Heblethwaite and some of the jurats were supposed to repent. We have seen in the previous chapter that the ability for the poor to collect fuel on the common wooded area called the Holmstone was ended in the 1550s. On 26 September 1574, the year before Barrowe's rescue and threat to Heblethwaite and others in the government, the common rights on the large grazing area called the Ripe were extinguished, and were replaced by a flock of sheep for the use of the town. Previously every tenant in the town had a right to a certain number of sheep to graze on the Ripe to support their household economies. This right would have become increasingly important given the reduction in available smallholdings elsewhere. This new flock of sheep would have generated profits for the town, perhaps providing the financial means to undertake its administrative duties. Apparently the commoners 'agreed' to forgo their rights on the commons, and this change was presented as an act of benevolence as the bailiff, jurats and commoners are said to have contributed 392 ewes to the flock. John Heblethwaite was singled out in the recording of this act, not only because he was bailiff at this time, but because he deserved extra praise for his contribution of six sheep 'notwithstanding his great loss in sheep last year', presumably due to disease (although possibly due to Barrowe).[26] It was of course when Heblethwaite was bailiff that Barrowe's trouble took place.

What are we to make of this? It was said that the forgoing of common rights was consented to by the bailiffs, jurats *and* the commoners. If by 'the commoners' the whole body of freemen were referred to, there were 56 freemen recorded as paying tax in 1571 as part of their obligation to the Cinque Ports.[27] If this number were allowed to vote for or against the extinguishing of common rights, only 22 of them would be required to join the bailiff and jurats to make a majority vote for it. However, the number of freemen eligible to vote in actual elections had been reduced to only 21 'combarons' in this period, and only 10 of these would need to vote with the government if those commoners

---

25   CKS, CP/B 2, pp. 18–19.

26   HMC 1896, p. 531.

27   TNA, E 179, 231–7.

eligible to vote for or against the commons was limited to the enfranchised combarons. Either way, those most in need of the commons would not have had a choice in their future. Arnold Barrowe may well have been a leading spokesperson for them, and perhaps not only them.

What may also be significant is that on 6 April 1575, some six or seven months after the foregoing of common rights in Lydd, a 'Special Guestling' (a form of Brodhull) was held and its proceedings were recorded in Lydd's assembly book. The latter recorded a decree which enacted that that during elections for bailiff in the Cinque Ports or their members, if any commoner voted for anyone other than a jurat in the port – that is, anyone other than a member of the permanent government – they were to be fined 40s. The implication of this decree, of course, is that some or many of the commoners, even though the number of commoners eligible to vote had been greatly reduced, were flagrantly upsetting this procedure in choosing someone outside of the government, possibly one of their favourites of the like of Arnold Barrowe. Barrowe in fact appears again in 1584, presented in court 'for an idle and suspicious person'.[28] The decree of 1575 also implies that a great deal of discontent was being felt even among the narrow range of commoners eligible to vote. It was these same commoners who as jurors had been presenting the jurats and big farmers in Lydd's court for infringing the statutes of the crown to no effect for the previous eight years at least. It is probably not a coincidence therefore that after 1575 the jury presentments cease to be recorded in the assembly book, if they were allowed to take place at all, and the only business exacted was that concerning allocations for ale houses and apprenticeships. The presentments return again in 1582 to coincide with the trial at Westminster of Godfrey and Berry.

The decades that followed the widespread rebellions between 1548 and 1551 saw a continuity of the class hatred witnessed then. Some outbursts by Kentish men caused them to be hauled before the quarter sessions. In 1568 a prophecy circulated in Kent foretelling that whoever still lived after the next year had passed 'shall not see one gentleman in England who was not killed or spoiled'. In 1584 Ralph Watson of Dover allegedly said that, 'this is a very evil land to live in except for a man with a very good occupation. I wish there was war. I know a great many rich men in the land; I would have some of their money if it were to come to pass'. Ten years later a Thomas Delman allegedly said that 'he did hope to see the rich churls pulled out of their houses and to see them together by the ears in England before next Candlemas day'.[29]

---

28   EKAC, Ly/Qs 1, p. 117.
29   Cited in Wood 2005, p. 171.

In conclusion, the thesis that there was a hiatus in engrossment and enclosure in England between 1530 and 1580 cannot be reconciled with the foregoing evidence of Browne's case against Godfrey and Berry, and with the cases brought by the jurors of Lydd against many other big farmers in these years. The resistance, legal and non-legal, made largely by those outside of the class of yeomen and gentry farmers and their 'lease-mongers' in this period, appears to have failed, just like the resistance in the 1460s against engrossment and enclosure that was described in the previous chapter failed. There is no indication that *any* element of the anti-enclosure statutes of the period between the 1530s and 1570s gained *any* traction in Lydd and its region. Robert Allen's contention that these statutes halted the earlier enclosure movement in its tracks and issued in during the seventeenth century a new golden age for English peasants is mistaken. The entirely opposite argument by Keith Wrightson that this hiatus meant that it was in the post-1580 period that the decisive steps towards agrarian capitalism were taken as the floodgates to enclosure were opened up again also does not sit well with the unusually good survival of evidence for Lydd and Romney Marsh. By 1580 agrarian capitalism was secure there. Historians should look again at Wordie's statistics on enclosure in the sixteenth century and make a recalculation which incorporates the consolidation of 'old enclosure', such as that in Kent, which amounted to 45 percent of England.

iii Postscript: Developments in the Seventeenth Century

Using comprehensive records that survive for the Level of Romney Marsh above the Rhee Wall in the period between 1587 and 1705, especially in the mid-seventeenth century, Stephen Hipkin reveals further increases in the size of farms and the reduction of the number of holders during the course of the seventeenth century. The majority of farms in the Level in contrast to the area below the Rhee Wall which contained Lydd were occupied by non-resident farmers. This was already the case, as Guildford said, in the 1520s, and so there was continuity in this phenomenon. In the late sixteenth and early seventeenth centuries, people who inhabited settlements within the Marsh Level accounted for about two-fifths of the occupiers. Many of these were smallholders supplementing other trades such as fishing. The figure was only a third by the end of the seventeenth century. While non-resident occupiers were spread all over Kent, the vast majority lived on the 'uplands' within 10 miles of their holdings. The attraction was rich sheep pastures. Of 24 inventories from the early seventeenth century only two mention grain crops and sheep dominated cattle by a ratio of 12:1.[30] In the early seventeenth century, those sheep graziers with over 500 sheep mostly resided within 10 miles of their holdings. The town of Ashford and its hinterland contained the wealthiest Romney Marsh sheep graziers whose wealth lay predominantly in the Level. Holdings were frequently between 200 and 300 acres. In 1687 Humphrey Wighwicke of Ashford, the occupier of 230 acres, held over 3,000 sheep and his inventory included another sum of over £3,000 he had received for corn, wool and other stock already sold. Henry Deedes of Hythe in 1699 owned 4,000 sheep spread across 561 acres in the Level and 749 acres in Walland Marsh. Another farmer of Tenterden occupied 981 acres within the level in 1650 and Hipkin thinks his inventory 'would have made good reading indeed' with regard to the number of sheep he farmed – it was not illegal by this time to farm over 2,000 sheep. George Witherden of Bethersden, occupier of 196 acres in Brenzett and Great Sedbrook in 1654 left 1,958 sheep and 86 cattle in 1670.

New Romney, three miles to the north of Lydd, was also 'home to some very substantial tenant farmers': flocks of over 900 sheep were kept in the 1660s by Jeremy Standford who held 111 acres in 1654, and Stephen Brett who held 163 acres in the same year. Hipkin says these 'were large by Jacobean standards, but modest by comparison with the 2,046 sheep possessed by fellow townsman Robert Wilcocke in 1665. Five years later, Thomas Chalker who held over 300 acres in 1654 left 3,526 sheep and 31 cattle. Hipkin concludes that a '[d]ecayed and depopulated town it may have been, but post-Restoration New Romney contained residents whose inventorial wealth dwarfed that of most of Canterbury's leading citizens', the latter being a main county town. Brett and Standford each left goods valued at more than £1,000, and Wilcocke's inventory was assessed at £1,829 and Chalker's at £2,989.

Hipkin has detected significant changes in the structure of landholding on the Level of Romney Marsh north of the Rhee Wall during the seventeenth century, although we must put this into the context of the massive and more qualitative changes that had taken place in the previous 150 years. In the late sixteenth and early seventeenth centuries those holding more than 200 acres occupied a fifth of the land. By the early 1650s they held a third, and by the beginning of the eighteenth century they farmed more than two fifths of the Level: '[t]he increase took place principally at the expense of middling groups of occupiers holding 20–99.5 acres' and occurred mainly in second quarter of the seventeenth century when the number of smaller – middling holders – fell by 25 percent. Larger and middling occupiers were farming similar proportions of Marsh in the late sixteenth and early seventeenth centuries, but by 1650 larger farmers occupied nearly twice as much. By 1705 there were just

---

30   Hipkin 2000, p. 662.

69 occupiers of less than 10 acres in the Level.[31] There was a 24 percent reduction in the number of occupiers between 1587 and 1705 and the main changes occurred in the earlier period when the population was rising rapidly. This meant a 33 percent increase in the mean average of acres held by each occupier. The average sheep flock was treble the size of flocks elsewhere in Kent in the early seventeenth century, and five times the size by the end of the century. We must remember however that those who held the large flocks on the Level also had smaller flocks in the upland areas where they resided. The causes of this consolidation may be seen in the rising rents and rising Marsh taxation. Rents rose from 8s per acre in 1570 to 12s by 1600, then sharply to a common experience of 20s by the 1610s, although often more.[32] Marsh scots (taxation for the maintenance of drainage and sea defence) that were set by committees of the larger holders rose higher than prices. The annual burden of wall-scot payments on occupiers rose from less than 1s per acre in the mid-1580s to 2s 6d by the 1620s and to 3s 6d in the early 1640s and early 1650s when large sums were spent on Dymchurch Wall which held back the sea on the eastern edge of the Level. There were drainage maintenance costs on top of this of 10d per acre in 1630s. So a middling tenant holding 50 acres had to find £9 per year merely for local tax.[33]

As we have seen in the previous chapter, in the 1520s at least a handful of Lydd's resident jurats would not have felt out of place in the Level in the mid-seventeenth century. In the 1580s even more of Lydd's farmers matched the remarkable wealth of the largest farmers of the Level from New Romney, Hythe and Ashford in the middle of the seventeenth century. By the 1580s, in terms of assessed wealth, Lydd had overtaken its historically much larger mercantile neighbour New Romney. Traditionally New Romney was charged with supplying five ships per year for the service of the Crown in return for its Cinque Port privileges, and Lydd had to contribute one given its limited size, wealth and relatively minor mercantile function. In 1588 a letter from the privy council of the Tudor state was sent to a number of tax assessors in relation to Cinque Port service and it ordered that Lydd 'should be taxed to the charge of shipping by ability and not according to any former composition' between Lydd and New Romney. This was because Lydd 'is presently in far better estate than it was in old times than New Romney is'.[34]

---

31   Hipkin 2000, p. 666.
32   Hipkin 2000, p. 667.
33   Hipkin 2000, p. 670.
34   Cited in Draper and Meddens 2009, p. 58.

Hipkin's evidence reveals that further engrossment of these already very large holdings and the proliferation of very large farmers also occurred south of the Rhee Wall – including Lydd – during the seventeenth century with a dozen people farming over 500 acres each among the 19,500 acres of Dengemarsh and Walland Marsh in 1699, and we know that some of them were farming a lot more than this 120 years earlier. More than a fifth of holders were farming over a hundred acres. The mean average of holdings in Dengemarsh and Walland was 83.7 acres compared to 66.9 acres within the Level.[35] Nevertheless the picture is of the prominence of very large capitalist farmers in the whole of the Romney Marsh and its region by the 1580s. Contrary to Hipkin's conclusion that his seventeenth-century evidence reveals the chronology of the emergence of the large tenant farmer of Romney Marsh, it is clear that these tenants had emerged a century before the period of his study begins: he has just traced further the logic of their existence.

---

35   Hipkin 2000, p. 674.

CHAPTER 13

Legitimising Social Transformation: The Festival of St. George

The rise of capitalist yeomen farmers and their counterparts in rural industry from the middle of the fifteenth century is central to discussions in the debate on the transition from feudalism to capitalism. Yet their political base in local government and connections to wider patronage networks is not sufficiently appreciated. To remedy this deficiency I have in previous chapters stressed the significance of office holding and developments in oligarchy in rural and small town society by the early sixteenth century. Even less understood is the potential of new distinct cultural productions to be associated with the economic and political successes of these farmers and clothiers. Was it possible for these new men to rule effectively in the first half of the sixteenth century through their monopoly of local government and patronage from greater gentry alone; particularly given the nature of the social transformation in the previous few generations, and the economic crisis in the 1520s? A major development took place in Lydd during years of economic crisis in the 1520s and early 1530s, and that was the development of a new play. In what follows I argue that the play and the four-day-long festival with which it was associated was developed for the purposes of legitimising the new regime in the eyes of the recently dispossessed population.

On 15 June 1532 two clerks of Lydd, Nicholas Pyx and Thomas Hewet, came to the borough court of Lydd and made the following deposition:

> John Bacon of Lydd said to them on Saint George's day last past [23 April 1532] that Thomas Strogull was a cankered churl and always envious against the said John Bacon; and moreover he said that if Thomas Strogull had got what he deserved he would have long before this time spoken even more fitting words.[1]

Following this entry in the court book is a plea made by Strogull himself that Bacon had acted 'contrary to the peace'. Bacon was destitute and died within the year, and his widow's poverty was such that she was unable to pay the town tax.[2] The little we know of Bacon is as follows. He was a freeman of the town

---

1   EKAC, Ly/JB 3, p. 47.
2   EKAC, Ly/fac 2, p. 191.

and he was paid with two others in 1512 to take up a ship in the king's service. He was therefore at least 40 years of age and a mariner or fisherman. William Cheyney, a leather maker from Hastings in East Sussex, owed him certain tools in 1530 and this indicates that he may also have had other skills.[3] The court record reveals that like so many others in Lydd he had often been in debt in the previous two decades, and some of these debts were quite substantial, including £4 6d 8d owed to Robert Horseley in 1519, £1 4s 6d to John Caxton in 1518, and £3 4d to James Robyn junior in 1530. In 1527 he, like many others identified in Chapter Eleven, began to have his town tax abated due to his inability to pay. It was abated for the minimum assessment for a freeman of 2d in 1527 and for 2d in 1528, and after this he was forgiven it due to his lack of means. A few years later in 1530 his poverty may have deepened because he was now forced to sell or pawn a laten basin, and the following year he had a fishing net appraised in the court for 5s in order to pay a debt. In the court held on 1 June 1532 – two weeks before Strogull's plea against him – he had a plea of trespass and a plea of debt brought against him. The magnitude of the debt is not recorded but the plea was brought by Sir Edward Guildford, knight, a leading member of the county gentry. It is curious that such a destitute man had such a relationship with Guildford, unless via intermediaries. It is also curious why Strogull's plea against Bacon was made almost two months after the offence was committed; and not least its juxtaposition to Guildford's plea. Strogull was, as we have seen in Chapter Eleven, one of the wealthiest men in Lydd, a multiple leaseholder and permanent member of the town oligarchy.

The context of Bacon's deepening poverty was the economic crisis which became worse from the middle of the 1520s. His outburst in April 1532 against Strogull took place five months after two other jurats had had their houses burned down. One of those acts was carried out by a man on the poor list. The economic crisis was apparently therefore causing a crisis of authority in the town. Bacon's insult took place on St. George's Day, a day when there would almost certainly have been some form of civic pageantry involving a procession by the elite of the town followed perhaps by other forms of drama, display and merriment. The word 'churl' that Bacon used to describe Strogull strikes me as important here because as well as being a simple term of abuse it would appear to de-legitimise Strogull's authority in the government, and on a day of ritual that might be designed to reinforce that authority. Andy Wood has found this term or phrases such as 'rich churl' frequently used in the sixteenth century against rich farmers. He suggests however that it was a *late* sixteenth-century phenomenon and that it marks a period when there was a decline in

---

3   EKAC, Ly/fac 2, p. 4; EKAC, Ly/JB 3, p. 21.

insurrection. The cause of this decline, he argues, was that these big fish in local communities no longer led rebellions against the gentry and had by this time come to associate with the latter in terms of both wealth and culture.[4] I argued in Chapter Six above that this separation had occurred much earlier and that the term was also used much earlier: Bacon's use of it in 1532 is another example of this.

Bacon's insult was more complex than a simple expression of class hatred. Coupled with the term 'churl' he used the terms 'cankered' and 'envious'. In the early modern period 'canker' could refer to corruption of mind or body, even of the body politic; but when it was associated with envy the suggestion was that a person was eating themselves from within with jealousy. It may well be that a more personal conflict between Strogull and Bacon was involved here and one cannot discount the possibility that personal animosities determined the whole of Bacon's meaning. Nevertheless the context of the disturbance during the crisis, Bacon's destitution, Strogull's great wealth and political position, and the symbolic nature of the day in which the disturbance took place should lead one to explore further. The symbolism of the day is particularly significant because during the crisis years the government of Lydd developed a new play incorporating a four-day festival of St. George which was eventually performed in 1533, the year – and almost certainly to the day – following Bacon's distur-bance. Before looking in detail at this development in Lydd it will be necessary first of all to provide some context of the nature of drama and spectacle in late medieval England.

While having substantial disagreements over the essence of social relations in the larger towns in the late fourteenth and fifteenth centuries, historians who have attempted to understand the social dynamics behind late medieval festivals and drama and other aspects of civic pageantry such as town founda-tion legends, myths, rituals and spectacles welcoming royal progresses, town entries and the like, recognise that they originate essentially within the ideo-logical ruminations of the ruling elite and are employed to a greater or lesser extent in their interests.[5] Hence Phythian-Adams, while laying great emphasis on what he perceives as the consensual, harmonious nature of urban social relations and urban cultural productions, concedes that 'many of the ceremo-nies instituted in the late fourteenth and fifteenth centuries, one suspects, were incidentally contrivances by the elite to enhance their position and so to preserve the social order on which their influence rested'; and Kermode, in a more recent study which identifies more generic structural conflict in the

---

4   Wood 2007, p. 204.

5   Anglo 1969; Phythian-Adams 1979; James 1983; Rubin 1991; Kermode 1998.

larger mercantile towns in this period, views these ceremonies as 'propagandist displays' and asserts that '[l]ocating the plays and the processions ... within the evidence of resistance and conflict surrounding them, makes it difficult to see them as anything other than politicised rituals reflecting the interests of the ruling groups of both city government and craft guilds'.[6] This latter point echoes other studies of urban ceremony as developed from the late fourteenth century, and has been made even more forcefully in terms of the 'political culture' of *post*-Reformation towns.[7]

Gervase Rosser reminds us that such media cannot be seen as simply in the political ownership of the dominant urban elite, because once in the public domain they provided a framework for negotiation between different social groups or classes that could empower those outside of official and economically successful circles. He prefers to see in this framework for negotiation a functional process in which all sectional and individual expressions may coexist in a 'positive' way – that is, in a contained way, 'within the dignity of a rich and common language'.[8] But this empowerment often facilitated through explicitly subversive interpretations and re-enactments of such media can also be seen as an *oppositional* force. This was something that was particularly significant and transparent in the struggle for symbolic authority or cultural hegemony in times of acute social disturbance such as that witnessed in the anti-processions at Bury St Edmonds and St Albans in 1381, at Norwich in the 1440s, and in the three anonymous bills nailed to Coventry's town hall in the 1490s. The latter called for the beheading of 'the rich churls' in the government who had appropriated the symbol of the town's identity, Lady Godiva, as a means of expressing the political dominance of their own merchant guilds.[9]

The rising dominance of the big merchants in the larger English towns such as Coventry and York – it occurred much earlier in the other provincial towns – and their related cultural productions, long predates that of the clothiers, yeomanry and minor gentry. The emergence of the latter becomes more noticeable by the late fifteenth and early sixteenth centuries when they increasingly dominated the countryside and small towns as a result of engrossment and enclosure.[10] The strategies which this new class employed with

---

6   Phythian-Adams 1969, p. 275; Kermode 1998, pp. 65–6.

7   McRee 1994; Lindenbaum 1994; Tittler 1998.

8   Rosser 2000, p. 369.

9   Dobson 1983, p. 236; Faith 1981; Hudson and Tingay 1906–10, pp. 328–56; Harris 1971, p. 567.

10   Dyer, 1980, chapter 17; Dyer 1994, pp. 424–9; Kumin 1996, pp. 238–9; Zell 1994; McIntosh 1998.

regard to cultural production in order to generate consent for its emerging authority are not at all obvious, and yet they potentially implicate a larger section of the population than the provincial urban merchants, and in a period of greater significance for social transformation.

Ronald Hutton, after an extensive trawling of fifteenth-century local church-wardens' accounts, and related sources from mostly rural and small town parishes, has found voluminous evidence for the introduction, geographical spread and elaboration of rituals and customs such as those relating to lords of misrule, Robin Hood, hocktide, midsummer watches, church ales and St. George. On this basis he has argued for 'the rise of merry England' during the fifteenth century. He also points to an increasing number of travelling groups of players and musicians by the early decades of the following century. The reason for this rise in activity for him is largely intractable, but he chooses to fall back on an interpretation which views these apparent developments simply in terms of an increasing general 'taste' for performance and ceremonial 'along traditional lines' in this period, only to be dampened down from above during the Reformation.[11] While it will be contested that Hutton's findings seem on the face of it dictated by the appearance of a new source (churchwardens' accounts) in the fifteenth century, Beat Kumin argues that the correlations between this increase in documented ritual activity and the development of parish institutions as well as the well-known communal 'spending spree' on church building – which is also well documented for Lydd as we have seen – are too striking to ignore. Using a range of comparative case studies, Kumin associates this apparent rise and spread of activity with an enhanced village self-assertiveness and *communal* motivation towards self-government in the context of a favourable socio-economic climate in the fifteenth century, during the golden age of the English peasantry. This was, he argues, before the enclosure movement had widened divisions in rural society towards the end of that century, and created social problems that were exacerbated by population and inflationary pressures in the period between 1520 and 1540 in which parish incomes, including those funds raised from church sales, peaked and declined.[12] Against Hutton, Kumin argues that this decline cannot be attributed to evangelical causes against Catholic rites because the latter only become evident in the 1530s, by which time incomes from traditional activities had already fallen markedly.

Kumin's interpretation is convincing, and it is indeed difficult to detect the particular pre-occupations of a narrow elite stratum within this increase in

---

11   Hutton 1994.
12   Kumin 1996.

ritual activity in these less socially differentiated communities in the fifteenth century. We could of course loosely speculate that this increasing activity may have been encouraged (with unpredictable results) as a means to social cohesion and control at a time of social and demographic restructuring, and particularly by the end of the century when the increasing social distance of the elite began to tell in the changing structures of authority. However, it is not the purpose of this study to deny the potential for the autonomous expression and organisation of the majority of people whose life experiences were outside of or marginal to elite circles.

Alternatively we may look for the potential cultural offspring of this emerging local authority within the dramatic political and cultural changes in and from the 1530s, display being largely refashioned into more sanitised and secularised formats, drama becoming more explicitly political if allowed at all. The potential relationship between this refashioning of cultural production, puritan ideology, and an emerging capitalist nexus with an uncluttered disposition towards religious and other social and economic practices has, of course, long been recognised. Indeed McIntosh, who has recently identified a strong relationship between the heightened concern over social 'misbehaviour' at the local level in England from the 1460s and 1470s, peaking in the 1520s and 1530s, and this emerging authority of 'the middling sort' in economically advanced areas and along important trade routes, has pointed to a determinate relationship between changing social practice and religious ideology in the sixteenth century.[13]

Bearing these arguments in mind, the rest of this chapter will focus on the development and performance of an unprecedented play at Lydd and explore its origins and purpose. The townspeople of Lydd had already been performing a St. George play from 1456 at the latest, before the social transformation.[14] Players and bann criers from Lydd visited other towns such as nearby Rye and New Romney and likewise received players and other performers from elsewhere. These visiting performers played under the auspices of royalty and aristocracy, and of town and village assemblies. In addition to the St. George play, Lydd and New Romney performed the traditional rituals of what Hutton described as 'Merry England' in each other's towns such as 'mays', lords of misrule and boy bishops. The first may of Lydd was recorded at New Romney in 1422.[15] These rituals involved a combination of the rites of fertility and rituals of social inversion known as 'the world turned upside down'.

---

13   McIntosh 1998, pp. 1–19, 210–11.

14   EKAC, Ly/fac 1, p. 46.

15   Hutton 1994, pp. 12, 29.

The relatively small amounts of money given to players and other performers as expenses in food and drink, often 6s 8d, suggests that these performances
were limited in scope and probably come under the umbrella of what is usually described as 'parish drama' – that is, small parish fund-raising activities,
like modern day fêtes. In the fifteenth century Lydd experienced between one
and five of these visiting performances each year, but there was an explosion in
numbers between 1516–7 and 1521–2 when no less than 67 groups came – an
average of over 11 in each of these years. These years almost exactly represent a
temporary hiatus in the crown's military exploits, and the increasing numbers
of travelling players at that time may reflect their political and diplomatic
importance – royal progresses in microcosm perhaps. Although we do not
know by which authority the earlier Lydd St. George play was chosen, the town
would no doubt have been pleased with its patronage of this particular saint as
a diplomatic and civic identity, because it was in 'Lydd' – according to *The
Golden Legend* – that George was buried, albeit in a place with the same name
in the classical East in the early fourth century.[16] Lydd's particular vulnerability
to attack from the sea, especially from the French, also made St. George a natural symbol for its identity, and perhaps rendered the collective disposition of
the commoners more receptive to nationalistic overtones as well.

It is at the same time that Lydd becomes swamped by visiting performers
that we are first introduced to some stirrings of activity that suggest changes in
the nature of performance were also being planned. Play books appear to have
become politicised and were withdrawn into official custody. In 1520–1 4s was
paid to Thomas Buntyng, town clerk, 'for the book of the play of St. George
which he said that he wrote himself', and 11s 6d to a certain Boson 'in reward
for bringing the said book of the Saint George's play in to the custody of the
town again, from where it was in the keeping of other men'.[17] The same occurred
at New Romney four years earlier in 1516 when 'Le Pleyboke' was delivered to
the common clerk, 'there, safely and securely to be kept to the use and behoof
of the said town'. The following year in 1517 the Lord Warden of the Cinque
Ports ordered that the jurats of New Romney 'ought not to play the play of the
Passion of Christ until they had the king's leave', and perhaps similar conditions of censorship were applied to Lydd and its St. George play, if a little later
(1520–1) for the less prestigious smaller town.[18] Then between 1526–7 and
1532–3 we find that a new play book was being worked upon against a back-
drop of meetings, mostly in London, between the leading jurats and clerks of

16   Di Voragine 1998, chapter twenty nine.
17   EKAC, Ly/fac 2, p. 56.
18   HMC 1896, p. 552.

Lydd and a certain Master Richard Gibson.[19] Gibson is understandably lauded by the historian of Tudor spectacle, because as sergeant of the royal tents and pillar of the 'Revels' department in the royal court, he was directly responsible for the magnificence of practically all of Henry VIII's festivals, tournaments, royal receptions and town entries until 1534, including the famous 'Field of the Cloth of Gold' in France in 1520, most of the evidence for which comes down to us in his accounts. From a lowly court interlude player in his youth, he was able to accomplish the ambitious projects of spectacular propaganda set for him by the Lord Chancellor Thomas Wolsey, projects that were crucial for the projection of the image of the young monarch in the further consolidation of the Tudor dynasty and in order to raise the relatively undistinguished national profile of England on the continent. Gibson also managed in the 1520s and 1530s to be solicitor of the Cinque Ports and jurat and MP for New Romney – to which Lydd was attached of course as a Cinque Port limb – and he counselled that town in its own substantial passion play in these years as well.[20]

Because 3s 4d was paid 'for three barrels of single beer on the first three play days and a firkyn the last play day' (no doubt set aside for the jurats), we can conclude that the performance at Lydd in 1533 was spread over four days.[21] Gibson's involvement, and the knowledge and materials at his disposal, imply that this was probably a very significant occasion, and one which no doubt attracted people from some distance and of some status. It may well be the case that the performance was indeed intended for the region as a whole, and that Lydd was chosen as a suitable location.

Remembering that the old play book was withdrawn into the custody of the town in 1520–1 at the outset of the meetings with Gibson, the chamberlains' account of 1526–7 records that 2s 4d was 'paid for a new book for "the lyfe of Saynt George"', and because the account after the performance in 1533 records a part payment of 3s to Lydd clerk Nicholas Purfote 'for writing the play book', and that this new book cost only 2s 4d, we might conclude that what was being referred to was a book of clean paper ready to be filled with the new text of 'the lyfe of Saynt George', or a version thereof.[22]

Regarding the content of this new playbook, I would tentatively wish to speculate that this new text may have derived in some form from Alexander

19   EKAC, Ly/fac 2, pp. 119–82.

20   Anglo, 1968, Volume II, Appendix III; Anglo, 1969, pp. 164, 179, 261; Bindoff 1982, Volume II, p. 207; Gibson 1996, p. 144.

21   EKAC, Ly/fac 2, p. 175.

22   EKAC, Ly/fac 2, pp. 122, 182.

Barclay's book of the *same name and spelling* as the account entry in 1526–7 and which was printed in 1515 by Pinson, Henry VIII's official printer.[23] This text is over 10 times the length of any other known contemporary St. George text in English, and it has a structure and a striking dramatic style that could relatively easily be made consistent with the cultural production in question.[24] Based on *The Golden Legend* version it splits nicely into four parts: first, the early life of George as a knight with superhuman qualities and his conversion to Christianity; second, the well known story of the dragon and the virgin; third, the transformation of George into a poor friar where he undergoes horrific torture under Dacian, a pagan tyrant; and finally, the events surrounding his final martyrdom and the death of Dacian. The text contains many dramatic confrontations, many interesting characters involved in long verbal exchanges, simple but visual and moving allegorical scenes, popular sermonising, and sections of commentary that could be accomplished by a standard chorus or messenger. With the language accessible and the tableaux nature of the descriptive text it is virtually a popular play as it stands. Also interesting is that the book seems to be referring to itself in some respects, *encouraging* performance and display. For example, after the dragon devil was slain, the people baptised, the land made fertile and the rivers full of fish, murals were painted on the walls of the saved city, a play was developed, and images of George and the virgin (the king's daughter) were constructed as memorials.

Designed to excite devotion for England's patron saint particularly among English youth and glorify the nation by showing 'Example of constancy, during extreme hardship', the book also delivers a crude xenophobic message, even at one point setting George above King Arthur, the latter being king of the British rather than of the English. The text is clearly relevant to the contemporary context of war and increasing poverty in Lydd as it exalts the traditional medieval and feudal themes of holy poverty and holy chivalry, stressing the moral equality between the two, and championing the qualities of faithfulness, meekness, and patience exemplified in George's martyrdom as the people's weapons against extreme and unimaginable suffering. The stress is also on unity between all ranks of society and a national common purpose and identity for all subjects. This sense of unity is illustrated in the scenes where all classes are equally responsible for drawing lots and providing the dragon with human sacrifices from their own class in order to divert the evil influence it has over the city. In addition, and equally important, the accountability of government and

---

23   Nelson 1960.
24   D'Evelyn and Foster 1970, pp. 410–57.

royalty to the people is promulgated as the king not surprisingly has second thoughts and wavers when his own daughter is chosen. He eventually bows to the 'grutching and murmuring' of the 'whole community', who require him to be a 'partner in their pain'.

The author Alexander Barclay, ironically a Scot, was close to the royal court and would also undoubtedly have known Gibson and probably worked with him commissioned as he (Barclay) was at the Field of Cloth of Gold, 'to devise stories and appropriate verities to flourish the buildings and banquet house'.[25] But even if this speculation concerning the relationship between Barclay's text and the performance of the St. George play in Lydd in 1533 is denied as too risky, it can be conceded that the outline of Barclay's vastly extended story and its themes, if in a less didactic and inflammatory form, are still provided in *The Golden Legend*, a version the town governors would almost certainly have known of because medieval churches were required to have one. Indeed Lydd's churchwardens' accounts record that a 'legente' was purchased for 12s in 1521 – the year Lydd's playbook was withdrawn into custody – and this almost certainly refers to the same book of Saints' lives.[26]

Referring to the Field of Cloth of Gold, the organisation and construction of which Gibson played such an important role, Sydney Anglo has asserted that 'The display and propaganda of 1520 seem, amidst the political machinations of the great powers, like some colossal anachronistic game which all the monarchs, all their ministers, and all their retinues had decided to play... The whole affair – with its romantic palaces and pavilions, its costly tournaments, and sumptuous banquets – seems a late flowering of the most extravagant medieval chivalry', and where 'every chivalric cliché was encountered'.[27] In an illuminating study of royal performance and the meaning of ritual, although of a later period, David Cannadine has argued that in times of change, crisis and dislocation, the 'preservation of anachronism' can act as 'a unifying symbol of permanence' and create a sense of 'national community'.[28] The anachronistic content of Barclay's text, as with other aspects of Tudor performance and ritual, may indeed have been charged with this function while at the same time providing a crucial, if mythical, historical basis for the regime's legitimacy.

At this stage of the analysis one could argue that the ideological origin of this cultural production at Lydd was the Tudor court or state. We can point to

---

25   Anglo 1969, p. 143; Fox 1989, pp. 37–55.
26   Finn 1912, p. 334.
27   Anglo 1969, p. 168.
28   Cannadine 1983, p. 122.

the explosion of those royal progresses in microcosm mentioned above from 1516, the state's lack of tolerance for unregulated performance in this region from the same year, the need to generate consent for the consolidation of its dynasty, its militaristic policy and its centralising tendencies, and of course the direct involvement of the royal court in the play in the form of Gibson – who also came to watch. However, most of the evidence we have of the play's organisation stems from the government of Lydd itself, and it would be premature to attribute too much to the state in this respect. It is true that the state may have had a hand in the sudden appearance of a rigid oligarchic governmental structure in Lydd around 1512. As Peter Clark has argued, the crown particularly wished to penetrate the freedoms and power centres of the Cinque Ports that were notoriously independent and yet crucial for the defence of the realm.[29] But this new oligarchy was also a creature of the social changes that had occurred within the previous couple of generations, and its rapid accumulations of wealth through agrarian capitalisation in the local manors and beyond by some of its members and its ancestors from the 1460s seriously implicated it in the acuteness of the crisis being experienced in the 1520s and 1530s. With regard to this crisis one is drawn into reading the evidence in the chamberlains' accounts as a form of narrative, and along with the developments for the play from 1526 the different aspects of its ominous developments fuse together in the narrative and appear entirely related. We need only to recall these developments and their tight chronology that have been presented in detail in Chapter Eleven. There could not be a closer congruity between the chronology of evidence for the economic crisis and for that of the play.

When the old play book was withdrawn in 1526 the oligarchy had only been in place for 14 years. The economic crisis and undoubtedly the political changes that had recently taken place limiting official participation generated social unrest across the Cinque Ports and this unrest was directed against the central governments of the towns in numerous ways. In 1526 the minutes of the Brodhull which was made up of representatives of these central governments record,

> that recently in many towns or in all of them there has been great dissentions, variances, vexations and trouble in choosing the king's head officers as mayors, bailiffs and jurats of every one of the said towns, not only at the day of election accustomed and used but also before the day in bands of unlawful confederacy and unlawful assemblies; and after the

---

29   Clark 1977, p. 20.

day by disdain and other great displeasures and grudges ... to the high
displeasure of almighty god and also breaking and disturbing of the king's
peace and against true justice to the great abusing and unquietness of the
well disposed [as in, 'wealthy'] people of the said towns, and also to the
great slander rebuke and decay of the said towns.[30]

Add to the economic and political crisis the threat of war and one may conclude that the authority of the oligarchy of new men was under threat. Hence
a possible attempt to appease a recently dispossessed population through such
ideological concessions as moral equality, accountable government, and unity
and common purpose as English people in defending the realm against demon-
ised foreigners – themes that were probably expressed in the performance or
spectacle of 1533 at Lydd. The St. George play at Lydd in 1533 can therefore be
seen as an interface between local and national politics, and something that in
many ways expressed the needs of the emerging structures of authority at both
levels, structures while in certain respects contradictory at this stage were
clearly complementary in others. Local governing groups, exemplified by the
jurats of Lydd, desired freedom in the processes of agrarian accumulation
through enclosure and engrossment and an increase in power at this level with
which to facilitate these interests. For stability at least, the Tudor state was
keen to keep these processes in check as the numerous anti-enclosure statutes
from 1489 bear witness, and yet in broadening the ruling class to include these
improving local groups it was reliant on their compliance in order to extend its
power in the provinces, neutralise the political ambitions of the aristocratic
feudal elite with which it was in competition, and create a more centralised
polity.

The answer to the question as to whether this cultural development was
successful and legitimised the new regime is more difficult. The subsequent
history of increasing political controls on the poor and disenfranchised in
Lydd, and serious legal challenges against the town's wealthiest inhabitants
and leading governors in the second half of the sixteenth century, reflects the
transparency of, and continued opposition to, the dispossession of both the
economic and political power of peasant society. That transparency was so
clear that I suspect it would need more than appeals to national unity to legitimise previous and ongoing dispossession. What this play represents is the dispossession of something else, namely the political expression of peasant
communities through cultural means, and this would have been damaging to

---

30   CKS, CP/B 1, pp. 206–7.

peasant social solidarities and the capacity of peasants to resist ongoing enclosure. Nevertheless, the new elites would have to rule without consent and face the consequences of what has been termed 'dominance without hegemony'.[31]

---

31   For a stimulating discussion of this concept with regard to state building by English, French and Indian bourgeoisies following the revolutions of 1642–8, 1789–1815 and 1947 respectively, see Chibber 2013, chapters two to four.

Conclusion

The essential difference between feudalism and capitalism lies, as Marx said, in the mode in which surplus labour is extracted from the producer. This mode takes fundamentally political or non-economic forms in feudalism and absolutism, and fundamentally economic forms in capitalism. The surplus is extracted from peasants by political force in feudalism and absolutism. In capitalism landless wage workers are compelled by market forces to give up their surplus to capitalist entrepreneurs.

This book has been concerned with how these distinct, structurally robust societies, were undermined, and with how the process of a transition from one to another began and was sustained. Following Robert Brenner's thesis my answer lies in the forms of struggle that were generated within feudal social-property relations. The origin of the process which set in train the transition to capitalism in England in the late medieval period was the unintended consequence of conflicting rules for reproduction both within and between the fundamental classes in feudalism, the peasants and lords. The debate over the northern Netherlands aside, the transition in England, a country which was relatively poorly developed commercially in the late medieval period, was the exception among other European feudal states. The origin of its exceptional characteristics can be traced back to the *comparatively* cohesive nature of its decentralised feudal lordships and monarchy that became established during the so-called 'Feudal Revolution' in the tenth and eleventh centuries, and the consequential logic of conflicting rules for reproduction between lords and peasants.

The crisis of feudalism in the early fourteenth century resulted from these conflicting rules for reproduction. In England peasant production was undermined by feudal lordship through its jurisdictional imperatives, the imposition of comparatively high levels of peasant enserfment after the Norman Conquest and in the decades around 1200, and the maintenance of these impositions during the thirteenth century. The origin of capitalism was aided by the comparatively greater controls English lords had over peasant tenure and over a very large proportion of England's productive land in the form of their comparatively large demesnes. While lords and state failed to pin back wage levels and maintain serfdom following the Black Death, lords were able to lease out their large home farms to wealthy peasants for temporary insecure terms and replace secure heritable – although hated – villein tenures with temporary insecure copyholds. This ability contrasted with the much smaller demesnes at the disposal of French and German lords and the hold the French and German peasants maintained on the land as relatively free proprietors protected by the state.

The origin of capitalism in England was driven by the mutual interests of lords and their increasingly large tenants. It was characterised by the symbiotic rise from the middle third of the fifteenth century of both a commercial land-lord class or capitalist aristocracy and a capitalist yeoman class. Capitalism was not driven from below by a revolutionary peasantry desiring to break the feudal fetters and create capitalism. While the peasantry desired to remove serfdom and even lordship as a whole, and improve their standard of living by accumulating modest amounts of land after the Black Death, the majority were bitterly opposed to large-scale engrossment and enclosure by the farmers and lords because it destroyed their long fought-for customs, undermined their means of subsistence, and created political imbalances locally. Although the transition was not simply lord-centred or lord-directed, it was effectively a top-down imposition by lords and their tenant farmers and manorial officials who together – sometimes autonomously and sometimes in collaboration – represented a new form of seigneurial authority. As such capitalism developed within the shell of the lords' developing capitalist estate system. The state – monarchy and aristocratic privy council – sought to check depopulation and damaging overspecialisation from the late fifteenth century. However the privy council itself included major enclosers, and by the late sixteenth century the state as a whole, including the monarchy, began to see the benefits of large scale enclosure of its domains. In doing so it bet its interests on the future of the new social-property structure even while the monarchy naturally remained fatally wedded to its maintenance of extra-economic powers.

The stimuli for the origin of capitalism in England were the decline of serf-dom and the increasing assertiveness of the peasantry following the rebellion of 1381, the development of copyhold from villein tenure, and the widespread transfer of 20 to 30 percent of the best land in England into the hands of the wealthiest peasants in the decades around 1400. For the majority of the subsis-tent peasantry, the first half of the fifteenth century has been described as a golden age, characterised as it was by the removal of servile disabilities and humiliations, high wages, low prices and available land. The widespread engrossment and enclosure to come was by no means inevitable or expected. The historic rupture which marked the origin of capitalism began however in the middle third of the fifteenth century with aggressive engrossment and enclosure by lords and farmers in the context of political upheavals, the emerg-ing demand for cloth on the continent, and domestic demand due to histori-cally high discretionary spending power for the majority of the population.

There was concerted resistance to engrossment and enclosure by the peasantry as exemplified in the evidence for Kent, and by the state from 1489, but this failed. By the middle of the sixteenth century, earlier in some places, the fundamental basis and blurred outline of the classic agrarian capitalist triad of commercial landlord, capitalist tenant farmer and wage labourer had emerged – particularly the first two elements. This blurred outline continued to sharpen as the population now rose rapidly, and engrossment and enclosure of smallholdings continued effectively unchecked by state legislation. By the middle of the sixteenth century, and in many places much earlier, the unintended historic rupture which marked the origin of capitalism became a more deliberate policy towards a new capitalist social-property structure now the benefits of that structure for lords and farmers were recognised. Increasing urbanisation and developing rural industry was fed both by a naturally growing population and increasing numbers of peasants who had either been evicted or forced to sell property due to accumulated debts. The consequence was increasing domestic demand for food, clothing and waged work from an increasingly large proportion of the population who would for the first time never have the opportunity to hold land and never be self-subsistent in their production. The stimulus of this demand determined a cycle of further accumulation and innovation leading to further evictions and sales. Increasing demand for land ensured rising rents which benefited the lords, and increasing demand for food, clothing and waged work ensured rising prices and declining real wages which benefited the farmers and clothiers. So began a new form of society with new distinct economic patterns and a new distinct logic. From this development of a capitalist social-property structure in agrarian society and rural industry on the capitalist putting-out system in England, the structural basis was created for a distinctive overseas empire in North America characterised by dispossessed white colonists from the metropolis,[1] a distinctive role in early modern geopolitics,[2] and the first so-called industrial revolution on capitalist lines.

---

1 Wood 2003, chapter 4; Blackburn 1997, chapter 6.

2 From the late seventeenth century, in contrast to the zero-sum gain of territorial conquest which was pursued by European absolutist states such as France, Teschke argues that 'Britain assumed the new role of balancer of the European pentarchy and disengaged from direct territorial claims on the Continent'. Although it was still tied up in the non-capitalist international system of warfare and mercantilism, the logic of its interests as a capitalist country lay more in economic competition and open markets. Hence '[a]fter 1713, British foreign policy no longer operated on the principle of "natural allies" – the "Old System", which allied

I do not speak of English exceptionalism from an Anglo-centric viewpoint which takes pride in these national developments. I do not see capitalism as a progressive, higher form of society, just a different one with both up-sides and down-sides. Before one takes a view on capitalism, its origin and development in its entirety needs to be placed under the lens, and this is what I have tried to do for the centuries between 1400 and 1600. Democratic institutions and rights in modern western Europe, for example, were won through centuries of struggle by working people, and are not to be confused with capitalism per se, a social system which is entirely compatible with non-democratic forms of state.[3] Nor do I view the development of capitalism from non-capitalist societies as inevitable or even necessarily desirable. The historic rupture which began in the middle of the fifteenth century in England was a catastrophe for the English peasantry who were the vast majority of English people. They are the ones that require first consideration in any assessment on the historical desirability of capitalism. I do not hold the orthodox Marxist view – in fact I firmly oppose it – that their suffering was for the greater good of progressive human history, and that capitalism is the *sine qua non* for a transition to socialism.

The detailed study of Lydd and its region reveals that, before the assault on customary holdings in the 1460s, there was the potential for an alternative future based on landholding, partial market integration and the withering away of lordship. With the maintenance of communal customary organisation in agriculture, relatively democratic local political organisations, an increasingly literate and legally astute population, there was the potential for something different to both feudalism and capitalism. The question is would such a society, the population of which was broadly supported by landholding, be subject to inevitable overpopulation and consequent economic and political crisis in the future in the form of a Malthusian cycle, something similar to that actually experienced on the non-capitalist continent? This would depend on the continuing relationship with lordship and the state – that is, on the continuity of exploitation. If the resistance mounted by highly committed individuals in Lydd in the middle third of the fifteenth century against engrossment,

---

England, the Dutch Republic, and Austria against France – but on the principle of rapidly changing coalitions, earning her on the Continent the epithet "Perfidious Albion" ... The new idea was to stop fighting once the weaker ally had recovered ... rather than to eliminate the common enemy': eliminating enemies weakens foreign markets and foreign demand for the eliminator's products: Teschke 2003, pp. 258–9.

3 Vivek Chibber makes this important point in his recent critique of postcolonial theorists who 'identify capitalism with its newly minted liberal incarnations': Chibber 2013, pp. 24–6.

enclosure and the related assault on custom would have been successful, and became widespread, the income of those lords involved would have increasingly suffered over time. Crucially there would also have been much less opportunity for the lords' tenant farmers to expand their enterprises in competition with others because the engrossment of customary holdings would not have been possible. This may well have led to the widespread fragmentation and distribution of the demesnes and would have provided the peasantry with an extra twenty to thirty percent of the best land. This land would have been spread more broadly among landholders, or run collectively by small and middling landholding communities. The latter would also have taken control of the wastes and used them for collective benefits. The weakening of jurisdictional controls would have allowed for peasant innovation in agriculture and industry and therefore substantial rises in labour productivity within a fundamentally subsistence-based regime. The rebellion of 1381 and Cade's rebellion of 1450 reveal that, when organised, peasants were a match for small armies of knights who on such occasions usually fled. If local democratic controls were maintained or even improved, and a potential emerging absolutist state resisted, it is an open question as to where this alternative society to feudalism and capitalism would have gone from there.

If capitalism in England was not the product of a revolutionary overthrow of the feudal ruling class from below, it also did not grow 'bit by bit' within the 'interstices' of feudalism as it is still sometimes thought.[4] Major economic and political concessions were forced out of the feudal ruling class as it sought new ways to restructure its channels of income. These concessions were implemented fairly rapidly and uniformly across virtually the whole country, the majority being granted within forty years (c. 1380–1420), and they contributed to an unintended consequence, a historic rupture, from which the whole of the society was transformed.

---

4 This view is of course derived from Marx's *Communist Manifesto*, and is implied by the urban-centred approach to the transition by orthodox Marxists. See also Harvey 2010, p. 135, and the critique by Chibber of postcolonial theorists who take this view as their Marxist reference: Chibber 2013, p. 10.

Appendix

Manuscript references to the 468 wills consulted for Lydd parish in Kent between 1455 and 1558, plus some later examples.

Date	Name	Class	Vol.	Folio
1455	Richard Cokered	PRC	1	73
1455	William Godfrey alias Fermour	PRC	1	74
1456	Henry Aleyn	PRC	1	98
1459	John Bate	PRC	2	6
1459	Agnes Howe	PRC	2	6
1460	Thomas Howgh	PRC	2	8
1460	Alice Bate	PRC	2	8
1460	Agnes Fermour	PRC	2	11
1460	Thomas Fermour	PRC	2	11
1460	Thomas Wynday	PRC	2	28
1461	James Ayllewyn	PRC	2	50
1462	John Lovecock	PRC	2	66
1463	Simon Fermour alias Godfrey	PRC	2	129
1463	Roger Jeken	PRC	2	84
1463	Richard Simon	PRC	2	132
1463	Juliane Tofte	PRC	2	133
1463	Simon Aleway	PRC	2	129
1463	William Danyell	PRC	2	130
1463	John Hunt	PRC	2	124
1464	John Pulton	PRC	2	275
1464	William Gros	PRC	2	143
1466	Thomas Ayllewyn	PRC	2	172
1469	William Stocham	PRC	2	197
1471	John Alchorn senior	PRC	2	214
1471	John Smyth	PRC	2	221
1473	William Rolf	PRC	2	264
1474	Richard William senior	PRC	2	268
1474	Simon Fisherman	PRC	2	286
1475	John Howe	PRC	2	305
1476	John Maket	PRC	2	322
1476	William Langhode	PRC	2	330

(Continued)

TABLE   *(Continued)*

Date	Name	Class	Vol.	Folio
1476	William Wanstall	PRC	2	341
1476	Richard Pulton	PRC	2	357
1476	John Serlis	PRC	2	353
1477	Joanne Wanstall, widow	PRC	2	365
1477	William Cok	PRC	2	37
1477	William Benet	PRC	2	390
1477	James Galeway	PRC	2	374
1478	William Benet	PRC	2	389
1478	Thomas Bradford	PRC	2	429
1478	Henry Bate	PRC	2	392
1479	John Cokered senior	PRC	2	429
1479	John Alwey	PRC	2	477
1479	Richard Rey	PRC	2	431
1480	William Elys	PRC	2	486
1480	Henry Colyn	PRC	2	525
1482	James Bagot	PRC	2	559
1482	William Broker	PRC	2	539
1483	Thomas Howslyd	PRC	2	550
1483	William Richard	PRC	2	551
1483	James Harry	PRC	2	575
1483	Henry Aleyn junior	PRC	2	584
1483	Henry Potyn	PRC	2	558
1483	Robert Clerke	PRC	2	563
1483	Thomas Blossom	PRC	2	572
1484	Joanne Houglot, widow	PRC	2	613
1484	Thomas Wynday	PRC	2	613
1484	Margery Pulton, widow	PRC	2	598
1484	Thomas Yong senior	PRC	2	608
1484	John Godfrey alias Fermour senior	PRC	2	597
1484	William Aleyn	PRC	2	617
1484	William Hayton	PRC	2	621
1484	Thomas Holderness	PRC	3	67
1484	Thomas Danyell senior	PRC	2	606
1485	Vincent Sedele	PRC	3	143
1485	John Godfrey	PRC	3	75

(Continued)

TABLE   (*Continued*)

Date	Name	Class	Vol.	Folio
1485	William Symond	PRC	3	88
1486	Thomas Beket	PRC	3	96
1486	Joanne Broker, widow	PRC	3	97
1486	James Maket	PRC	3	92
1486	John Galaunt	PRC	3	92
1486	Agnes Moryng	PRC	3	122
1486	Thomas Bate	PRC	3	90
1486	William Maket junior	PRC	3	82
1486	John Waren	PRC	3	82
1486	Joanne Serlis	PRC	3	93
1487	John Danyell	PRC	3	135
1487	Robert Bownde	PRC	3	135
1487	Agnes Howlyn, widow	PRC	3	176
1487	Robert Howgh	PRC	3	135
1487	John Stocham	PRC	3	173
1488	John Hunt	PRC	3	196
1488	Henry Pulton	PRC	3	201
1488	John the 'men Sutor'	PRC	3	202
1488	Margery Cokeram	PRC	3	203
1488	William Wattes	PRC	3	213
1488	John William	PRC	3	188
1488	Robert Lambard	PRC	3	192
1488	Thomas Bagot	PRC	3	192
1489	John Lucas	PRC	3	225
1489	James Lucas	PRC	3	226
1489	John Peret	PRC	3	227
1489	Stephen Colyn	PRC	3	225
1489	Stephen Cheseman alias Hogge senior	PRC	3	219
1490	Joanne Danyell, widow	PRC	3	248
1490	Margaret Bate, widow	PRC	3	275
1490	John Roper	PRC	3	275
1490	John Lewys	PRC	3	245
1490	Thomas Bate	PRC	3	278
1490	William Gylberd	PRC	3	288

(Continued)

TABLE *(Continued)*

Date	Name	Class	Vol.	Folio
1491	Joanne Cokered, widow	PRC	3	289
1491	William Nicholl	PRC	3	289
1491	Simon Menwood	PRC	3	302
1492	Alexander Clerke	PRC	3	321
1492	James Bate	PRC	3	311
1492	Richard White	PRC	3	326
1492	Thomas Shalwell	PRC	3	340
1492	William Butcher	PRC	3	330
1493	John Walter	PRC	3	353
1493	Thomas Hall	PRC	3	345
1493	John Pollard	PRC	3	354
1494	Richard Benefeld	PRC	4	3
1494	Robert Benton	PRC	4	17
1494	Richard Broker	PRC	4	18
1494	James Hills	PRC	4	2
1494	John Crocheman	PRC	4	31
1494	Stephen Wyderden	PRC	4	4
1494	Stephen Spooner	PRC	4	29
1494	Margaret Colyn	PRC	4	19
1494	John Swan	PRC	4	20
1494	Richard Rolf	PRC	4	65
1494	John Kempe	PRC	4	80
1495	John Parker senior	PRC	4	41
1494	John Ederyk	PRC	4	55
1494	Isabelle Wyderden, widow	PRC	4	56
1494	William Laurens	PRC	4	65
1495	Thomas Caxton	PRC	4	44
1495	William Maket	PRC	4	43
1496	William Gerard	PRC	4	176
1496	Stephen Sefogyl	PRC	4	99
1496	Agnes Roper, widow	PRC	4	91
1496	Michael Godfrey	PRC	4	136
1496	Thomas Godfrey	PRC	4	146
1496	John Holme	PRC	4	91
1496	Edward Fowle	PRC	4	93

(Continued)

TABLE   (*Continued*)

Date	Name	Class	Vol.	Folio
1496	John Deme	PRC	4	101
1496	James Base	PRC	4	126
1496	John Wolvyn	PRC	4	135
1496	Nicholas Lucas	PRC	4	135
1496	Richard Huglott	PRC	4	145
1496	John Cottor	PRC	4	146
1497	Joanne Wolyn, widow	PRC	4	159
1497	John Decon	PRC	4	146
1497	John Payn	PRC	4	145
1497	Laurence Gros	PRC	4	178
1497	John Adam	PRC	4	135
1497	Stephen Lovecock	PRC	4	174
1498	Elizabeth Dyne, widow	PRC	4	208
1498	Peter Cheseman	PRC	4	185
1498	John Bate	PRC	4	185
1498	Elena Howe	PRC	5	3
1498	Nicholas Kenet	PRC	4	188
1498	Edmund Hogan	PRC	4	189
1499	John Blossom	PRC	5	17
1499	Elena Stephen, widow	PRC	5	17
1499	John Pulton senior	PRC	5	32
1499	Thomas Tolkyn	PRC	5	32
1499	John Alchorn senior	PRC	5	33
1499	Marion Durdson, widow	PRC	5	33
1499	William Crocheman	PRC	5	35
1499	Thomas Sefogyl	PRC	5	35
1499	Thomas Pargate	PRC	5	36
1499	Thomas Godfrey	PRC	5	31
1499	Margery Bate, widow	PRC	5	34
1499	Martin Cayser	PRC	5	36
1499	William Stephen	PRC	5	26
1499	Agnes Lucas, widow	PRC	5	60
1500	James Johnson	PRC	6	1
1501	Thomas a Gate	PRC	7	6
1501	Thomas Shalwell	PRC	7	6

(*Continued*)

TABLE   (*Continued*)

Date	Name	Class	Vol.	Folio
1501	John Symon	PRC	7	6
1501	Thomas Lucas	PRC	7	7
1501	William Ardern	PRC	7	8
1501	Roger Bekynton	PRC	7	8
1501	Matthew Hauler	PRC	7	19
1501	Thomas Barre	PRC	7	19
1501	Thomas Brokhyll	PRC	7	20
1501	Stephen Gerard	PRC	6	32
1501	Thomas Galeway	PRC	6	34
1501	John Breggis	PRC	6	24
1501	Thomas Gros	PRC	7	5
1501	John Gerard	PRC	7	7
1501	William Danyell	PRC	7	11
1501	Thomas Danyell	PRC	7	19
1501	Richard Danyell	PRC	7	21
1503	William Godfrey alias Fermour	PRC	8	25
1503	Thomas Ederyk	PRC	8	25
1503	Thomas Pemsey senior	PRC	7	53
1503	John Alkyn	PRC	7	58
1503	John Hamond	PRC	7	63
1504	Thomas Thorpe	PRC	8	19
1504	Henry Palmer	PRC	8	25
1504	Thomas Holme	PRC	8	30
1504	Laurence Elys	PRC	8	44
1504	Richard Gerard	PRC	8	54
1504	John Harry	PRC	8	55
1504	Stephen Hogge alias Cheseman	PRC	8	59
1504	John Amys	PRC	8	59
1505	John Hayton	PRC	8	69
1505	John Godfrey	PRC	8	93
1505	Thomas Holderness	PRC	8	129
1505	John Olyver	PRC	8	71
1505	Laurence a Downe	PRC	8	71
1505	John a Downe	PRC	8	72
1505	Alys Richard	PRC	8	73

(*Continued*)

TABLE   *(Continued)*

Date	Name	Class	Vol.	Folio
1505	John Hynxell	PRC	8	89
1505	John at Wood	PRC	8	91
1505	William Brokhill	PRC	8	91
1505	Joanna Kenet, widow	PRC	8	130
1505	Alice Brokhill, widow	PRC	8	131
1505	Agnes Alchorn, widow	PRC	8	131
1505	Clement Maykyn	PRC	9	62
1506	Margaret Ederyk, widow	PRC	9	4
1506	William Hoorne	PRC	9	5
1506	John Mayne	PRC	9	5
1506	Simon Alkyn	PRC	8	130
1506	Edward Alway	PRC	9	11
1507	William Cokered	PRC	9	73
1507	Robert Alway	PRC	9	68
1507	Joanne Alway, widow	PRC	9	60
1507	Joanne Gros	PRC	9	51
1507	Laurence Holderness	PRC	9	44
1507	Agness Shalwell, widow	PRC	9	43
1507	William Lucas	PRC	9	10
1507	Agnes Ame, widow	PRC	9	15
1508	John Swetyng	PRC	9	61
1508	Beatrice Alway	PRC	9	44
1508	Isabelle Cokered, widow	PRC	9	63
1508	John Kempe	PRC	9	77
1508	Joanne Swetyng, widow	PRC	9	62
1508	Alice Thorpe	PRC	9	63
1508	Stephen Ederyk	PRC	9	63
1508	Robert Cockeram	PRC	9	78
1508	James Inglott	PRC	9	85
1508	Richard Dyne	PRC	9	86
1508	Margaret Tofte	PRC	9	86
1508	John Mighell	PRC	9	115
1509	William Boinfilde	PRC	9	124
1509	John Maykyn	PRC	9	154
1509	Stephen May	PRC	9	173

(Continued)

TABLE   *(Continued)*

Date	Name	Class	Vol.	Folio
1509	Thomas Hunt	PRC	10	22
1509	Richard William	PRC	9	133
1509	Sir John Walker, priest	PRC	10	32
1510	Agnes Holme, widow	PRC	10	38
1510	John Stockton	PRC	10	38
1510	Henry Inglott	PRC	10	53
1510	Richard Notye	PRC	10	53
1510	Simon Wolvyn	PRC	10	75
1510	John Godfrey junior	PRC	10	55
1510	John Crocheman	PRC	10	31
1510	Thomas Inglott	PRC	10	113
1511	Hamon Colyn	PRC	10	137
1511	John Robyn	PRC	10	134
1511	Margery Robyn, widow	PRC	10	133
1511	Thomas Godfrey	PRC	10	120
1511	Joanne Horsley	PRC	10	113
1511	John Alchorn	PRC	10	121
1511	Thomas Bulle	PRC	10	128
1511	Alice Barbour, widow	PRC	11	15
1511	John Kempe	PRC	11	2
1512	Thomas Simond	PRC	11	9
1512	John Tye	PRC	11	9
1512	Margaret Pulton, widow	PRC	11	39
1512	William Strete	PRC	11	52
1512	Robert Colyn	PRC	11	40
1512	Isabelle Godfrey	PRC	11	52
1513	John Smyth	PRC	11	63
1513	Edmund Robyn	PRC	11	78
1513	Andrew Bate	PRC	11	59
1513	Robert Michill	PRC	11	67
1513	Thomas Hamon	PRC	11	67
1513	William Caxton	PRC	11	68
1513	John a Fyld	PRC	11	68
1513	William Heed	PRC	11	76
1513	William Longe	PRC	11	77

(Continued)

TABLE   *(Continued)*

Date	Name	Class	Vol.	Folio
1513	John Fynem	PRC	11	77
1513	Thomas Colyn	PRC	11	77
1513	John Raye	PRC	11	78
1513	William Thorpe	PRC	11	84
1513	William Wanstall	PRC	11	88
1513	Eden Adam, widow	PRC	11	116
1513	John Pulton	PCC, CANT.23 FETISPLACE, QUIRE 17		
1514	Edward Maket	PRC	11	117
1513	Reynold Colt	PRC	11	97
1515	Simon Watte	PRC	12	1
1516	Stephen Marden	PRC	12	25
1516	Isabelle Fermour	PRC	12	4
1517	Thomas Danyell the elder	PRC	12	27
1517	Agnes Godfrey, widow	PRC	12	35
1517	William Hall	PRC	12	35
1518	William Maket	PRC	12	70
1518	Margaret Martin	PRC	12	104
1519	Henry Maket	PRC	12	153
1519	Richard Laurence	PRC	12	160
1519	Sir John Ward, clerk	PRC	12	170
1519	Adrian Dyne	PRC	12	171
1520	John Godfrey	PRC	13	7
1520	Nicholas Bate	PRC	13	29
1520	Vincent Danyell	PRC	13	32
1520	James Swan the elder	PRC	13	35
1520	John Crosse	PRC	13	6
1520	Florence Dyne, widow	PRC	13	40
1520	Margaret Bosom	PRC	13	49
1521	John Boldyng	PRC	13	42
1521	Aimes Jerveyse (Gerves), widow	PRC	13	70
1521	William Clerke	PRC	13	86
1521	John Bate	PRC	14	7
1521	Richard Danyell	PRC	13	84
1522	John Bate	PRC	13	115

(Continued)

TABLE *(Continued)*

Date	Name	Class	Vol.	Folio
1522	Thomas William	PRC	13	140
1522	William Warde	PRC	13	120
1523	Simon Byrkyn	PRC	13	153
1523	William Makemete	PRC	13	153
1523	Simon Dodde	PRC	13	153
1523	Robert Horseley	PRC	13	155
1523	Peter Bakke	PRC	13	169
1523	John Watte	PRC	13	179
1523	John Nicholl	PRC	13	154
1523	Thomas Elys	PRC	13	209
1523	John Becham	PRC	14	138
1524	John Claiche	PRC	14	94
1524	John Benton	PRC	14	27
1524	Edward Hewet	PRC	14	56
1524	John Cutthorn alias Roper	PRC	14	67
1524	John Elyott	PRC	14	89
1525	Richard Watte	PRC	14	108
1525	Alice Swan, widow	PRC	14	122
1526	Thomas Robyn	PRC	14	140
1526	John Menwood	PRC	14	153
1526	Simon Rolf	PRC	14	178
1526	Robert Stuard	PRC	14	154
1527	John Bruer	PRC	14	190
1527	Robert Huglott	PRC	14	191
1527	John Brand	PRC	14	192
1527	Alice Brand, widow	PRC	14	233
1527	Richard Gunter	PRC	14	222
1527	John Dyne the elder	PRC	14	222
1527	John Langley	PRC	15	5
1527	Thomas Godfrey alias Fermour	PRC	14	223
1527	William Hyx	PRC	15	3
1527	William Adam	PRC	15	40
1528	Agnes Clache	PRC	15	25
1528	John Bate the elder	PRC	15	58
1528	Roger Myles	PRC	15	27

(Continued)

TABLE   *(Continued)*

Date	Name	Class	Vol.	Folio
1529	John Godfrey	PRC	15	70
1530	Richard Style	PRC	15	114
1531	Henry Whatman	PRC	15	135
1531	Julyan Bate	PRC	15	162
1532	John Danyell	PRC	15	70
1532	Andrew Bate	PRC	15	219
1532	James Bowmforth	PRC	15	171
1532	John Playden	PRC	15	171
1532	John Barmyng	PRC	15	192
1532	John Everden	PRC	15	193
1532	John Mychell	PRC	15	194
1533	Henry Smyth	PRC	15	193
1533	Alice Huglyn	PRC	15	192
1533	Sir Simon Leche	PRC	15	206
1533	Alice Inglott, widow	PRC	15	231
1534	Thomas Inglott	PRC	15	231
1534	John Purduwax	PRC	15	266
1534	William Style	PRC	15	267
1534	Ame Everden	PRC	15	231
1534	Thomas Smyth	PRC	15	264
1535	John Colyn	PRC	15	280
1535	Richard Maket	PRC	15	317
1535	Robert Mayow (Mayhew)	PRC	15	367
1536	Agnes Mayowe, widow	PRC	15	348
1537	Robert Potman	PRC	15	365
1537	Thomas Bate the younger	PRC	15	380
1537	Margaret Nicholl	PRC	15	377
1538	Thomas Bate the elder	PRC	17	28
1538	Luke Jerves	PRC	17	25
1538	Robert Woodrouse	PRC	17	14
1538	Andrew Boye	PRC	17	28
1538	William Lawless	PRC	17	28
1540	Thomas a Gate	PRC	17	60
1540	John Johnson	PRC	17	86
1540	John Smyth	PRC	17	59

(Continued)

TABLE   *(Continued)*

Date	Name	Class	Vol.	Folio
1540	John Caxton	PRC	17	95
1540	John Mighell	PRC	17	94
1540	Thomas Michell	PRC	17	96
1540	John Moyse	PRC	17	97
1540	Richard Dent	PRC	17	103
1540	Joanna Mighell	PRC	17	103
1540	Alice Newman, widow	PRC	17	103
1540	Robert Butcher	PRC	18	7
1540	John Hasilden	PRC	18	3
1540	Richard Stuppeny the elder	PRC	17	68
1541	Thomas Payne	PRC	18	16
1541	Alice Boye, widow	PRC	17	91
1541	Robert Sperpoynt	PRC	17	93
1541	Isabelle Bate, widow	PRC	18	1
1541	Richard Huglyng	PRC	18	48
1542	Thomas Clache	PRC	19	3
1542	James Miller	PRC	18	14
1543	Margaret Dyne	PRC	19	13
1543	John Inglott	PRC	19	18
1543	Thomas Godfrey the elder	PRC	19	14
1543	Marion Hewett	PRC	19	13
1544	William Maykyn	PRC	20	11
1544	Clement Rolf	PRC	19	51
1545	William Cheriton	PRC	20	21
1545	Richard Dyne	PRC	19	67
1545	Simon Bate	PRC	20	30
1545	Thomas Hall	(ADM.)C. ACT	1	55
1545	James Robyn	(ADM.)C. ACT	1	55
1545	William Bate	(ADM.)C. ACT	1	60
1546	William Marden	PRC	20	38
1546	Margery Cockerel, widow	PRC	20	70
1546	George Newman	PRC	20	32
1546	Thomas Welche	PRC	20	39
1547	Simon Nicholl	(ADM.)C. ACT	1	79
1547	Agnes Cockerel, widow	PRC	21	52

(Continued)

TABLE   (*Continued*)

Date	Name	Class	Vol.	Folio
1548	Robert May	PRC	22	12
1548	John Dyne the elder	PRC	21	98
1548	Robert Menwood	PRC	22	133
1549	Robert Lucas	PRC	22	12
1549	James Bate	PRC	22	90
1549	Philip Martin	PRC	22	20
1549	William Reche	PRC	22	28
1549	Thomas a Tye	PRC	22	16
1549	Joanne a Tye, widow	PRC	22	80
1550	Margaret Gerves, widow	PRC	22	120
1550	Stephen Clarke	PRC	22	129
1550	Simon Typpe	PRC	22	131
1550	Sir William Langley, curate	PRC	22	98
1550	Simon May the elder	PRC	22	92
1550	Elizabeth Gerard, widow	PRC	22	127
1550	John Bate	(ADM.)C. ACT	97	97
1551	Peter Elys	(ADM.)C. ACT	1	99
1551	Robert Robyn	PRC	24	9
1551	Edward Godfrey	PRC	24	14
1551	Sebastian Caxton	PRC	24	56
1551	Edward Austin	PRC	23	24
1551	Thomas Browne	PRC	23	44
1551	John Dyne the elder	PRC	23	35
1551	Robert Miller	PRC	23	36
1551	Alan Epse	PRC	24	2
1551	Thomas Strogull	PRC	24	16
1552	George Ember	PRC	24	87
1552	Margaret Playden, widow	PRC	24	25
1552	William Pett	PRC	24	31
1552	Richard Sebrand	PRC	24	33
1552	John Saunder	PRC	25	3
1552	Agnes Elys, widow	PRC	24	35
1553	Robert Caxton	PRC	25	14
1553	Thomas Robyns	(ADM.)C. ACT	2	22
1553	Robert Bitover	PRC	25	13

(*Continued*)

TABLE   *(Continued)*

Date	Name	Class	Vol.	Folio
1553	Thomas Harley	PRC	25	14
1553	John Huglen	PRC	25	34
1553	Robert Clarke	PRC	25	53
1553	Nicholas Adam	PRC	25	54
1554	Robert Bolland	PRC	25	58
1554	Simon Mott	PRC	25	58
1554	William Colyn	PRC	25	67
1554	Richard Awgosse	PRC	25	58
1554	William Greneway	PRC	26	8
1554	Thomas Danyell	PRC	26	7
1555	William Barrowe	PRC	26	66
1555	Ralph Wilcockes	PCC, CANT.38 MORE, QUIRE 37		
1556	Robert Colyn	PRC	26	122
1556	Andrew Awkinge	PRC	26	170
1556	Thomas Pisinge	PRC	26	123
1557	Thomas Colyn	PRC	27	24
1557	Thomas Harte	PRC	26	155
1558	Nicholas Owrel, priest and curate	PRC	27	123
1558	Laurence Stuppeny (New Romney)	PRC	27	11
1560	Thomas Cuttard	PRC	28	1
1560	Augustine Caxton	PRC	28	68
1563	John Kempe	PRC	29	105
1565	John Robyn	PRC	29	281
1566	William Smyth	PRC	29	409
1569	Peter Godfrey	PRC	32	124
1577	Thomas Bate	PRC	33	87
1588	John Hebylthwaite	PRC	36	92
1592	John Berry	PRC	38	313
1612	Katherine Berry	PRC	42	241
1624	Thomas Godfrey junior	PRC	46	281

References

Primary Sources: Manuscripts

British Library (BL), London
Additional Charters: Title Deeds
Additional Manuscript: 37,018, Belgar Rental of 1380
Harleian Manuscripts: 77, 78 Grants
Harleian Roll S.34 Grant

Canterbury Cathedral Library (CCL)
Literature Manuscript: B2 (Compilation including a copy of Lydd's custumal)

Centre For Kentish Studies (CKS), Maidstone
Manorial U1043/M4 Old Langport Rental of 1551
U442/M72 New Langport Rental, 'Septvans Roll' of 1394
Drainage S/W, AZ 2 'North Walland Boundary Book'
S/W, FAe 1 Dengemarsh Expenditor Accounts 1586–1611
Wills for Canterbury Diocese PRC 32/1–46
Canterbury Archdeaconry Court Act Books: PRC 1; PRC 2
Cinque Ports CP/B1–2 (White and Black Books of the Cinque Ports)
Wage Regulations NR/Z, Pr 37, Pr 43

Lambeth Palace Library (LPL), London
Estate Documents 137, 138

Lydd Borough Archive, East Kent Archive Collection (EKAC), Dover
Ly/fac Chamberlains' Accounts
Ly/ZP Churchwardens' Accounts
Ly/JB Borough Court Books
Ly/ZM Manorial (Aldington 'Bishop's Rent' Rental of 1556)
Ly/JQs Assembly Books
Ly/LC Custumals
Ly/T Title Deeds
Ly/AL Muster Lists
Ly/FR Town Scot Assessments
Ly/I Incorporation
Ly/ZS Sewers Accounts
Ly/ZR Sewers Scot Assessments

The National Archives (TNA), London
C 2 Chancery Proceedings
E 179 Cinque Port Barons' Taxation
E 315 Rentals and Surveys
PRC Prerogative Court Canterbury Wills
SC 2 Court Rolls
SC 6 Ministers Accounts

Trinity College, Cambridge
V1.1.13 *The Lyfe of Saynt George* by Alexander Barclay

Printed Primary and Secondary Sources

Allen, Robert C. 1992, *Enclosure and the Yeoman: The Agricultural Development of the South Midlands*, Oxford: Clarendon Press.

Almond, Richard and A.J. Pollard 2001, 'The Yeomanry of Robin Hood and Social Terminology in Fifteenth-Century England', *Past and Present*, 170: 52–77.

Andreas, Joel 2012, 'Sino-Seismology', *New Left Review*, 76: 128–35.

Anglo, Sydney 1968, 'Introduction' to *The Great Tournament Roll of Westminster*, 2 Volumes, edited by The College of Arms, London: Clarendon Press.

——— 1969, *Spectacle, Pageantry and Early Tudor Policy*, Oxford: Clarendon Press.

Bailey, Mark 2009, 'Villeinage in England: a Regional Case Study, c. 1250–1349', *Economic History Review*, 62, 2: 430–57.

Bisson, Thomas N. 2009, *The Crisis of the Twelfth Century: Power, Lordship and the Origins of European Government*, Princeton: Princeton University Press.

Blackburn, Robin 1988, *The Overthrow of Colonial Slavery, 1776–1848*, London: Verso.

——— 1997, *The Making of New World Slavery: From the Baroque to the Modern, 1492–1800*, London: Verso.

Bois, Guy 1976, *The Crisis of Feudalism: Economy and Society in Eastern Normandy c. 1300–1550*, Cambridge: Cambridge University Press.

——— 1985, 'Against the Neo-Malthusian Orthodoxy', in *The Brenner Debate: Agrarian Class Structure and Economic Development in Pre-Industrial Europe*, Cambridge: Cambridge University Press.

Brenner, Robert 1977, 'The Origins of Capitalist Development: a Critique of Neo-Smithian Marxism', *New Left Review*, 104: 25–93.

——— 1978, 'Dobb on the Transition from Feudalism to Capitalism', *Cambridge Journal of Economics*, 2: 121–40.

—————— 1985a, 'Agrarian Class Structure and Economic Development in Pre-Industrial Europe', in *The Brenner Debate: Agrarian Class structure and Economic Development in Pre-Industrial Europe*, edited by T.H. Aston and C.H.E. Philpin, Cambridge: Cambridge University Press.

—————— 1985b, 'The Agrarian Roots of European Capitalism', in *The Brenner Debate: Agrarian Class structure and Economic Development in Pre-Industrial Europe*, edited by T.H. Aston and C.H.E. Philpin, Cambridge: Cambridge University Press.

—————— 1986, 'The Social Basis of Economic Development', in *Analytical Marxism*, edited by John Roemer, Cambridge: Cambridge University Press.

—————— 1989, 'Bourgeois Revolution and the Transition to Capitalism', in *The First Modern Society: Essays in English History in Honour of Lawrence Stone*, edited by A.L. Beier, David Cannadine and James M. Rosenheim, Cambridge: Cambridge University Press.

—————— 1991, 'Economic Backwardness in Eastern Europe in Light of Developments in the West', in *The Origins of Backwardness in Eastern Europe: Economics and Politics from the Middle Ages until the Early Twentieth Century*, edited by Daniel Chirot, Berkeley, CA: University of California Press.

—————— 1996, 'The Rises and Declines of Serfdom in Medieval and Early Modern Europe', in *Serfdom and Slavery: Studies in Legal Bondage*, edited by M.L. Bush, London: Longman.

—————— 2001, 'The Low Countries in the Transition to Capitalism', in *Peasants into Farmers? The Transformation of Rural Economy and Society in the Low Countries (Middle Ages–19th Century) in Light of the Brenner Debate*, edited by Peter Hoppenbrouwers and Jan Luiten van Zanden, Turnout: Brepols.

—————— 2003, *Merchants and Revolution: Commercial Change, Political Conflict, and London's Overseas Traders, 1550–1653*, London: Verso.

—————— 2007, 'Property and Progress: Where Adam Smith Went Wrong', in *Marxist History Writing for the Twenty-First Century*, edited by Chris Wickham, Oxford: Oxford University Press.

Brewer, John 1990, *The Sinews of Power: War, Money and the English State, 1688–1783*, Harvard: Harvard University Press.

Britnell, Richard H. 1996, *The Commercialisation of English Society, 1000–1500*, Manchester: Manchester University Press.

—————— 1993, 'Commerce and Capitalism in Late Medieval England: Problems of Description and Theory', *Journal of Historical Sociology*, 6: 359–76.

Butcher, Andrew 1974, 'The Origins of Romney Freemen, 1433–1523', in *Economic History Review*, 15: 16–27.

Byres, Terence 2006, 'Differentiation of the Peasantry Under Feudalism and the Transition to Capitalism: In Defence of Rodney Hilton', *Journal of Agrarian Change*, 6: 17–68.

Caley John, and Hunter, Joseph (eds.) 1810–34, *Valor Ecclesiasticus*, 6 Volumes, London: George Eyre and Andrew Spottiswood.

Campbell, Bruce M.S. 2005, 'The Agrarian Problem in the Early Fourteenth Century', *Past and Present*, 188: 3–70.

———— 2006, 'The Land', in *A Social History of England, 1200–1500*, edited by Rosemary Horrox and W. Mark Ormrod, Cambridge: Cambridge University Press.

Cannadine, David 1983, 'The Context, Performance and Meaning of Ritual: The British Monarchy and the "Invention of Tradition" c. 1820–1977', in *The Invention of Tradition*, edited by Eric Hobsbawm and Terence Ranger, Cambridge: Cambridge University Press.

Chibber, Vivek 2013, *Postcolonial Theory and the Specter of Capital*, London: Verso.

Clark, Peter 1977, *English Provincial Society from the Reformation to the Revolution: Politics and Society in Kent*, Sussex: Harvester Press.

Clark, Peter 2000, *The Cambridge Urban History of Britain, Volume II: 1540–1840*, Cambridge: Cambridge University Press.

Cohen, Gerald A. 1986, 'Forces and Relations of Production' in *Analytical Marxism*, edited by John Roemer, Cambridge: Cambridge University Press.

Cohn, Samuel K. Jr. 2006, *Lust for Liberty: The Politics of Social Revolt in Medieval Europe, 1200–1425: Italy, France, and Flanders*, Cambridge, MA: Harvard University Press.

Comninel, George C. 1987, *Rethinking The French Revolution: Marxism and the Revisionist Challenge*, London: Verso.

———— 2000, 'English Feudalism and the Origins of Capitalism', *Journal of Peasant Studies*, 27: 1–53.

Croft, Justin 1997, 'The Custumals of the Cinque Ports c. 1290–c. 1500: Studies in the Cultural Production of the Urban Record', University of Kent at Canterbury: Unpublished Doctoral Thesis.

Daniel-Tysen, John R., and Michael A. Lower 1886, 'A Translation of a Latin Roll Dated 31st Edward III., Relating to the Liberties and Immunities of Battel Abbey', *Sussex Archaeological Collections*, 24: 152–92.

Darby, Henry C. 1977, *Domesday England*, Cambridge: Cambridge University Press.

Davidson, Neil 2004a, 'The Scottish Path to Capitalist Agriculture 1: From the Crisis of Feudalism to the Origins of Agrarian Transformation (1688–1746)', *Journal of Agrarian Change*, 4: 227–68.

———— 2004b, 'The Scottish Path to Capitalist Agriculture 2: The Capitalist Offensive (1747–1815)', *Journal of Agrarian Change*, 4: 411–66.

———— 2012, *How Revolutionary Were the Bourgeois Revolutions?*, Chicago: Haymarket Books.

D'Evelyn, Charlotte, and Foster, Frances A. 1970, 'Saints' Legends', in *A Manual of Writings in Middle English 1050–1500*, Volume II, edited by J. Burke-Severs, Connecticut: The Connecticut Academy of Arts and Sciences.

Dewald, Jonathan, and Vardi, Liana 1998, 'The Peasantries of France, 1400–1789', in *The Peasantries of Europe from the Fourteenth to the Eighteenth Centuries*, edited by Tom Scott, New York: Addison Wesley Longman Limited.

Dimmock, Spencer 2001, 'English Small Towns and the Emergence of Capitalist Relations', *Urban History*, 28: 5–24.

———— 2007a, 'English Towns and The Transition', in *Rodney Hilton's Middle Ages: An Exploration of Historical Themes*, edited by Christopher Dyer, Peter Coss and Chris Wickham, Oxford: Oxford University Press.

———— 2007b, 'Review Article' of *The Development of Agrarian Capitalism: Land and Labour in Norfolk: 1440–1580*, by Jane Whittle, *Historical Materialism*, 15.

———— 2010, 'Review' of *Agriculture and Rural Society after the Black Death: Common Themes and Regional Variations*, edited by Ben Dodds and Richard Britnell, *Journal of Agrarian Change*, 10.

Di Voragine, Jacobo, and Christopher Stace (eds.) 1998, *The Golden Legend: Selections*, London: Penguin Classics.

Dobb, Maurice 1963, *Studies in the Development of Capitalism*, Revised Edition, London: Routledge.

Dobson, Richard Barrie (ed.) 1983, *The Peasants' Revolt of 1381*, Second Edition, Basingstoke: Macmillan.

Dodds, Ben, and Richard Britnell (eds.) 2008, *Agriculture and Rural Society after the Black Death: Common Themes and Regional Variations*, Hatfield: University of Hertfordshire Press.

Draper, Gillian M. 1998, 'The Farmers of Canterbury Cathedral Priory and All Souls College on Romney Marsh c. 1443–1545', in *Romney Marsh: Environmental Change and Human Occupation in a Coastal Lowland*, edited by Jill Eddison, Mark Gardiner and Anthony Long, OUCA Monograph 46.

———— 2009, *Rye: A History of a Sussex Cinque Port to 1660*, Chichester: Phillimore & Co. Ltd.

Draper, Gillian M. and Frank Meddens 2009, *The Sea and the Marsh: The Medieval Cinque Port of New Romney*, London: Pre-Construct Archaeology Ltd.

Draper, Gillian M. 2010, 'Timber and Iron: Natural Resources for the Late Medieval Shipbuilding Industry in Kent', in *Later Medieval Kent 1220–1540*, edited by Sheila Sweetinburgh, Woodbridge, Suffolk: Boydell Press.

Du Boulay, Francis R.H. 1965, 'Who was farming the English Demesnes at the end of the Middle Ages?', *English Historical Review*, 17: 95–108.

———— 1966, *The Lordship of Canterbury: An Essay on Medieval Society*, London: Nelson.

Dugdale, William 1662, *History of Drainage and Imbanking*, London.

Dulley, A.J.F. 1966, 'Four Kent Towns at the End of the Middle Ages', *Archaeologia Cantiana*, 81: 95–108.

———— 1969, 'The Early History of the Rye Fishing Industry', *Sussex Archaeological Collections*, 107: 36–64.

Duplessis, Robert 1997, *Transitions to Capitalism in Early Modern Europe*, Cambridge: Cambridge University Press.

Dyer, Christopher 1980, *Lords and Peasants in a Changing Society: The Estates of the Bishopric of Worcester, 680–1540*, Cambridge: Cambridge University Press.

———— 1992, 'Small-Town Conflict in the Later Middle Ages: Events at Shipston-on-Stour, *Urban History*, 19: 183–210.

———— 1994, 'The English Medieval Community and its Decline', *Journal of British Studies*, 33: 407–29.

———— 1996, 'Memories of Unfreedom: Attitudes Towards Serfdom in England, 1200–1350', in *Serfdom and Slavery: Studies in Legal Bondage*, edited by M.L. Bush, London: Longman.

———— 2000, 'Trade, Urban Hinterlands and Market Integration, 1300–1600', in *Trade, Urban Hinterlands and Market Integration c. 1300–1600*, edited by James A. Galloway,

———— 2002, *Making a Living in the Middle Ages: The People of Britain, 850–1520*, New Haven: Yale University Press.

———— 2007, *An Age of Transition? Economy and Society in England in the Later Middle Ages*, Oxford: Oxford University Press.

———— 2012, *A Country Merchant, 1495–1520: Trading and Farming at the End of the Middle Ages*, Oxford: Oxford University Press.

Elks, Sally 1989, 'Lydd 1540–1644: A Demographic Study', Unpublished M.A. Thesis, University of Kent at Canterbury.

Epstein, Stephan R. 1998, 'The Peasantries of Italy', in *The Peasantries of Europe from the Fourteenth to the Eighteenth Centuries*, edited by Tom Scott, New York: Addison Wesley Longman Limited.

———— 2000, *Freedom and Growth: The Rise of States and Markets in Europe, 1300–1750*, London: Routledge.

———— 2007, 'Rodney Hilton, Marxism and the Transition from Feudalism to Capitalism', in *Rodney Hilton's Middle Ages: An Exploration of Historical Themes*, edited by Christopher Dyer, Peter Coss and Chris Wickham, Oxford: Oxford University Press.

Faith, Rosamond 1981, 'The Class Struggle in Fourteenth-Century England', in *People's History and Socialist Theory*, edited by Ralph Samuel, London: Routledge and Kegan Paul.

———— 1997, *The English Peasantry and the Growth of Lordship*, London: Leicester University Press.

Fenwick, Carolyn C. (ed.) 1998, *The Poll Taxes of 1377, 1379 and 1381: Part 1 Bedfordshire-Leicestershire*, Oxford: Oxford University Press.

Finn, Arthur (ed.) 1911, *Records of Lydd*, Ashford: Kentish Express.

Fleming, Peter 2004, 'Scott Family (*per.* c. 1400–c. 1525)', in *Oxford Dictionary of National Biography*, Oxford: Oxford University Press.

———— 2010, 'The Landed Elite, 1300–1500', in *Later Medieval Kent 1220–1540*, edited by Sheila Sweetinburgh, Woodbridge, Suffolk: Boydell Press.

Fox, Alistair 1989, *Politics and Literature in the Reigns of Henry VII and Henry VIII*, Oxford: Basil Blackwell.

French, Henry R. and Richard W. Hoyle 2007, *The Character of English Rural Society: Earls Colne, 1550–1750*, Manchester: Manchester University Press.

Fryde, Edmund B. and Natalie Fryde 1991, 'Peasant Rebellion and Peasant Discontents', in *The Agrarian History of England and Wales, Volume III, 1348–1500*, edited by Edward Miller, Cambridge: Cambridge University Press.

Gardiner, Mark 1998, 'Settlement Change on Denge and Walland Marshes, 1400–1550', in *Romney Marsh: Environmental Change and Human Occupation in a Coastal Lowland*, edited by Jill Eddison, Mark Gardiner and Anthony Long, OUCA Monograph 46.

Gibson, James M. 1996, 'Interludum Passionis Dominum: Parish Drama in Medieval New Romney', in *English Parish Drama*, edited by Alexandra F. Johnston and Wim Husken, Amsterdam: Rodopi B.V. Editions.

Glennie, Paul 1988, 'In Search of Agrarian Capitalism: Manorial Land Markets and the Acquisition of Land in the Lea Valley, 1450–1560', *Continuity and Change*, 3: 11–40.

Gott, Richard 2011, *Britain's Empire: Resistance, Repression and Revolt*, London: Verso.

Griffiths, Ralph A. 1998, *The Reign of King Henry VI*, Second Edition, Stroud: Sutton Publishing Limited.

Hanley, Hugh A. and Christopher W. Chalkin, (eds.) 1964, *The Kent Lay Subsidy Roll of 1334–5*, in *Documents Illustrative of Medieval Kentish Society*, Kent Records, Volume 18, edited by Francis R.H. Du Boulay, 58–170.

Harris, Mary Dormer 1907–8, *Coventry Leet Book or Mayor's Register, Parts I–II*, Early English Text Society, 134–5, London: Kegan Paul, Trench, Trubner & Co.

Harriss, Gerald 2005, *Shaping the Nation: England 1360–1461*, Oxford University Press: Oxford.

Harman, Chris 1998, *Marxism and History*, London: Bookmarks Publications Ltd.

———— 2008, 'Review Article' of Christopher Dyer's, *An Age of Transition? Economy and Society in England in the Later Middle Ages* and John Landers, *The Field and the Forge: Population, Production and Power in the Pre-Industrial West*, *Historical Materialism*, 16: 185–99.

Harvey, David 2010, *The Enigma of Capital and the Crises of Capitalism*, London: Profile Books Ltd.

Harvey, I.M.W. 1991, *Jack Cade's Revolt*, Oxford: Oxford University Press.

Hasted, Edward 1972, *The History and Topographical Survey of the County of Kent*, Volume IV, Wakefield: E.P. Publishing Ltd.

Hatcher, John 1981, 'English Serfdom and Villeinage: Towards a Reassessment', *Past and Present*, 90: 3–39.

Hatcher, John and Mark Bailey 2001, *Modelling the Middle Ages: The History and Theory of England's Economic Development*: Oxford: Oxford University Press.

Heller, Henry 2011, *The Birth of Capitalism. A Twenty-First-Century Perspective*, London: Pluto Press.

Hilton, Rodney H. 1973, *Bond Men Made Free: Medieval Peasant Movements and The English Rising of 1381*, London: Routledge.

——— 1976 (ed.), *The Transition from Feudalism to Capitalism*, London: Verso.

——— 1976, 'Freedom and Villeinage in England', in *Peasants, Knights and Heretics*, by Rodney H. Hilton, Cambridge: Cambridge University Press.

——— 1985, 'A Crisis of Feudalism', in *The Brenner Debate: Agrarian Class Structure and Economic Development in Pre-Industrial Europe*, edited by T.H. Aston and C.H.E. Philpin, Cambridge: Cambridge University Press.

——— 1985, 'Medieval Market Towns and Simple Commodity Production', *Past and Present*, 109: 3–23.

——— 1990a, 'Peasant Movements in England Before 1381', in *Class Conflict and the Crisis of Feudalism*, Revised Edition, edited by Rodney Hilton, London: Verso.

——— 1990b, 'Reasons for Inequality Among Medieval Peasants', in *Class Conflict and the Crisis of Feudalism*, Revised Edition, edited by Rodney Hilton, London: Verso.

——— 1991, 'Feudal Society', in *A Dictionary of Marxist Thought*, Second Edition, edited by Tom Bottomore, Oxford: Blackwell.

——— 1992, *English and French Towns in Feudal Society: A Comparative Study*, Cambridge: Cambridge University Press.

Hipkin, Stephen 1995, 'The Impact of Marshland Drainage on Rye Harbour c. 1550–1650', in *The Debatable Ground*, edited by Jill Eddison, OUCA Monograph 41.

——— 2000, 'Tenant farming and short term leasing on Romney Marsh, 1587–1705', *Economic History Review*, 53: 646–76.

Hoffman, Philip T. 1996, *Growth in a Traditional Society: The French Countryside, 1450–1815*, Princeton: Princeton University Press.

Hoyle, Richard W. 1990, 'Tenure and Land Market in Early Modern England: or a Late Contribution to The Brenner Debate', *Economic History Review*, 43: 1–20.

Hudson, William and John C. Tingay (eds.) 1906–10, *Records of the City of Norwich*, 2 Volumes, Norwich and London: Jarrold and Sons Ltd.

Hutton, Ronald 1994, *The Rise and Fall of Merry England: The Ritual Year, 1400–1700*, Oxford: Oxford University Press.

Hyams, Paul R. 1980, *Kings, Lords and Peasants in the Twelfth and Thirteenth Centuries* Oxford: Oxford University Press.

James, Mervyn 1983, 'Ritual, Drama and Social Body in the Late Medieval English Town', *Past and Present*, 98: 3–29.

Jones, Philip 1997, *The Italian City-State: From Commune to Signoria*, Oxford: Oxford University Press.

Jones, P.M. 1988, *The Peasantry in the French Revolution*, Cambridge: Cambridge University Press.

Kanzaka, Junichi 2002, 'Villein Rents in Thirteenth-Century England: An Analysis of the Hundred Rolls of 1279–80, *Economic History Review*, 55: 593–618.

Keen, Maurice 2003, *England in the Later Middle Ages: A Political History*, Second Edition, London: Routledge.

Kermode, Jennifer 1998, *Medieval Merchants: York, Beverley and Hull in the Later Middle Ages*, Cambridge: Cambridge University Press.

Kerridge, Eric 1969, *Agrarian Problems in the Sixteenth Century and After*, London: George Allen and Unwin.

Kriedte, Peter 1983, *Peasants, Landlords and Merchant Capitalists: Europe and the World Economy, 1500–1800*, Leamington Spa: Berg publishers.

Killingray, David, and Terry Lawson 2010, *An Historical Atlas of Kent*, Andover: Phillimore and Co. Ltd.

Kosminsky, Evgenij. A. 1956, *Studies in the Agrarian History of England in the Thirteenth Century*, edited by Rodney H. Hilton, Oxford: Basil Blackwell.

Kumin, Beat A. 1996, *The Shaping of a Community: The Rise and Reformation of the English Parish c. 1400–1560*, Aldershot: Scolar Press.

Lindenbaum, Sheila 1994, 'Ceremony and Oligarchy: The London Midsummer Watch', in *City and Spectacle in Medieval Europe*, edited by Barbara A. Hanawalt and Kathryn L. Reyerson, Minneapolis: University of Minnesota Press.

Markoff, John 1996, *The Abolition of Feudalism: Peasants, Lords and Legislators in the French Revolution*, University Park: Pennsylvania State University Press.

Marx, Karl 1970 [1859], 'Preface' to *A Contribution to the Critique of Political Economy*, New York: International Publishers.

———— 1990 [1867], *Capital, Volume I*, London: Penguin Classics.

———— 1991 [1894], *Capital, Volume III*, London: Penguin Classics.

———— 1992 [1850], 'Review of Guizot's Book on the English Revolution', in *Karl Marx: Surveys From Exile: Political Writings: Volume 2*, edited by David Fernbach, London: Penguin Classics.

———— 1993 [1848], 'Manifesto of the Communist Party', in *Karl Marx: The Revolutions of 1848, Political Writings: Volume 1*, edited by David Fernbach, London: Penguin Classics.

———— 1998 [1845], *The German Ideology*, New York: Prometheus Books.

Mate, Mavis E. 1987, 'Pastoral Farming in South-East England in the Fifteenth Century', *The Economic History Review*, 40: 523–36.

——— 1991, 'The Occupation of the Land: Kent and Sussex', in *The Agrarian History of England and Wales, Volume III, 1348–1500*, edited by Edward Miller, Cambridge: Cambridge University Press.

——— 1993, 'The East Sussex Land Market and Agrarian Class Structure in the Late Middle Ages', *Past and Present*, 139: 46–65.

——— 2006, *Trade and Economic Developments, 1450–1550: The Experience of Kent, Surrey and Sussex*, Woodbridge, Suffolk: Boydell Press.

——— 2010, 'The Economy of Kent, 1200–1500: The Aftermath of the Black Death', in *Later Medieval Kent*, edited by Sheila Sweetinburgh, Woodbridge, Suffolk: The Boydell Press.

Mayhew, Graham 1987, *Tudor Rye*, Falmer: University of Sussex.

McIntosh, Marjorie Keniston 1986, *Autonomy and Community: The Royal Manor of Havering, 1200–1500*, Cambridge: Cambridge University Press.

——— 1991, *A Community Transformed: The Manor and Liberty of Havering, 1500–1620*, Cambridge: Cambridge University Press.

——— 1998, *Controlling Misbehaviour in England, 1370–1600*, Cambridge: Cambridge University Press.

McRee, Benjamin R. 1994, 'Unity or Division? The Social Meaning of Guild Ceremony in Urban Communities', in *City and Spectacle in Medieval Europe*, edited by Barbara A. Hanawalt and Kathryn L. Reyerson, Minneapolis: University of Minnesota Press.

Moreton, C. E. 1992, *The Townshends and their World: Gentry, Law and Land in Norfolk c. 1450–1551*, Oxford: Oxford University Press.

Murray, K. M. E. 1935, *The Constitutional History of the Cinque Ports*, Manchester: Manchester University Press.

Neal, Larry and Jeffrey J. Williamson (eds) 2014, *The Cambridge History of Capitalism: Volume I: The Rise of Capitalism: From Ancient Origins to 1848*, Cambridge: Cambridge University Press.

Nelson, William 1960, *The Life of St. George by Alexander Barclay, Early English Text Society*, Oxford: Oxford University Press.

Neeson, Jeanette M. 1993, *Commoners: Common Right, Enclosure and Social Change in England, 1700–1820*, Cambridge: Cambridge University Press.

Palliser, David M. (ed.) 2000, *The Cambridge Urban History of Britain, Volume I: 600–1540*, Cambridge: Cambridge University Press.

Phythian-Adams, Charles 1979, *Desolation of a City: Coventry and the Urban Crisis of the Late Middle Ages*, Cambridge: Cambridge University Press.

Post, Charles 2002, 'Comments on the Brenner-Wood Exchange on the Low Countries', *Journal of Agrarian Change*, 2: 88–95.

Post, Charles 2011, *The American Road to Capitalism: Studies in Class-Structure, Economic Development and Political Conflict, 1620–1877*, Leiden: Brill.

Price, Roger 1983, *The Modernization of Rural France: Communications Networks and Agricultural Market Structures in Nineteenth-Century France*, New York: St. Martin's Press.

Razi, Zvi 2007, 'Serfdom and Freedom in Medieval England: A Reply to the Revisionists', in *Rodney Hilton's Middle Ages: an Exploration of Historical Themes*, edited by Christopher Dyer, Peter Coss and Chris Wickham, Oxford: Oxford University Press.

Rigby, Steve H. 1995, *English Society in the Later Middle Ages: Class, Status and Gender*, Basingstoke and London: Macmillan.

———— 1998, *Marxism and History: A Critical Introduction*, Second Edition, Manchester: Manchester University Press.

———— 1999, 'Medieval England: to Have and Have Not', *New Left Review*, 236: 154–9.

———— 2006, 'Introduction: Social Structure and Economic Change in Late Medieval England', in *A Social History of England, 1200–1500*, edited by Rosemary Horrox and W. Mark Ormrod, Cambridge: Cambridge University Press.

Robertson, Scott 1880, 'Churches on Romney Marsh', *Archaeologia Cantiana*, 13: 427–50.

Robisheaux, Thomas 1998, 'The Peasantries of Western Germany, 1300–1750', in *The Peasantries of Europe from the Fourteenth to the Eighteenth Centuries*, edited by Tom Scott, New York: Addison Wesley Longman Limited.

Rollison, David 1992, *The Local Origins of Modern Society: Gloucestershire 1500–1800*, London: Routledge.

———— 2001, 'Discourse and Class Struggle: The Politics of Industry in Early Modern England', *Social History*, 26: 166–89.

———— 2010, *A Commonwealth of the People: Popular Politics and England's Long Social Revolution, 1066–1649*, Cambridge: Cambridge University Press.

Rosenthal, Jean-Laurent 1992, *The Fruits of Revolution: Property Rights, Litigation and French Agriculture, 1700–1860*, Cambridge: Cambridge University Press.

Rosser, Gervase 2000, 'Urban Culture and the Church 1300–1540', in *The Cambridge Urban History of Britain, Volume I, 600–1540*, edited by D.M. Palliser, Cambridge: Cambridge University Press.

Royal Commission on Historical Manuscripts, Fifth Report 1896, London: Eyre and Spottiswood for Her Majesty's Stationery Office.

Rubin, Miri 1991, *Corpus Christi: The Eucharist in Late Medieval Culture*, Cambridge: Cambridge University Press.

Saville, John 1987, *1848: The British State and the Chartist Movement*, Cambridge: Cambridge University Press.

Scargill-Bird, Samuel R. (ed.) 1887, *Custumals of Battle Abbey, in the Reigns of Edward I and Edward II (1283–1312)*, printed for the Camden Society.

Scott, Tom 1998 (ed.), *The Peasantries of Europe from the Fourteenth to the Eighteenth Centuries*, New York: Addison Wesley Longman Limited.

———— 2002, *Society and Economy in Germany, 1300–1600*, Basingstoke and New York, Palgrave.

———— 2012, *The City-State in Europe, 1000–1600*, Oxford: Oxford University Press.

Searle, Eleanor 1974, *Lordship and Community: Battle Abbey and its Banlieu 1066–1538*, Toronto: Pontifical Institute of Mediaeval Studies.

Shagan, Ethan 2003, *Popular Politics and the English Reformation*, Cambridge: Cambridge University Press.

Smith, Richard M. 1984, 'Families and Their Land in an Area of Partible Inheritance: Redgrave, Suffolk 1260–1320', in *Land, Kinship and Life-Cycle*, edited by Richard M. Smith, Cambridge: Cambridge University Press.

Sweetinburgh, Sheila 2002, 'Landholding and the Landmarket in a Fifteenth Century Peasant Community: Appledore, 1400–1470', in *Romney Marsh: Coastal and Landscape Change Through The Ages,* edited by Anthony Long, Stephen Hipkin, and Helen Clarke, OUCA Monograph 56.

Tawney, Richard H. 1912, *The Agrarian Problem in the Sixteenth Century*, London: Longmans, Green and Co.

Teichman-Derville, Max 1936, *The Level and Liberty of Romney Marsh*, Ashford: Invicta Press.

Teschke, Benno 2003, *The Myth of 1648: Class, Geopolitics and the Making of Modern International Relations*, London: Verso.

Thirsk, Joan 1967, 'Enclosing and Engrossing', in *The Agrarian History of England and Wales, Volume 4, 1500–1640*, edited by Joan Thirsk, Cambridge: Cambridge University Press.

———— 1978, *Economic Policy and Projects: The Development of a Consumer Society in Early Modern England*, Oxford: Oxford Clarendon Press.

Thompson, Edward P. 1978, 'The Poverty of Theory or an Orrery of Errors' in *The Poverty of Theory and Other Essays*, London: The Merlin Press Ltd.

———— 1991, *The Making of the English Working Class*, London: Penguin Books.

———— 1991, *Customs in Common*, London: The Merlin Press Ltd.

Tittler, Robert 1998, *The Reformation and the Towns in England: Politics and Political Culture, c. 1540–1640*, Oxford: Oxford Clarendon Press.

Van Bavel, Bas 2001, 'Elements in the transition of the rural economy. Factors contributing to the emergence of large farms in the Dutch river area (15th–16th centuries)', in *Peasants into Farmers? The Transformation of Rural Economy and Society in the Low Countries (Middle Ages–19th Century) in Light of the Brenner Debate*, edited by Peter Hoppenbrouwers and Jan Luiten van Zanden, Turnout: Brepols.

———— 2010, *Manors and Markets: Economy and Society in the Low Countries, 500–1600*, Oxford and New York: Oxford University Press.

Whitney, Kenneth P. 2000, *The Survey of Archbishop Pecham's Kentish Manors, 1283–1285*, Maidstone: Kent Archaeological Society.

Whittle, Jane 2000, *The Development of Agrarian Capitalism: Land and Labour in Norfolk, 1440–1580*, Oxford: Clarendon Press.

———— 2004, 'Tenure and Landholding in England 1440–1580: A Crucial Period for the Development of Agrarian Capitalism?', in *Landholding and Land Transfer in the North Sea Area (Late Middle Ages–19th Century)*, edited by Bas J.P. Van Bavel and Peter Hoppenbrouwers, Turnout: Brepols.

———— 2010, 'Lords and Tenants in Kett's Rebellion 1549', *Past and Present*, 207: 3–52.

Wickham, Chris 2007, 'Memories of Underdevelopment: What Has Marxism Done for Medieval History, and What Can it Still Do?', in *Marxist History Writing for the Twenty-First Century*, edited by Chris Wickham, Oxford: Oxford University Press.

———— 2009, *The Inheritance of Rome: A History of Europe from 400 to 1000*, London: Allen Lane.

Wood, Andy 1999, *The Politics of Social Conflict: The Peak Country, 1520–1770*, Cambridge: Cambridge University Press.

———— 2002, *Riot, Rebellion and Popular Politics in Early Modern England*, Basingstoke and New York: Palgrave.

———— 2007, *The 1549 Rebellions and the Making of Early Modern England*, Cambridge: Cambridge University Press.

Wood, Ellen Meiksins 1995, *Democracy Against Capitalism: Renewing Historical Materialism*, Cambridge: Cambridge University Press.

———— 2002, *The Origin of Capitalism: A Longer View*, London: Verso.

———— 2002, 'The Question of Market Dependence', *Journal of Agrarian Change*, 2: 50–87.

———— 2003, *Empire of Capital*, London: Verso.

———— 2012, *Liberty and Property: A Social History of Western Political Thought from Renaissance to Enlightenment*, London: Verso.

Wordie, J. Ross 1983, 'The Chronology of English Enclosure, 1500–1914', *Economic History Review*, 36: 483–505.

Wrightson, Keith 2000, *Earthly Necessities: Economic Lives in Early Modern Britain, 1470–1750*, New Haven and London: Yale University Press.

Wrigley, Edward Anthony 1985, 'Urban Growth and Agricultural Change: England and the Continent in the Early Modern Period', *Journal of Interdisciplinary History*, 15: 673–728.

Zell, Michael 1994, *Industry in the Countryside: Wealden Society in the Sixteenth Century*, Cambridge: Cambridge University Press.

———— 2000, 'Landholding and the Land Market in Early Modern Kent', in *Early Modern Kent, 1540–1640*, edited by Michael Zell, Woodbridge, Suffolk: Boydell Press.

Index

Lucàcs, Georg   169

Malthus, Thomas   11
manors
    customs of   283–4, 286–7, 315
    demesnes in   26, 41, 81–3, 87, 92–3, 111,
        114, 129, 130–2, 146, 176, 279–81, 284,
        286
    landmarket within   108, 131, 145, 186, 242,
        283
    officials of   123–4, 187, 293–4
    relationship to villages   45
    See also peasants and rural artisans
Markoff, John   72n, 194n, 224n, 224n2
Marxism   4
    'British'   82, 170n
    'orthodox Marxism'   4, 7, 14–19, 44, 48, 64,
        156, 157–232, 263, 279, 366, 367n
    'political Marxism'   4, 7, 157–232
    For the orthodox approach see also
        commercialisation theories
Marx, Karl   14, 14n, 16, 21n, 41n, 65, 65n,
    128–9, 129n, 130, 157, 159–60, 160n, 164–9,
    171, 182, 192, 192n, 193–4, 194n, 194n2, 195,
    205–7, 367n
Mate, Mavis   101, 102, 102n, 107, 107n, 118,
    118n, 140, 140n, 145, 151, 151n, 152, 152n,
    152n2, 152n3, 239–40, 239n, 239n2, 240n,
    240n2, 242, 274n
McIntosh, Marjorie K.   150–1, 151n, 353n, 355,
    355n
McRee, Benjamin R.   353n
Mill, J.S.   42, 47
Murray, K.M.E.   239n, 264–5, 264n, 265n,
    266n

Neal, Larry   1n
Neeson, Jeanette   64, 64n, 140n
New World   139n, 140, 155–6, 175, 207

Overton, Mark   189n

Palliser, David   200n
Parker, David   95, 95n, 107, 107n, 116, 227
peasants and rural artisans
    comparisons of, across Europe   29, 31–2,
        38–41, 44–7, 73–4, 80, 149–50, 182–3,
        221, 229
    differentiation within   63, 108, 112, 113n,
        135, 153, 181, 182–6, 188–191

expropriation of   4, 6, 27, 61, 63–4, 128–9,
    131, 133, 139n, 149, 166, 171–2, 182, 187,
    198, 201, 203, 207–8, 220, 220n, 226–7,
    231
personal status of: serfdom and freedom
    6, 26, 39, 41, 45–6, 54, 65–72, 73n, 75–88,
    105–6, 187, 210, 230
political communities of   19–20, 45–6,
    73, 81, 87, 179, 185, 191, 195, 215, 224, 261
rebellion and resistance by   3, 27, 67, 76,
    97, 99, 102–3, 120–7, 146, 153–6, 184–5,
    188–9, 191, 213, 215, 217, 220, 222–6, 245,
    257–8, 261–3, 272–300, 331–50, 364–5,
    367
subsistence farming and reproduction
    strategies of   1–2, 4, 20–3, 27, 50–2, 61,
    75, 78, 140n, 164–5, 184, 190, 193–8, 215,
    227, 237, 250–1, 253, 281–2, 367
See also agriculture; feudalism; manors;
    waged labour; tenures
Phythian-Adams, Charles   352, 352n, 353n
'pluralist' historical perspectives   5, 34, 42,
    64
Pollard, A.J.   111n
Portugal   206–8
Post, Charles   2n, 3n, 158
Postan, Michael   11, 14
Pounds, Norman   209–11, 211n
Price, Roger   194n

Razi, Zvi   80, 81n, 83n
Ricardo, David   11
Rigby, Steve   3n, 37, 42–8, 66, 66n, 158, 158n,
    173
Robertson, Scott   275n, 275n2
Robisheaux, Thomas   215–16, 215n, 215n2,
    216n, 217n
Rollison, David   139n
Rosenthal, Jean-Laurent   194n
Rosser, Gervase   353, 353n
Rous, John   141–2, 141n, 144, 299
Rubin, Miri   352n
Russia   170

Saville, John   170n
Scotland   160–1, 171–2, 176–7, 188, 190, 195–6
Scott, Tom   209–11, 211n, 214, 214n, 214n2,
    215n, 215n2, 215n3, 216n, 217n, 217n2
Searle, Eleanor   279n, 280n, 290, 290n
Shagan, Ethan   155n, 260n

www.ingramcontent.com/pod-product-compliance
Lightning Source LLC
Chambersburg PA
CBHW060020030426
42334CB00019B/2114

9 781608 464852